CISCO

IT Essentials Course Booklet

PC Hardware and Software

Version 4.1

ciscopress.com

Cisco | Networking Academy
Mind Wide Open

IT Essentials: PC Hardware and Software Course Booklet, Version 4.1
Cisco Networking Academy

Copyright© 2010 Cisco Systems, Inc.

Published by:
Cisco Press
800 East 96th Street
Indianapolis, IN 46240 USA

Printed in the United States of America

First Printing April 2010

Library of Congress Cataloging-in-Publication Data is available upon request.

ISBN-13: 978-1-58713-261-2

ISBN-10: 1-58713-261-3

Warning and Disclaimer

This book is designed to provide information about PC Hardware and Software. Every effort has been made to make this book as complete and as accurate as possible, but no warranty or fitness is implied.

The information is provided on an "as is" basis. The authors, Cisco Press, and Cisco Systems, Inc. shall have neither liability nor responsibility to any person or entity with respect to any loss or damages arising from the information contained in this book or from the use of the discs or programs that may accompany it.

The opinions expressed in this book belong to the author and are not necessarily those of Cisco Systems, Inc.

Publisher
Paul Boger

Associate Publisher
Dave Dusthimer

Cisco Representative
Erik Ullanderson

Cisco Press Program Manager
Anand Sundaram

Executive Editor
Mary Beth Ray

Managing Editor
Sandra Schroeder

Project Editor
Tonya Simpson

Editorial Assistant
Vanessa Evans

Designer
Sandra Schroeder

Composition
Mark Shirar

CISCO

Trademark Acknowledgments

All terms mentioned in this book that are known to be trademarks or service marks have been appropriately capitalized. Cisco Press or Cisco Systems, Inc., cannot attest to the accuracy of this information. Use of a term in this book should not be regarded as affecting the validity of any trademark or service mark.

Feedback Information

At Cisco Press, our goal is to create in-depth technical books of the highest quality and value. Each book is crafted with care and precision, undergoing rigorous development that involves the unique expertise of members from the professional technical community.

Readers' feedback is a natural continuation of this process. If you have any comments regarding how we could improve the quality of this book, or otherwise alter it to better suit your needs, you can contact us through email at feedback@ciscopress.com. Please make sure to include the book title and ISBN in your message.

We greatly appreciate your assistance.

Contents at a Glance

Contents

Command Syntax Conventions

The conventions used to present command syntax in this book are the same conventions used in the IOS Command Reference. The Command Reference describes these conventions as follows:

- **Boldface** indicates commands and keywords that are entered literally as shown. In actual configuration examples and output (not general command syntax), boldface indicates commands that are manually input by the user (such as a **show** command).

- *Italic* indicates arguments for which you supply actual values.

- Vertical bars (|) separate alternative, mutually exclusive elements.

- Square brackets ([ ]) indicate an optional element.

- Braces ({ }) indicate a required choice.

- Braces within brackets ([{ }]) indicate a required choice within an optional element.

About This Course Booklet

Your Cisco Networking Academy Course Booklet is designed as a study resource you can easily read, highlight, and review on the go, wherever the Internet is not available or practical:

- The text is extracted directly, word-for-word, from the online course so you can highlight important points and take notes in the "Your Chapter Notes" section.

- Headings with the exact page correlations provide a quick reference to the online course for your classroom discussions and exam preparation.

- An icon system directs you to the online curriculum to take full advantage of the images imbedded within the Networking Academy online course interface and reminds you to perform the labs, worksheets, interactive activities, Packet Tracer activities, and chapter quizzes.

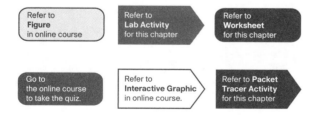

Introduction to the Personal Computer

Introduction

Information technology (IT) is the design, development, implementation, support, and management of computer hardware and software applications. An IT professional is knowledgeable about computer systems and operating systems. This chapter will review IT certifications and the components of a basic personal computer system.

After completing this chapter, you will meet these objectives:

- Explain IT industry certifications.

- Describe a computer system.

- Identify the names, purposes, and characteristics of cases and power supplies.

- Identify the names, purposes, and characteristics of internal components.

- Identify the names, purposes, and characteristics of ports and cables.

- Identify the names, purposes, and characteristics of input devices.

- Identify the names, purposes, and characteristics of output devices.

- Explain system resources and their purposes.

1.1 Explain IT industry certifications

Refer to
Figure
in online course

This course will focus on desktop and laptop computers. It will also discuss electronic devices, such as personal digital assistants and cell phones.

Training and experience will qualify a technician to service these computers and personal electronic devices. You will gain the specialized technical skills needed to install, maintain, and repair computers. Earning an industry-standard certification will give you confidence and increase your opportunities in IT.

This course is focused on the following two industry-standard certifications:

- CompTIA A+

- European Certification of Informatics Professional (EUCIP) IT Administrator Certification (Modules 1 and 2)

After completing this section, you will meet these objectives:

- Identify education and certifications.

- Describe the A+ Certification.

- Describe the EUCIP Certification.

Refer to
Figure
in online course

1.1.1 Identify education and certifications

Information Technology (IT) is a term that encompasses the relationship between hardware, software, networks, and technical assistance provided to users. **IT Essentials: PC Hardware and Software** covers the information that a technician needs to be successful in IT. This course covers the following topics:

- Personal computers
- Safe lab procedures
- Troubleshooting
- Operating systems
- Laptop computers
- Printers and scanners
- Networks
- Security
- Communication skills

The IT Essentials course focuses on two hardware and software skills-based industry certifications: CompTIA A+ and EUCIP. This course is only an introduction into the world of IT. A technician may continue to study and earn the following certifications:

- CCNA – Cisco Certified Networking Associate
- CCNP – Cisco Certified Networking Professional
- CCIE – Cisco Certified Internetworking Expert
- CISSP – Certified Information Systems Security Professional
- MCP – Microsoft Certified Professional
- MCSA – Microsoft Certified Systems Administrator
- MCSE – Microsoft Certified Systems Engineer
- Network+ – CompTIA Network Certification
- Linux+ – CompTIA Linux Certification

IT certifications can be used as credits for university and college degrees in areas such as computer science and telecommunications.

Refer to
Figure
in online course

1.1.2 Describe the A+ certification

Computing Technology Industry Association (CompTIA) developed the A+ Certification program. A CompTIA A+ certification, as shown in Figure 1, signifies that a candidate is a qualified PC hardware and software technician. CompTIA certifications are known throughout the IT community as one of the best ways to enter the information technology field and build a solid career.

The latest version of CompTIA A+ is CompTIA A+ 2009 Edition. Two exams are necessary to be certified: CompTIA A+ Essentials, exam code 220-701; and CompTIA A+ Practical Application, exam code 220-702.

CompTIA A+ Essentials measures the necessary competencies of an entry-level IT professional with at least 500 hours of hands-on experience in the lab or field. It tests for the fundamentals of computer technology, networking and security, as well as the communication skills and professionalism now required of all entry-level IT professionals.

CompTIA A+ Practical Application is an extension of the knowledge and skills identified in CompTIA A+ Essentials, with more of a hands-on orientation focused on scenarios in which troubleshooting and tools must be applied to resolve problems.

Refer to
Worksheet
for this chapter

Job Opportunities
Gather information for jobs in the computer service and repair field.

Refer to
Figure
in online course

1.1.3 Describe the EUCIP certification

The EUCIP IT Administrator program offers a recognized certification of competence in IT. The certification covers the standards prescribed by the Council of European Professional Informatics Societies (CEPIS). The EUCIP IT Administrator Certification consists of five modules, with a corresponding exam for each module. This course will prepare you for Modules 1 and 2.

Module 1: PC Hardware

The PC Hardware module requires that the candidate understand the basic makeup of a personal computer and the functions of the components. The candidate should be able to effectively diagnose and repair hardware problems. The candidate should be able to advise customers of the appropriate hardware to buy.

Module 2: Operating Systems

The Operating Systems module requires that the candidate be familiar with the procedures for installing and updating most common operating systems and applications. The candidate should know how to use system tools for troubleshooting and repairing operating systems.

Module 3: Local Area Network and Network Services

This module is beyond the scope of the IT Essentials course, although some of the topics are covered. The Local Area Network and Network Services module requires that the candidate be familiar with the procedure of installing, using, and managing local area networks. The candidate should be able to add and remove users and shared resources. The candidate should know how to use system tools for troubleshooting and repairing networks.

Module 4: Expert Network Use

This module is beyond the scope of the IT Essentials course, although some of the topics are covered. The Expert Network Use module requires that the candidate understand LAN communication.

Module 5: IT Security

This module is beyond the scope of the IT Essentials course, although some of the topics are covered. The IT Security module requires that the candidate be familiar with security methods and features that are available for a standalone or networked computer.

Refer to
Figure
in online course

1.2 Describe a computer system

A computer system consists of hardware and software components. Hardware is the physical equipment such as the case, storage drives, keyboards, monitors, cables, speakers, and printers. The term software includes the operating system and programs. The operating system instructs the computer how to operate. These operations may include identifying, accessing, and processing information. Programs or applications perform different functions. Programs vary widely depending on the type of information that will be accessed or generated. For example, instructions for balancing a checkbook are very different from instructions for simulating a virtual reality world on the Internet.

The rest of this chapter discusses the hardware components found in a computer system.

Refer to
Figure
in online course

1.3 Identify the names, purposes, and characteristics of cases and power supplies

The computer case provides protection and support for the internal components of the computer. All computers need a power supply to convert alternating-current (AC) power from the wall socket into direct-current (DC) power. The size and shape of the computer case is usually determined by the motherboard and other internal components.

You can select a large computer case to accommodate additional components that may be required in the future. Other users may select a smaller case that requires minimal space. In general, the computer case should be durable, easy to service, and have enough room for expansion.

The power supply must provide enough power for the components that are currently installed and allow for additional components that may be added at a later time. If you choose a power supply that powers only the current components, it may be necessary to replace the power supply when other components are upgraded.

After completing this section, you will meet these objectives:

- Describe cases.
- Describe power supplies.

Refer to
Figure
in online course

1.3.1 Describe cases

A computer case contains the framework to support the internal components of a computer while providing an enclosure for added protection. Computer cases are typically made of plastic, steel, and aluminum and are available in a variety of styles.

The size and layout of a case is called a form factor. There are many types of cases, but the basic form factors for computer cases include desktop and tower. Desktop cases may be slimline or full-sized, and tower cases may be mini or full-sized, as shown in Figure 1.

Computer cases are referred to in a number of ways:

- Computer chassis
- Cabinet
- Tower
- Box

- Housing

In addition to providing protection and support, cases also provide an environment designed to keep the internal components cool. Case fans are used to move air through the computer case. As the air passes warm components, it absorbs heat and then exits the case. This process keeps the components of the computer from overheating.

There are many factors that must be considered when choosing a case:

- The size of the motherboard

- The number of external or internal drive locations called bays

- Available space

See Figure 2 for a list of features.

In addition to providing protection from the environment, cases help to prevent damage from static electricity. Internal components of the computer are grounded by attachment to the case.

Note

You should select a case that matches the physical dimensions of the power supply and motherboard.

Refer to
Figure
in online course

1.3.2 Describe power supplies

The power supply, shown in Figure 1, converts alternating-current (AC) power coming from a wall outlet into direct-current (DC) power, which is a lower voltage. DC power is required for all of the components inside the computer.

A computer can tolerate slight fluctuations in power, but a significant deviation can cause the power supply to fail. An uninterruptible power supply (UPS) can protect a computer from problems caused by changes in power. A UPS provides power for a computer using a power inverter. A power inverter provides AC power to the computer from a built-in battery by converting the DC current of the UPS battery into AC power.

Connectors

Most connectors today are keyed connectors. Keyed connectors are designed to be inserted in only one direction. Each part of the connector has a colored wire with a different voltage running through it, as seen in Figure 2. Different connectors are used to connect specific components to various ports on the motherboard:

- A Molex connector is a keyed connector used to connect to an optical drive or a hard drive.

- A Berg connector is a keyed connector used to connect to a floppy drive. A Berg connector is smaller than a Molex connector.

- A 20-pin or 24-pin slotted connector is used to connect to the motherboard. The 24-pin slotted connector has two rows of 12 pins each, and the 20-pin slotted connector has two rows of 10 pins each.

- A 4-pin to 8-pin auxiliary power connector has two rows of two to four pins and supplies power to all areas of the motherboard. The 4-pin to 8-pin auxiliary power connector is the same shape as the main power connector, but smaller.

- Older standard power supplies used two connectors called P8 and P9 to connect to the motherboard. P8 and P9 were unkeyed connectors. They could be installed backwards, potentially damaging the motherboard or power supply. The installation required that the connectors were lined up with the black wires together in the middle.

Note

If you have a difficult time inserting a connector, try a different way, or check to make sure that there are no bent pins or foreign objects in the way. Remember, if it seems difficult to plug in any cable or other part, something is wrong. Cables, connectors, and components are designed to fit together snugly. Never force any connector or component. The connectors that are plugged in incorrectly will damage the plug and the connector. Take your time and make sure that you are handling the hardware correctly.

Electricity and Ohm's Law

These are the four basic units of electricity:

- Voltage (**V**)
- Current (**I**)
- Power (**P**)
- Resistance (**R**)

Voltage, current, power, and resistance are electronic terms that a computer technician must know:

- Voltage is a measure of the force required to push electrons through a circuit.
- Voltage is measured in volts (V). A computer power supply usually produces several different voltages.
- Current is a measure of the amount of electrons going through a circuit.
- Current is measured in amperes, or amps (A). Computer power supplies deliver different amperages for each output voltage.
- Power is a measure of the pressure required to push electrons through a circuit, called voltage, multiplied by the number of electrons going through that circuit, called current. The measurement is called watts (W). Computer power supplies are rated in watts.
- Resistance is the opposition to the flow of current in a circuit. Resistance is measured in ohms. Lower resistance allows more current, and therefore more power, to flow through a circuit. A good fuse will have low resistance or a measurement of almost 0 ohms.

There is a basic equation that expresses how three of the terms relate to each other. It states that voltage is equal to the current multiplied by the resistance. This is known as Ohm's Law.

$V = IR$

In an electrical system, power (P) is equal to the voltage multiplied by the current.

$P = VI$

In an electrical circuit, increasing the current or the voltage will result in higher power.

As an example of how this works, imagine a simple circuit that has a 9V light bulb hooked up to a 9V battery. The power output of the light bulb is 100W. Using the equation above, we can calculate how much current in amps would be required to get 100W out of this 9V bulb.

To solve this equation, we know the following information:

- **P = 100W**

- **V = 9V**

- **I = 100W / 9V = 11.11A**

What happens if a 12V battery and a 12V light bulb are used to get 100W of power?

100W / 12V = 8.33A

This system produces the same power, but with less current.

Computers normally use power supplies ranging from 250W to 650W output capacity. However, some computers may need 850W and higher capacity power supplies. When building a computer, select a power supply with sufficient wattage to power all of the components. Each component inside the computer uses a certain amount of power. Obtain the wattage information for the components from the manufacturer's documentation. When deciding on a power supply, make sure to choose a power supply that has more than enough power for the current components. A power supply with a higher wattage rating has more capacity; therefore, it can handle more devices.

On the back of the power supply is a small switch called the voltage selector switch. This switch sets the input voltage to the power supply to either 110V / 115V or 220V / 230V. The correct voltage setting is determined by the country where the power supply will be used. Setting the voltage switch to the incorrect input voltage could damage the power supply and other parts of your computer. If a power supply does not have the voltage selector switch, your power supply will automatically detect and set the correct voltage.

Caution

Do not open a power supply. Electronic capacitors located inside of a power supply, shown in Figure 3, can hold a charge for extended periods of time.

Refer to
Figure
in online course

1.4 Identify the names, purposes, and characteristics of internal components

This section discusses the names, purposes, and characteristics of the internal components of a computer.

After completing this section, you will meet these objectives:

- Identify the names, purposes, and characteristics of motherboards.

- Explain the names, purposes, and characteristics of CPUs.

- Identify the names, purposes, and characteristics of cooling systems.

- Identify the names, purposes, and characteristics of ROM and RAM.

- Identify the names, purposes, and characteristics of adapter cards.

- Identify the names, purposes, and characteristics of storage drives.

- Identify the names, purposes, and characteristics of internal cables.

Refer to
Figure
in online course

1.4.1 Identify the names, purposes, and characteristics of motherboards

The motherboard is the main printed circuit board and contains the buses, or electrical pathways, found in a computer. These buses allow data to travel between the various components that comprise a computer. Figure 1 shows a variety of motherboards. A motherboard is also known as the system board, the backplane, or the main board.

The motherboard accommodates the central processing unit (CPU), RAM, expansion slots, heat sink/fan assembly, BIOS chip, chipset, and the embedded wires that interconnect the motherboard components. Sockets, internal and external connectors, and various ports are also placed on the motherboard.

The form factor of motherboards pertains to the size and shape of the board. It also describes the physical layout of the different components and devices on the motherboard. The form factor determines how individual components attach to the motherboard and the shape of the computer case. Various form factors exist for motherboards, as shown in Figure 2.

The most common form factor in desktop computers was the AT, based on the IBM AT motherboard. The AT motherboard can be up to approximately one foot wide. This cumbersome size led to the development of smaller form factors. The placement of heat sinks and fans often interferes with the use of expansion slots in smaller form factors.

A newer motherboard form factor, ATX, improved on the AT design. The ATX case is designed to accommodate the integrated I/O ports on the ATX motherboard. The ATX power supply connects to the motherboard via a single 20-pin connector instead of the confusing P8 and P9 connectors used with some earlier form factors. Instead of using a physical toggle switch, the ATX power supply can be powered on and off using signaling from the motherboard.

Some manufacturers have proprietary form factors based on the ATX design. This causes some motherboards, power supplies, and other components to be incompatible with standard ATX cases.

An important set of components on the motherboard is the chipset. The chipset is composed of various integrated circuits attached to the motherboard that control how system hardware interacts with the CPU and motherboard. The CPU is installed into a slot or socket on the motherboard. The socket on the motherboard determines the type of CPU that can be installed.

The chipset of a motherboard allows the CPU to communicate and interact with the other components of the computer, and to exchange data with system memory, or RAM, hard disk drives, video cards, and other output devices. The chipset establishes how much memory can be added to a motherboard. The chipset also determines the type of connectors on the motherboard.

Most chipsets are divided into two distinct components, Northbridge and Southbridge. What each component does varies from manufacturer to manufacturer. In general, the Northbridge controls access to the RAM, video card, and the speeds at which the CPU can communicate with them. The video card is sometimes integrated into the Northbridge. AMD and Intel have chips that integrate the memory controller onto the CPU die, which improves performance and power consumption. The Southbridge, in most cases, allows the CPU to communicate with the hard drives, sound card, USB ports, and other I/O ports.

Refer to
Figure
in online course

1.4.2 Identify the names, purposes, and characteristics of CPUs

The central processing unit (CPU) is considered the brain of the computer. It is sometimes referred to as the processor. Most calculations take place in the CPU. In terms of computing power, the CPU is the most important element of a computer system. CPUs come in different form factors, each style requiring a particular slot or socket on the motherboard. Common CPU manufacturers include Intel and AMD.

The CPU socket or slot is the connector that interfaces between the motherboard and the processor. Most CPU sockets and processors in use today are built around the pin grid array (PGA) architecture, in which the pins on the underside of the processor are inserted into the socket, usually with zero insertion force (ZIF). ZIF refers to the amount of force needed to install a CPU into the motherboard socket or slot. Slot-based processors are cartridge-shaped and fit into a slot that looks similar to an expansion slot. Figure 1 lists common CPU socket specifications.

The CPU executes a program, which is a sequence of stored instructions. Each model of processor has an instruction set, which it executes. The CPU executes the program by processing each piece of data as directed by the program and the instruction set. While the CPU is executing one step of the program, the remaining instructions and the data are stored nearby in a special memory called cache. There are two major CPU architectures related to instruction sets:

- *Reduced Instruction Set Computer (RISC)–* Architectures use a relatively small set of instructions, and RISC chips are designed to execute these instructions very rapidly.

- *Complex Instruction Set Computer (CISC)–* Architectures use a broad set of instructions, resulting in fewer steps per operation.

Some CPUs incorporate hyperthreading to enhance the performance of the CPU. With hyperthreading, the CPU has multiple pieces of code being executed simultaneously on each pipeline. To an operating system, a single CPU with hyperthreading performs as though there are two CPUs.

The power of a CPU is measured by the speed and the amount of data that it can process. The speed of a CPU is rated in cycles per second. The speed of current CPUs is measured in millions of cycles per second, called megahertz (MHz), or billions of cycles per second, called gigahertz (GHz). The amount of data that a CPU can process at one time depends on the size of the processor data bus. This is also called the CPU bus or the front side bus (FSB). The wider the processor data bus width, the more powerful the processor is. Current processors have a 32-bit or a 64-bit processor data bus.

Overclocking is a technique used to make a processor work at a faster speed than its original specification. Overclocking is not a reliable way to improve computer performance and can result in damage to the CPU. The opposite of overclocking is CPU throttling. CPU throttling is a technique used when the processor runs at less than the rated speed to conserve power or produce less heat. Throttling is commonly used on laptops and other mobile devices.

MMX is a set of multimedia instructions built into Intel processors. MMX enabled microprocessors can handle many common multimedia operations that are normally handled by a separate sound or video card. However, only software specifically written to call MMX instructions can use the MMX instruction set. In Intel CPUs, MMX has been replaced by Streaming Single-instruction-multi-data Extensions (SSE), which is an enhancement to the instruction set. There are many versions of SSE, each of which includes additional instructions.

The latest processor technology has resulted in CPU manufacturers finding ways to incorporate more than one CPU core onto a single chip. Figure 2 lists the most common multiple core processors. These CPUs are capable of processing multiple instructions concurrently:

- *Single Core CPU–* One core inside a single CPU that handles all of the processing capability. A motherboard manufacturer may provide sockets for more than one single processor, providing the ability to build a powerful, multi-processor computer.

- *Dual Core CPU–* Two cores inside a single CPU in which both cores can process information at the same time.

- *Triple Core CPU*– Three cores inside a single CPU that is actually a quad-core processor with one of the cores disabled.

- *Quad Core CPU*– Four cores inside a single CPU in which all cores can process information simultaneously for enhanced software applications.

Refer to **Figure** in online course

1.4.3 Identify the names, purposes, and characteristics of cooling systems

Electronic components generate heat. Heat is caused by the flow of current within the components. Computer components perform better when kept cool. If the heat is not removed, the computer may run slower. If too much heat builds up, computer components can be damaged.

Increasing the air flow in the computer case allows more heat to be removed. A case fan, shown in Figure 1, is installed in the computer case to make the cooling process more efficient.

In addition to case fans, a heat sink draws heat away from the core of the CPU. A fan on top of the heat sink, shown in Figure 2, moves the heat away from the CPU.

Other components are also susceptible to heat damage and are sometimes equipped with fans. Video adapter cards also produce a great deal of heat. Fans are dedicated to cool the graphics-processing unit (GPU), as seen in Figure 3.

Computers with extremely fast CPUs and GPUs may use a water-cooling system. A metal plate is placed over the processor and water is pumped over the top to collect the heat that the CPU creates. The water is pumped to a radiator to be cooled by the air, and then re-circulated.

Refer to **Figure** in online course

1.4.4 Identify the names, purposes, and characteristics of ROM and RAM

ROM

Read-only memory (ROM) chips are located on the motherboard. ROM chips contain instructions that can be directly accessed by the CPU. Basic instructions for booting the computer and loading the operating system are stored in ROM. ROM chips retain their contents even when the computer is powered down. The contents cannot be erased or changed by normal means. The different types of ROM are described in Figure 1.

Note

ROM is sometimes called firmware. This is misleading because firmware is actually the software that is stored in a ROM chip.

RAM

Random access memory (RAM) is the temporary storage for data and programs that are being accessed by the CPU. RAM is volatile memory, which means that the contents are erased when the computer is powered off. The more RAM in a computer, the more capacity the computer has to hold and process large programs and files, as well as enhance system performance. The different types of RAM are described in Figure 2.

Memory Modules

Early computers had RAM installed on the motherboard as individual chips. The individual memory chips, called dual inline package (DIP) chips, were difficult to install and often became loose on the motherboard. To solve this problem, designers soldered the memory chips on a special circuit board called a memory module. The different types of memory modules are described in Figure 3.

Note

Memory modules can be single-sided or double-sided. Single-sided memory modules only contain RAM on one side of the module. Double-sided memory modules contain RAM on both sides of the module.

The speed of memory has a direct impact on how much data a processor can process because faster memory improves the performance of the processor. As processor speed increases, memory speed must also increase. For example, single-channel memory is capable of transferring data at 64 bits. Dual-channel memory increases speed by using a second channel of memory, creating a data transfer rate of 128 bits.

Double Data Rate (DDR) technology doubles the maximum bandwidth of SDRAM. DDR2 offers faster performance while using less energy. DDR3 operates at even higher speeds than DDR2; however, none of these DDR technologies are backward- or forward-compatible. See Figure 4 for a chart comparing different memory types and speeds.

Cache

SRAM is used as cache memory to store the most frequently used data. SRAM provides the processor with faster access to the data than retrieving it from the slower DRAM, or main memory. The three types of cache memory are described in Figure 5.

Error Checking

Memory errors occur when the data is not stored correctly in the RAM chips. The computer uses different methods to detect and correct data errors in memory. Figure 6 describes three different methods of memory error checking.

Refer to
Figure
in online course

1.4.5 Identify the names, purposes, and characteristics of adapter cards

Adapter cards increase the functionality of a computer by adding controllers for specific devices or by replacing malfunctioning ports. Figure 1 shows several types of adapter cards. Adapter cards are used to expand and customize the capability of the computer:

- *Network Interface Card (NIC)*– Connects a computer to a network using a network cable

- *Wireless NIC*– Connects a computer to a network using radio frequencies

- *Sound adapter*– Provides audio capability

- *Video adapter*– Provides graphic capability

- *Capture card*– Sends a video signal to a computer so that the signal can be recorded to the computer hard drive with Video Capture software

- *TV tuner*– Provides the ability to watch and record TV signals on a PC by connecting a TV source, such as cable TV, satellite, or an antenna, to the installed tuner card

- *Modem adapter*– Connects a computer to the Internet using a phone line

- *Small Computer System Interface (SCSI) adapter*– Connects SCSI devices, such as hard drives or tape drives, to a computer

- **Redundant Array of Independent Disks (RAID) adapter–** Connects multiple hard drives to a computer to provide redundancy and to improve performance

- **Universal Serial Bus (USB) port–** Connects a computer to peripheral devices

- **Parallel port–** Connects a computer to peripheral devices

- **Serial port–** Connects a computer to peripheral devices

Computers have expansion slots on the motherboard to install adapter cards. The type of adapter card connector must match the expansion slot. A riser card was used in computer systems with the LPX form factor to allow adapter cards to be installed horizontally. The riser card was mainly used in slim-line desktop computers. The different types of expansion slots are shown in Figure 2.

Refer to
Figure
in online course

1.4.6 Identify the names, purposes, and characteristics of storage drives

Storage drives, as shown in Figure 1, read or write information to magnetic or optical storage media. The drive can be used to store data permanently or to retrieve information from a media disk. Storage drives can be installed inside the computer case, such as a hard drive. For portability, some storage drives can connect to the computer using a USB port, a FireWire port, or an SCSI port. These portable storage drives are sometimes referred to as removable drives and can be used on multiple computers. Here are some common types of storage drives:

- Floppy drive

- Hard drive

- Optical drive

- Flash drive

Floppy Drive

A floppy drive, or floppy disk drive, is a storage device that uses removable 3.5-inch floppy disks. These magnetic floppy disks can store 720 KB or 1.44 MB of data. In a computer, the floppy drive is usually configured as the A: drive. The floppy drive can be used to boot the computer if it contains a bootable floppy disk. A 5.25-inch floppy drive is older technology and is seldom used.

Hard Drive

A hard drive, or hard disk drive, is a magnetic storage device that is installed inside the computer. The hard drive is used as permanent storage for data. In a Windows computer, the hard drive is usually configured as the C: drive and contains the operating system and applications. The hard drive is often configured as the first drive in the boot sequence. The storage capacity of a hard drive is measured in billions of bytes, or gigabytes (GB). The speed of a hard drive is measured in revolutions per minute (RPM). Multiple hard drives can be added to increase storage capacity.

Traditional hard drives are magnetic. Magnetic hard drives have drive motors designed to spin magnetic platters and the drive heads. In contrast, the newer solid state drives (SSDs) do not have moving parts. Because there are no drive motors and moving parts, the SSD uses far less energy than the magnetic hard drive. Non-volatile flash memory chips manage all storage on an SSD, which results in faster access to data, higher reliability, and reduced power usage. SSDs have the same form factor as magnetic hard drives and use ATA or SATA interfaces. SSDs can be installed as a replacement for magnetic drives.

Optical Drive

An optical drive is a storage device that uses lasers to read data on the optical media. There are three types of optical drives:

- Compact Disc (CD)

- Digital versatile Disc (DVD)

- Blu-ray Disc (BD)

CD, DVD, and BD media can be pre-recorded (read-only), recordable (write once), or re-recordable (read and write multiple times). CDs have a data storage capacity of approximately 700 MB. DVDs have a data storage capacity of approximately 4.3 GB on a single-layer disc, and approximately 8.5 GB on a dual-layer disc. BDs have a storage capacity of 25 GB on a single-layer disc, and 50 GB on a dual-layer disc.

There are several types of optical media:

- CD-ROM – CD read-only memory media that is pre-recorded.

- CD-R – CD recordable media that can be recorded one time.

- CD-RW – CD rewritable media that can be recorded, erased, and re-recorded.

- DVD-ROM – DVD read-only memory media that is pre-recorded.

- DVD-RAM – DVD random access memory media that can be recorded, erased, and re-recorded.

- DVD+/-R – DVD recordable media that can be recorded one time.

- DVD+/-RW – DVD rewritable media that can be recorded, erased, and re-recorded.

- BD-ROM – BD read-only media that is pre-recorded with movies, games, or software.

- BD-R – BD recordable media that can record HD video and PC data storage one time.

- BD-RE – BD rewritable format for HD video recording and PC data storage.

External Flash Drive

An external flash drive, also known as a thumb drive, is a removable storage device that connects to a USB port. An external flash drive uses the same type of non-volatile memory chips as solid state drives and does not require power to maintain the data. These drives can be accessed by the operating system in the same way that other types of drives are accessed.

Types of Drive Interfaces

Hard drives and optical drives are manufactured with different interfaces that are used to connect the drive to the computer. To install a storage drive in a computer, the connection interface on the drive must be the same as the controller on the motherboard. Here are some common drive interfaces:

- *IDE–* Integrated Drive Electronics, also called Advanced Technology Attachment (ATA) is an early drive controller interface that connects computers and hard disk drives. An IDE interface uses a 40-pin connector.

- *EIDE–* Enhanced Integrated Drive Electronics, also called ATA-2, is an updated version of the IDE drive controller interface. EIDE supports hard drives larger than 512 MB, enables Direct Memory Access (DMA) for speed, and uses the AT Attachment Packet Interface

(ATAPI) to accommodate optical drives and tape drives on the EIDE bus. An EIDE interface uses a 40-pin connector.

- *PATA–* Parallel ATA refers to the parallel version of the ATA drive controller interface.

- *SATA–* Serial ATA refers to the serial version of the ATA drive controller interface. A SATA interface uses a 7-pin data connector.

- *eSATA–* External Serial ATA provides a hot-swappable, external interface for SATA drives. The eSATA interface connects an external SATA drive using a 7-pin connector. The cable can be up to two meters (6.56 ft.) in length.

- *SCSI–* Small Computer System Interface is a drive controller interface that can connect up to 15 drives. SCSI can connect both internal and external drives. An SCSI interface uses a 50-pin, 68-pin, or 80-pin connector.

RAID provides a way to store data across multiple hard disks for redundancy. To the operating system, RAID appears as one logical disk. See Figure 2 for a comparison of the different RAID levels. The following terms describe how RAID stores data on the various disks:

- *Parity–* A method used to detect data errors.

- *Striping–* A method used to write data across multiple drives.

- *Mirroring–* A method of storing duplicate data to a second drive.

Refer to
Figure
in online course

1.4.7 Identify the names, purposes, and characteristics of internal cables

Drives require both a power cable and a data cable. A power supply will have a SATA power connector for SATA drives, a Molex power connector for PATA drives, and a Berg 4-pin connector for floppy drives. The buttons and the LED lights on the front of the case connect to the motherboard with the front panel cables.

Data cables connect drives to the drive controller, which is located on an adapter card or on the motherboard. Here are some common types of data cables:

- *Floppy disk drive (FDD) data cable–* Data cable has up to two 34-pin drive connectors and one 34-pin connector for the drive controller.

- *PATA (IDE/EIDE) 40-conductor data cable–* Originally, the IDE interface supported two devices on a single controller. With the introduction of Extended IDE, two controllers capable of supporting two devices each were introduced. The 40-conductor ribbon cable uses 40-pin connectors. The cable has two connectors for the drives and one connector for the controller.

- *PATA (EIDE) 80-conductor data cable–* As the data rates available over the EIDE interface increased, the chance of data corruption during transmission increased. An 80-conductor cable was introduced for devices transmitting at 33.3 MB/s and over, allowing for a more reliable balanced data transmission. The 80-conductor cable uses 40-pin connectors.

- *SATA data cable–* This cable has seven conductors, one keyed connector for the drive, and one keyed connector the drive controller.

- *eSATA data cable–* The eSATA external disk connects to the eSATA interface using a 7-pin data cable. This cable does not supply any power to the eSATA external disk. A separate power cable provides power to the disk.

■ *SCSI data cable*– There are three types of SCSI data cables. A narrow SCSI data cable has 50 conductors, up to seven 50-pin connectors for drives, and one 50-pin connector for the drive controller, also called the host adapter. A wide SCSI data cable has 68 conductors, up to 15 68-pin connectors for drives, and one 68-pin connector for the host adapter. An Alt-4 SCSI data cable has 80 conductors, up to 15 80-pin connectors for drives, and one 80-pin connector for the host adapter.

Note

A colored stripe on a cable identifies Pin 1 on the cable. When installing a data cable, always ensure that Pin 1 on the cable aligns with Pin 1 on the drive or drive controller. Some cables may be keyed and therefore they can only be connected one way to the drive and drive controller.

Research Computer Components

Gather information about the components you will need to complete your customer's computer.

1.5 Identify the names, purposes, and characteristics of ports and cables

Input/output (I/O) ports on a computer connect peripheral devices, such as printers, scanners, and portable drives. The following ports and cables are commonly used:

■ Serial

■ USB

■ FireWire

■ Parallel

■ SCSI

■ Network

■ PS/2

■ Audio

■ Video

Serial Ports and Cables

A serial port can be either a DB-9, as shown in Figure 1, or a DB-25 male connector. Serial ports transmit one bit of data at a time. To connect a serial device, such as a modem or printer, a serial cable must be used. A serial cable has a maximum length of 50 feet (15.2 m).

Modem Ports and Cables

In addition to the serial cable used to connect an external modem to a computer, a telephone cable is used to connect a modem to a telephone outlet. This cable uses an RJ-11 connector, as shown in Figure 2. A traditional setup of an external modem using a serial cable and a telephone cable is shown in Figure 3.

USB Ports and Cables

The Universal Serial Bus (USB) is a standard interface that connects peripheral devices to a computer. It was originally designed to replace serial and parallel connections. USB devices are hot-swappable, which means that users can connect and disconnect the devices while the computer is powered on. USB connections can be found on computers, cameras, printers, scanners, storage devices, and many other electronic devices. A USB hub is used to connect multiple USB devices. A single USB port in a computer can support up to 127 separate devices with the use of multiple USB hubs. Some devices can also be powered through the USB port, eliminating the need for an external power source. Figure 4 shows USB cables with connectors.

USB 1.1 allowed transmission rates of up to 12 Mbps in full-speed mode and 1.5 Mbps in low-speed mode. USB 2.0 allows transmission speeds up to 480 Mbps. USB devices can only transfer data up to the maximum speed allowed by the specific port.

FireWire Ports and Cables

FireWire is a high-speed, hot-swappable interface that connects peripheral devices to a computer. A single FireWire port in a computer can support up to 63 devices. Some devices can also be powered through the FireWire port, eliminating the need for an external power source. FireWire uses the IEEE 1394 standard and is also known as i.Link.

The IEEE 1394a standard supports data rates up to 400 Mbps and cable lengths up to 15 feet (4.5 m). This standard uses a 6-pin connector or a 4-pin connector. The IEEE 1394b standard allows for a greater range of connections, including CAT5 UTP and optical fiber. Depending on the media used, data rates are supported up to 3.2 Gbps over a 100m distance. Figure 5 shows FireWire cables with connectors.

Parallel Ports and Cables

A parallel port on a computer is a standard Type A DB-25 female connector. The parallel connector on a printer is a standard Type B 36-pin Centronics connector. Some newer printers may use a Type C high-density 36-pin connector. Parallel ports can transmit 8 bits of data at one time and use the IEEE 1284 standard. To connect a parallel device, such as a printer, a parallel cable must be used. A parallel cable, as shown in Figure 6, has a maximum length of 15 feet (4.5 m).

SCSI Ports and Cables

A SCSI port can transmit parallel data at rates in excess of 320 MBps and can support up to 15 devices. If a single SCSI device is connected to an SCSI port, the cable can be up to 80 feet (24.4 m) in length. If multiple SCSI devices are connected to an SCSI port, the cable can be up to 40 (12.2 m) feet in length. An SCSI port on a computer can be one of three different types, as shown in Figure 7:

- 80-pin connector
- 50-pin connector
- 68-pin connector

Note

SCSI devices must be terminated at the endpoints of the SCSI chain. Check the device manual for termination procedures.

Caution

Some SCSI connectors resemble parallel connectors. Be careful not to connect the cable to the wrong port. The voltage used in the SCSI format may damage the parallel interface. SCSI connectors should be clearly labeled.

Network Ports and Cables

A network port, also known as an RJ-45 port, connects a computer to a network. The connection speed depends on the type of network port. Standard Ethernet can transmit up to 10 Mbps, Fast Ethernet can transmit up to 100 Mbps, and Gigabit Ethernet can transmit up to 1000 Mbps. The maximum length of network cable is 328 feet (100 m). A network connector is shown in Figure 8.

PS/2 Ports

A PS/2 port connects a keyboard or a mouse to a computer. The PS/2 port is a 6-pin mini-DIN female connector. The connectors for the keyboard and mouse are often colored differently, as shown in Figure 9. If the ports are not color-coded, look for a small figure of a mouse or keyboard next to each port.

Audio Ports

An audio port connects audio devices to the computer. Some of the following audio ports are commonly used, as shown in Figure 10:

- Line In – Connects to an external source, such as a stereo system

- Microphone – Connects to a microphone

- Line Out – Connects to speakers or headphones

- Sony/Philips Digital Interface Format (S/PDIF) – Connects to fiber optic cable to support digital audio

- TosLink – Connects to coaxial cable to support digital audio

- Gameport/MIDI – Connects to a joystick or MIDI-interfaced device

Video Ports and Connectors

A video port connects a monitor cable to a computer. Figure 11 shows three common video ports. There are several video port and connector types:

- *Video Graphics Array (VGA)*– VGA has a 3-row, 15-pin female connector and provides analog output to a monitor.

- *Digital Visual Interface (DVI)*– DVI has a 24-pin female connector or a 29-pin female connector and provides an uncompressed digital output to a monitor. DVI-I provides both analog and digital signals. DVI-D provides digital signals only.

- *High-Definition Multimedia Interface (HDMi)–* HDMi has a 19-pin connector and provides digital video and digital audio signals.

- *S-Video–* S-Video has a 4-pin connector and provides analog video signals.

- *Component/RGB–* RGB has three shielded cables (red, green, blue) with RCA jacks and provides analog video signals.

Refer to
Figure
in online course

1.6 Identify the names, purposes, and characteristics of input devices

An input device is used to enter data or instructions into a computer. Here are some examples of input devices:

- Mouse and keyboard

- Digital camera and digital video camera

- Biometric authentication device

- Touch screen

- Scanner

The mouse and keyboard are the two most commonly used input devices. The mouse is used to navigate the graphical user interface (GUI). The keyboard is used to enter text commands that control the computer.

A keyboard, video, mouse (KVM) switch is a hardware device that can be used to control more than one computer using a single keyboard, monitor, and mouse. KVM switches provide cost-efficient access to multiple servers using a single keyboard, monitor, and mouse for businesses. Home users can save space using a KVM switch to connect multiple computers to one keyboard, monitor, and mouse. See Figure 1.

Newer KVM switches have added the capability to share USB devices and speakers with multiple computers. Typically, by pressing a button on the KVM switch, the user can change the control from one connected computer to another connected computer. Some models of the switch transfer control from one computer to another computer using a specific key sequence on a keyboard, such as CNTL > CNTL > A > ENTER to control the first computer connected to the switch, then CNTL > CNTL > B > ENTER to transfer control to the next computer.

Digital cameras and digital video cameras, shown in Figure 2, create images that can be stored on magnetic media. The image is stored as a file that can be displayed, printed, or altered.

Biometric identification makes use of features that are unique to an individual user, such as fingerprints, voice recognition, or a retinal scan. When combined with ordinary usernames, biometrics guarantees that the authorized person is accessing the data. Figure 3 shows a laptop that has a built-in fingerprint scanner. By measuring the physical characteristics of the fingerprint of the user, the user is granted access if the fingerprint characteristics match the database and the correct login information is supplied.

A touch screen has a pressure-sensitive transparent panel. The computer receives instructions specific to the place on the screen that the user touches.

A scanner digitizes an image or document. The digitization of the image is stored as a file that can be displayed, printed, or altered. A bar code reader is a type of scanner that reads universal product code (UPC) bar codes. It is widely used for pricing and inventory information.

Refer to
Figure
in online course

1.7 Identify the names, purposes, and characteristics of output devices

An output device is used to present information to the user from a computer. Here are some examples of output devices:

- Monitors and Projectors

- Printers, scanners, and fax machines

- Speakers and headphones

Monitors and Projectors

Monitors and projectors are primary output devices for a computer. There are different types of monitors, as shown in Figure 1. The most important difference between these monitor types is the technology used to create an image:

- *CRT–* The cathode-ray tube (CRT) has three electron beams. Each beam directs colored phosphor on the screen that glows either red, blue, or green. Areas not struck by an electron beam do not glow. The combination of glowing and non-glowing areas creates the image on the screen. This technology is also used by most televisions. CRTs usually have a degauss button on the front that the user can press to remove discoloration caused by magnetic interference.

- *LCD–* Liquid crystal display is commonly used in flat panel monitors, laptops, and some projectors. It consists of two polarizing filters with a liquid crystal solution between them. An electronic current aligns the crystals so that light can either pass through or not pass through. The effect of light passing through in certain areas and not in others is what creates the image. LCD comes in two forms, active matrix and passive matrix. Active matrix is sometimes called thin film transistor (TFT). TFT allows each pixel to be controlled, which creates very sharp color images. Passive matrix is less expensive than active matrix but does not provide the same level of image control. Passive matrix is not commonly used in laptops.

- *DLP–* Digital light processing is another technology used in projectors. DLP projectors use a spinning color wheel with a microprocessor-controlled array of mirrors called a digital micromirror device (DMD). Each mirror corresponds to a specific pixel. Each mirror reflects light toward or away from the projector optics. This creates a monochromatic image of up to 1024 shades of gray in between white and black. The color wheel then adds the color data to complete the projected color image.

Monitor resolution refers to the level of image detail that can be reproduced. Figure 2 is a chart of common monitor resolutions. Higher resolution settings produce better image quality. Several factors are involved in monitor resolution:

- *Pixel–* The term pixel is an abbreviation for picture element. Pixels are the tiny dots that comprise a screen. Each pixel consists of red, green, and blue.

- *Dot pitch–* Dot pitch is the distance between pixels on the screen. A lower dot pitch number produces a better image.

- *Contrast ratio–* The contrast ratio is a measurement of the difference in intensity of light between the brightest point (white) and the darkest point (black). A 10,000:1 contrast ratio shows dimmer whites and lighter blacks than a monitor with a contrast ratio of 1,000,000:1.

- *Refresh rate–* The refresh rate is how often per second the image is rebuilt. A higher refresh rate produces a better image and reduces the level of flicker.

- *Interlace/Non-Interlace–* Interlaced monitors create the image by scanning the screen two times. The first scan covers the odd lines, top to bottom, and the second scan covers the even lines. Non-interlaced monitors create the image by scanning the screen, one line at a time from top to bottom. Most CRT monitors today are non-interlaced.

- *Horizontal Vertical Colors (HVC)–* The number of pixels in a line is the horizontal resolution. The number of lines in a screen is the vertical resolution. The number of colors that can be reproduced is the color resolution.

- *Aspect ratio–* Aspect ratio is the horizontal to vertical measurement of the viewing area of a monitor. For example, a 4:3 aspect ratio would apply to a viewing area that is 16 inches wide by 12 inches high. A 4:3 aspect radio would also apply to a viewing area that is 24 inches wide by 18 inches high. A viewing area that is 22 inches wide by 12 inches high has an aspect ratio of 11:6.

- *Native resolution–* Native resolution is the number of pixels that a monitor has. A monitor with a resolution of 1280x1024 has 1280 horizontal pixels and 1024 vertical pixels. Native mode is when the image sent to the monitor matches the native resolution of the monitor.

Monitors have controls for adjusting the quality of the image. Here are some common monitor settings:

- Brightness – Intensity of the image

- Contrast – Ratio of light to dark

- Position – Vertical and horizontal location of image on the screen

- Reset – Returns the monitor settings to factory settings

Adding additional monitors increases the number of windows that are visible on the desktop. Many computers have built-in support for multiple monitors. See Figure 3 for more information about configuring multiple monitors.

All-in-One Printer

Printers are output devices that create hard copies of computer files. Some printers specialize in particular applications, such as printing color photographs. Other all-in-one type printers, like the one shown in Figure 4, are designed to provide multiple services such as printing, scanning, faxing, and copying.

Speakers and Headphones

Speakers and headphones are output devices for audio signals. Most computers have audio support either integrated into the motherboard or on an adapter card. Audio support includes ports that allow input and output of audio signals. The audio card has an amplifier to power headphones and external speakers, which are shown in Figure 5.

Refer to
Figure
in online course

1.8 Explain system resources and their purposes

System resources are used for communication purposes between the CPU and other components in a computer. There are three common system resources:

- Interrupt Requests (IRQ)

- Input/Output (I/O) Port Addresses

- Direct Memory Access (DMA)

Interrupt Requests

IRQs are used by computer components to request information from the CPU. The IRQ travels along a wire on the motherboard to the CPU. When the CPU receives an interrupt request, the CPU determines how to fulfill this request. The priority of the request is determined by the IRQ number assigned to that computer component. Older computers only had eight IRQs to assign to devices. Newer computers have 16 IRQs, which are numbered 0 to 15, as shown in Figure 1. As a general rule, each component in the computer must be assigned a unique IRQ. IRQ conflicts can cause components to stop functioning and even cause the computer to crash. Today, most IRQ numbers are assigned automatically with plug and play (PnP) operating systems and the implementation of PCI slots, USB ports, and FireWire ports. With the numerous components that can be installed in a computer, it is difficult to assign a unique IRQ to every component. PCI devices can now share IRQs without conflict.

Input/Output (I/O) Port Addresses

Input/output (I/O) port addresses are used to communicate between devices and software. The I/O port address is used to send and receive data for a component. As with IRQs, each component will have a unique I/O port assigned. There are 65,535 I/O ports in a computer, and they are referenced by a hexadecimal address in the range of 0000h to FFFFh. Figure 2 shows a chart of common I/O ports.

Direct Memory Access

DMA channels are used by high-speed devices to communicate directly with main memory. These channels allow the device to bypass interaction with the CPU and directly store and retrieve information from memory. Only certain devices can be assigned a DMA channel, such as SCSI host adapters and sound cards. Older computers only had four DMA channels to assign to components. Newer computers have eight DMA channels that are numbered 0 to 7, as shown in Figure 3.

Summary

This chapter introduced the IT industry, options for training and employment, and some of the industry-standard certifications. This chapter also covered the components that comprise a personal computer system. Much of the content in this chapter will help you throughout this course:

- Information Technology encompasses the use of computers, network hardware, and software to process, store, transmit, and retrieve information.

- A personal computer system consists of hardware components and software applications.

- The computer case and power supply must be chosen carefully to support the hardware inside the case and allow for the addition of components.

- The internal components of a computer are selected for specific features and functions. All internal components must be compatible with the motherboard.

- You should use the correct type of ports and cables when connecting devices.

- Typical input devices include the keyboard, mouse, touch screen, and digital cameras.

- Typical output devices include monitors, printers, and speakers.

- System resources must be assigned to computer components. System resources include IRQs, I/O port addresses, and DMAs.

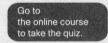
Go to
the online course
to take the quiz.

Chapter 1 Quiz

Take the chapter quiz to test your knowledge.

Your Chapter Notes

Safe Lab Procedures and Tool Use

Introduction

This chapter covers basic safety practices for the workplace, hardware and software tools, and the disposal of hazardous materials. Safety guidelines help protect individuals from accidents and injury and protect equipment from damage. Some of these guidelines are designed to protect the environment from contamination by discarded materials. Stay alert to situations that could result in injury or damage to equipment. Warning signs are designed to alert you to danger. Always watch for these signs and take the appropriate action according to the warning given.

After completing this chapter, you will meet these objectives:

- Explain the purpose of safe working conditions and procedures.

- Identify tools and software used with personal computer components and their purposes.

- Implement proper tool use.

Refer to
Figure
in online course

2.1 Explain the purpose of safe working conditions and procedures

Safe working conditions help to prevent injury to people and damage to computer equipment. A safe workspace is clean, organized, and properly lighted. Everyone must understand and follow safety procedures.

Follow proper procedures for handling computer equipment to reduce the risk of personal injury, damage to property, and loss of data. Any damage or loss may result in claims for damage from the owner of the property and data.

The proper disposal or recycling of hazardous computer components is a global issue. Make sure to follow regulations that govern how to dispose of specific items. Organizations that violate these regulations can be fined or face expensive legal battles.

After completing this section, you will meet these objectives:

- Identify safety procedures and potential hazards for users and technicians.

- Identify safety procedures to protect equipment from damage and data from loss.

- Identify safety procedures to protect the environment from contamination.

Refer to
Figure
in online course

2.1.1   Identify safety procedures and potential hazards for users and technicians

General Safety Guidelines

Follow the basic safety guidelines to prevent cuts, burns, electrical shock, and damage to eyesight. As is best practice, make sure that a fire extinguisher and first-aid kit are available in case of fire or injury. Poorly placed or unsecured cables usually cause tripping hazards in a network installation. Cables should be installed in conduit or cable trays to prevent hazards to users. Figure 1 shows a list of general safety guidelines.

Electrical Safety Guidelines

Follow electrical safety guidelines to prevent electrical fires, injuries, and fatalities in the home and the workplace. Power supplies and monitors contain very high voltage. Only experienced technicians should attempt to repair power supplies and monitors, while most users should simply replace them. Do not wear the antistatic wrist strap when repairing power supplies or monitors.

Some printer parts may become very hot when in use, and other parts may contain very high voltages. Make sure that the printer has had time to cool before making the repair. Check the printer manual for locations of various components that may contain high voltages. Some components may retain high voltages even after the printer is turned off.

Electrical devices have certain power requirements. For example, AC adapters are manufactured for specific laptops. Exchanging power cords with a different type of laptop or device may cause damage to both the AC adapter and the laptop.

Fire Safety Guidelines

Follow fire safety guidelines to protect lives, structures, and equipment. To avoid an electrical shock, and to prevent damage to the computer, turn off and unplug the computer before beginning a repair.

Fire can spread rapidly and be very costly. Proper use of a fire extinguisher can prevent a small fire from getting out of control. When working with computer components, always consider the possibility of an accidental fire and know how to react. You should be alert for odors emitting from computers and electronic devices. When electronic components overheat or short out, they will emit a burning odor. If there is a fire, you should follow these safety procedures:

- Never fight a fire that is out of control or not contained.

- Always have a planned fire escape route before beginning any work.

- Get out of the building quickly.

- Contact emergency services for help.

- Be sure to locate and read the instructions on the fire extinguishers in your workplace before you have to use them. Safety training may be available in your organization.

In the United States, there are four classifications for fire extinguishers. A different letter, color, and shape identify each fire extinguisher classification, as shown in Figure 2. Each type of fire extinguisher has specific chemicals to fight different types of fires:

Class A – Paper, wood, plastics, cardboard

Class B – Gasoline, kerosene, organic solvents

Class C – Electrical equipment

Class D – Combustible metals

What types of fire extinguisher classifications are there in your country?

It is important to know how to use a fire extinguisher. Use the memory aid P-A-S-S to help you remember the basic rules of fire extinguisher operation:

P -   Pull the pin.

A -   Aim at the base of the fire, not at the flames.

S -   Squeeze the lever.

S -   Sweep the nozzle from side to side.

Refer to
Figure
in online course

2.1.2 Identify safety procedures to protect equipment from damage and data from loss

Electrostatic discharge (ESD), harsh climates, and poor-quality sources of electricity can cause damage to computer equipment. Follow proper handling guidelines, be aware of environmental issues, and use equipment that stabilizes power to prevent equipment damage and data loss.

ESD

Static electricity is the buildup of an electric charge resting on a surface. This buildup may jump to a component and cause damage. This is known as electrostatic discharge (ESD). ESD can be destructive to the electronics in a computer system.

At least 3,000 volts of static electricity must build up before a person can feel ESD. For example, static electricity can build up on you as you walk across a carpeted floor. When you touch another person, you both receive a shock. If the discharge causes pain or makes a noise, the charge was probably above 10,000 volts. By comparison, less than 30 volts of static electricity can damage a computer component.

ESD Protection Recommendations

ESD can cause permanent damage to electrical components. Follow these recommendations to help prevent ESD damage:

■ Keep all components in antistatic bags until you are ready to install them.

■ Use grounded mats on workbenches.

■ Use grounded floor mats in work areas.

■ Use antistatic wrist straps when working on computers.

EMI

Electromagnetic Interference (EMI) is the intrusion of outside electromagnetic signals in a transmission media, such as copper cabling. In a network environment, EMI distorts the signals so that the receiving devices have difficulty interpreting them.

EMI does not always come from expected sources such as cellular phones. Other types of electric equipment can emit a silent, invisible electromagnetic field that can extend for more than a mile.

As shown in Figure 1, there are many sources of EMI:

■ Any source designed to generate electromagnetic energy

■ Man-made sources like power lines or motors

- Natural events such as electrical storms or solar and interstellar radiations

Wireless networks are affected by Radio Frequency Interference (RFI). RFI is the interference caused by radio transmitters and other devices transmitting in the same frequency. For example, a cordless telephone can cause problems with a wireless network when both devices use the same frequency. Microwaves can also cause interference when positioned in close proximity to wireless networking devices.

Climate

Climate affects computer equipment in a variety of ways:

- If the environment temperature is too high, equipment can overheat.
- If the humidity level is too low, the chance of ESD increases.
- If the humidity level is too high, equipment can suffer from moisture damage.

Figure 2 shows how environmental conditions increase or decrease the risk of ESD.

Power Fluctuation Types

Voltage is the force that moves electrons through a circuit. The movement of electrons is called current. Computer circuits need voltage and current to operate electronic components. When the voltage in a computer is not accurate or steady, computer components may not operate correctly. Unsteady voltages are called power fluctuations.

The following types of AC power fluctuations can cause data loss or hardware failure:

- *Blackout*– Complete loss of AC power. A blown fuse, damaged transformer, or downed power line can cause a blackout.
- *Brownout*– Reduced voltage level of AC power that lasts for a period of time. Brownouts occur when the power line voltage drops below 80% of the normal voltage level. Overloading electrical circuits can cause a brownout.
- *Noise*– Interference from generators and lightning. Noise results in unclean power, which can cause errors in a computer system.
- *Spike*– Sudden increase in voltage that lasts for a very short period and exceeds 100% of the normal voltage on a line. Spikes can be caused by lightning strikes, but can also occur when the electrical system comes back on after a blackout.
- *Power surge*– Dramatic increase in voltage above the normal flow of electrical current. A power surge lasts for a few nanoseconds, or one-billionth of a second.

Power Protection Devices

To help shield against power fluctuation issues, use protection devices to protect the data and computer equipment:

- *Surge suppressor*– Helps protect against damage from surges and spikes. A surge suppressor diverts extra electrical voltage on the line to the ground.
- *Uninterruptible Power Supply (UPS)*– Helps protect against potential electrical power problems by supplying electrical power to a computer or other device. The battery is

constantly recharging while the UPS is in use. The UPS is able to supply a consistent quality of power when brownouts and blackouts occur. Many UPS devices are able to communicate directly with the operating system on a computer. This communication allows the UPS to safely shut down the computer and save data prior to the UPS losing all electrical power.

- *Standby Power Supply (SPS)*– Helps protect against potential electrical power problems by providing a backup battery to supply power when the incoming voltage drops below the normal level. The battery is on standby during the normal operation. When the voltage decreases, the battery provides DC power to a power inverter, which converts it to AC power for the computer. This device is not as reliable as a UPS because of the time it takes to switch over to the battery. If the switching device fails, the battery will not be able to supply power to the computer. Figure 3 shows some examples of surge suppressors, UPS, and SPS devices.

Caution

Never plug a printer into a UPS device. UPS manufacturers suggest never plugging a printer into a UPS for fear of overloading the UPS.

Refer to **Figure** in online course

2.1.3 Identify safety procedures to protect the environment from contamination

Computers and peripherals, as shown in Figure 1, contain materials that can be harmful to the environment. Hazardous materials are sometimes called toxic waste. These materials can contain high concentrations of heavy metals such as cadmium, lead, or mercury. The regulations for the disposal of hazardous materials vary according to state or country. Contact the local recycling or waste removal authorities in your community for information about disposal procedures and services.

Material Safety and Data Sheet

A Material Safety and Data Sheet (MSDS) is a fact sheet that summarizes information about material identification, including hazardous ingredients that can affect personal health, fire hazards, and first aid requirements. In Figure 2, the MSDS sheet contains chemical reactivity and incompatibility information that includes spill, leak, and disposal procedures. It also includes protective measures for the safe handling and storage of materials.

To determine if a material is classified as hazardous, consult the manufacturer's MSDS. In the U.S., the Occupational Safety and Health Administration (OSHA) requires that all hazardous materials must be accompanied by an MSDS when transferred to a new owner. The MSDS information included with products purchased for computer repairs or maintenance can be relevant to computer technicians. OSHA also requires that employees be informed about the materials that they are working with and be provided with material safety information. In the United Kingdom, Chemicals Hazard Information and Packaging for Supply Regulations 2002 (CHIP3) oversees the handling of hazardous materials. CHIP3 requires chemical suppliers to safely package and transport dangerous chemicals and to include a data sheet with the product.

Note

The MSDS is valuable in determining how to dispose of any potentially hazardous materials in the safest manner. Always check local regulations concerning acceptable disposal methods before disposing of any electronic equipment.

Which organization governs the use of hazardous chemicals in your country? Are MSDS sheets mandatory?

The MSDS contains valuable information:

- The name of the material
- The physical properties of the material
- Any hazardous ingredients contained in the material
- Reactivity data, such as fire and explosion data
- Procedures for spills or leaks
- Special precautions
- Health hazards
- Special protection requirements

Computers and other computing devices are eventually discarded because of one of the following reasons:

- Parts or components begin to fail more frequently as the device ages.
- The computer becomes obsolete for the application for which it was originally intended.
- Newer models have improved features.

Before discarding a computer or any of its components, it is crucial to consider safe disposal of each separate component.

Proper Disposal of Batteries

Batteries often contain rare earth metals that can be harmful to the environment. Batteries from portable computer systems may contain lead, cadmium, lithium, alkaline manganese, and mercury. These metals do not decay and will remain in the environment for many years. Mercury is commonly used in the manufacturing of batteries and is extremely toxic and harmful to humans.

Recycling batteries should be a standard practice for a technician. All batteries, including lithium-ion, nickel-cadmium, nickel-metal hydride, and lead-acid are subject to disposal procedures that comply with local environmental regulations.

Proper Disposal of Monitors or CRTs

Handle monitors and CRTs with care. Extremely high voltage can be stored in monitors and CRTs, even after being disconnected from a power source. CRTs contain glass, metal, plastics, lead, barium, and rare earth metals. According to the U.S. Environmental Protection Agency (EPA), CRTs may contain approximately 4 lbs (1.8 kg) of lead. Monitors must be disposed of in compliance with environmental regulations.

Proper Disposal of Toner Kits, Cartridges, and Developers

Used printer toner kits and printer cartridges must be disposed of properly or recycled. Some toner cartridge suppliers and manufacturers will take empty cartridges for refilling. There are also companies that specialize in refilling empty cartridges. Kits to refill inkjet printer cartridges are available but are not recommended, because the ink may leak into the printer, causing irreversible damage. This can be especially costly because using refilled inkjet cartridges may also void the inkjet printer warranty.

Proper Disposal of Chemical Solvents and Aerosol Cans

Contact the local sanitation company to learn how and where to dispose of the chemicals and solvents used to clean computers. Never dump chemicals or solvents down a sink or dispose of them in any drain that connects to public sewers.

The cans or bottles that contain solvents and other cleaning supplies must be handled carefully. Make sure that they are identified and treated as special hazardous waste. For example, some aerosol cans may explode when exposed to heat if the contents are not completely used.

Refer to **Figure** in online course

2.2 Identify tools and software used with personal computer components and their purposes

For every job there is the right tool. Make sure that you are familiar with the correct use of each tool and that the right tool is used for the current task. Skilled use of tools and software makes the job less difficult and ensures that tasks are performed properly and safely.

Software tools are available that help diagnose problems. Use these tools to determine which computer device is not functioning correctly.

A technician must document all repairs and computer problems. The documentation can then be used as a reference for future problems or for other technicians who may not have encountered the problem before. The documents may be paper-based, but electronic forms are preferred because they can be easily searched for specific problems.

After completing this section, you will meet these objectives:

- Identify hardware tools and their purpose.
- Identify software tools and their purpose.
- Identify organizational tools and their purpose.

Refer to **Figure** in online course

2.2.1 Identify hardware tools and their purpose

A toolkit should contain all of the tools necessary to complete hardware repairs. As you gain experience, you will learn which tools to have available for different types of jobs. Hardware tools are grouped into these four categories:

- ESD tools
- Hand tools
- Cleaning tools
- Diagnostic tools

ESD Tools

There are two ESD tools: the antistatic wrist strap and the antistatic mat. The antistatic wrist strap protects computer equipment when grounded to a computer chassis. The antistatic mat protects computer equipment by preventing static electricity from accumulating on the hardware or on the technician. Click each of the items in Figure 1 for more information on ESD tools.

Hand Tools

Most tools used in the computer assembly process are small hand tools. They are available individually or as part of a computer repair toolkit. Toolkits range widely in size, quality, and price. Click each of the items in Figure 2 for more information on hand tools.

Cleaning Tools

Having the appropriate cleaning tools is essential when maintaining or repairing computers. Using these tools ensures that computer components are not damaged during cleaning. Click each of the items in Figure 3 for more information on cleaning tools.

Diagnostic Tools

A digital multimeter and a loopback adapter are used to test hardware. Click each of the items in Figure 4 for more information on diagnostic tools.

Refer to
Figure
in online course

2.2.2   Identify software tools and their purpose

A technician must be able to use a range of software tools to help diagnose problems, maintain hardware, and protect the data stored on a computer.

Disk Management Tools

You must be able to identify which software to use in different situations. Disk management tools help detect and correct disk errors, prepare a disk for data storage, and remove unwanted files.

Click each of the buttons in Figure 1 to see screen shots of the following disk management tools:

- *Fdisk or Disk Management–* Creates and deletes partitions on a hard drive

- *Format–* Prepares a hard drive to store information

- *Scandisk or Chkdsk–* Checks the integrity of files and folders on a hard drive by scanning the file system. These tools may also check the disk surface for physical errors

- *Defrag–* Optimizes space on a hard drive to allow faster access to programs and data

- *Disk Cleanup–* Clears space on a hard drive by searching for files that can be safely deleted

- *Disk Management–* Initializes disks, creates partitions, and formats partitions

- *System File Checker (SFC)–* Scans the operating system critical files and replaces any files that are corrupted

Use the Windows XP boot disk for troubleshooting and repairing corrupted files. The Windows XP boot disk is designed to repair Windows system files, restore damaged or lost files, and reinstall the operating system. Third-party software tools are available to assist in troubleshooting problems.

Protection Software Tools

Each year, viruses, spyware, and other types of malicious attacks infect millions of computers. These attacks can damage an operating system, application, and data. Computers that have been infected may even have problems with hardware performance or component failure.

To protect data and the integrity of the operating system and hardware, use software designed to guard against attacks and to remove malicious programs.

Various types of software are used to protect hardware and data. Click each of the buttons in Figure 2 to see screen shots of these protection software tools:

- *Windows XP Security Center–* Checks the status of essential security settings. The Security Center continuously checks to make sure that the software firewall and antivirus programs are running. It also ensures that automatic updates are set to download and install automatically.

- *Antivirus program–* Protects against virus attacks.

- *Spyware remover–* Protects against software that sends information about web surfing habits to an attacker. Spyware can be installed without the knowledge or consent of the user.

- *Firewall program–* Runs continuously to protect against unauthorized communications to and from your computer.

Refer to **Worksheet** for this chapter

Diagnostic Software

Gather information about a hard drive diagnostic program.

Refer to **Figure** in online course

2.2.3 Identify organizational tools and their purpose

It is important that a technician document all services and repairs. These documents need to be stored centrally and made available to all other technicians. The documentation can then be used as reference material for similar problems that are encountered in the future. Good customer service includes providing the customer with a detailed description of the problem and the solution.

Personal Reference Tools

Personal reference tools include troubleshooting guides, manufacturer manuals, quick reference guides, and repair journals. In addition to an invoice, a technician keeps a journal of upgrades and repairs. The documentation in the journal should include descriptions of the problem, possible solutions that have been attempted, and the steps taken to repair the problem. Be sure to note any configuration changes made to the equipment and any replacement parts used in the repair. This documentation will be valuable when you encounter similar situations in the future.

- *Notes–* Make notes as you go through the investigation and repair process. Refer to these notes to avoid repeating previous steps and to determine what steps to take next.

- *Journal–* Document the upgrades and repairs that you perform. The documentation should include descriptions of the problem, possible solutions that have been tried in order to correct the problem, and the steps taken to repair the problem. Be sure to note any configuration changes made to the equipment and any replacement parts used in the repair. Your journal, along with your notes, can be valuable when you encounter similar situations in the future.

- *History of repairs–* Make a detailed list of problems and repairs, including the date, replacement parts, and customer information. The history allows a technician to determine what work has been performed on a computer in the past.

Internet Reference Tools

The Internet is an excellent source of information about specific hardware problems and possible solutions:

- Internet search engines
- News groups
- Manufacturer FAQs
- Online computer manuals
- Online forums and chat
- Technical websites

Figure 1 shows an example of a technical website.

Miscellaneous Tools

With experience, you will discover many additional items to add to the toolkit. Figure 2 shows how a roll of masking tape can be used to label parts that have been removed from a computer when a parts organizer is not available.

A working computer is also a valuable resource to take with you on computer repairs in the field. A working computer can be used to research information, download tools or drivers, or communicate with other technicians.

Figure 3 shows the types of computer replacement parts to include in a toolkit. Make sure that the parts are in good working order before you use them. Using known good components to replace possible bad ones in computers will help you quickly determine which component may not be working properly.

Refer to
Figure
in online course

2.3 Implement proper tool use

Safety in the workplace is everyone's responsibility. You are much less likely to injure yourself or damage components when using the proper tool for the job.

Before cleaning or repairing equipment, check to make sure that your tools are in good condition. Clean, repair, or replace any items that are not functioning adequately.

After completing this section, you will meet these objectives:

- Demonstrate proper use of an antistatic wrist strap.
- Demonstrate proper use of an antistatic mat.
- Demonstrate proper use of various hand tools.
- Demonstrate proper use of cleaning materials.

Refer to
Figure
in online course

2.3.1 Demonstrate proper use of an antistatic wrist strap

As discussed previously, an example of ESD is the small shock that you receive when you walk across a room with carpet and touch a doorknob. Although the small shock is harmless to you, the same electrical charge passing from you to a computer can damage its components. Wearing an antistatic wrist strap can prevent ESD damage to computer components.

The purpose of an antistatic wrist strap is to equalize the electrical charge between you and the equipment. The antistatic wrist strap is a conductor that connects your body to the equipment that you are working on. When static electricity builds up in your body, the connection made by the wrist strap to the equipment, or ground, channels the electricity through the wire that connects the strap.

As shown in Figure 1, the wrist strap has two parts and is easy to wear:

Step 1.   Wrap the strap around your wrist and secure it using the snap or Velcro. The metal on the back of the wrist strap must remain in contact with your skin at all times.

Step 2.   Snap the connector on the end of the wire to the wrist strap, and connect the other end either to the equipment or to the same grounding point that the antistatic mat is connected to. The metal skeleton of the case is a good place to connect the wire. When connecting the wire to equipment that you are working on, choose an unpainted metal surface. A painted surface does not conduct the electricity as well as unpainted metal.

Note

Attach the wire on the same side of the equipment as the arm wearing the antistatic wrist strap. This will help to keep the wire out of the way while you are working.

Although wearing a wrist strap will help to prevent ESD, you can further reduce the risks by not wearing clothing made of silk, polyester, or wool. These fabrics are more likely to generate a static charge.

Note

Technicians should roll up their sleeves, remove scarfs or ties, and tuck in their shirts to prevent interference from clothing. Ensure that earrings, necklaces, and other loose jewelry are properly secured.

Caution

Never wear an antistatic wrist strap if you are repairing a monitor or a power supply unit.

Refer to **Figure** in online course

2.3.2 Demonstrate proper use of an antistatic mat

You may not always have the option to work on a computer in a properly equipped workspace. If you can control the environment, try to set up your workspace away from carpeted areas. Carpets can cause the buildup of electrostatic charges. If you cannot avoid the carpeting, ground yourself to the unpainted portion of the case of the computer on which you are working before touching any components.

Antistatic Mat

An antistatic mat is slightly conductive. It works by drawing static electricity away from a component and transferring it safely from equipment to a grounding point, as shown in Figure 1:

Step 1.   Lay the mat on the workspace next to or under the computer case.

Step 2.   Clip the mat to the case to provide a grounded surface on which you can place parts as you remove them from the system.

Reducing the potential for ESD reduces the likelihood of damage to delicate circuits or components.

Note

Always handle components by the edges.

Workbench

When you are working at a workbench, ground the workbench and the antistatic floor mat. By standing on the mat and wearing the wrist strap, your body has the same charge as the equipment and reduces the probability of ESD.

Refer to
Figure
in online course

2.3.3 Demonstrate proper use of various hand tools

A technician needs to be able to properly use each tool in the toolkit. This topic covers many of the various hand tools used when repairing computers.

Screws

Match each screw with the proper screwdriver. Place the tip of the screwdriver on the head of the screw. Turn the screwdriver clockwise to tighten the screw and counterclockwise to loosen the screw, as shown in Figure 1.

Screws can become stripped if you over-tighten them with a screwdriver. A stripped screw, shown in Figure 2, may get stuck in the screw hole, or it may not tighten firmly. Discard stripped screws.

Flat Head Screwdriver

As shown in Figure 3, use a flat head screwdriver when you are working with a slotted screw. Do not use a flat head screwdriver to remove a Phillips head screw. Never use a screwdriver as a pry bar. If you cannot remove a component, check to see if there is a clip or latch that is securing the component in place.

Caution

If excessive force is needed to remove or add a component, something is probably wrong. Take a second look to make sure that you have not missed a screw or a locking clip that is holding the component in place. Refer to the device manual or diagram for additional information.

Phillips Head Screwdriver

As shown in Figure 4, use a Phillips head screwdriver with crosshead screws. Do not use this type of screwdriver to puncture anything. This will damage the head of the screwdriver.

Hex Driver

As shown in Figure 5, use a hex driver to loosen and tighten bolts that have a hexagonal (six-sided) head. Hex bolts should not be over-tightened because the threads of the bolts can be stripped. Do not use a hex driver that is too large for the bolt that you are using.

Caution

Some tools are magnetized. When working around electronic devices, be sure that the tools you are using have not been magnetized. Magnetic fields can be harmful to data stored on magnetic media. Test your tool by touching the tool with a screw. If the screw is attracted to the tool, do not use the tool.

Part Retriever, Needle-Nose Pliers, or Tweezers

As shown in Figure 6, the part retriever, needle-nose pliers, and tweezers can be used to place and retrieve parts that may be hard to reach with your fingers. Do not scratch or hit any components when using these tools.

Caution

Pencils should not be used inside the computer to change the setting of switches or to pry off jumpers. The pencil lead can act as a conductor and may damage the computer components.

> Refer to
> **Figure**
> in online course

2.3.4 Demonstrate proper use of cleaning materials

Keeping computers clean inside and out is a vital part of a maintenance program. Dirt can cause problems with the physical operation of fans, buttons, and other mechanical components. Figure 1 shows severe dust buildup on computer components. On electrical components, an excessive buildup of dust will act like an insulator and trap the heat. This insulation will impair the ability of heat sinks and cooling fans to keep components cool, causing chips and circuits to overheat and fail.

Caution

When compressed air is used to clean inside the computer, the air should be blown around the components with a minimum distance of four inches from the nozzle. The power supply and the fan should be cleaned from the back of the case.

Caution

Before cleaning any device, turn it off and unplug the device from the power source.

Computer Cases and Monitors

Clean computer cases and the outside of monitors with a mild cleaning solution on a damp, lint-free cloth. Mix one drop of dishwashing liquid with four ounces of water to create the cleaning solution. If any water drips inside the case, allow enough time for the liquid to dry before powering on the computer.

LCD Screens

Do not use ammoniated glass cleaners or any other solution on an LCD screen, unless the cleaner is specifically designed for the purpose. Harsh chemicals will damage the coating on the screen. There is no glass protecting these screens, so be gentle when cleaning them and do not press firmly on the screen.

CRT Screens

To clean the screens of CRT monitors, dampen a soft, clean, lint-free cloth with distilled water and wipe the screen from top to bottom. Then use a soft, dry cloth to wipe the screen and remove any streaking after you have cleaned the monitor.

Clean dusty components with a can of compressed air. Compressed air does not cause electrostatic buildup on components. Make sure that you are in a well-ventilated area before blowing the dust out of the computer. A best practice is to wear a dust mask to make sure that you do not breathe in the dust particles.

Blow out the dust using short bursts from the can. Never tip the can or use the compressed air can upside down. Do not allow the fan blades to spin from the force of the compressed air. Hold the fan in place. Fan motors can be ruined from spinning when the motor is not turned on.

Component Contacts

Clean the contacts on components with isopropyl alcohol. Do not use rubbing alcohol. Rubbing alcohol contains impurities that can damage contacts. Make sure that the contacts do not collect any lint from the cloth or cotton swab. Blow any lint off the contacts with compressed air before reinstallation.

Keyboard

Clean a desktop keyboard with compressed air or a small, hand-held vacuum cleaner with a brush attachment.

Caution

Never use a standard vacuum cleaner inside a computer case. The plastic parts of the vacuum cleaner can build up static electricity and discharge to the components. Use only a vacuum approved for electronic components.

Mouse

Use glass cleaner and a soft cloth to clean the outside of the mouse. Do not spray glass cleaner directly on the mouse. If cleaning a ball mouse, you can remove the ball and clean it with glass cleaner and a soft cloth. Wipe the rollers clean inside the mouse with the same cloth. Do not spray any liquids inside the mouse.

The chart in Figure 2 indicates the computer items that you should clean and the cleaning materials that you should use in each case.

Refer to
Lab Activity
for this chapter

Computer Disassembly
Disassemble a computer.

Summary

This chapter discussed safe lab procedures, correct tool usage, and the proper disposal of computer components and supplies. You have familiarized yourself in the lab with many of the tools used to build, service, and clean computer and electronic components. You have also learned the importance of organizational tools and how these tools help you work more efficiently.

The following are some of the important concepts to remember from this chapter:

- Work in a safe manner to protect both users and equipment.

- Follow all safety guidelines to prevent injuries to yourself and to others.

- Know how to protect equipment from ESD damage.

- Know about and be able to prevent power issues that can cause equipment damage or data loss.

- Know which products and supplies require special disposal procedures.

- Familiarize yourself with MSDS sheets for both safety issues and disposal restrictions to help protect the environment.

- Be able to use the correct tools for the task.

- Know how to clean components safely.

- Use organizational tools during computer repairs.

Chapter 2 Quiz

Go to
the online course
to take the quiz.

Take the chapter quiz to test your knowledge.

Your Chapter Notes

Computer Assembly - Step by Step

Introduction

Assembling computers is a large part of a technician's job. As a technician, you will need to work in a logical, methodical manner when working with computer components. As with any learned trade, computer assembly skills will improve dramatically with practice.

After completing this chapter, you will meet these objectives:

- Open the case.
- Install the power supply.
- Attach the components to the motherboard and install the motherboard.
- Install internal drives.
- Install drives in external bays.
- Install adapter cards.
- Connect all internal cables.
- Re-attach the side panels and connect external cables to the computer.
- Boot the computer for the first time.

Refer to
Figure
in online course

3.1 Open the case

Computer cases are produced in a variety of form factors. Form factors refer to the size and shape of the case.

Prepare the workspace before opening the computer case. There should be adequate lighting, good ventilation, and a comfortable room temperature. The workbench or table should be accessible from all sides. Avoid cluttering the surface of the workbench or table with tools and computer components. An antistatic mat on the table will help prevent physical and ESD damage to equipment. Small containers can be used to hold small screws and other parts as they are being removed.

There are different methods for opening cases. To learn how to open a particular computer case, consult the user manual or manufacturer's website. Most computer cases are opened in one of the following ways:

- The computer case cover can be removed as one piece.
- The top and side panels of the case can be removed.
- The top of the case may need to be removed before the side panels can be removed.

Refer to
Figure
in online course

3.2 Install the power supply

A technician may be required to replace or install a power supply. Most power supplies can only fit one way in the computer case. There are usually three or four screws that attach the power supply to the case. Power supplies have fans that can vibrate and loosen screws that are not secured. When installing a power supply, make sure that all of the screws are used and that they are properly tightened.

These are the power supply installation steps:

Step 1.   Insert the power supply into the case.

Step 2.   Align the holes in the power supply with the holes in the case.

Step 3.   Secure the power supply to the case using the proper screws.

Refer to
Interactive Graphic
in online course.

Virtual Desktop: Power Supply

System requirements for the virtual desktop include a minimum of 512 MB RAM and Windows 2000 or Windows XP operating system.
Complete the power supply layer in the virtual desktop.

Refer to
Lab Activity
for this chapter

Install the Power Supply

Install a power supply in a computer case.

Refer to
Figure
in online course

3.3 Attach the components to the motherboard and install the motherboard

This section details the steps to install components on the motherboard and then install the motherboard into the computer case.

After completing this section, you will meet these objectives:

- Install a CPU and a heat sink/fan assembly.
- Install the RAM.
- Install the motherboard.

Refer to
Figure
in online course

3.3.1 Install a CPU and a heat sink/fan assembly

The CPU and the heat sink/fan assembly may be installed on the motherboard before the motherboard is placed in the computer case.

CPU

Figure 1 shows a close-up view of the CPU and the motherboard. The CPU and motherboard are sensitive to electrostatic discharge. When handling a CPU and motherboard, make sure that you place them on a grounded antistatic mat. You should wear an antistatic wrist strap while working with these components.

Caution

When handling a CPU, do not touch the CPU contacts at any time.

The CPU is secured to the socket on the motherboard with a locking assembly. The CPU sockets today are ZIF sockets. You should be familiar with the locking assembly before attempting to install a CPU into the socket on the motherboard.

Thermal compound helps to conduct heat away from the CPU. Figure 2 shows thermal compound being applied to the CPU.

When you are installing a used CPU, clean the CPU and the base of the heat sink with isopropyl alcohol. Doing this removes all traces of old thermal compound. The surfaces are now ready for a new layer of thermal compound. Follow all manufacturer recommendations about applying the thermal compound.

Heat Sink/Fan Assembly

Figure 3 shows the heat sink/fan assembly. It is a two-part cooling device. The heat sink draws heat away from the CPU. The fan moves the heat away from the heat sink. The heat sink/fan assembly usually has a 3-pin power connector.

Figure 4 shows the connector and the motherboard header for the heat sink/fan assembly.

Follow these instructions for CPU and heat sink/fan assembly installation:

> Refer to
> **Figure**
> in online course

1. Align the CPU so that the Connection 1 indicator is lined up with Pin 1 on the CPU socket. Doing this ensures that the orientation notches on the CPU are aligned with the orientation keys on the CPU socket.

2. Place the CPU gently into the socket.

3. Close the CPU load plate and secure it in place by closing the load lever and moving it under the load lever retention tab.

4. Apply a small amount of thermal compound to the CPU and spread it evenly. Follow the application instructions provided by the manufacturer.

5. Align the heat sink/fan assembly retainers with the holes on the motherboard.

6. Place the heat sink/fan assembly onto the CPU socket, being careful not to pinch the CPU fan wires.

7. Tighten the heat sink/fan assembly retainers to secure the assembly in place.

8. Connect the heat sink/fan assembly power cable to the header on the motherboard.

3.3.2 Install the RAM

Like the CPU and the heat sink/fan assembly, RAM is installed in the motherboard before the motherboard is secured in the computer case. Before you install a memory module, consult the motherboard documentation or website of the manufacturer to ensure that the RAM is compatible with the motherboard.

RAM provides temporary data storage for the CPU while the computer is operating. RAM is volatile memory, which means that its contents are lost when the computer is shut down. Typically, more RAM will enhance the performance of your computer.

Follow these steps for RAM installation:

1. Align the notches on the RAM module to the keys in the slot and press down until the side tabs click into place.

2. Make sure that the side tabs have locked the RAM module. Visually check for exposed contacts.

Repeat these steps for additional RAM modules.

Refer to **Figure** in online course

3.3.3 Install the motherboard

The motherboard is now ready to install in the computer case. Plastic and metal standoffs are used to mount the motherboard and to prevent it from touching the metal portions of the case. You should install only the standoffs that align with the holes in the motherboard. Installing any additional standoffs may prevent the motherboard from being seated properly in the computer case.

Follow these steps for motherboard installation:

1. Install standoffs in the computer case.

2. Align the I/O connectors on the back of the motherboard with the openings in the back of the case.

3. Align the screw holes of the motherboard with the standoffs.

4. Insert all of the motherboard screws.

5. Tighten all of the motherboard screws.

Refer to **Interactive Graphic** in online course.

Virtual Desktop: Motherboard

System requirements for the virtual desktop include a minimum of 512 MB RAM and Windows 2000 or Windows XP operating system.

Complete the motherboard assembly in the virtual desktop motherboard layer.

Refer to **Lab Activity** for this chapter

Install the Motherboard

Install a CPU, a heat sink/fan assembly, and a RAM module on the motherboard.

Refer to **Figure** in online course

3.4 Install internal drives

Drives that are installed in internal bays are called internal drives. A hard disk drive (HDD) is an example of an internal drive.

Follow these steps for HDD installation:

1. Position the HDD so that it aligns with the 3.5-inch drive bay.

2. Insert the HDD into the drive bay so that the screw holes in the drive line up with the screw holes in the case.

3. Secure the HDD to the case using the proper screws.

Refer to **Interactive Graphic** in online course.

Virtual Desktop: Internal Drives

System requirements for the virtual desktop include a minimum of 512 MB RAM and Windows 2000 or Windows XP operating system.

Complete the hard drive installation in the virtual desktop internal drive layer.

Refer to **Figure** in online course

3.5 Install drives in external bays

Drives, such as optical drives and floppy drives, are installed in drive bays that are accessed from the front of the case. Optical drives and floppy drives store data on removable media. Drives in external bays allow access to the media without opening the case.

After completing this section, you will meet these objectives:

- Install the optical drive.
- Install the floppy drive.

Refer to
Figure
in online course

3.5.1 Install the optical drive

An optical drive is a storage device that reads and writes information to CDs and DVDs. A Molex power connector provides the optical drive with power from the power supply. A PATA cable connects the optical drive to the motherboard.

Follow these steps for optical drive installation:

Refer to
Figure
in online course

1. Position the optical drive so that it aligns with the 5.25-inch drive bay.

2. Insert the optical drive into the drive bay so that the optical drive screw holes align with the screw holes in the case.

3. Secure the optical drive to the case using the proper screws.

3.5.2 Install the floppy drive

A floppy disk drive (FDD) is a storage device that reads and writes information to a floppy disk. A Berg power connector provides the FDD with power from the power supply. A floppy data cable connects the FDD to the motherboard.

A floppy disk drive fits into the 3.5-inch bay on the front of the computer case.

Follow these steps for FDD installation:

1. Position the FDD so that it aligns with the 3.5-inch drive bay.

2. Insert the FDD into the drive bay so that the FDD screw holes align with the screw holes in the case.

3. Secure the FDD to the case using the proper screws.

Refer to
Interactive Graphic
in online course.

Virtual Desktop: Drives in External Bays
System requirements for the virtual desktop include a minimum of 512 MB RAM and Windows 2000 or Windows XP operating system.
Complete the optical and floppy drive installation in the virtual desktop drives in external bays layer.

Refer to
Lab Activity
for this chapter

Install the Drives
Install the hard disk drive, the optical drive, and the floppy drive.

Refer to
Figure
in online course

3.6 Install adapter cards

Adapter cards are installed to add functionality to a computer. Adapter cards must be compatible with the expansion slot. This section focuses on the installation of three types of adapter cards:

- PCIe x1 NIC

- PCI wireless NIC

- PCIe x16 video adapter card

After completing this section, you will meet these objectives:

- Install the NIC.

- Install the wireless NIC.

- Install the video adapter card.

Refer to
Figure
in online course

3.6.1 Install the NIC

A NIC enables a computer to connect to a network. NICs use PCI and PCIe expansion slots on the motherboard.

Follow these steps for NIC installation:

Refer to
Figure
in online course

1. Align the NIC to the appropriate expansion slot on the motherboard.

2. Press down gently on the NIC until the card is fully seated.

3. Secure the NIC PC mounting bracket to the case with the appropriate screw.

3.6.2 Install the wireless NIC

A wireless NIC enables a computer to connect to a wireless network. Wireless NICs use PCI and PCIe expansion slots on the motherboard. Some wireless NICs are installed externally with a USB connector.

Follow these steps for wireless NIC installation:

Refer to
Figure
in online course

1. Align the wireless NIC to the appropriate expansion slot on the motherboard.

2. Press down gently on the wireless NIC until the card is fully seated.

3. Secure the wireless NIC PC mounting bracket to the case with the appropriate screw.

3.6.3 Install the video adapter card

A video adapter card is the interface between a computer and a display monitor. An upgraded video adapter card can provide better graphic capabilities for games and graphic programs. Video adapter cards use PCI, AGP, and PCIe expansion slots on the motherboard.

Follow these steps for video adapter card installation:

1. Align the video adapter card to the appropriate expansion slot on the motherboard.

2. Press down gently on the video adapter card until the card is fully seated.

3. Secure the video adapter card PC mounting bracket to the case with the appropriate screw.

Refer to
Interactive Graphic
in online course.

Virtual Desktop: Adapter Cards
System requirements for the virtual desktop include a minimum of 512 MB RAM and Windows 2000 or Windows XP operating system.
Complete the NIC, wireless NIC, and video adapter card installation in the virtual desktop adapter card layer.

Refer to
Lab Activity
for this chapter

Install Adapter Cards
Install a NIC, a wireless NIC, and a video adapter card.

Refer to
Figure
in online course

3.7 Connect all internal cables

Power cables are used to distribute electricity from the power supply to the motherboard and other components. Data cables transmit data between the motherboard and storage devices, such as hard drives. Additional cables connect the buttons and link lights on the front of the computer case to the motherboard.

After completing this section, you will meet these objectives:

- Connect the power cables.
- Connect the data cables.

Refer to
Figure
in online course

3.7.1 Connect the power cables

Motherboard Power Connections

Just like other components, motherboards require power to operate. The Advanced Technology Extended (ATX) main power connector will have either 20 or 24 pins. The power supply may also have a 4-pin or 6-pin Auxiliary (AUX) power connector that connects to the motherboard. A 20-pin connector will work in a motherboard with a 24-pin socket.

Follow these steps for motherboard power cable installation:

1. Align the 20-pin ATX power connector to the socket on the motherboard. [Figure 1]
2. Gently press down on the connector until the clip clicks into place.
3. Align the 4-pin AUX power connector to the socket on the motherboard. [Figure 2]
4. Gently press down on the connector until the clip clicks into place.

SATA Power Connectors

SATA power connectors use a 15-pin connector. SATA power connectors are used to connect to hard disk drives, optical drives, or any devices that have a SATA power socket.

Molex Power Connectors

Hard disk drives and optical drives that do not have SATA power sockets use a Molex power connector.

Caution

Do not use a Molex connector and a SATA power connector on the same drive at the same time.

Berg Power Connectors

The 4-pin Berg power connector supplies power to a floppy drive.

Follow these steps for power connector installation:

Refer to
Figure
in online course

1. Plug the SATA power connector into the HDD. [Figure 3]
2. Plug the Molex power connector into the optical drive. [Figure 4]
3. Plug the 4-pin Berg power connector into the FDD. [Figure 5]
4. Connect the 3-pin fan power connector into the appropriate fan header on the motherboard, according to the motherboard manual. [Figure 6]
5. Plug the additional cables from the case into the appropriate connectors according to the motherboard manual.

3.7.2 Connect the data cables

Drives connect to the motherboard using data cables. The drive being connected determines the type of data cable used. The types of data cables are PATA, SATA, and floppy disk.

PATA Data Cables

The PATA cable is sometimes called a ribbon cable because it is wide and flat. The PATA cable can have either 40 or 80 conductors. A PATA cable usually has three 40-pin connectors. One connector at the end of the cable connects to the motherboard. The other two connectors connect to drives. If multiple hard drives are installed, the master drive connects to the end connector. The slave drive connects to the middle connector.

A stripe on the data cable denotes the location of pin 1. Plug the PATA cable into the drive with the pin 1 indicator on the cable aligned to the pin 1 indicator on the drive connector. The pin 1 indicator on the drive connector is usually closest to the power connector on the drive. Many motherboards have two PATA drive controllers, providing support for a maximum of four PATA drives.

SATA Data Cables

The SATA data cable has a 7-pin connector. One end of the cable is connected to the motherboard. The other end is connected to any drive that has a SATA data connector.

Floppy Data Cables

The floppy drive data cable has a 34-pin connector. Like the PATA data cable, the floppy drive data cable has a stripe to denote the location of pin 1. A floppy drive cable usually has three 34-pin connectors. One connector at the end of the cable connects to the motherboard. The other two connectors connect to drives. If multiple floppy drives are installed, the A: drive connects to the end connector. The B: drive connects to the middle connector.

Plug the floppy drive data cable into the drive with the pin 1 indicator on the cable aligned to the pin 1 indicator on the drive connector. Motherboards have one floppy drive controller, providing support for a maximum of two floppy drives.

Note

If pin 1 on the floppy drive data cable is not aligned with pin 1 on the drive connector, the floppy drive does not function. This misalignment does not damage the drive, but the drive activity light displays continuously. To fix this problem, turn off the computer and reconnect the data cable so that pin 1 on the cable and pin 1 on the connector are aligned. Reboot the computer.

Follow these steps for data cable installation:

1. Plug the motherboard end of the PATA cable into the motherboard socket. [Figure 1]

2. Plug the connector at the far end of the PATA cable into the optical drive. [Figure 2]

3. Plug one end of the SATA cable into the motherboard socket. [Figure 3]

4. Plug the other end of the SATA cable into the HDD. [Figure 4]

5. Plug the motherboard end of the FDD cable into the motherboard socket. [Figure 5]

6. Plug the connector at the far end of the FDD cable into the floppy drive. [Figure 6]

Refer to
Interactive Graphic
in online course.

Virtual Desktop: Internal Cables

System requirements for the virtual desktop include a minimum of 512 MB RAM and Windows 2000 or Windows XP operating system.

Complete the internal cable installation in the virtual desktop internal cable layer.

Refer to
Lab Activity
for this chapter

Install Internal Cables

Install the internal power and data cables in the computer.

Refer to
Figure
in online course

3.8 Re-attach the side panels and connect external cables to the computer

Now that all the internal components have been installed and connected to the motherboard and power supply, the side panels are re-attached to the computer case. The next step is to connect the cables for all computer peripherals and the power cable.

After completing this section, you will meet these objectives:

- Re-attach the side panels to the case.
- Connect external cables to the computer.

Refer to
Figure
in online course

3.8.1 Re-attach the side panels to the case

Most computer cases have two panels, one on each side. Some computer cases have one three-sided cover that slides down over the case frame.

When the cover is in place, make sure that it is secured at all screw locations. Some computer cases use screws that are inserted with a screwdriver. Other cases have knob-type screws that can be tightened by hand.

If you are unsure about how to remove or replace the computer case, refer to the documentation or website of the manufacturer for more information.

Caution

Handle case parts with care. Some computer case covers have sharp or jagged edges.

Refer to
Figure
in online course

3.8.2 Connect external cables to the computer

After the case panels have been re-attached, connect the cables to the back of the computer. Here are some common external cable connections:

- Monitor
- Keyboard
- Mouse
- USB
- Ethernet
- Power

When attaching cables, ensure that they are connected to the correct locations on the computer. For example, some mouse and keyboard cables use the same type of PS/2 connector.

Caution

When attaching cables, never force a connection.

Note

Plug in the power cable after you have connected all other cables.

Follow these steps for external cable installation:

1. Attach the monitor cable to the video port. [Figure 1]

2. Secure the cable by tightening the screws on the connector.

3. Plug the keyboard cable into the PS/2 keyboard port. [Figure 2]

4. Plug the mouse cable into the PS/2 mouse port. [Figure 3]

5. Plug the USB cable into a USB port. [Figure 4]

6. Plug the network cable into the network port. [Figure 5]

7. Connect the wireless antenna to the antenna connector. [Figure 6]

8. Plug the power cable into the power supply. [Figure 7]

Figure 8 shows all of the external cables plugged into the back of the computer.

> Refer to
> **Interactive Graphic**
> in online course.

Virtual Desktop: External Cables

System requirements for the virtual desktop include a minimum of 512 MB RAM and Windows 2000 or Windows XP operating system.

Complete the external cable installation in the virtual desktop external cable layer.

> Refer to
> **Lab Activity**
> for this chapter

Complete the Computer Assembly

Install the side panels and the external cables on the computer.

> Refer to
> **Figure**
> in online course

3.9 Boot the computer for the first time

When the computer is booted, the basic input/output system (BIOS) performs a check on all of the internal components. This check is called a power-on self test (POST).

After completing this section, you will meet these objectives:

- Identify beep codes.
- Describe BIOS setup.

> Refer to
> **Figure**
> in online course

3.9.1 Identify beep codes

POST checks to see that all of the hardware in the computer is operating correctly. If a device is malfunctioning, an error or a beep code alerts the technician that there is a problem. Typically, a single beep denotes that the computer is functioning properly. If there is a hardware problem, the computer might emit a series of beeps. Each BIOS manufacturer uses different codes to indicate hardware problems. Figure 1 shows a sample chart of beep codes. The beep codes for your computer might be different. Consult the motherboard documentation to view beep codes for your computer.

Refer to
Figure
in online course

3.9.2 Describe BIOS setup

The BIOS contains a setup program used to configure settings for hardware devices. The configuration data is saved to a special memory chip called a Complementary Metal Oxide Semiconductor (CMOS), as shown in Figure 1. CMOS is maintained by the battery in the computer. If this battery dies, all BIOS setup configuration data will be lost. If this occurs, replace the battery and reconfigure the BIOS settings.

To enter the BIOS setup program, you must press the proper key or key sequence during POST. Most computers use the DEL key. Your computer might use another key or combination of keys.

Figure 2 shows an example of a BIOS setup program. Here are some common BIOS setup menu options:

- Main – System time, date, HDD type, etc.

- Advanced – Infrared port settings, parallel port settings, etc.

- Security – Password settings to setup utility

- Others – Low battery alarm, system beep, etc.

- Boot – Boot order of the computer

- Exit – Setup utility exit

Refer to
Lab Activity
for this chapter

Boot the Computer

Boot the computer for the first time, explore the BIOS setup program, and change the boot order sequence.

Summary

This chapter detailed the steps used to assemble a computer and to boot the system for the first time. These are some important points to remember:

- Computer cases come in a variety of sizes and configurations. Many of the components of the computer must match the form factor of the case.

- The CPU is installed on the motherboard with a heat sink/fan assembly.

- RAM is installed in RAM slots found on the motherboard.

- Adapter cards are installed in PCI and PCIe expansion slots found on the motherboard.

- Hard disk drives are installed in 3.5-inch drive bays located inside the case.

- Optical drives are installed in 5.25-inch drive bays that can be accessed from outside the case.

- Floppy drives are installed in 3.5-inch drive bays that can be accessed from outside the case.

- Power supply cables are connected to all drives and the motherboard.

- Internal data cables transfer data to all drives.

- External cables connect peripheral devices to the computer.

- Beep codes signify when hardware malfunctions.

- The BIOS setup program is used to display information about the computer components and allows the user to change system settings.

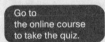

Chapter 3 Quiz

Take the chapter quiz to test your knowledge.

Your Chapter Notes

Basics of Preventive Maintenance and Troubleshooting

Introduction

This chapter introduces preventive maintenance and the troubleshooting process. Preventive maintenance is a regular and systematic inspection, cleaning, and replacement of worn parts, materials, and systems. Preventive maintenance helps to prevent failure of parts, materials, and systems by ensuring that they are in good working condition. Troubleshooting is a systematic approach to locating the cause of a fault in a computer system. With fewer faults, there is less troubleshooting to do, thus saving an organization time and money.

Troubleshooting is a learned skill. Not all troubleshooting processes are the same, and technicians tend to refine their own troubleshooting skills based on knowledge and personal experience. Use the guidelines in this chapter as a starting point to help develop your troubleshooting skills. Although each situation is different, the process described in this chapter will help you to determine your course of action when you are trying to solve a technical problem for a customer.

After completing this chapter, you will meet these objectives:

- Explain the purpose of preventive maintenance.
- Identify the steps of the troubleshooting process.

> Refer to
> **Figure**
> in online course

4.1 Explain the purpose of preventive maintenance

Preventive maintenance reduces the probability of hardware or software problems by systematically and periodically checking hardware and software to ensure proper operation.

Hardware

Check the condition of cables, components, and peripherals. Clean components to reduce the likelihood of overheating. Repair or replace any components that show signs of abuse or excess wear. Use the tasks listed in Figure 1 as a guide to create a hardware maintenance program.

What additional hardware maintenance tasks can you add to the list?

Software

Verify that installed software is current. Follow the policies of the organization when installing security updates, operating system updates, and program updates. Many organizations do not allow updates until extensive testing has been completed. This testing is done to confirm that the update will not cause problems with the operating system and software. Use the tasks listed in Figure 2 as a guide to create a software maintenance schedule that fits the needs of your computer equipment.

What other software maintenance tasks can you add to the list?

Benefits

Be proactive in computer equipment maintenance and data protection. By performing regular maintenance routines, you can reduce potential hardware and software problems. Regular maintenance routines reduce computer downtime and repair costs.

A preventive maintenance plan is developed based on the needs of the equipment. A computer exposed to a dusty environment, such as a construction site, needs more attention than equipment in an office environment. High-traffic networks, such as a school network, might require additional scanning and removal of malicious software or unwanted files. Document the routine maintenance tasks that must be performed on the computer equipment and the frequency of each task. This list of tasks can then be used to create a maintenance program.

Some benefits of preventive maintenance are listed in Figure 3. Can you think of any other benefits that preventive maintenance provides?

Refer to
Figure
in online course

4.2 Identify the steps of the troubleshooting process

Troubleshooting requires an organized and logical approach to problems with computers and other components. A logical approach to troubleshooting allows you to eliminate variables in a systematic order. Asking the right questions, testing the right hardware, and examining the right data helps you understand the problem. This helps you form a proposed solution to try.

Troubleshooting is a skill that you will refine over time. Each time you solve another problem, you will increase your troubleshooting skills by gaining more experience. You will learn how and when to combine, as well as skip, steps to reach a solution quickly. The troubleshooting process is a guideline that can be modified to fit your needs.

In this section, you will learn an approach to problem solving that can be applied to both hardware and software. Many of the steps can also be applied to problem solving in other work-related areas.

Note

The term customer, as used in this course, is any user that requires technical computer assistance.

After completing this section, you will meet these objectives:

- Explain the purpose of data protection.
- Identify the problem.
- Establish a theory of probable causes.
- Test the theory to determine an exact cause.
- Establish a plan of action to resolve the problem and implement the solution.
- Verify full system functionality, and if applicable, implement preventive measures.
- Document findings, actions and outcomes.

Refer to
Figure
in online course

4.2.1 Explain the purpose of data protection

Before you begin troubleshooting problems, always follow the necessary precautions to protect data on a computer. Some repairs, such as replacing a hard drive or reinstalling an operating system, might put the data on the computer at risk. Make sure that you do everything possible to prevent data loss while attempting repairs.

Caution

Although data protection is not one of the six troubleshooting steps, you must protect data before beginning any work on a customer's computer. If your work results in data loss for the customer, you or your company could be held liable.

Data Backup

A data backup is a copy of the data on a computer hard drive that is saved to media such as a CD, DVD, or tape drive. In an organization, backups are routinely done on a daily, weekly, and monthly basis.

If you are unsure that a backup has been done, do not attempt any troubleshooting activities until you check with the customer. Here is a list of items to verify with the customer about data backups:

- Date of the last backup
- Contents of the backup
- Data integrity of the backup
- Availability of all backup media for a data restore

If the customer does not have a current backup and you are not able to create one, you should ask the customer to sign a liability release form. A liability release form should contain at least the following information:

- Permission to work on the computer without a current backup available
- Release from liability if data is lost or corrupted
- Description of the work to be performed

Refer to
Figure
in online course

4.2.2 Identify the problem

During the troubleshooting process, gather as much information from the customer as possible. The customer should provide you with the basic facts about the problem. Figure 1 lists some of the important information to gather from the customer.

Conversation Etiquette

When you are talking to the customer, you should follow these guidelines:

- Ask direct questions to gather information.
- Do not use industry jargon when talking to customers.
- Do not talk down to the customer.
- Do not insult the customer.
- Do not accuse the customer of causing the problem.

By communicating effectively, you will be able to elicit the most relevant information about the problem from the customer.

Open-Ended Questions

Open-ended questions are used to obtain general information. Open-ended questions allow customers to explain the details of the problem in their own words. Figure 2 shows some examples of open-ended questions.

Closed-Ended Questions

Based on the information from the customer, you can proceed with closed-ended questions. Closed-ended questions generally require a "yes" or "no" answer. These questions are intended to get the most relevant information in the shortest time possible. Figure 3 shows some examples of closed-ended questions.

Documenting Responses

Document the information obtained from the customer in the work order and in the repair journal. Write down anything that you think might be important for you or another technician. Often, the small details can lead to the solution of a difficult or complicated problem. It is now time to verify the customer's description of the problem by gathering data from the computer.

Event Viewer

When system, user, or software errors occur on a computer, the Event Viewer is updated with information about the errors. The Event Viewer application shown in Figure 4 records the following information about the problem:

- What problem occurred
- Date and time of the problem
- Severity of the problem
- Source of the problem
- Event ID number
- Which user was logged in when the problem occurred

Although the Event Viewer lists details about the error, you might need to further research the solution.

Device Manager

The Device Manager shown in Figure 5 displays all of the devices that are configured on a computer. Any device that the operating system determines to be acting incorrectly is flagged with an error icon. This type of error has a yellow circle with an exclamation point (!). If a device is disabled, it is flagged with a red circle and an "X". A yellow question mark (?) indicates that the hardware is not functioning properly because the system does not know which driver to install for the hardware.

Beep Codes

Each BIOS manufacturer has a unique beep sequence for hardware failures. When troubleshooting, power on the computer and listen. As the system proceeds through the POST, most computers emit one beep to indicate that the system is booting properly. If there is an error, you might hear multiple beeps. Document the beep code sequence, and research the code to determine the specific hardware failure.

BIOS Information

If the computer boots and stops after the POST, investigate the BIOS settings to determine where to find the problem. A device might not be detected or configured properly. Refer to the motherboard manual to make sure that the BIOS settings are accurate.

Diagnostic Tools

Conduct research to determine which software is available to help diagnose and solve problems. There are many programs available that can help you troubleshoot hardware. Often, manufacturers of system hardware provide diagnostic tools of their own. For instance, a hard drive manufacturer, might provide a tool that you can use to boot the computer and diagnose why the hard drive does not boot Windows.

Refer to
Figure
in online course

4.2.3 Establish a theory of probable causes

The second step in the troubleshooting process is to establish a theory of probable causes. First, create a list of the most common reasons why the error would occur. Even though the customer may think that there is a major problem, start with the obvious issues before moving to more complex diagnoses. List the easiest or most obvious causes at the top with the more complex causes at the bottom. You will test each of these causes in the next steps of the troubleshooting process.

Refer to
Figure
in online course

4.2.4 Determine an exact cause

The next step in the troubleshooting process is to determine an exact cause. You determine an exact cause by testing your theories of probable causes one at a time, starting with the quickest and easiest. Figure 1 identifies some common quick tests. After identifying an exact cause of the problem, determine the steps to resolve the problem. As you become more experienced at troubleshooting computers, you will work through the steps in the process faster. For now, practice each step to better understand the troubleshooting process.

If the exact cause of the problem has not been determined after you have tested all your theories, establish a new theory of probable causes and test it. If necessary, escalate the problem to a technician with more experience. Before you escalate, document each test that you try. Information about the tests is vital if the problem needs to be escalated to another technician, as shown in Figure 2.

Refer to
Figure
in online course

4.2.5 Implement the solution

After you have determined the exact cause of the problem, establish a plan of action to resolve the problem and implement the solution. Sometimes quick procedures can determine the exact cause of the problem or even correct the problem. If a quick procedure does correct the problem, you can go to step 5 to verify the solution and full system functionality. If a quick procedure does not correct the problem, you might need to research the problem further to establish the exact cause.

Evaluate the problem and research possible solutions. Figure 1 lists possible research locations. Divide larger problems into smaller problems that can be analyzed and solved individually. Prioritize solutions starting with the easiest and fastest to implement. Create a list of possible solutions and implement them one at a time. If you implement a possible solution and it does not work, reverse the solution and try another.

Refer to
Figure
in online course

4.2.6 Verify solution and full system functionality

After the repairs to the computer have been completed, continue the troubleshooting process by verifying full system functionality and implementing any preventive measures if needed. Verifying full system functionality confirms that you have solved the original problem and ensures that you have not created another problem while repairing the computer. Whenever possible, have the customer verify the solution and system functionality.

Refer to
Figure
in online course

4.2.7 Document findings

After the repairs to the computer have been completed, finish the troubleshooting process by closing with the customer. Communicate the problem and the solution to the customer verbally and in all documentation. Figure 1 shows the steps to be taken when you have finished a repair and are closing with the customer.

Verify the solution with the customer. If the customer is available, demonstrate how the solution has corrected the computer problem. Have the customer test the solution and try to reproduce the problem. When the customer can verify that the problem has been resolved, you can complete the documentation for the repair in the work order and in your journal. The documentation should include the following information:

- Description of the problem
- Steps to resolve the problem
- Components used in the repair

Summary

This chapter discussed the concepts of preventive maintenance and the troubleshooting process.

- Regular preventive maintenance reduces hardware and software problems.

- Before beginning any repair, back up the data on a computer.

- The troubleshooting process is a guideline to help you solve computer problems in an efficient manner.

- Document everything that you try, even if it fails. The documentation that you create will become a useful resource for you and other technicians.

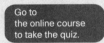

Chapter 4 Quiz

Take the chapter quiz to test your knowledge.

Your Chapter Notes

Fundamental Operating Systems

Introduction

The operating system (OS) controls almost all functions on a computer. In this chapter, you will learn about the components, functions, and terminology related to the Windows 2000, Windows XP, and Windows Vista operating systems.

After completing this chapter, you will meet these objectives:

- Explain the purpose of an operating system.
- Describe and compare operating systems to include purpose, limitations, and compatibilities.
- Determine the operating system based on customer needs.
- Install an operating system.
- Navigate a Graphical User Interface (GUI).
- Identify and apply common preventive maintenance techniques for operating systems.
- Troubleshoot operating systems.

Refer to
Figure
in online course

5.1 Explain the purpose of an operating system

All computers rely on an OS to provide the interface for interaction between users, applications, and hardware. The OS boots the computer and manages the file system. Almost all modern operating systems can support more than one user, task, or CPU.

After completing this section, you will meet these objectives:

- Describe the characteristics of modern operating systems.
- Explain operating system concepts.

Refer to
Figure
in online course

5.1.1 Describe characteristics of modern operating systems

Regardless of the size and complexity of the computer and the operating system, all operating systems perform the same four basic functions. Operating systems control hardware access, manage files and folders, provide a user interface, and manage applications.

Control Hardware Access

The operating system manages the interaction between applications and the hardware. To access and communicate with the hardware, the operating system installs a device driver for each hardware component. A device driver is a small program written by the hardware manufacturer and supplied with the hardware component. When the hardware device is installed, the device driver is also installed, allowing the OS to communicate with the hardware component.

The process of assigning system resources and installing drivers can be performed with Plug and Play (PnP). The PnP process was introduced in Windows 95 to simplify the installation of new hardware. All modern operating systems are PnP-compatible. With PnP, the operating system automatically detects the PnP-compatible hardware and installs the driver for that component. The operating system then configures the device and updates the registry, which is a database that contains all the information about the computer.

Note

The registry contains information about applications, users, hardware, network settings, and file types.

File and Folder Management

The operating system creates a file structure on the hard disk drive to allow data to be stored. A file is a block of related data that is given a single name and treated as a single unit. Program and data files are grouped together in a directory. The files and directories are organized for easy retrieval and use. Directories can be kept inside other directories. These nested directories are referred to as subdirectories. Directories are called folders in Windows operating systems, and subdirectories are called subfolders.

User Interface

The operating system enables the user to interact with software and hardware. There are two types of user interfaces:

- Command Line Interface (CLI) – The user types commands at a prompt, as shown in Figure 1.

- Graphical User Interface (GUI) – The user interacts with menus and icons, as shown in Figure 2.

Most operating systems, such as Windows 2000 and Windows XP, include both a GUI and a CLI.

Application Management

The operating system locates an application and loads it into the RAM of the computer. Applications are software programs, such as word processors, databases, spreadsheets, games, and many other applications. The operating system ensures that each application has adequate system resources.

An Application Programming Interface (API) is a set of guidelines used by programmers to ensure that the application they are developing is compatible with an operating system. Here are two examples of APIs:

- Open Graphics Library (OpenGL) – Cross-platform standard specification for multimedia graphics

- DirectX – Collection of APIs related to multimedia tasks for Microsoft Windows

Refer to
Figure
in online course

5.1.2 Explain operating system concepts

To understand the capabilities of an operating system, it is important to understand some basic terms. The following terms are often used when comparing operating systems:

- *Multi-user–* Two or more users can work with programs and share peripheral devices, such as printers, at the same time.

- *Multi-tasking–* The computer is capable of operating multiple applications at the same time.

- *Multi-processing–* The computer can have two or more central processing units (CPUs) that programs share.

- *Multi-threading–* A program can be broken into smaller parts that can be loaded as needed by the operating system. Multi-threading allows individual programs to be multi-tasked.

Almost all modern operating systems are multi-user and multi-tasking, and they support multi-processing and multi-threading.

Modes of Operation

All modern CPUs can run in different modes of operation. The mode of operation refers to the capability of the CPU and the operating environment. The mode of operation determines how the CPU manages applications and memory. Figure 1 shows an example of the logical memory allocation. The four common modes of operation are real mode, protected mode, virtual real mode, and compatible mode.

Real Mode

A CPU that operates in real mode can only execute one program at a time, and it can only address 1 MB of system memory. Although all modern processors have real mode available, it is only used by DOS and DOS applications in old operating systems or by 16-bit operating environments, such as Windows 3.x.

Protected Mode

A CPU that operates in protected mode has access to all of the memory in the computer, including virtual memory. Virtual memory is hard disk space that is used to emulate RAM. Operating systems that use protected mode can manage multiple programs simultaneously. Protected mode provides 32-bit access to memory, drivers, and transfers between input and output (I/O) devices. Protected mode is used by 32-bit operating systems, such as Windows 2000 or Windows XP. In protected mode, applications are protected from using the memory reserved for another application that is currently running.

Virtual Real Mode

A CPU that operates in virtual real mode allows a real-mode application to run within a protected-mode operating system. This can be demonstrated when a DOS application runs in a 32-bit operating system, such as Windows XP. Figure 2 is a chart of some common DOS commands that can still be used in modern operating systems, such as Windows XP.

Compatibility Mode

Compatibility mode creates the environment of an earlier operating system for applications that are not compatible with the current operating system. As an example, an application that checks the version of the operating system might be written for Windows NT and require a particular service pack. Compatibility mode can create the proper environment or version of the operating system to allow the application to run as if it is in the intended environment.

Although Windows Vista is highly compatible with previous versions of Windows, two particularly useful features are available. The first feature is Windows XP Service Pack 2 (SP2) compatibility mode. This allows applications that are not compatible with Windows Vista to be executed as if the operating system were Windows XP SP2. The second feature is a method to override the

User Account Control (UAC). This allows an application to be run even if the user does not have the required administrative privileges.

32-bit vs. 64-bit

There are three main differences between 32-bit and 64-bit operating systems. A 32-bit operating system, such as Windows XP Professional, is capable of addressing only 4 GB of RAM, while a 64-bit operating system can address more than 128 GB of RAM. Memory management is also different between these two types of operating systems, resulting in enhanced performance of 64-bit programs. A 64-bit operating system, such as Windows Vista 64-bit, has additional security features such as Kernel Patch Protection and mandatory Driver Signing. With Kernel Patch Protection, third-party drivers cannot modify the kernel. With mandatory Driver Signing, unsigned drivers cannot be used.

Processor Architecture

There are two common architectures used by CPUs to process data: x86 (32-bit architecture) and x64 (64-bit architecture). x86 uses a Complex Instruction Set Computer (CISC) architecture to process multiple instructions with a single request. Registers are storage areas used by the CPU when performing calculations. x86 processors use fewer registers than x64 processors. x64 architecture is backward compatible with x86 and adds additional registers specifically for instructions that use a 64-bit address space. The additional registers of the x64 architecture allow the computer to process much more complex instructions at a much higher rate.

Refer to
Figure
in online course

5.2 Describe and compare operating systems to include purpose, limitations, and compatibilities

A technician might be asked to choose and install an operating system for a customer. The type of OS selected depends on the customer's requirements for the computer. There are two distinct types of operating systems: desktop operating systems and network operating systems. A desktop operating system is intended for use in a Small Office/Home Office (SOHO) with a limited number of users. A Network Operating System (NOS) is designed for a corporate environment serving multiple users with a wide range of needs.

After completing this section, you will meet these objectives:

- Describe desktop operating systems.
- Describe network operating systems.

Refer to
Figure
in online course

5.2.1 Describe desktop operating systems

A desktop OS has the following characteristics:

- Supports a single user
- Runs single-user applications
- Shares files and folders on a small network with limited security

In the current software market, the most commonly used desktop operating systems fall into three groups: Microsoft Windows, Apple Mac OS, and UNIX/Linux.

Microsoft Windows

Windows is one of the most popular operating systems today. The following products are desktop versions of the Microsoft Windows operating systems:

- Windows XP Professional – Used on most computers that will connect to a Windows Server on a network

- Windows XP Home Edition – Used on home computers and has very limited security

- Windows XP Media Center – Used on entertainment computers for viewing movies and listening to music

- Windows XP Tablet PC Edition – Used for tablet PCs

- Windows XP 64-bit Edition – Used for computers with 64-bit processors

- Windows 2000 Professional – Older Windows operating system that has been replaced by Windows XP Professional

- Windows Vista Home Basic – Used on home computers for basic computing

- Windows Vista Home Premium – Used on home computers to expand personal productivity and digital entertainment beyond the basics

- Windows Vista Business – Used on small business computers for enhanced security and enhanced mobility technology

- Windows Vista Ultimate – Used on computers to combine all the needs of both home and business users

Apple Mac OS

Apple computers are proprietary and use an operating system called Mac OS. Mac OS is designed to be a user-friendly GUI operating system. Current versions of Mac OS are now based on a customized version of UNIX.

UNIX/Linux

UNIX, which was introduced in the late 1960s, is one of the oldest operating systems. There are many different versions of UNIX today. One of the most recent is the extremely popular Linux. Linux was developed by Linus Torvalds in 1991, and it is designed as an open-source operating system. Open-source programs allow the source code to be distributed and changed by anyone as a free download or from developers at a much lower cost than other operating systems.

Note

In this course, all command paths refer to Windows XP unless otherwise noted.

Refer to
Figure
in online course

5.2.2 Describe network operating systems

A network OS has the following characteristics:

- Supports multiple users

- Runs multi-user applications

- Is robust and redundant

■ Provides increased security compared to desktop operating systems

These are the most common network operating systems:

■ *Microsoft Windows*– Network operating systems offered by Microsoft are Windows 2000 Server, Windows Server 2003, and Windows Server 2008. Windows Server operating systems use a central database called Active Directory to manage network resources.

■ *Novell NetWare*– Novell NetWare was the first OS to meet network OS requirements and enjoy widespread deployment in PC-based Local Area Networks (LANs) back in the 1980s.

■ *Linux*– Linux operating systems include Red Hat, Caldera, SUSE, Debian, Fedora, Ubuntu, and Slackware.

■ *UNIX*– Various corporations offer proprietary operating systems based on UNIX.

NOS Certifications and Jobs
Gather information about network operating system certifications and jobs that require these certifications.

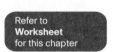

Refer to
Worksheet
for this chapter

Refer to
Figure
in online course

5.3 Determine operating system based on customer needs

To select the proper operating system to meet the requirements of your customer, you need to understand how the customer wants to use the computer. The operating system that you recommend should be compatible with any applications that will be used and should support all hardware that is installed in the computer. If the computer will be attached to a network, the new operating system should also be compatible with other operating systems on the network.

After completing this section, you will meet these objectives:

■ Identify applications and environments that are compatible with an operating system.

■ Determine minimum hardware requirements and compatibility with the OS platform.

Refer to
Figure
in online course

5.3.1 Identify applications and environments that are compatible with an operating system

An operating system should be compatible with all applications that are installed on a computer. Before recommending an OS to your customer, investigate the types of applications that your customer will be using. If the computer will be part of a network, the operating system must also be compatible with the operating systems of the other computers in the network. The network type determines which operating systems are compatible. Microsoft Windows networks can have multiple computers using different versions of Microsoft operating systems. These are some guidelines that will help you determine the best operating system for your customer:

■ Does the computer have "off-the-shelf" applications or customized applications that were programmed specifically for this customer? If the customer will be using a customized application, the programmer of that application will specify which operating system is compatible with it. Most off-the-shelf applications specify a list of compatible operating systems on the outside of the application package.

- Are the applications programmed for a single user or multiple users? This information helps you decide whether to recommend a desktop OS or a network OS. If the computer will be connected to a network, make sure to recommend the same OS platform that the other computers on the network use.

- Are any data files shared with other computers, such as a laptop or home computer? To ensure compatibility of file formats, recommend the same OS platform that the other data file-sharing computers use.

As an example, your customer has a Windows network installed and wants to add more computers to the network. In this case, you should recommend a Windows OS for the new computers. If the customer does not have any existing computer equipment, the choice of available OS platforms increases. To make an OS recommendation, you must review budget constraints, learn how the computer will be used, and determine which types of applications will be installed.

Refer to
Figure
in online course

5.3.2 Determine minimum hardware requirements and compatibility with the OS platform

Operating systems have minimum hardware requirements that must be met for the OS to install and function correctly. Figure 1 and Figure 2 provide a chart of the minimum hardware requirements and features for the various Windows operating systems.

Identify the equipment that your customer has in place. If hardware upgrades are necessary to meet the minimum requirements for an OS, conduct a cost analysis to determine the best course of action. In some cases, it might be less expensive for the customer to purchase a new computer than to upgrade the current system. In other cases, it might be cost-effective to upgrade one or more of the following components:

- RAM

- Hard disk drive

- CPU

- Video adapter card

Note

In some cases, the application requirements might exceed the hardware requirements of the operating system. For the application to function properly, it is necessary to satisfy the additional requirements.

After you have determined the minimum hardware requirements for an OS, ensure that all hardware in the computer is compatible with the operating system that you have selected for your customer.

Hardware Compatibility List

Most operating systems have a Hardware Compatibility List (HCL) that can be found on the manufacturer's website, as shown in Figure 3. These lists provide a detailed inventory of hardware that has been tested and is known to work with the operating system. If any of your customer's existing hardware is not on the list, those components might need to be upgraded to match components on the HCL.

Note

An HCL might not be continuously maintained and therefore might not be a comprehensive reference.

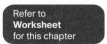

Refer to
Worksheet
for this chapter

Refer to
Figure
in online course

Upgrade Hardware Components
Gather information about hardware components.

5.4 Install an operating system

As a technician, you might have to perform a clean installation of an operating system. Perform a clean install in the following situations:

- When a computer is passed from one employee to another

- When the operating system is corrupted

- When a new replacement hard drive is installed in a computer

After completing this section, you will meet these objectives:

- Identify hard drive setup procedures.

- Prepare the hard drive.

- Install the operating system using default settings.

- Create user accounts.

- Complete the installation.

- Describe custom installation options.

- Identify the boot sequence files and Registry files.

- Describe how to manipulate operating system files.

- Describe directory structures.

Refer to
Figure
in online course

5.4.1 Identify hard drive setup procedures

The installation and initial booting of the operating system is called the operating system setup. Although it is possible to install an operating system over a network from a server or from a local hard drive, the most common installation method is with CDs and DVDs. To install an OS from a CD or DVD, first configure the BIOS setup to boot the system from the CD or DVD.

Partitioning and Formatting

Before installing an operating system on a hard drive, the hard drive must be partitioned and formatted. When a hard drive is partitioned, it is logically divided into one or more areas. When a hard drive is formatted, the partitions are prepared to hold files and applications. During the installation phase, most operating systems automatically partition and format the hard drive. A technician should understand the process relating to hard drive setup. The following terms are used when referring to hard drive setup:

- *Primary partition*– This partition is usually the first partition. A primary partition cannot be subdivided into smaller sections. There can be up to four partitions per hard drive.

- *Active partition*– This partition is the partition used by the operating system to boot the computer. Only one primary partition can be marked active.

- *Extended partition–* This partition normally uses the remaining free space on a hard drive or takes the place of a primary partition. There can be only one extended partition per hard drive, and it can be subdivided into smaller sections called logical drives.

- *Logical drive–* This drive is a section of an extended partition that can be used to separate information for administrative purposes.

- *Formatting–* This process prepares a file system in a partition for files to be stored.

- *Sector–* A sector contains a fixed number of bytes, generally at least 512.

- *Cluster–* A cluster is also called a file allocation unit. It is the smallest unit of space used for storing data. It is made up of one or more sectors.

- *Track–* A track is one complete circle of data on one side of a hard drive platter. A track is broken into groups of sectors.

- *Cylinder–* A cylinder is a stack of tracks lined up one on top of another to form a cylinder shape.

- *Drive mapping–* Drive mapping is a letter assigned to a physical or logical drive.

Refer to **Figure** in online course

5.4.2 Prepare hard drive

A clean installation of an operating system proceeds as if the disk were brand new; there is no attempt to preserve any information that is currently on the hard drive. The first phase of the installation process entails partitioning and formatting the hard drive. This process prepares the disk to accept the file system. The file system provides the directory structure that organizes the user's operating system, application, configuration, and data files.

The Windows XP operating system can use one of two file systems:

- *File Allocation Table, 32-bit (FAT32)–* A file system that can support partition sizes up to 2 TB or 2,048 GB. The FAT32 file system is supported by Windows 9.x, Windows Me, Windows 2000, and Windows XP.

- *New Technology File System (NTFS)–* A file system that can support partition sizes up to 16 exabytes, in theory. NTFS incorporates more file system security features and extended attributes than the FAT file system.

Figure 1 shows the steps required to partition and format a drive in Windows XP. Click the **Start** button in the lower right corner to see the hard drive setup steps.

The Windows Vista operating system will automatically create a partition on the entire hard drive, format it for you, and begin installing Windows if you do not create your own partitions using the **New** option, as shown in Figure 2. If you decide to create and format your own partitions, the process is the same as Windows XP, except that Windows Vista does not provide a choice of file systems. NTFS formats the partition in which Windows Vista will be installed.

Refer to **Lab Activity** for this chapter

Refer to **Lab Activity** for this chapter

Install Windows XP
Install the Windows XP operating system.

Install Windows Vista
Install the Windows Vista operating system.

Refer to **Figure** in online course

5.4.3 Install the operating system using default settings

When installing Windows XP, as shown in Figure 1, the installation wizard gives the option to install using typical (default) settings or custom settings. Using the typical settings increases the likelihood of a successful installation. However, the user must still provide the following information during the setup:

- Standards and formats that define currency and numerals
- Text input language
- Name of the user and company
- Product key
- Computer name
- Administrator password
- Date and time settings
- Network settings
- Domain or workgroup information

When a computer boots up with the Windows installation disc, the Windows XP installation starts with three options:

- *Setup XP–* To run the setup and install the XP operating system, press **ENTER.**
- *Repair XP–* To repair an installation, press **R** to open the Recovery Console. The Recovery Console is a troubleshooting tool. It can be used to create and format partitions and repair the boot sector or Master Boot Record. It can also perform basic file operations on operating system files and folders. The Recovery Console configures services and devices to start or not start the next time the computer boots up.
- *Quit–* To quit Setup without installing Windows XP, press **F3**.

For this section, select the Setup XP option.

Windows setup searches for existing Windows installations. If no existing installation is found, you can perform a clean installation of Windows. If an existing installation is found, you have the option of performing a repair installation. A repair installation fixes the current installation using the original files from the Windows XP installation disc. Before performing a repair installation, back up any important files to a different physical location such as a second hard drive, CD, or USB storage device.

After a repair installation begins, Windows setup copies installation files to the hard drive and reboots. Following the reboot, a message to press any key to boot from CD appears. Do not press any keys at this time. Setup continues to install Windows as if it were a clean install, but any applications that you have installed and any settings that you have configured remains unchanged.

When a computer boots up with the Windows Vista installation disc, Windows Vista installation starts with three options:

- *Upgrade–* Keep your files, settings, and programs and upgrade Windows. Also use this option to repair an installation.
- *Custom (advanced)–* Install a clean copy of Windows, select where you want to install it, or make changes to disks and partitions.
- *Quit–* To quit Setup, click the x in the Close box.

If no existing Windows installations are found, the Upgrade option is disabled, as shown in Figure 2.

Refer to
Figure
in online course

5.4.4 Create accounts

An administrator account is automatically created when Windows XP is installed. The default administrator account is named "administrator". For security purposes, change this name as soon as possible. Use this privileged account to manage the computer only. Do not use it as a daily account. People have accidentally made drastic changes while using the administrator account instead of a regular user account. Attackers seek out the administrator account because it is so powerful.

Create a user account when prompted during the installation process. Unlike the administrator account, user accounts can be created at any time. A user account has fewer permissions than the computer administrator. For example, users may have the right to read, but not modify, a file.

Refer to
Figure
in online course

5.4.5 Complete the installation

After the Windows installation copies all of the necessary operating system files to the hard drive, the computer reboots and prompts you to log in for the first time.

You must register Windows XP. As shown in Figure 1, you must also complete the verification that ensures that you are using a legal copy of the OS. Doing so enables you to download patches and service packs. Performing this step requires a connection to the Internet.

Depending on the age of the media at the time of your installation, there might be updates to install. As shown in Figure 2, you can use the Microsoft Update Manager from the Start menu to scan for new software and to do the following:

- Install all service packs.

- Install all patches.

Start > All Programs > Accessories > System Tools > Windows Update

In Windows Vista, use the following path to access Windows Update:

Start > All Programs > Windows Update

You should also verify that all hardware is installed correctly. As shown in Figure 3, you can use Device Manager to locate problems and to install the correct or updated drivers using the following path:

Start > Control Panel > System > Hardware > Device Manager

In Device Manager, warning icons are represented by a yellow exclamation point or a red "X". A yellow exclamation point represents a problem with the device. To view the problem description, right-click the device and select **Properties**. A red "X" represents a device that has been disabled. To enable the device, right-click the disabled device and select **Enable**. To open a category that is not yet expanded, click the plus (+) sign.

Note

When Windows detects a system error, Windows reporting displays a dialog box. If you choose to send the report, Microsoft Windows Error Reporting (WER) collects information about the application and the module involved in the error and sends the information to Microsoft.

Refer to
Lab Activity
for this chapter

Refer to
Lab Activity
for this chapter

Refer to
Figure
in online course

Create Accounts and Check For Updates in Windows XP
Create user accounts and configure the operating system for automatic updates.

Create Accounts and Check For Updates in Windows Vista
Create user accounts and configure the operating system for automatic updates.

5.4.6 Describe custom installation options

Installing an operating system on a single computer takes time. Imagine the time it would take to install operating systems on multiple computers, one at a time, in a large organization. To simplify this activity, you can use the Microsoft System Preparation (Sysprep) tool to install and configure the same operating system on multiple computers. Sysprep prepares an operating system that will be used on computers with different hardware configurations. With Sysprep and a disk cloning application, technicians are able to quickly install an operating system, complete the last configuration steps for the OS setup, and install applications.

Disk Cloning

Disk cloning creates an image of a hard drive in a computer. Follow these steps for disk cloning:

1. Create a master installation on one computer. This master installation includes the operating system, software applications, and configuration settings that will be used by the other computers in the organization.

2. Run Sysprep.

3. Create a disk image of the configured computer using a third-party disk-cloning program.

4. Copy the disk image onto a server. When the destination computer is booted, a shortened version of the Windows setup program runs. The setup creates a new system security identifier (SID), installs drivers for hardware, creates user accounts, and configures network settings to finish the OS install.

Network Installation

Windows can also be installed over a network:

Step 1.   Prepare the computer by creating a FAT or FAT32 partition of at least 1.5 GB. You must also make the partition bootable and include a network client. You can also use a boot disk that contains a network client so that the computer can connect to a file server over the network.

Step 2.   Copy the Windows XP installation files (the I386 folder from the installation disc) to the network server and make sure to share the directory so that clients can connect and use the files.

Step 3.   Boot the computer and connect to the shared directory.

Step 4.   From the shared directory, run the setup program, WINNT.EXE. The setup program copies all of the installation files from the network share onto your hard drive. After the installation files have been copied, the installation continues much the same as if the installation were performed from a disc.

Recovery Disc

You can use a recovery disc when there has been a system failure and other recovery options have failed, such as booting in Safe Mode or booting a Last Known Good. An Automated System Recovery (ASR) set must be created before a recovery can be performed. Use the ASR Wizard in

Backup to create the ASR set. The ASR Wizard creates a backup of the system state, services, and operating system components. The ASR Wizard also creates a file that contains information about your disks, the backup, and how to restore the backup.

To restore the ASR, press F2 after booting the Windows XP installation disc. ASR reads the set and restores the disks that are needed to start the computer. After the basic disk information has been restored, ASR installs a basic version of Windows and begins restoring the backup created by the ASR Wizard.

Factory Recovery Partition

Some computers that have Windows XP pre-installed from the factory contain a section of disk that is inaccessible to the user. This partition on the disk contains an image of the bootable partition, created when the computer was built. This partition is called a factory recovery partition and can be used to restore the computer to its original configuration. Occasionally, the option to reach this partition for restoration is hidden and a special key or key combination must be used when the computer is being started. The option to restore from the factory recovery partition can also be found in the BIOS of some computers. Contact the manufacturer to find out how you can access the partition and restore the original configuration of the computer.

Refer to **Figure** in online course

5.4.7 Identify the boot sequence files and Registry files

You should know the process that Windows XP uses when booting. Understanding these steps can help you to troubleshoot boot problems. Figure 1 shows the boot sequence for Windows XP.

Windows XP Boot Process

To begin the boot process, you first turn on the computer, which is called a cold boot. The computer performs the Power On Self Test (POST). Because the video adapter has not yet been initialized, any errors that occur at this point in the boot process are reported by a series of audible tones, called beep codes.

After POST, the BIOS locates and reads the configuration settings that are stored in the CMOS. This configuration setting, called the boot device priority, is the order in which devices are checked to see if an operating system is located there. The boot device priority, as shown in Figure 2, is set in the BIOS and can be arranged in any order. The BIOS boots the computer using the first drive that contains an operating system.

One common boot order is floppy drive, CD-ROM drive, and then the hard drive. This order allows you to use removable media to boot the computer. The BIOS checks the floppy drive, the CD-ROM, and finally the hard drive for an operating system to boot the computer. Network drives, USB drives, and even removable magnetic media, such as CompactFlash or Secure Digital (SD) cards, can also be used in the boot order, depending on the capabilities of the motherboard. Some BIOS also have a boot device priority menu that can be accessed using a special key combination while the computer is starting but before the boot sequence begins. You can use this menu to choose the device that you want to boot, which is useful if multiple drives can boot the computer.

When the drive with the operating system is located, the BIOS locates the Master Boot Record (MBR). The MBR locates the operating system boot loader. For Windows XP, the boot loader is called NT Loader (NTLDR).

NTLDR and the Windows Boot Menu

At this point, NTLDR controls several installation steps. For instance, if more than one OS is present on the disk, BOOT.INI gives the user a chance to select which one to use. If there are no other operating systems, or if the user does not make a selection before the timer expires, the following steps occur:

- NTLDR runs NTDETECT.COM to get information about the installed hardware.

- NTLDR then uses the path specified in the BOOT.INI to find the boot partition.

- NTLDR loads two files that make up the core of XP: NTOSKRNL.EXE and HAL.DLL.

- NTLDR reads the Registry files, chooses a hardware profile, and loads the device drivers.

Windows Registry

The Windows Registry files are an important part of the Windows XP boot process. These files are recognized by their distinctive names, which begin with HKEY_, as shown in Figure 3, followed by the name of the portion of the operating system under their control. Every setting in Windows—from the background of the desktop and the color of the screen buttons to the licensing of applications—is stored in the Registry. When a user makes changes to the Control Panel settings, File Associations, System Policies, or installed software, the changes are stored in the Registry.

Each user has a unique section of the Registry. The Windows login process pulls system settings from the Registry to reconfigure the system to the state that it was in the last time that the user turned it on.

NT Kernel

At this point, the NT kernel, the heart of the Windows operating system, takes over. The name of this file is NTOSKRNL.EXE. It starts the login file called WINLOGON.EXE and displays the XP welcome screen.

Note
If a SCSI drive will boot the computer, Windows copies the NTBOOTDD.SYS file during installation. This file is not copied if SCSI drives are not being used.

Refer to
Figure
in online course

5.4.8 Describe how to manipulate operating system files

After you have installed Windows XP, you might want to make changes to the configuration. The following applications are used extensively for post-installation diagnostics and modifications:

- *Msconfig–* This boot configuration utility allows you to set the programs that run at startup and to edit configuration files. It also offers simplified control over Windows Services, as shown in Figure 1. Figure 2 shows Msconfig in Windows Vista.

- *Regedit–* This application allows you to edit the registry, as shown in Figure 3.

- *Msinfo32–* This utility displays a complete system summary of your computer including hardware components and details, and installed software and settings, as shown in Figure 4.

- *Dxdiag–* This utility shows details about all of the DirectX components and drivers that are installed in your computer, as shown in Figure 5. You can use this utility to ensure that DirectX is installed properly and configured correctly.

- *Cmd–* This command opens a command window when it is entered in the **Run...** box, as shown in Figure 6. This is used to execute command line programs and utilities.

Note

REGEDT32.EXE was used with Windows NT. In Windows XP, and Windows Server 2003, the REGEDT32.EXE file is a shortcut to the REGEDIT.EXE command. In Windows XP, you can enter REGEDT32.EXE or REGEDIT.EXE; both commands run the same program.

Caution

Using REGEDT32.EXE or REGEDIT.EXE incorrectly might cause configuration problems that could require you to reinstall the operating system.

Startup Modes

You can boot Windows in one of many different modes. Pressing the F8 key during the boot process opens the Windows Advanced Startup Options menu, which allows you to select how to boot Windows. The following startup options are commonly used:

- *Safe Mode–* Starts Windows but only loads drivers for basic components, such as the keyboard and display.

- *Safe Mode with Networking Support–* Starts Windows identically to Safe Mode and also loads the drivers for network components.

- *Safe Mode with Command Prompt–* Starts Windows and loads the command prompt instead of the GUI.

- *Last Known Good Configuration–* Enables a user to load the configuration settings of Windows that were used the last time that Windows started successfully . It does this by accessing a copy of the registry that is created for this purpose.

Note

Last Known Good Configuration is not useful unless it is applied immediately after a failure occurs. If the machine is restarted and, despite its difficulties, manages to open Windows, the registry key for Last Known Good Configuration will probably be updated with the faulty information.

Refer to
Lab Activity
for this chapter

Managing System Files with Built-in Utilities in Windows XP
Use Windows built-in utilities to gather information about the system and to troubleshoot system resources.

Refer to
Lab Activity
for this chapter

Managing System Files with Built-in Utilities in Windows Vista
Use Windows built-in utilities to gather information about the system and to troubleshoot system resources.

Refer to
Figure
in online course

5.4.9 Describe directory structures

File Extensions and Attributes

In Windows, files are organized in a directory structure. The root level of the Windows partition is usually labeled drive C:\. Next, there is an initial set of standardized directories, called folders, for the operating system, applications, configuration information, and data files. Following the initial installation, users can install most applications and data in whichever directory they choose.

Files in the directory structure adhere to a Windows naming convention:

- Maximum of 255 characters can be used.

- Characters such as a slash or a backslash (/ \) are not allowed.

- An extension of three or four letters is added to the filename to identify the file type.

- Filenames are not case sensitive.

The following filename extensions are commonly used:

- .doc – Microsoft Word

- .txt – ASCII text only

- .jpg – Graphics format

- .ppt – Microsoft PowerPoint

- .zip – Compression format

The directory structure maintains a set of attributes for each file that controls how the file can be viewed or altered. These are the most common file attributes:

- R – The file is read-only.

- A – The file will be archived the next time that the disk is backed up.

- S – The file is marked as a system file, and a warning is given if an attempt is made to delete or modify the file.

- H – The file is hidden in the directory display.

You can view the filenames, extensions, and attributes by entering the ATTRIB command in a DOS window, as shown in Figure 1. Use the following path:

Start > Run > Type **cmd** and Press **Enter**

In Windows Vista, use the following path:

Start > Start Search > Type **cmd** and Press **Enter**

Navigate to the folder that contains the file that you are interested in. Type ATTRIB followed by the file name. Use a wildcard such as *.* to view many files at once. The attributes of each file appear in the left column of the screen. To get information about the ATTRIB command, type the following at the command prompt:

ATTRIB/?

You can access the Windows equivalent of ATTRIB by right-clicking a file in Windows Explorer and choosing **Properties**.

Note

To see the properties of a file in Windows Explorer, you must first set Windows Explorer to Show Hidden Files. Use this path:

Right-click **Start > Explore > Tools > Folder Options > View**

In Windows Vista, use this path:

Right-click **Start > Explore > Organize > Folder and Search Options > View**

NTFS and FAT32

Windows XP and Windows 2000 use FAT32 and NTFS, while Windows Vista uses NTFS. Security is one of the most important differences between these file systems. NTFS can support more and larger files than FAT32 and provides more flexible security features for files and folders. Figures 2 and 3 show the file permission properties for FAT32 and NTFS.

To use the extra security advantages of NTFS, you can convert partitions from FAT32 to NTFS using the CONVERT.EXE utility. To restore an NTFS partition back to a FAT32 partition, reformat the partition and restore the data from a backup.

Caution

Before converting a file system, remember to back up the data.

Refer to
Worksheet
for this chapter

Refer to
Figure
in online course

Answer NTFS and FAT32 Questions

Answer questions about the NTFS and FAT32 file systems.

5.5 Navigate a GUI (Windows)

The operating system provides a user interface that allows you to interact with the computer. There are two methods that you can use to navigate the file system and run applications within an operating system:

- A Graphical User Interface (GUI) provides graphical representations (icons) of all of the files, folders, and programs on a computer. You manipulate these icons using a pointer that is controlled with a mouse or similar device. The pointer allows you to move icons by dragging and dropping, and execute programs by clicking.

- A Command Line Interface (CLI) is text-based. You must type commands to manipulate files and execute programs.

After completing this section, you will meet these objectives:

- Manipulate items on the desktop.

- Explore Control Panel applets.

- Explore Administrative Tools.

- Install, navigate, and uninstall an application.

- Describe upgrading operating systems.

Refer to
Figure
in online course

5.5.1 Manipulate items on the desktop

After the operating system has been installed, the desktop can be customized to suit individual needs. A desktop on a computer is a graphical representation of a workspace. The desktop has icons, toolbars, and menus to manipulate files. The desktop can be customized with images, sounds, and colors to provide a more personalized look and feel. All of these customizable items together make up a theme. Windows Vista has a special theme called Aero, as shown in Figure 1. Aero is the default theme and has translucent window borders, numerous animations, and live icons that are thumbnail images of the contents of a file. Because of the advanced graphics needed, the Aero theme can only be used on computers that meet certain hardware requirements.

Note

Windows Vista Home Basic does not include the Aero theme.

In Windows Vista, a feature called the Sidebar, as shown in Figure 2, can also be personalized. The Sidebar is a graphical pane on the desktop that keeps small programs called gadgets organized.

Gadgets are small applications such as games, sticky notes, or a clock. Gadgets, like interfaces to web information such as weather maps or contacts on a social networking site, can also be added.

Desktop Properties

To customize the Windows XP GUI of your desktop, right-click the desktop and choose Properties. The Display Properties window, as shown in Figure 3, has five tabs: Themes, Desktop, Screen Saver, Appearance, and Settings. Click any of these tabs to customize your display settings. In Windows Vista, right-click the desktop and choose Personalize. The Personalization window, as shown in Figure 4, has seven links: Window Color and Appearance, Desktop Background, Screen Saver, Sounds, Mouse Pointers, Themes, and Display Settings. Click any of these links to customize your display settings.

Desktop Items

There are several items on the desktop that can be customized, such as the Taskbar and Recycle Bin. To customize any item, right-click the item and then choose **Properties**.

Start Menu

On the desktop, the Start menu is accessed by clicking the **Start** button. The Start menu, shown in Figure 5, displays all of the applications installed in the computer, a list of recently opened documents, and a listing of other elements, such as a search feature, help center, and system settings. The Start menu can also be customized. There are two styles of Start menu: XP and Classic. The XP-style Start menu is used throughout this course for demonstrating command sequences.

My Computer

To access the various drives installed in the computer, double-click the **My Computer** icon that appears on the desktop. To customize certain settings, right-click **My Computer** and choose **Properties**. Settings that can be customized include the following:

- Computer name
- Hardware settings
- Virtual memory
- Automatic updates
- Remote access

Note

In Windows Vista, My Computer is called Computer. To customize certain settings, click the **Start** button then right-click **Computer** and choose **Properties**. Access installed drives in Windows Vista with the following path:

Start > Computer

Launching Applications

You can launch applications in several ways:

- Click the application on the Start menu.

- Double-click the application shortcut icon on the desktop.

- Double-click the application executable file in My Computer.

- Launch the application from the Run window or command line.

My Network Places

To view and configure network connections, right-click the **My Network Places** icon on the desktop. In My Network Places, you can connect to or disconnect from a network drive. Click **Properties** to configure existing network connections, such as a wired or wireless LAN connection.

> **Note**
>
> In Windows Vista, My Network Places is called Network.

Refer to
Lab Activity
for this chapter

Run Commands in Windows XP

Open the same program by using Windows Explorer and the "Run..." command.

Refer to
Lab Activity
for this chapter

Run Commands in Windows Vista

Open the same program by using Windows Explorer and the "Run..." command.

Refer to
Figure
in online course

5.5.2 Explore Control Panel applets

Windows centralizes the settings for many features that control the behavior and appearance of the computer. These settings are categorized in applets, or small programs, found in the Control Panel, as shown in Figure 1. Adding or removing programs, changing network settings, and changing the security settings are some of the configuration options available in the Control Panel.

Control Panel Applets

The names of various applets in the Control Panel differ slightly depending on the version of Windows installed. In Windows XP, the icons are grouped into categories:

- *Appearance and Themes–* applets that control the look of windows:
  - Display
  - Taskbar and Start menu
  - Folder options
- *Network and Internet Connections–* applets that configure all of the connection types:
  - Internet options
  - Network connections
- *Add or Remove Programs–* applet to add or remove programs and windows components safely

- *Sounds, Speech, and Audio Devices–* applets that control all of the settings for sound:
  - Sounds and audio devices
  - Speech
  - Portable Media Devices
- *Performance and Maintenance–* applets to find information about your computer or perform maintenance:
  - Administrative tools
  - Power options
  - Scheduled tasks
  - System

- *Printers and Other Hardware–* applets to configure devices connected to your computer:
  - Game controllers
  - Keyboard
  - Mouse
  - Phone and modem options
  - Printers and faxes
  - Scanners and cameras
- *User Accounts–* applets to configure options for users and their e-mail:
  - E-mail
  - User accounts
- *Date, Time, Language, and Regional Options–* applets to change settings based on your location and language:
  - Date and time
  - Regional and language options
- *Accessibility Options–* wizard used to configure windows for vision, hearing, and mobility needs

- *Security Center–* applet used to configure security settings for:
  - Internet options
  - Automatic updates
  - Windows firewall

Display Settings

You can change the display settings by using the Display Settings applet. Change the appearance of the desktop by modifying the resolution and color quality, as shown in Figure 2. You can change more advanced display settings, such as wallpaper, screen saver, power settings, and other options, with the following path:

Start > Control Panel > Display > Settings tab > Advanced

Use the following path in Windows Vista:

Start > Control Panel > Personalization > Display Settings > Advanced Settings button

Refer to
Figure
in online course

5.5.3 Explore administrative tools

Computer Management

The Computer Management console, shown in Figure 1, allows you to manage many aspects of both your computer and remote computers. The Computer Management console addresses three main areas of administration: System Tools, Storage, and Services and Applications. You must have administrative privileges to access the Computer Management console. To view the Computer Management console, use the following path:

Start > Control Panel > Administrative Tools > Computer Management

To view the Computer Management console for a remote computer, right-click **Computer Management (Local)** in the console tree and click **Connect to another computer....** In the **Another computer:** box, type the name of the computer or click **Browse...** to find a computer you want to manage.

Device Manager

The Device Manager, shown in Figure 2, allows you to view all of the settings for devices in the computer. A common task for technicians is to view the values assigned for the IRQ, I/O address, and the DMA setting for all of the devices in the computer. To view the system resources in the Device Manager, use the following path:

Start > Control Panel > System > Hardware > Device Manager > View > Resources

In Windows Vista, use the following path:

Start > Control Panel > System > Device Manager > Continue > View > Resources

From the Device Manager, you can quickly view the properties of any device in the system by double-clicking the device name. You can view which version of the driver is installed in your computer, view driver file details, update a driver, or even roll back or uninstall a device driver. You can compare the driver version listed here with the version available from the website of your device manufacturer.

Task Manager

The Task Manager, shown in Figure 3, allows you to view all applications that are currently running and to close any applications that have stopped responding. The Task Manager allows you to monitor the performance of the CPU and virtual memory, view all processes that are currently running, and view information about the network connections. To view information in the Task Manager, use the following path:

CTRL-ALT-DEL > Task Manager

In Windows Vista, use the following path:

CTRL-ALT-DEL > Start Task Manager

Services

Services are executable programs that require little or no user input. Services can be set to run automatically when Windows starts, or manually when required. The Services console, shown in Figure 4, allows you to manage all of the services on your computer and remote computers. You can start, stop, or disable services. You can also change how a service starts, or define actions for the computer to perform automatically when a service fails. You must have administrative privileges to access the Services console. To view the Services console, use the following path:

Start > Control Panel > Administrative Tools > Services

To view the Services console for a remote computer, right-click **Services (Local)** in the console tree and click **Connect to another computer** In the **Another computer:** box, type the name of the computer or click **Browse...** to find a computer you want to manage.

Performance Monitor

The Performance Monitor console, shown in Figure 5, has two distinct parts: the System Monitor and Performance Logs and Alerts. The System Monitor displays real-time information about the processors, disks, memory, and network usage for your computer. You can easily summarize these activities through histograms, graphs, and reports.

Performance Logs and Alerts allow you to record the performance data and configure alerts. The alerts will notify you when a specified usage falls below or rises above a specified threshold. You can set alerts to create entries in the event log, send a network message, begin a performance log, run a specific program, or any combination of these. You must have administrative privileges to access the Performance Monitor console. To view the Performance Monitor console in Windows XP, use the following path:

Start > Control Panel > Administrative Tools > Performance

In Windows Vista, use the following path:

Start > Control Panel > Administrative Tools > Reliability and Performance Monitor > Continue

Event Viewer

The Event Viewer, shown in Figure 6, logs a history of events regarding applications, security, and the system. These log files are a valuable troubleshooting tool. To access the Event Viewer, use the following path:

Start > Control Panel > Administrative Tools > Event Viewer

In Windows Vista, use the following path:

Start > Control Panel > Administrative Tools > Event Viewer > Continue

MMC

The Microsoft Management console (MMC), shown in Figure 7, allows you to organize management tools, called snap-ins, in one location for easy administration. Web page links, tasks, ActiveX controls, and folders can also be added to the MMC. After you have configured an MMC, save it to keep all the tools and links in that MMC. You can create as many customized MMCs as needed, each with a different name. This is useful when multiple administrators manage different aspects of the same computer. Each administrator can have an individualized MMC for monitoring and configuring computer settings. You must have administrative privileges to access the MMC. To view the MMC in Windows XP, use the following path:

Start > Run > Type **mmc** and Press **Enter**

In Windows Vista, use the following path:

Start > Start Search > Type **mmc** and Press **Enter**

Remote Desktop

The Remote Desktop allows one computer to remotely take control of another computer. Remote technicians can use this troubleshooting feature to repair and upgrade computers. For Windows XP, Remote Desktop is available on Windows XP Professional only. To access the Remote Desktop in Windows XP Professional, use the following path:

Start > All Programs > Accessories > Communications > Remote Desktop Connection

In Windows Vista, use the following path:

Start > All Programs > Accessories > Remote Desktop Connection

Performance Settings

To enhance the performance of the operating system, you can change some of the settings that your computer uses, such as virtual memory configuration settings, which are shown in Figure 8. To change the virtual memory setting in Windows XP, use the following path:

Start > Control Panel > System > Advanced > Performance area > Settings button

In Windows Vista, use the following path:

Start > Control Panel > System > Advanced system settings > Continue > Advanced tab > Performance area > Settings button > Advanced

Refer to
Lab Activity
for this chapter

Refer to
Lab Activity
for this chapter

Refer to
Figure
in online course

Managing Administrative Settings and Snap-ins in Windows XP

Use administrative tools to monitor system resources and build a custom console to manage storage devices.

Managing Administrative Settings and Snap-ins in Windows Vista

Use administrative tools to monitor system resources and build a custom console to manage storage devices.

5.5.4 Install, navigate, and uninstall an application

As a technician, you will be responsible for adding and removing software from your customers' computers. Most applications use an automatic installation process when an application CD is inserted in the optical drive. The installation process updates the Add or Remove Programs utility. The user is required to click through the installation wizard and provide information when requested.

Add or Remove Programs Applet

Microsoft recommends that users always use the Add or Remove Programs utility, as shown in Figure 1, when installing or removing applications. When you use the Add or Remove Programs utility to install an application, the utility tracks installation files so that the application can be uninstalled completely, if desired. To open the Add or Remove Programs applet in Windows XP, use the following path:

Start > Control Panel > Add or Remove Programs

In Windows Vista, use the following path:

Start > Control Panel > Programs and Features

Add an Application

If a program or application is not automatically installed when the CD is inserted, you can use the Add or Remove Programs applet to install the application in Windows XP, as shown in Figure 2. Click the **Add New Programs** button and select the location where the application is located. Windows installs the application for you. In Windows Vista, insert the CD or DVD, and the program installer should start. If the program does not start, browse the CD or DVD and run the "setup" or "install" file to begin installation.

After the application is installed, the application can be started from the Start menu or a shortcut icon that the application installs on the desktop. Check the application to ensure that it is functioning properly. If there are problems with the application, make the repair or uninstall the application. Some applications, such as Microsoft Office, provide a repair option in the install process. You can use this function to try to correct a program that is not working properly.

Uninstall an Application

If an application is not uninstalled properly, you may be leaving files on the hard drive and unnecessary settings in the registry. This might not cause any problems, but it depletes available hard drive space, system resources, and the speed at which the registry is read. Figure 3 shows the Add or Remove Programs applet to use to uninstall programs in Windows XP. The wizard guides you through the software removal process and removes every file that was installed.

Refer to
Lab Activity
for this chapter

Refer to
Lab Activity
for this chapter

Refer to
Figure
in online course

Install Third-Party Software in Windows XP

Install and remove a third-party software application.

Install Third-Party Software in Windows Vista

Install and remove a third-party software application.

5.5.5 Describe upgrading an operating system

Sometimes it might be necessary to upgrade an operating system. Before upgrading the operating system, check the minimum requirements of the new operating system to ensure that the computer meets the minimum specifications. Check the HCL to ensure that the hardware is compatible with the new operating system. Back up all data before upgrading the operating system in case there is a problem with the installation.

The process of upgrading a computer system from Windows 2000 to Windows XP is quicker than performing a new installation of Windows XP. The Windows XP setup utility replaces the existing Windows 2000 files with Windows XP files during the upgrade process. However, existing applications and settings are saved.

Upgrading the Operating System to Windows XP

1. Insert the Windows XP disc into the optical drive to start the upgrade process. Select **Start > Run**.

2. In the Run box, where D is the drive letter for the optical drive, type **D:\i386\winnt32** and press **Enter**. The Welcome to the Windows XP Setup Wizard displays.

3. Choose **Upgrade to Windows XP** and click **Next**. The License Agreement page displays.

4. Read the license agreement and click the button to accept this agreement.

5. Click **Next**. The Upgrading to the Windows XP NTFS File System page displays.

6. Follow the prompts and complete the upgrade. When the install is complete, the computer will restart.

Note

The Windows XP Setup Wizard might automatically start when the disc is inserted into the optical drive.

Note

Before you can upgrade from Windows XP to Windows Vista, you must install Windows XP Service Pack 2.

Upgrading the Operating System to Windows Vista

1. Insert the Windows Vista disc into the optical drive. The Set Up window appears.

2. Select **Install Windows Vista**.

3. You are prompted to download any important updates for Windows Vista.

4. Enter your **Product Key** and then agree to the **End User License Agreement (EULA)**.

5. You are presented with two choices, **Custom** or **Upgrade**.

6. Click **Upgrade** and setup will begin copying installation files.

7. Follow the prompts and complete the upgrade. When the install is complete, the computer will restart.

In some cases, you cannot upgrade to a newer operating system. Figure 1 shows which Windows operating systems can be upgraded to other versions of Windows. If your operating system cannot be upgraded, you must perform a new installation.

When a new installation of Windows is needed, you can use the Windows User State Migration Tool (USMT) to migrate all of the current user files and settings to the new operating system. The USMT allows users to restore the configurations and customizations from their current computer to the newly installed Windows operating system. Download and install USMT from Microsoft to create a store of user files and settings onto a separate drive or partition. After the new operating system is installed, download and install USMT again to restore the user files and settings to the new operating system.

Refer to
Figure
in online course

5.6 Identify and apply common preventive maintenance techniques for operating systems

Preventive maintenance for an operating system includes organizing the system, defragmenting the hard drive, keeping applications current, removing unused applications, and checking the system for errors.

After completing this section, you will meet these objectives:

- Create a preventive maintenance plan.

- Schedule a task.

- Back up the hard drive.

Refer to
Figure
in online course

5.6.1 Create a preventive maintenance plan

The goal of an operating system preventive maintenance plan is to avoid problems in the future. Perform preventive maintenance regularly, and record all actions taken and observations made. Some preventative maintenance should take place when it causes the least amount of disruption to the people who use the computers. This often means scheduling tasks at night, early in the morning, or over the weekend. There are also tools and techniques that can automate many preventive maintenance tasks.

Preventive Maintenance Planning

Preventive maintenance plans should include detailed information about the maintenance of all computers and network equipment, with emphasis on equipment that could impact the organization the most. Preventive maintenance includes the following important tasks:

- Hard drive backup [Figure 1]

- Hard drive defragmentation [Figure 2]

- Updates to the operating system and applications [Figure 3]

- Updates to antivirus and other protective software [Figure 4]

- Hard drive error checking [Figure 5]

A preventive maintenance program that is designed to fix things before they break, and to solve small problems before they affect productivity, can provide the following benefits to users and organizations:

- Decreased downtime

- Improved performance

- Improved reliability

- Decreased repair costs

An additional part of preventive maintenance is documentation. A repair log helps you determine which equipment is the most or least reliable. It also provides a history of when a computer was last fixed, how it was fixed, and what the problem was.

Device Driver Updates

Manufacturers occasionally release new drivers to address issues with the current drivers. As a best practice, you should check for updated drivers regularly. Check for updated drivers when your hardware does not work properly or to prevent future problems. It is also important to update drivers that patch or correct security problems. Updating device drivers should be part of your preventive maintenance program to ensure that your drivers are always current. If a driver update does not work properly, use the Roll Back Driver feature to revert back to the previously installed driver.

Firmware Updates

Manufacturers occasionally release new firmware updates to address issues that might not be fixed with driver updates. Firmware updates are less common than driver updates. They can increase the speed of certain types of hardware, enable new features, or increase the stability of a product. Follow the manufacturer's instructions carefully when performing a firmware update to avoid making the hardware unusable. Research the firmware updates completely because it might not be possible to revert to the original firmware. Checking for firmware updates should be part of your preventive maintenance program.

Operating System Updates

Microsoft releases updates to address security issues and other functionality problems. You can install individual updates manually from the Microsoft website or automatically using the Windows Automatic Update utility.

Downloads that contain multiple updates are known as service packs. A service pack usually contains all of the updates for an operating system. Installing a service pack is a good way to bring your operating system up to date quickly. Set a restore point and back up critical data prior to installing a service pack. Add operating system updates to your preventive maintenance program to ensure that your operating system has the latest functionality and security fixes.

Security

Security is an important aspect of your preventive maintenance program. Install virus and malware protection software and perform regular scans on your computer to help ensure that your computer remains free of malicious software. Use the Windows Malicious Software Removal Tool to check a computer for specific, prevalent malicious software. If an infection is found, the tool removes it. Each time a new version of the tool is available from Microsoft, download it and scan your computer for new threats. This should be a standard item in your preventive maintenance program along with regular updates to your antivirus and spyware removal tools.

Startup Programs

Some programs, such as antivirus scanners and spyware removal tools, do not automatically start when the computer boots up. To ensure that these programs run each time the computer is booted, add the program to the Startup folder of the Start menu. Many programs have switches to allow the program to perform a specific action, start up without being displayed, or go to the Windows Tray. Check the documentation to determine if your programs allow the use of special switches.

Refer to **Figure** in online course

5.6.2 Schedule a task

Some preventive maintenance consists of cleaning, inspecting, and doing minor repairs. Some preventive maintenance uses application tools that are either already in the operating system or can be loaded onto the user's hard drive. Most preventive maintenance applications can be set to run automatically according to a schedule.

Windows has the following utilities that launch tasks when you schedule them:

- The DOS AT command launches tasks at a specified time using the CLI.
- The Windows Task Scheduler launches tasks at a specified time using a GUI.

Information about the AT command is available at this path in Windows XP:

Start > Run > Type **cmd** and press **Enter**

Then type **AT /?** at the command line.

In Windows Vista, access the command line using the following path:

Start > Start Search > Type **cmd** and press **Enter**

Access the Windows Task Scheduler by following this path in Windows XP:

Start > All Programs > Accessories > System Tools > Scheduled Tasks

In Windows Vista, follow this path:

Start > All Programs > Accessories > System Tools > Task Scheduler

Both of these tools allow you to run a command once at a specific time or schedule a command to run on selected days or times. The Windows Task Scheduler, shown in Figure 1, is easier to learn and use than the AT command, especially when it comes to recurring tasks and deleting tasks already scheduled.

System Utilities

Several utilities included with DOS and Windows help maintain system integrity. Two utilities that are useful tools for preventive maintenance are:

- *ScanDisk or CHKDSK–* ScanDisk (Windows 2000) and CHKDSK (Windows XP and Vista) check the integrity of files and folders and scan the hard disk surface for physical errors. Consider using ScanDisk or CHKDSK at least once a month and also whenever a sudden loss of power causes the system to shut down.

■ *Defrag–* As files increase in size, some data is written to the next available space on the disk. In time, data becomes fragmented, or spread all over the hard drive. It takes time to seek each section of the data. Defrag gathers the noncontiguous data into one place, making files run faster.

You can access both of these utilities by using this path in Windows XP:

Start > All Programs > Accessories > System Tools > Disk Defragmenter

In Windows Vista, use this path:

Start > Computer > right-click **Drive x > Properties > Tools**

Automatic Updates

If every maintenance task had to be scheduled every time it was run, repairing computers would be much harder than it is today. Fortunately, tools such as the Scheduled Task Wizard allow many functions to be automated. But how can you automate the update of software that has not been written?

Operating systems and applications are constantly being updated for security purposes and for added functionality. It is important that Microsoft and others provide an update service, as shown in Figure 2. The update service can scan the system for needed updates and then recommend what should be downloaded and installed. The update service can download and install updates as soon as they are available, or it can download updates as required, and install them when the computer is next rebooted. The Microsoft Update Wizard is available at this path in Windows XP:

Start > Control Panel > System > Automatic Updates

In Windows Vista, it is available at this path:

Start > Control Panel > Windows Update

Most antivirus software contains its own update facility. It can update both its application software and its database files automatically. This feature allows it to provide immediate protection as new threats develop.

Restore Point

An update can sometimes cause serious problems. Perhaps an older program is in the system that is not compatible with the current operating system. An automatic update might install code that works for most users but does not work with your system.

You can solve this problem by creating a restore point, which is an image of the computer settings. If the computer crashes or an update causes system problems, the computer can roll back to a previous configuration. You can use the Windows Restore Point utility, as shown in Figure 3, to create and revert to a restore point.

A technician should always create a restore point before updating or replacing the operating system. Restore points should also be created at the following times:

■ When an application is installed

■ When a driver is installed

Note

A restore point backs up drivers, system files, and registry settings but not application data.

To restore or create a restore point, use the following path:

Start > All Programs > Accessories > System Tools > System Restore

Backup Status and Configuration

Windows Vista has the Backup Status and Configuration tool for backing up photos, music, email, and other types of user data. Backups can be set to run automatically at regular intervals. Back up your data to a drive other than the drive that contains the operating system. The Backup Status and Configuration tool is not used to back up system settings. Windows Vista Home Basic does not include the option to set automatic backups. To access the Backup Status and Configuration tool, use the following path:

Start > All Programs > Accessories > System Tools > Backup Status and Configuration

ERD and ASR

Windows 2000 offers the ability to create an emergency repair disk (ERD) that saves critical boot files and configuration information necessary to troubleshoot problems in Windows. Windows XP offers the same features with the Automated System Recovery (ASR) wizard. Although both ERD and ASR are powerful troubleshooting tools, they should never replace a good backup.

A recovery disc contains the essential files used to repair the system after a serious issue, such as a hard drive crash. The recovery disc can contain the original version of Windows, hardware drivers, and application software. When the recovery disc is used, the computer is restored to the original default configuration.

Refer to Lab Activity for this chapter

Restore Points in Windows XP

Create a restore point and return your computer back to that point in time.

Refer to Lab Activity for this chapter

Restore Points in Windows Vista

Create a restore point and return your computer back to that point in time.

Refer to Figure in online course

5.6.3 Back up the hard drive

Just as the system restore points allow the restoration of OS configuration files, backup tools allow the recovery of data. You can use the Microsoft Backup Utility, shown in Figure 1, to perform back ups as required. It is important to establish a backup strategy that includes data recovery. The organization's requirements will determine how often the data must be backed up and the type of backup to perform.

It can take a long time to run a backup. If the backup strategy is followed carefully, it will not be necessary to back up every file at every backup. It is only necessary to make copies of the files that have changed since the last backup. For this reason, there are several different types of backups.

Normal Backup

A normal backup is also called a full backup. During a normal backup, all selected files on the disk are archived to the backup medium. These files are marked as having been archived by clearing the archive bit.

Copy Backup

A copy backup copies all selected files. It does not mark the files as having been archived.

Differential Backup

A differential backup backs up all the files and folders that have been created or modified since either the last normal backup or the last incremental backup (see below). The differential backup does not mark the files as having been archived. Copies are made from the same starting point until the next incremental or full backup is performed. Making differential backups is important because only the last full and differential backups are needed to restore all the data.

Incremental Backup

An incremental backup procedure backs up all the files and folders that have been created or modified since either the last normal or incremental backup. It marks the files as having been archived by clearing the archive bit. This has the effect of advancing the starting point of differential backups without having to re-archive the entire contents of the drive. If you must perform a system restore, restore the last full backup first, then restore each incremental backup in order, and finally, restore the differential backups made since the last incremental backup.

Daily Backup

Daily backups only back up the files that are modified on the day of the backup. Daily backups do not modify the archive bit.

To access the daily backup utility on a Windows XP Professional system, use the following path:

Start > All Programs > Accessories > System Tools > Backup

To access the daily backup utility in Windows Vista, use the following path:

Start > All Programs > Accessories > System Tools > Backup Status and Configuration

Backup Media

Many types of backup media are available for computers:

- Tape drives are devices that are used for data backup on a network server drive. Tapes drives are an inexpensive way to store a lot of data.

- The Digital Audio Tape (DAT) tape standard uses 4 mm digital audiotapes to store data in the Digital Data Storage (DSS) format.

- Digital Linear Tape (DLT) technology offers high-capacity and relatively high-speed tape backup capabilities.

- USB flash memory can hold hundreds of times the data that a floppy disk can hold. USB flash memory devices are available in many capacities and offer better transfer rates than tape devices.

- Optical media, such as CDs, DVDs, and Blu-ray Discs, are plastic discs used to store data. Many formats and capacities of optical media are available. A DVD holds much more data than a CD, and a Blu-ray Disc holds much more data than a DVD.

- External Hard Disk Drives (HDDs) are hard drives that are connected to your computer using a USB, FireWire, or external Serial ATA (eSATA) connection. External HDDs can hold very large amounts of data and can transfer data very quickly.

Refer to
Lab Activity
for this chapter

Registry Backup and Recovery in Windows XP

Back up a computer registry and perform a recovery of a computer registry.

Refer to
Figure
in online course

5.7 Troubleshoot operating systems

Most operating systems contain utilities to assist in the troubleshooting process. These utilities help technicians determine why the computer crashes or does not boot properly. The utilities also help identify the problem and how to resolve it.

Follow the steps outlined in this section to accurately identify, repair, and document the problem. The troubleshooting process is shown in Figure 1.

After completing this section, you will meet these objectives:

- Review the troubleshooting process.
- Identify common problems and solutions.

Refer to **Figure** in online course

5.7.1 Review the troubleshooting process

Operating system problems can result from a combination of hardware, application, and configuration issues. Computer technicians must be able to analyze the problem and determine the cause of the error to repair the operating system. This process is called troubleshooting.

The first step in the troubleshooting process is to identify the problem. Figure 1 lists open-ended and closed-ended questions to ask the customer.

After you have talked to the customer, you should establish a theory of probable causes. Figure 2 lists some common causes of operating system problems.

After a theory of probable causes has been established, try to determine an exact cause of the problem. Figure 3 lists common steps to determine the cause of operating system problems.

If you were unable to determine the cause of the problem, use Step 4 in the troubleshooting process to research the problem more thoroughly. Figure 4 shows sources of information to gather additional information to resolve an issue.

At this point, you will be able to verify the solution and the full system functionality. Figure 5 shows how to validate your implementation of the solution.

After you have solved the operating system problem, document your findings. Figure 6 is a list of the tasks required to complete this step.

Refer to **Figure** in online course

Refer to **Lab Activity** for this chapter

Refer to **Lab Activity** for this chapter

Refer to **Figure** in online course

5.7.2 Identify common problems and solutions

Operating system problems can be attributed to hardware, application, or configuration issues, or to some combination of the three. You will resolve some types of operating system problems more often than others. Figure 1 is a chart of common operating system problems and solutions.

Managing Device Drivers with Device Manager in Windows XP
Use Windows Device Manager to gather information about different drivers and learn how Device Manager manages drivers.

Managing Device Drivers with Device Manager in Windows Vista
Use Windows Device Manager to gather information about different drivers and learn how Device Manager manages drivers.

Summary

This chapter introduced computer operating systems. As a technician, you should be skilled at installing, configuring, and troubleshooting an operating system. The following concepts from this chapter are important to remember:

- Several different operating systems are available, and you must consider the customer's needs and environment when choosing an operating system.

- The main steps in setting up a customer's computer include preparing the hard drive, installing an operating system, creating user accounts, and configuring installation options.

- A GUI shows icons of all files, folders, and applications on the computer. A pointing device, such as a mouse, is used to navigate in a GUI desktop.

- You should establish a backup strategy that allows for the recovery of data. Normal, copy, differential, incremental, and daily backups are all optional backup tools available in Windows operating systems.

- Preventive maintenance techniques help to ensure optimal operation of the operating system.

- Some of the tools available for troubleshooting an operating system problem include Windows Advanced Options menu, event logs, device manager, and system files.

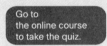

Chapter 5 Quiz

Take the chapter quiz to test your knowledge.

Your Chapter Notes

Fundamental Laptops and Portable Devices

Introduction

Do you know when the first laptops were developed? Who do you think used the early laptops?

One of the original laptops was the GRiD Compass 1101. It was used by astronauts on space missions in the early 1980s. It weighed 11 lb (5 kg) and cost US $8,000 - $10,000! Laptops today often weigh less than one-half the weight and cost less than one-third the price of the GRiD. The compact design, convenience, and evolving technology of laptops have made them as popular as desktops.

Laptops, Personal Digital Assistants (PDAs), and smartphones are becoming more popular as their prices decrease and technology continues to progress. As a computer technician, you need to have knowledge of portable devices of all kinds. This chapter focuses on the differences between laptops and desktops and describes the features of PDAs and smartphones.

After completing this chapter, you will meet these objectives:

- Describe laptops and other portable devices.
- Identify and describe the components of a laptop.
- Compare and contrast desktop and laptop components.
- Explain how to configure laptops.
- Compare the different mobile phone standards.
- Identify common preventive maintenance techniques for laptops and portable devices.
- Describe how to troubleshoot laptops and portable devices.

Refer to
Figure
in online course

6.1 Describe laptops and other portable devices

Note

Notebooks, laptops, and tablets are types of portable computers. For clarity and consistency in this course, all portable computers are called laptops.

Laptops

Early laptops were heavy and expensive. Today, laptops are very popular because advances in technology have resulted in laptops that cost less, weigh less, and have improved capabilities. Many laptops can be configured with an additional video port, a FireWire port, an infrared port, or an integrated camera.

PDAs and Smartphones

PDAs and smartphones are examples of portable, handheld devices that are becoming more popular. PDAs offer features such as games, web surfing, e-mail, instant messaging, and many other features offered by PCs. Smartphones are cell phones with many built-in PDA capabilities. PDAs and smartphones can run some of the same software as laptops.

After completing this section, you will meet these objectives:

- Identify some common uses of laptops.
- Identify some common uses of PDAs and smartphones.

Refer to
Figure
in online course

6.1.1 Identify some common uses of laptops

The most significant feature of a laptop is its compact size. The design of the laptop places the keyboard, screen, and internal components into a small, portable case.

Another popular feature of the laptop is its portability. A rechargeable battery allows the laptop to function when it is disconnected from an AC power source.

The first laptops were used primarily by business people who needed to access and enter data when they were away from the office. The use of laptops was limited due to expense, weight, and limited capabilities compared to less expensive desktops.

Today, laptops have lower prices and increased capabilities. A laptop is now a real alternative to a desktop computer.

Here are some common uses for the laptop:

- Taking notes in school or researching papers
- Presenting information in business meetings
- Accessing data away from home or the office
- Playing games while traveling
- Watching movies while traveling
- Accessing the Internet in a public place
- Sending and receiving e-mail in a public place

Can you think of other uses for laptops?

Refer to
Figure
in online course

6.1.2 Identify some common uses of PDAs and smartphones

The concept of the PDA has existed since the 1970s. The earliest models were computerized personal organizers designed to have a touch screen or a keyboard. Today, some models have both a touch screen and a keyboard and use an operating system that is similar to operating systems used on desktop computers.

The PDA is an electronic personal organizer with tools to help organize information:

- Address book

- Calculator

- Alarm clock

- Internet access

- E-mail

- Global positioning

The smartphone is a mobile phone with PDA capabilities. Smartphones combine cell phone and computer functions in a single, handheld device. The technology of the PDA and the technology of the smartphone continue to merge.

Smartphones may include these additional options:

- Built-in camera

- Document access

- E-mail

- Abbreviated note-taking

- Television

Smartphone connectivity and PDA connectivity include Bluetooth and regular USB cable connections.

Can you think of other uses for the PDA and the smartphone?

Research Laptops, Smartphones, and PDAs
Gather information, and record the specifications for a laptop, smartphone, and PDA.

Refer to
Worksheet
for this chapter

Refer to
Figure
in online course

6.2 Identify and describe the components of a laptop

What are some common laptop features?

- They are small and portable.

- They have an integrated display screen in the lid.

- They have an integrated keyboard in the base.

- They run on AC power or a rechargeable battery.

- They support hot-swappable drives and peripherals.

- Most laptops can use docking stations and port replicators to connect peripherals.

In this section, you will look closely at the components of a laptop. You will also examine a docking station. Remember, laptops and docking stations come in many models. Components might be located in different places on different models.

After completing this section, you will meet these objectives:

- Describe the components found on the outside of the laptop.

- Describe the components found on the inside of the laptop.

- Describe the components found on the laptop docking station.

Refer to
Figure
in online course

6.2.1 Describe the components found on the outside of the laptop

Laptop and desktop computers use the same types of ports so that peripherals can be interchangeable. These ports are specifically designed for connecting peripherals, providing network connectivity, and providing audio access.

Ports, connections, and drives are located on the front, back, and sides of the laptop due to the compact design. Laptops contain PC Card or ExpressCard slots to add functionality such as more memory, a modem, or a network connection.

Laptops require a port for external power. Laptops can operate using either a battery or an AC power adapter. This port can be used to power the computer or to charge the battery.

Status indicators, ports, slots, connectors, bays, jacks, vents, and a keyhole are on the exterior of the laptop. Click the highlighted areas in Figures 1 to 7 to discover additional information about each of these components.

Figure 1 shows three LEDs on the top of the laptop. Click the three highlighted areas for more information about what the LEDs indicate:

Step 1.   Bluetooth

Step 2.   Battery

Step 3.   Standby

Note

LED displays vary among laptops. Technicians should consult the laptop manual for a list of specific status displays.

Figure 2 shows three components on the back of the laptop. Click the three highlighted areas for more information about the components:

Step 1.   Parallel port

Step 2.   AC power connector

Step 3.   Battery bay

A laptop operates using either a battery or an AC power adapter. Laptop batteries are manufactured in various shapes and sizes. They use different types of chemicals and metals to store power. Refer to Figure 3 to compare rechargeable batteries.

The left side of the laptop shown in Figure 4 has ten components. Click the ten highlighted areas for more information about the components:

Step 1.   Security keyhole

Step 2.   USB

Step 3.   S-video connector

Step 4.   Modem RJ-11

Step 5.   Ethernet RJ-45

Step 6.   Network LEDs

Step 7.   Stereo headphone jack

Step 8.   Microphone jack

Step 9.   Ventilation

Step 10.   PC combo expansion slot

The front of the laptop shown in Figure 5 has the components listed here. Click the four highlighted areas for more information about the components:

Step 1.   Ventilation

Step 2.   Speakers

Step 3.   Infrared port

Step 4.   Laptop latch

The right side of the laptop shown in Figure 6 contains four components. Click the four highlighted areas for more information about the components:

Step 1.   VGA port

Step 2.   Drive bay status indicator

Step 3.   Optical drive activity indicator

Step 4.   Optical drive

The bottom of the laptop shown in Figure 7 has the components listed here. Click the five highlighted areas for more information about the components:

Step 1.   Docking station connector

Step 2.   Battery latches (two areas)

Step 3.   RAM access panel

Step 4.   Hard drive access panel

Refer to
Interactive Graphic
in online course.

Virtual Laptop: Explore Laptop

System requirements for the virtual laptop include a minimum of 512 MB RAM and Windows 2000 or Windows XP operating system.

Explore the different views of the virtual laptop.

Refer to
Figure
in online course

6.2.2 Describe the components found on the inside of the laptop

Laptops use input devices to add functionality to the laptop. Installing input devices might require downloading drivers from the manufacturer's website. There are a variety of input devices:

- Stylus or digitizer
- Tablet

- Barcode reader

- Scanner

- Light pen

- Web camera

- PC game device

Some input devices might need to be configured or optimized for speed, sensitivity, scrolling, or the number of taps needed. To gain access to these configuration utilities for input devices, use the following path:

Start > Control Panel > Mouse

Not all devices can be configured through the Control Panel. When you install the software for some devices, programs might be installed in the All Programs section of the Start menu. These programs are used to configure more advanced settings.

Some input devices are built into the laptop. Typically, the laptop is closed when not in use. By opening the lid of the laptop, you can access a variety of input devices, LEDs, and a display screen. Click the five highlighted areas in Figure 1 for more information about the input devices:

- Keyboard

- Input devices

- Fingerprint reader

- Volume controls

- Power button

Refer to Figure 1. Do you know which of these devices perform the following functions?

- Move the pointer.

- Turn up the volume.

- Log on to the laptop.

- Type a document.

- Turn on the laptop.

- Switch to the external monitor.

At the bottom of the screen is a row of LEDs that shows the status of specific functions. Click the eight highlighted areas in Figure 2 for more information on these LEDs:

- Wireless

- Bluetooth

- Num Lock

- Caps Lock

- Hard drive activity

- Power on

- Battery status

- Hibernate/Standby

Note

Indicators vary by laptop.

A laptop monitor is a built-in LCD. It is similar to a desktop LCD monitor, except that the resolution, brightness, and contrast settings can be adjusted using software or button controls. The laptop monitor cannot be adjusted for height and distance because it is integrated into the lid of the case. A desktop monitor can be added to a laptop. An Fn key on the laptop keyboard toggles between the laptop display and the desktop monitor, as shown in Figure 3.

The purpose of the Fn key is to activate a second function on a dual-purpose key. The feature that is accessed by pressing and holding the Fn key is printed on another key in a smaller font or different color. There are several functions that can be accessed:

- Volume setting

- Display brightness

- Sleep states

- Wireless functionality

- Check battery status

The Fn key must not be confused with function keys F1 through F12. These keys are typically located in a horizontal row across the top of the keyboard. Their function depends on the operating system and application that is running when they are pressed. Each key can be made to perform up to seven separate operations. The key can be pressed alone or with one or more combinations of the Shift, Control, and Alt keys.

On many laptops, a small pin on the laptop cover contacts a switch when the case is closed, called an LCD cutoff switch. The LCD cutoff switch tells the CPU to conserve power by extinguishing the backlight and turning off the LCD. If this switch breaks or is dirty, the LCD remains dark while the laptop is open. Carefully clean this switch to restore normal operation.

Refer to
Interactive Graphic
in online course.

Virtual Laptop: Keyboard
System requirements for the virtual laptop include a minimum of 512 MB RAM and Windows 2000 or Windows XP operating system.
Explore the virtual laptop keyboard.

Refer to
Figure
in online course

6.2.3 Describe the components found on the laptop docking station

A base station is a device that attaches to AC power and to desktop peripherals. When you plug the laptop into the base station, you have convenient access to power and the attached peripherals.

There are two types of base stations: docking stations and port replicators. Docking stations and port replicators are used for the same purpose. Port replicators are usually smaller than docking stations and do not have speakers or PCI slots. Docking stations and port replicators use a variety of connection types:

- Manufacturer- and model-specific

- USB or FireWire
- PC-Card or ExpressCard

Figures 1 to 3 illustrate a docking station.

Click the three highlighted areas in Figure 1 for more information about components on the top of the docking station:

- Power button
- Eject button
- Docking connector

Some docking stations include the following drive bays and ports to provide additional functionality:

- Parallel
- USB
- Ethernet
- Video
- Audio

The back of the docking station contains ports and connectors used to attach to desktop peripherals such as a mouse, a monitor, or a printer. A vent is also necessary to expel hot air from the docking station. Click the 15 highlighted areas in Figure 2 for more information about the components located on the back of the docking station:

- Exhaust vent
- AC power connector
- PC Card or ExpressCard slot
- VGA port
- DVI port
- Line In connector
- Headphone connector
- USB port
- Mouse port
- Keyboard port
- External-diskette-drive connector
- Parallel port
- Serial port
- Modem port
- Ethernet port

Secure the laptop to the docking station with a key lock. Click the highlighted area in Figure 3 for more information about the key lock located on the right side of the docking station.

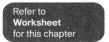

Refer to
Worksheet
for this chapter

Refer to
Interactive Graphic
in online course.

Refer to
Figure
in online course

Complete Docking Stations True or False Questions

Print and complete this worksheet.

Virtual Laptop: Docking Station

System requirements for the virtual laptop include a minimum of 512 MB RAM and Windows 2000 or Windows XP operating system.

Explore the different views of the docking station.

6.3 Compare and contrast desktop and laptop components

Most of the functions that a desktop can perform can also be performed by a laptop. However, these two kinds of computers are built very differently and the parts are not interchangeable. As an example, a plane and a helicopter can each travel to the same destination, but they cannot be repaired with the same spare parts. This is also true for laptops and desktops. Few components can be shared between desktops and laptops.

Desktop components tend to be standardized. They usually meet universal form factors. Desktops made by different manufacturers can often use the same components. A DVD/CD-RW drive is an example of a desktop component that has a standard form factor.

Laptop components are much more specialized than desktop components. This difference is because laptop manufacturers focus on refining components to make them more efficient and compact. As a result, manufacturers design laptop components to follow their own specific form factors. Laptop components are proprietary. You might not be able to use components made by one laptop manufacturer to repair a laptop made by another manufacturer.

Note

Technicians might have to obtain certification for each laptop manufacturer that they support.

After completing this section, you will meet these objectives:

- Compare and contrast desktop and laptop motherboards.
- Compare and contrast desktop and laptop processors.
- Compare and contrast desktop and laptop power management.
- Compare and contrast desktop and laptop expansion capabilities.

Refer to
Figure
in online course

6.3.1 Compare and contrast desktop and laptop motherboards

Desktop motherboards have standard form factors. The standard size and shape allow motherboards from different manufacturers to be interchangeable.

Laptop motherboards vary by manufacturer and are proprietary. When you repair a laptop, it is strongly recommended that you obtain a replacement motherboard from the manufacturer of the laptop. Figure 1 shows a desktop motherboard and a laptop motherboard.

Laptop motherboards and desktop motherboards are designed differently. Components designed for a laptop generally cannot be used in a desktop. Figure 2 shows a few examples of the design differences.

Laptops, some printers, and routers have space restrictions; therefore, they use Small Outline Dual In-line Memory Modules (SODIMMs), as shown in Figure 3.

Refer to
Figure
in online course

6.3.2 Compare and contrast desktop and laptop processors

The CPU is the brain of the computer. The CPU interprets and processes instructions that are used to manipulate data.

Laptop processors are designed to use less power and create less heat than desktop processors. As a result, laptop processors do not require cooling devices that are as large as those found in desktops. Laptop processors also use CPU throttling to modify the clock speed as needed to reduce power consumption and heat. This results in a slight decrease in performance. It also increases the lifespan of some components. These specially designed processors allow laptops to operate for a longer period of time when using a battery power source. Figure 1 shows laptop processor specifications.

Note

Technicians should refer to the laptop manual for processors that can be used as replacement processors and for processor replacement instructions.

Refer to
Figure
in online course

6.3.3 Compare and contrast desktop and laptop power management

Power management controls the flow of electricity to the components of a computer.

Desktops are usually set up in a location where they remain plugged into a power source. Desktop power management distributes electricity from the source to the components of the desktop. There is also a small battery in the desktop that provides electricity to maintain the internal clock and BIOS settings when the desktop is powered off.

Laptops are small and portable. This portability feature is achieved by combining the small size and weight of a laptop with the ability to operate from a battery. Unlike a desktop computer power supply, laptops can accept only DC power. AC adapters convert unregulated AC power to the regulated DC power required to run the laptop and charge the laptop battery.

When the laptop is plugged in, laptop power management sends electricity from the AC power source to the laptop components. The laptop power management also recharges the battery. When the laptop is unplugged, laptop power management takes electricity from the battery and sends it to the laptop components.

There are two methods of power management:

- Advanced Power Management (APM)

- Advanced Configuration and Power Interface (ACPI)

APM is an earlier version of power management. With APM, the BIOS was used to control the settings for power management.

ACPI has replaced APM. ACPI offers additional power management features. With ACPI, the operating system controls power management.

Refer to
Figure
in online course

6.3.4 Compare and contrast desktop and laptop expansion capabilities

Expansion capabilities add functionality to a computer. Many expansion devices can be used with both laptops and desktops:

- External drives

- Modems

- Network cards

- Wireless adapters

- Printers

- Other peripherals

Expansion devices are attached to laptops and desktops differently. A desktop attaches these devices with serial, parallel, USB, and FireWire ports. A laptop attaches these devices with the same ports and PC Cards.

The standardized use of USB and FireWire ports makes it possible to connect many types of external components to laptops, docking stations, port replicators, and desktops. The USB and FireWire standards make it possible to connect and remove external components without the need to power off the system. USB and FireWire ports are used to connect a range of external components:

- Printers

- Scanners

- Floppy disk drives

- Mice

- Cameras

- Keyboards

- Hard drives

- Flash drives

- Optical drives

- MP3 players

Laptops and desktops have similar expansion capabilities. It is the difference in form factor between the computers that determines which type of expansion device is used. Desktops have internal bays that support 5.25" and 3.5" drives. Additionally, there is space to install other permanent expansion drives. Laptops have limited space; therefore, the expansion bays on laptops are designed to allow different types of drives to fit into the same bay. Drives are hot-swappable and are inserted or removed as needed. Figure 1 shows a comparison of desktop and laptop expansion components.

Expansion devices used for data storage use three types of storage methods:

- Magnetic

- Flash

- Optical

Traditional hard drives are magnetic. Magnetic hard drives have drive motors designed to spin magnetic platters and the drive heads.

A flash drive uses a special type of memory that requires no power to maintain the data. Flash memory chips manage all storage on a Solid State Drive (SSD), which results in faster access to data, higher reliability, and reduced power usage. SSDs do not have moving parts. Because there are no drive motors and moving parts, the SSD uses far less energy than the magnetic hard drive.

The optical drive is a storage device that uses lasers to read data on the optical medium. Optical drives have moving parts like hard drives. They have drive motors designed to spin a platter and move a drive head. There are three types of optical drives:

- CD

- DVD

- Blu-ray Disc (BD)

CD, DVD, and BD media can be pre-recorded (read-only), recordable (write once), or re-recordable (read and write multiple times). CDs have a data storage capacity of approximately 700 MB. DVDs have a data storage capacity of approximately 8.5 GB on one side of the disc. BDs have a storage capacity of 25 GB on a single-layer disc, and 50 GB on a dual-layer disc.

Laptops use the PC Card slot to add functionality. The PC Card slot uses an open standard interface to connect to peripheral devices using the CardBus standard. Here are some examples of devices that connect using PC Cards:

- Memory

- Modems

- Hard drives

- Network cards

PC Cards follow the PCMCIA standard. They come in three types: Type I, Type II, and Type III. Each type of PC Card is different in size and can attach to different devices. A newer type of PC Card is called the PC ExpressCard. Figure 2 shows a comparison of PC Cards and PC Express-Cards. The PC ExpressCard comes in 34mm and 54mm widths. Figure 3 shows an example of a PC Card and PC ExpressCards.

Suppose that you need to purchase a wireless NIC for a laptop. Which type of PC Card would you select?

Answer Laptop Expansion Questions

Print and complete this worksheet.

Refer to
Worksheet
for this chapter

Refer to
Figure
in online course

6.4 Explain how to configure laptops

To allow applications and processes to run smoothly, it might be necessary to configure and allocate system resources, install additional components and plug-ins, or change environmental settings to match software requirements. Adding external components is usually accomplished through the use of Plug and Play, but occasionally driver installation and additional configuration might be required. Proper configuration of the power settings helps you get the maximum performance from a laptop, such as increasing the length of time the laptop can be used on battery power.

With laptops, it might be necessary to exchange components as needed to accomplish different tasks and respond to changing situations and needs. A laptop can be customized for specific purposes by adding external components. For example, a second hard drive can be installed in a laptop to provide additional storage capacity. Components need to be carefully inserted or connected to bays, connectors, and proprietary expansion areas to avoid damage to the equipment. It is important to follow safe removal procedures when disconnecting hot-swappable and non-hot-swappable devices.

After completing this section, you will meet these objectives:

- Describe how to configure power settings.

- Describe the safe installation and removal of laptop components.

Refer to **Figure** in online course

6.4.1 Describe how to configure power settings

One of the most popular features of a laptop is the ability to operate using batteries. This feature allows laptops to operate in locations where AC power is not available or is inconvenient. Advances in power management and battery technology are increasing the time that laptop users can remain disconnected from AC power. Current batteries can last anywhere between 2 to 10 hours without recharging. Managing the power by configuring the power settings on a laptop is important to ensure that the battery charge is used efficiently.

The ACPI standards create a bridge between the hardware and OS and allow technicians to create power management schemes to get the best performance from the computer. The ACPI standards can be applicable to most computers, but they are particularly important when managing power in laptops. Click the power states in Figure 1 to view more information about each power state.

Note

When working in Windows XP or Windows Vista, the ACPI power management mode must be enabled in BIOS to allow the OS to configure all of the power management states.

Technicians frequently are required to configure power settings by changing the settings found in BIOS. Configuring power settings in BIOS affects the following conditions:

- System states

- Battery and AC modes

- Thermal management

- CPU PCI bus power management

- Wake-On-LAN (WOL)

Note

WOL might require a cable connection inside the computer from the network adapter to the motherboard.

Figure 2 shows an example of power settings in BIOS.

Note

There is no standard name for each power management state. Manufacturers might use different names for the same state.

Here are the steps to check the ACPI settings in BIOS:

Step 1. Enter BIOS setup by pressing the appropriate key or key combination while the computer is booting. Typically this is the **Delete** key or the **F2** key, but there are several other options.

Step 2. Locate and enter the Power Management settings menu item.

Step 3. Use the appropriate keys to enable ACPI mode.

Step 4. Save and exit BIOS setup.

Note

These steps are common to most laptops and should be used only as a guideline. Be sure to check your laptop manual for specific configuration settings.

The Power Options feature in Windows XP or Windows Vista allows you to reduce the power consumption of a number of devices or of the entire system. Use Power Options to control the power management features of the following:

- Hard drive
- Display
- Shut Down, Hibernate, and Suspend modes (Windows XP)
- Shut Down, Hibernate, and Sleep modes (Windows Vista)
- Low-battery warnings

Configuring Power Settings in Windows XP and Windows Vista

You can adjust power management by using Power Options in the Control Panel. The Power Options displays only the options that can be controlled.

Note

Power Options automatically detects devices that might be unique to your computer; therefore, the Power Options windows might vary by the hardware that is detected.

To configure your power settings, click:

Start > Control Panel > Power Options

Managing Power Usage

Power Schemes and Power Plans are a collection of hardware and system settings that manage the power usage of the computer. These power settings can help you save energy, maximize system performance, or achieve a balance between the two. Both the hard drive and the display consume large amounts of power. They can be configured under the Power Schemes tab in Windows XP and the Change Plan settings in Windows Vista.

When you open Power Options, you will notice that Windows XP has preset power schemes and Windows Vista has preset power plans. These are the default settings and were created when the operating system was installed. You can use the default setting, or create customized schemes or plans that are based on specific work requirements. Customized sleep timers are shown in Figure 3 for Windows XP Power Scheme and in Figure 4 for Windows Vista Power Plan.

To configure sleep timers in Windows XP, click:

Start > Control Panel > Power Options > select the time you want.

To configure sleep timers in Windows Vista, click:

Start > Control Panel > Power Options > click the link **Change when the computer sleeps >** select the time you want.

Power Management for the Hard Drive and the Display

One of the biggest power consumers on a laptop is the hard drive. In our example, the hard drive is not accessed often. The "Turn off hard disks" time is set for 1 hour when the laptop is plugged in, and 3 minutes when the laptop is "Running on batteries". You can also set the LCD to turn off after a specified period of time.

You decide that Windows XP default settings for the Standby and Hibernate modes are acceptable and no changes are made. In Windows Vista these settings are Sleep, Hybrid Sleep, and Hibernate. Power Schemes and Power Plans can be saved with a customized name. Saving the new setting with a custom name allows the user to easily switch back to the default settings. In Figure 5 and Figure 6, the new settings are saved with the name Research.

Setting the Laptop Power Options

If you do not want to completely shut down the laptop, you have two options in Windows XP: Standby and Hibernate.

- *Standby–* Documents and applications are saved in RAM, allowing the computer to power on quickly.

- *Hibernate–* Documents and applications are saved to a temporary file on the hard drive, and takes a little longer than Standby to power on.

Figure 7 shows Hibernate enabled in the Power Options properties.

If you do not want to completely shut down the laptop, you have three options in Windows Vista: Sleep, Hybrid Sleep and Hibernate.

- *Sleep–* Documents and applications are saved in RAM, allowing the computer to power on quickly.

- *Hybrid Sleep–* Documents and applications are saved in RAM and data is written to the hard disk, and takes a little longer than Sleep to power on.

- *Hibernate–* Documents and applications are saved to a temporary file on the hard drive, and takes a little longer than Hybrid Sleep to power on.

Adjusting Low Battery Warnings

In Windows XP, you can set the low battery warnings. There are two levels: Low Battery Alarm and Critical Battery Alarm. The Low Battery Alarm warns you that the battery is low. The Critical Battery Alarm initiates a forced standby, hibernate, or shut down mode, as shown in Figure 8. Standby is called Sleep in Windows Vista.

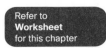

Match ACPI Standards

Print and complete this worksheet.

Refer to
Figure
in online course

6.4.2 Describe the safe installation and removal of laptop components

Some components of a laptop might need to be replaced. Remember always to make sure that you have the correct replacement component and tools as recommended by the manufacturer. Some components are hot-swappable, which means that they can be removed and replaced while the computer is on. These are some components that might need to be replaced:

- AC adapter
- Battery
- Optical drive
- Hard drive
- Memory
- PC expansion cards

Figure 1 shows an example of a laptop.

Note

Each laptop manufacturer uses unique hardware installation and removal procedures. Check the laptop manual for specific installation information and follow safety installation and ESD precautions.

Caution

Always disconnect power and remove the battery before installing or removing laptop components that are not hot-swappable.

AC adapters must be compatible with the manufacturer and model of laptop that you have. AC adapters are either auto-switching or fixed input. Auto-switching AC adapters can switch between 110V and 220V, while a fixed input AC adapter only operates under a specific voltage. Auto switching allows the power supply to be used in different countries.

Battery Replacement Steps
[Figure 2]

Remove the battery from the battery bay:

1. Move the battery lock to the unlocked position.
2. Hold the release lever in the unlock position and remove the battery.

Install the battery into the battery bay:

1. Insert the battery.
2. Make sure that both battery levers are locked.

Optical Drive Replacement Steps
[Figure 3]

Remove the DVD/CD-RW drive:

1. Press the button to open the drive and remove any media in the drive. Close the tray.

2. Slide the latch to release the lever that secures the drive.

3. Pull on the lever to expose the drive. Remove the drive.

Install the DVD/CD-RW drive:

1. Insert the drive securely.

2. Push the lever inward.

Hard Drive Replacement Steps
[Figure 4]

Remove the hard drive:

1. On the bottom of the laptop, remove the screw that holds the hard drive in place.

2. Slide the assembly outward. Remove the hard drive assembly.

3. Remove the hard drive faceplate from the hard drive.

Install the hard drive:

1. Attach the hard drive faceplate to the hard drive.

2. Slide the hard drive into the hard drive bay.

3. On the bottom of the laptop, install the screw that holds the hard drive in place.

Expansion Memory Replacement Steps
[Figure 5]

Laptop expansion memory is also called SODIMM. Remove the existing SODIMM if there are no available slots for the new SODIMM:

1. Remove screw to expose the SODIMM.

2. Press outward on the clips that hold the sides of the SODIMM.

3. Lift up to loosen the SODIMM from the slot and remove the SODIMM.

Install the SODIMM:

1. Align the notch at a 45-degree angle.

2. Gently press down until clips lock.

3. Replace cover and install screw.

PC Expansion Card Replacement Steps
[Figure 6]

All PC expansion cards, including ExpressCards, are inserted and removed using similar steps.

To remove the PC expansion card, press the top eject button to release it.

Note

There are two buttons. The bottom blue button ejects the Type II PC card.

Install the PC expansion card:

1. Press the blue button inward.

2. Insert the PC expansion card into the express slot.

Caution

On some laptops, the PC Card, optical drive, and USB devices are hot-swappable. However, the internal hard drive, RAM, and battery are NOT hot-swappable.

Hot-Swappable Device Removal Steps

1. Left-click the Safely Remove Hardware icon in the Windows system tray to ensure that the device is not in use.

2. Left-click the device that you want to remove. A message pops up to tell you that it is safe to remove the device.

3. Remove the hot-swappable device from the laptop.

Refer to
Interactive Graphic
in online course.

Virtual Laptop: Components and Devices
System requirements for the virtual laptop include a minimum of 512 MB RAM and Windows 2000 or Windows XP operating system.
Replace components and devices in the virtual laptop.

Refer to
Figure
in online course

6.4.3 Laptop communication hardware installation and configuration

Laptops use several different communication methods:

- Ethernet

- Wireless Ethernet

- Modem

- Bluetooth

- Infrared

- Cellular WAN

Ethernet Installation and Configuration Steps

1. Plug the Ethernet cable into the NIC port.

2. Configure IP address information.

Windows XP:

Start > Control Panel > Network Connections > right click **Local Area Connection > Properties > TCP/IP > Properties** > configure IP setting > **OK > OK**.

Windows Vista:

Start > Control Panel > Network and Sharing Center > Manage network connections > right-click the connection that you want to set up **> Properties > TCP/IPv4 > Properties >** configure IP setting **> OK > OK**.

Wireless Ethernet Installation and Configuration

Wireless Ethernet NICs can be built into the laptop or attached to the laptop through one of the various laptop expansion ports. Wireless NIC IP address information is configured in the same way as wired NICs.

Modem Installation and Configuration Steps
[Figure 1]

1. Make sure the modem is installed and turned on if an external modem is attached.

2. Attach a phone cable from the wall outlet to the appropriate RJ-11 modem port.

3. Use the Install New Modem Wizard to add the modem.

Windows XP:

Start > Control Panel > Phone and Modem Options > specify the dialing information for your location **> OK > Add Hardware Wizard** starts **> Modems > Add > Next > Add Hardware Wizard** installs the device **> Finish.**

Windows Vista:

Start > Control Panel > Phone and Modem Options > specify the dialing information for your location **> OK > Add Hardware Wizard** starts **> Modems > Add >** if prompted for permission click **Continue > Next > Add Hardware Wizard** installs the device **> Finish.**

You can use the Phone and Modem Options tabs to configure settings:

- *Dialing Rules–* List, add, edit, and delete dialing locations.

- *Modems–* Add, remove a device, or view the properties of a device.

- *Advanced–* List, add, remove, and configure telephony providers installed on the computer.

Note

To configure an installed modem, open **Phone and Modem Options** in the Control Panel. On the Modems tab, click the modem you want to configure, and then click **Properties**.

Bluetooth Installation and Configuration Steps
[Figure 2]

Windows activates Bluetooth connections by default. If the connection is not active, look for a switch on the front face or on the side of the laptop to enable the connection. Figure 3 shows the LED status for Bluetooth.

1. Make sure Bluetooth is enabled in the BIOS before installing and configuring the device.

2. Turn on the device and make it discoverable to Windows. Check the device documentation to learn how to make your device discoverable.

3. Use the Bluetooth Wizard to search and discover any Bluetooth devices that are in Discoverable mode.

Windows XP:

Start > Control Panel > Bluetooth Devices > Device > Add > Add Bluetooth Device Wizard starts **> My device is set up and ready to be found > Next >** select the discovered device **> Next >** if prompted, enter a passkey **> Next > Finish**.

Windows Vista:

Start > Control Panel > Network and Internet > Set up a Bluetooth enabled device > Device > Add > if prompted, click **Continue > Add Bluetooth Device Wizard** starts **> My device is set up and ready to be found > Next >** select the discovered device **> Next >** if prompted, enter a passkey **> Finish**.

You can use the Bluetooth Devices tabs to configure Bluetooth settings:

- *Device–* Adds, removes a device, or views the properties of a device.
- *Options–* Controls how devices discover and connect to your computer.
- *COM Ports–* Sets up new incoming and outgoing serial ports.
- *Hardware–* Lists Bluetooth devices that are installed on your computer.

Infrared Installation and Configuration Steps [Figure 4]

1. Make sure infrared is enabled in the BIOS before installing and configuring the device.

2. Turn on the device to make it discoverable to Windows.

3. Align your devices so that the infrared transceivers are within one meter of each other, and the transceivers are pointing at each other.

4. When the devices are correctly aligned, an icon appears on the taskbar with a pop-up message.

5. Click the pop-up message to display the Infrared dialog box.

In both Windows XP and Windows Vista the Infrared dialog box can be accessed in the Control Panel.

Laptops without an internal infrared device can connect a serial infrared transceiver to a serial port or a USB port. Figure 5 shows an internal infrared port transceiver.

You can use the Infrared dialog box tabs to configure infrared settings:

- *Infrared–* Control how you are notified about an infrared connection, and control how files are transferred.
- *Image Transfer–* Control how images are transferred from a digital camera.
- *Hardware–* Lists infrared devices that are installed on your computer.

Cellular WAN Installation and Configuration Steps

Laptops with integrated cellular WAN capabilities require no software installation and no additional antenna or accessories. When you turn on the laptop, the integrated WAN capabilities are ready to be used. If the connection is not active, look for a switch on the front face or on the side of the laptop to enable the connection.

1. Make sure cellular WAN is enabled in the BIOS before installing and configuring the device.

2. Install the manufacturer's broadband card utility software.

3. Use the utility software to manage the network connection.

The cellular WAN utility software can be located in the taskbar or in **Start > Programs**.

Refer to
Figure
in online course

6.5 Compare the different mobile phone standards

When people began to use cell phones, there were few industry-wide standards applying to cell phone technology. Without standards, it was difficult and expensive to make calls to people that were on another network. Today, cell phone providers use industry standards, which makes it easier to use cell phones to make calls.

When the industry started, most cell phone standards were analog. Today, cell phone standards are mostly digital.

Note

Cell phone standards have not been adopted uniformly around the world. Some cell phones are capable of using multiple standards, whereas others can use only one standard. As a result, some cell phones can operate in many countries, and other cell phones can only be used locally.

The first generation (1G) of cell phones began service in the 1980s. First-generation phones primarily used analog standards, including Advanced Mobile Phone System (AMPS) and Nordic Mobile Telephone (NMT). In an analog system, the voice information is sent by varying the radio signals used by the phone in the same pattern as the speakers' voices. Unfortunately, this means that interference and noise, which also vary the signal, cannot easily be separated from the voice in the signal. This factor limits the usefulness of analog systems.

Digital signals convert the speakers' voices into a series of ones and zeros. This technology degrades the signal a little, because ones and zeros are not a faithful representation of your voice. However, the digital signal is robust. It can be fixed using error correction routines if there is interference. Also, digital signals can be compressed, making the systems much more efficient than analog.

In the 1990s, the second generation (2G) of cell phones was marked by a switch from analog to digital standards. Second-generation cell standards included Global System for Mobile (GSM), Integrated Digital Enhanced Network (iDEN), and Code Division Multiple Access (CDMA).

Third-generation standards enable cell phones to go beyond simple voice and data communications. It is now common for cell phones to send and receive text, photos, and video. It is also common for 3G cell phones to access the Internet and to use the Global Positioning System (GPS).

Note

As 3G cell phone standards were being developed, extensions to the existing 2G standards were added. These transitional standards are known as 2.5G standards.

Fourth-generation (4G) standards have been championed by many users in response to the availability of increased data rates. Higher data rates will allow users to download files, such as video and music, faster than what was available with standards of previous generations.

Click the five generation tabs in Figure 1 to view more information about the different cell phone standards.

New technologies that add multimedia and networking functionality can be bundled with cell phone standards. Figure 2 lists common technologies that can be added to the cell phone bundle of services. Most cell phone providers charge extra for adding these features.

Refer to
Figure
in online course

6.6 Identify common preventive maintenance techniques for laptops and portable devices

Because laptops are mobile, they are used in different types of environments. Some environments can be hazardous to a laptop. Even eating or drinking around a laptop creates a potentially hazardous condition.

Consider what would happen if a drink were spilled onto the keyboard of a laptop. Many components are placed in a very small area directly beneath the keyboard. Spilling liquid or dropping debris onto the keyboard can result in severe internal damage.

It is important to keep a laptop clean and to ensure that it is being used in the most optimal environment possible. This section covers preventive maintenance techniques for the laptop.

After completing this section, you will meet these objectives:

- Identify appropriate cleaning procedures.
- Identify optimal operating environments.

Refer to
Figure
in online course

6.6.1 Identify appropriate cleaning procedures

Proper routine cleaning is the easiest, least expensive way to protect and to extend the life of a laptop. It is very important to use the right products and procedures when cleaning a laptop. Always read all warning labels on the cleaning products. The components are very sensitive and should be handled with care. Consult the laptop manual for additional information and cleaning suggestions.

Laptop Keyboard Cleaning Procedures

1. Turn off the laptop.
2. Disconnect all of the attached devices.
3. Disconnect the laptop from the electrical outlet.
4. Remove all of the installed batteries.
5. Wipe the laptop and the keyboard with a soft, lint-free cloth that is lightly moistened with water or computer-screen cleaner.

Ventilation Cleaning Procedures

1. Turn off the laptop.
2. Disconnect all of the attached devices.
3. Disconnect the laptop from the electrical outlet.
4. Remove all of the installed batteries.
5. Use compressed air or a non-electrostatic vacuum to clean out the dust from the vents and from the fan behind the vent.
6. Use tweezers to remove any debris.

LCD Cleaning Procedures

1. Turn off the laptop.

2. Disconnect all of the attached devices.

3. Disconnect the laptop from the electrical outlet.

4. Remove all of the installed batteries.

5. Wipe the display with a soft, lint-free cloth that is lightly moistened with a mild cleaning solution.

Caution

Do not spray cleaning solution directly onto the LCD display. Use products specifically designed for cleaning LCD displays.

Touch Pad Cleaning Procedures

1. Turn off the laptop.

2. Disconnect all of the attached devices.

3. Disconnect the laptop from the electrical outlet.

4. Remove all of the installed batteries.

5. Wipe the surface of the touch pad gently with a soft, lint-free cloth that is moistened with an approved cleaner. Never use a wet cloth.

The small screen of a PDA or smartphone requires special care. The user operates these devices by touching the screen with a stylus. If dirt is present, the PDA might not accurately detect the stylus position or movement. The dirt can also scratch the screen. Clean the screen with a small amount of non-abrasive cleaning solution on a soft cloth. To protect the screen surface from a stylus, use self-adhesive screen covers.

Caution

Use a soft, lint-free cloth with an approved cleaning solution to avoid damaging laptop surfaces. Apply the cleaning solution to the lint-free cloth, not directly to the laptop.

Floppy Drive Cleaning Procedures

Use a commercially-available cleaning kit to clean a floppy drive. Floppy drive cleaning kits include pre-treated floppy discs that remove contaminants from the floppy drive heads that have accumulated through normal operation.

1. Remove all of the media from the floppy drive.

2. Insert the cleaning disc and let it spin for the suggested amount of time.

Optical Drive Cleaning Procedures

Dirt, dust, and other contaminants can collect in the optical drives. Contaminated drives can cause malfunctions, missing data, error messages, and lost productivity.

1. Use a commercially-available CD or DVD drive cleaning disc. Many floppy disc cleaning kits include an optical disc cleaner. Like the floppy disc cleaner, optical disc cleaner kits contain a cleaning solution and a non-abrasive disc that is inserted into the optical drive.

2. Remove all of the media from the optical drive.

3. Insert the cleaning disc and let it spin for the suggested amount of time to clean all contact areas.

Cleaning a CD or DVD Disc

Inspect the disc for scratches. Replace discs that contain deep scratches because they can create data errors. If you notice problems such as skipping or degraded playback quality with your CDs or DVDs, clean the discs. Commercial products are available that clean discs and provide protection from dust, fingerprints, and scratches. Cleaning products for CDs are safe to use on DVDs.

Step 1.   Hold the disc by the outer edge or by the inside edge.

Step 2.   Gently wipe the disc with a lint-free cotton cloth. Never use paper or any material that can scratch the disc or leave streaks.

Step 3.   Wipe from the center of the disc outward. Never use a circular motion.

Step 4.   Apply a commercial CD or DVD cleaning solution to the lint-free cotton cloth, and wipe again if any contaminates remain on the disc.

Step 5.   Allow the disc to dry before it is inserted into the drive.

Refer to
Figure
in online course

6.6.2 Identify optimal operating environments

An optimal operating environment for a laptop is clean, free of potential contaminants, and within the temperature and humidity range specified by the manufacturer. Figure 1 shows examples of operating environments. With most desktop computers, the operating environment can be controlled. However, due to the portable nature of laptops, it is not always possible to control the temperature, humidity, and working conditions. Laptops are built to resist adverse environments, but technicians should always take precautions to protect the equipment from damage and loss of data.

It is important to transport or ship laptops carefully. Use a padded laptop case to store your laptop. When you carry it, use an approved computer bag. If the laptop is shipped, use sufficient packing material. Figure 2 shows examples of laptop carrying cases and packing boxes.

Caution

Be sure to pack laptops and all accessories securely to prevent damage during transport.

Laptops are transported to many types of environments. Dust particles, temperature, and humidity can affect the performance of a laptop.

Follow these guidelines to help ensure optimal operating performance from your laptop:

- Clean the laptop frequently to remove dust and potential contaminants.

- Do not obstruct vents or airflow to internal components. A laptop can overheat if air circulation is obstructed.

- Keep the room temperature between 45 to 90 degrees Fahrenheit (7 to 32 degrees Celsius).

- Keep the humidity level between 10 to 80 percent.

Caution

Use a soft, lint-free cloth with an approved cleaning solution to avoid damaging laptop surfaces. Apply the cleaning solution to the lint-free cloth, not directly to the laptop.

Temperature and humidity recommendations vary by laptop manufacturer. You should research these recommended values, especially if you plan to use the laptop in extreme conditions. Refer to Figure 3 for humidity and temperature examples.

Refer to
Figure
in online course

6.7 Describe how to troubleshoot laptops and portable devices

When troubleshooting problems with laptops or portable devices, you should determine if a repair is cost-effective. To determine the best course of action, compare the cost of the repair with the replacement cost of the laptop or portable device, less the salvage value.

Because many portable devices change rapidly in design and functionality, they are often more expensive to repair than to replace. For this reason, portable devices are usually replaced, whereas laptops can be replaced or repaired.

Follow the steps outlined in this section to accurately identify, repair, and document the problem. The troubleshooting process is shown in Figure 1.

After completing this section, you will meet these objectives:

- Review the troubleshooting process.
- Identify common problems and solutions.

Refer to
Figure
in online course

6.7.1 Review the troubleshooting process

Computer problems can result from a combination of hardware, software, and network issues. Computer technicians must be able to analyze the problem and determine the cause of the error to repair the computer. This process is called troubleshooting.

The first step in the troubleshooting process is to identify the problem. Figure 1 is a list of open-ended and closed-ended questions to ask the customer.

After you have talked to the customer, you can establish a theory of probable causes. Figure 2 is a list of some common probable causes for printer problems.

After you have developed some theories about what is wrong, test your theories to determine the cause of the problem. Figure 3 is a list of quick procedures that can determine the exact cause of the problem or even correct the problem. If a quick procedure does correct the problem, you can go to step 5 to verify full system functionality. If a quick procedure does not correct the problem, you may need to research the problem further to establish the exact cause.

After you have determined the exact cause of the problem, establish a plan of action to resolve the problem and implement the solution. Figure 4 shows sources of information to gather additional information to resolve an issue.

After you have corrected the problem, verify full functionality and, if applicable, implement preventive measures. Figure 5 is a list of the steps to verify the solution.

In the final step of the troubleshooting process, you must document your findings, actions, and outcomes. Figure 6 is a list of the tasks required to document the problem and the solution.

Refer to
Figure
in online course

Refer to
Worksheet
for this chapter

Refer to
Figure
in online course

6.7.2 Identify common problems and solutions

Computer problems can be attributed to hardware, software, networks, or some combination of the three. You will resolve some types of computer problems more often than others. Figure 1 is a chart of common laptop problems and solutions.

Research Laptop Problems

Print and complete this worksheet.

Summary

This chapter discussed the features of laptops, portable devices, and smartphones. The following concepts from this chapter are important to remember:

- Laptops and PDAs are becoming increasingly popular due to reduced costs, lighter weights, increased capabilities, and battery power for portability.

- PDAs and smartphones are small, handheld devices with many of the capabilities of a computer, such as an address book, calendar, e-mail, and Internet access.

- Laptops and desktops have ports that are virtually the same; therefore, the peripherals are interchangeable. Laptops can use docking stations or port replicators to quickly connect to desktop peripherals and AC power.

- Desktop and laptop components, such as motherboards, are not interchangeable. Additionally, laptop components tend to be proprietary to each manufacturer and designed with unique form factors.

- The laptop CPU is designed to use less power and create less heat than the desktop computer. It uses CPU throttling to reduce power consumption and heat.

- Functionality of the laptop can be expanded by adding components via PC Card or ExpressCard slots and USB, FireWire, or parallel ports.

- An important component of laptop portability is the ability to run on battery power. The current method of managing power is through the operating system with the Advanced Configuration and Power Interface (ACPI). The ACPI standard defines six power management states.

- Some components of a laptop might need to be replaced. Steps are defined to replace the battery, optical drive, hard drive, memory, and PC Cards.

- Cell phone standards were developed in the 1980s. The current third-generation standards enable cell phones to share some laptop functions, such as e-mail, Internet access, address, and calendar functions. Standards have not been adopted worldwide.

- Preventive maintenance will ensure optimal operation of the laptop. It is important to keep the laptop clean and in safe environments. It is critical to use the correct materials and techniques when cleaning the various components of a laptop. Procedures for cleaning the components are presented.

- Dust, temperature, and humidity can affect laptop performance. Basic guidelines are to keep the laptop clean, with good ventilation, and room temperature between 45 and 90 degrees F (7 to 32 degrees C) and humidity levels in the range of 10 to 80 percent.

- Always verify that repair of a laptop is cost-effective.

- Troubleshooting laptop problems requires the technician to identify, repair, and document the problem. Troubleshooting steps include: Gather data from customer, verify the obvious issues, try quick solutions first, gather data from the computer, evaluate the problem, implement the solution, and close with the customer.

- When troubleshooting wireless-capable devices, check all status LEDs and signal strength indicators. Remove all unnecessary peripherals to isolate the problem.

- Check for external problems, such as connection errors, power errors, and function key errors. Connection errors can often be solved by removing and reinserting components. Check in the Device Manager for errors. Power errors can be caused by the use of incorrect adaptors, damaged batteries, damaged AC adaptors, or dead wall outlets. Check components controlled by function keys.

- Try quick solutions first to solve laptop problems. Reboot and verify the BIOS settings, start the laptop in safe mode, and use the Last Known Good Configuration option.

- For problem resolution, gather information from the computer from the Device Manager, Network Settings, Power Options, Event Viewer, and System Configuration.

- Resources for troubleshooting should include other technicians, Internet resources, manufacturers' FAQs, and online forums.

- The final steps in the troubleshooting process are to test the laptop in all scenarios, discuss the solution with the customer, fill out all necessary paperwork and billing documents, and document the solution.

The Advanced Laptops and Portable Devices chapter will focus on troubleshooting more difficult problems.

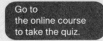

Chapter 6 Quiz

Take the chapter quiz to test your knowledge.

Your Chapter Notes

Fundamental Printers and Scanners

Introduction

This chapter provides essential information about printers and scanners. You will learn how printers operate, what to consider when purchasing a printer, and how to connect printers to an individual computer or to a network.

Printers produce paper copies of electronic files. Scanners allow users to convert paper documents into electronic files. Many government regulations require physical records; therefore, hard copies of computer documents are often as important today as they were when the paperless revolution began several years ago.

You must understand the operation of various types of printers and scanners to be able to install and maintain them, as well as troubleshoot any problems that arise.

After completing this chapter, you will meet these objectives:

- Describe the types of printers currently available.
- Describe the installation and configuration process for printers.
- Describe the types of scanners currently available.
- Describe the installation and configuration process for scanners.
- Identify and apply common preventive maintenance techniques for printers and scanners.
- Troubleshoot printers and scanners.

Refer to
Figure
in online course

7.1 Describe the types of printers currently available

As a computer technician, you might be required to purchase, repair, or maintain a printer. The customer might request that you perform the following tasks:

- Select a printer.
- Install and configure a printer.
- Troubleshoot a printer.

After completing this section, you will meet these objectives:

- Describe characteristics and capabilities of printers.
- Describe printer-to-computer interfaces.
- Describe laser printers.
- Describe impact printers.
- Describe inkjet printers.

- Describe solid-ink printers.

- Describe other printer types.

Refer to
Figure
in online course

7.1.1 Describe characteristics and capabilities of printers

Printers available today are usually either laser printers using electrophotographic technology or inkjet printers using electrostatic spray technology. Dot matrix printers using impact technology are used in applications that require carbon copies. Figure 1 shows a list of printer selection criteria.

Capacity and Speed

Printer capacity and speed are factors to consider when selecting a printer. Inkjet printers are usually slower, but they might be adequate for a home or small office. The speed of a printer is measured in pages per minute (ppm). The speed of an inkjet printer is 2–6 ppm. The speed of a laser printer is 8–200 ppm.

Color or Black and White

A computer monitor produces colors through the additive mixing of dots that are displayed on the screen. The eye picks up the colors directly. The dots produce the color range using red, green, and blue (RGB) dots.

A printer produces colors using subtractive mixing. The eye sees a color that reflects from the combination of colors on the paper. Figure 2 shows a CMYK color wheel.

The choice between a black-and-white printer and a color printer depends on the needs of your customer. If your customer is primarily printing letters and does not need color capability, a black-and-white printer is sufficient. However, an elementary school teacher might need a color printer to add excitement to lessons.

Quality

The quality of printing is measured in dots per inch (dpi). The more dpi, the higher the resolution. When the resolution is higher, text and images are usually clearer. To produce the best high-resolution images, you should use both high-quality ink or toner and high-quality paper.

Reliability

A printer should be reliable. Because there are so many types of printers on the market, research the specifications of several printers before selecting one. Here are some of the options available from the manufacturer:

- *Warranty*– Identify what is covered within the warranty.

- *Scheduled servicing*– Servicing is based on expected usage. Information is found in the manual or on the manufacturer's website.

- *Mean time between failures (MTBF)*– There is an average length of time that the printer works without failing. Information is found in the manual or on the manufacturer's website.

Total Cost of Ownership

Consider the cost when selecting hardware. When buying a printer, there is more than just the initial cost of the printer to consider. The total cost of ownership (TCO) includes a number of factors:

- Initial purchase price

- Cost of supplies, such as paper and ink

- Price per page

- Maintenance costs

- Warranty costs

When calculating the TCO, you should also consider the amount of material printed and the expected lifetime of the printer.

Refer to
Figure
in online course

7.1.2 Describe printer to computer interfaces

A computer must have a compatible interface with the printer to be able to print documents. Typically, printers connect to home computers using a parallel, USB, or wireless interface. Corporate printers might connect to a network using a network cable.

Serial

Serial data transfer is the movement of single bits of information in a single cycle. A serial connection can be used for dot matrix printers because the printers do not require high-speed data transfer.

Parallel

Parallel data transfer is faster than serial data transfer. Parallel data transfer is the movement of multiple bits of information in a single cycle. The path is wider for information to move to or from the printer.

IEEE 1284 is the current standard for parallel printer ports. Enhanced Parallel Port (EPP) and Enhanced Capabilities Port (ECP) are two modes of operation within the IEEE 1284 standard that allow bi-directional communication.

SCSI

Small Computer System Interface (SCSI) is a type of interface that uses parallel communication technology to achieve high data-transfer rates.

USB

USB is a common interface for printers and other devices. The speed and simple setup has made USB very practical. Newer operating systems offer PnP USB support. When a USB device is added to a computer system supporting PnP, the device is automatically detected and starts the driver installation process.

FireWire

FireWire, also known as i.LINK or IEEE 1394, is a high-speed communication bus that is platform independent. FireWire connects digital devices such as digital printers, scanners, digital cameras, and hard drives.

FireWire allows a peripheral device, such as a printer, to seamlessly plug into a computer. It also allows a device such as printer to be hot-swappable. FireWire provides a single plug-and-socket connection that can attach up to 63 devices. FireWire has a data transfer rate of up to 400 Mbps.

Ethernet

Printers can be shared over a network. Connecting a printer to the network requires cabling that is compatible with both the existing network and the network port installed in the printer. Most network printers use an RJ-45 interface to connect to a network.

Wireless

Wireless printing technology is available in infrared, Bluetooth, and wireless fidelity (Wi-Fi) technology.

For infrared communication to take place between a printer and a computer, transmitters and receivers are required on both devices. There must be a clear line of sight between the transmitter and receiver on both devices, with a maximum distance of 12 feet (3.7 m). Infrared uses a type of light that is invisible to the human eye.

Bluetooth technology uses an unlicensed radio frequency for short-range communication and is popular for wireless headsets and synching PDAs to laptops and desktop computers. A Bluetooth adapter allows a Bluetooth device to connect to a printer, usually by using a USB port.

Wi-Fi is the popular name for a relatively new technology that allows the connection of computers to a network without using cables. There are two common standards for Wi-Fi technology, both of which begin with the number of the IEEE standard 802.11:

- 802.11b transfers data at a rate of 11 Mbps.

- 802.11g transfers data at a rate of 54 Mbps. 802.11g products are backward-compatible with 802.11b.

Refer to **Figure** in online course

7.1.3 Describe laser printers

A laser printer is a high-quality, fast printer that uses a laser beam to create an image. The central part of the laser printer is its electrophotographic drum. The drum is a metal cylinder that is coated with a light-sensitive insulating material. When a beam of laser light strikes the drum, it becomes a conductor at the point where the light hits it. As the drum rotates, the laser beam draws an electrostatic image upon the drum, called the image. The undeveloped or latent image is passed by a supply of dry ink or toner that is attracted to it. The drum turns and brings this image in contact with the paper, which attracts the toner from the drum. The paper is passed through a fuser that is made up of hot rollers, which melts the toner into the paper.

Printing Process

The laser printer process involves six steps to print information onto a single sheet of paper.

Step 1: Cleaning

When an image has been deposited on the paper and the drum has separated from the paper, any remaining toner must be removed from the drum. A printer may have a blade that scrapes all excess toner from the drum. Some printers use an AC voltage on a wire that removes the charge from the drum surface and allows the excess toner to fall away from the drum. The excess toner is stored in a used toner container that is either emptied or discarded.

Step 2: Conditioning

This step involves removing the old latent image from the drum and conditioning the drum for a new latent image. Conditioning is done by placing a special wire, grid, or roller that receives a negative charge of approximately –600 volts DC uniformly across the surface of the drum. The charged wire or grid is called the primary corona. The roller is called a conditioning roller.

Step 3: Writing

The writing process involves scanning the photosensitive drum with the laser beam. Every portion of the drum that is exposed to the light has the surface charge reduced to about –100 volts DC.

This electrical charge has a lower negative charge than the remainder of the drum. As the drum turns, an invisible latent image is created on the drum.

Step 4: Developing

In the developing phase, the toner is applied to the latent image on the drum. The toner is a negatively-charged combination of plastic and metal particles. A control blade holds the toner at a microscopic distance from the drum. The toner then moves from the control blade to the more positively-charged latent image on the drum.

Step 5: Transferring

In this step, the toner attached to the latent image is transferred to the paper. The transfer, or secondary corona, places a positive charge on the paper. Because the drum was charged negatively, the toner on the drum is attracted to the paper. The image is now on the paper and is held in place by the positive charge.

Step 6: Fusing

In this step, the toner is permanently fused to the paper. The printing paper is rolled between a heated roller and a pressure roller. As the paper moves through the heated roller and the pressure roller, the loose toner is melted and fused with the fibers in the paper. The paper is then moved to the output tray as a printed page.

The following mnemonic can help you memorize the order of the steps of the laser printing process: Continuous Care Will Delay Trouble Forever (Cleaning, Conditioning, Writing, Developing, Transferring, Fusing).

Warning

The primary corona wire or grid, or the conditioning roller, can be very dangerous. The voltage runs as high as –6000 volts. Only certified technicians should work on the unit. Before working inside a laser printer, you should make sure that voltage is properly discharged.

Refer to
Figure
in online course

7.1.4 Describe impact printers

Impact printers are very basic printers. Impact printers have print heads that strike the inked ribbon, causing characters to be imprinted on the paper. Dot matrix and daisy wheel are examples of impact printers.

The following are some advantages of an impact printer:

- Uses inexpensive consumables
- Uses continuous feed paper
- Has carbon-copy printing ability

The following are some disadvantages of an impact printer:

- Noisy
- Low-resolution graphics
- Limited color capability
- Slow printing, normally in the range of 32 to 76 characters per second (cps)

Types of Impact Printers

In the daisy wheel printer, the wheel contains the letters, numbers, and special characters. The wheel is rotated until the required character is in place, and an electromechanical hammer pushes the character into the ink ribbon. The character then strikes the paper, imprinting the character on the paper.

The dot matrix printer is similar to the daisy wheel printer, except that instead of a wheel containing the characters, a print head contains pins that are surrounded by electromagnets. When energized, the pins push forward onto the ink ribbon, creating a character on the paper.

The number of pins on a print head, 9 or 24, indicates the quality of the print. The highest quality of print that is produced by the dot matrix printer is referred to as near letter quality (NLQ).

Most dot matrix printers use continuous feed paper. The paper has perforations between each sheet and perforated strips on the side used to feed the paper and to prevent skewing or shifting. Sheet feeders that print one page at a time are available in some of the higher-quality office printers. A large roller, called the platen, applies pressure to keep the paper from slipping. If a multiple-copy paper is used, the platen gap can be adjusted to the thickness of the paper.

Refer to
Figure
in online course

7.1.5 Describe inkjet printers

Inkjet printers produce high-quality prints. Inkjet printers are easy to use and inexpensive compared to laser printers. The print quality of an inkjet printer is measured in dots per inch (dpi). Higher dpi numbers provide greater image details. Figure 1 shows an all-in-one device that contains an inkjet printer. Figure 2 shows ink jet printer components.

Inkjet printers use ink-filled cartridges that spray ink onto a page through tiny holes. The tiny holes are called nozzles. The ink is sprayed in a pattern on the page.

There are two types of inkjet nozzles:

- *Thermal–* A pulse of electrical current is applied to heating chambers around the nozzles. The heat creates a bubble of steam in the chamber. The steam forces ink out through the nozzle and onto the paper.

- *Piezoelectric–* Piezoelectric crystals are located in the ink reservoir at the back of each nozzle. A charge is applied to the crystal, causing it to vibrate. This vibration of the crystal controls the flow of ink onto the paper.

Inkjet printers use plain paper to make economical prints. Special-purpose paper can be used to create high-quality prints of photographs. When the inkjet print is complete and the paper leaves the printer, the ink is often wet. You should avoid touching printouts for 10 to 15 seconds to prevent the images from smearing.

These are some advantages of an inkjet printer:

- Low cost

- High resolution

- Quick to warm up

These are some disadvantages of an inkjet printer:

- Nozzles are prone to clogging.

- Ink cartridges are expensive.

- Ink is wet after printing.

Refer to
Figure
in online course

7.1.6 Describe solid-ink printers

Solid-ink printers use solid sticks of ink rather than toner or ink cartridges. Solid-ink printers produce high-quality images. The ink sticks are nontoxic and can be handled safely.

Solid-ink printers melt ink sticks and spray the ink through nozzles. The ink is sprayed onto a drum. The drum transfers the ink to paper.

These are some advantages of solid-ink printers:

- Produces vibrant color prints

- Easy to use

- Can use many different paper types

These are some disadvantages of solid-ink printers:

- Printers are expensive.

- Ink is expensive.

- They are slow to warm up.

Refer to
Figure
in online course

7.1.7 Describe other printer types

Two other printing technologies that you might work with are thermal and dye-sublimation.

Thermal Printers

Some retail cash registers or older fax machines might contain thermal printers, as shown in Figure 1. The thermal paper used in thermal printers is chemically treated and has a waxy quality. Thermal paper becomes black when heated. Most thermal printer print heads are the width of the paper. Areas of the print head are heated as required to make the pattern on the paper. The paper is supplied in the form of a roll.

A thermal printer has the following advantage:

- Longer life because there are few moving parts

A thermal printer has the following disadvantages:

- Paper is expensive.

- Paper has a short shelf life.

- Images are poor quality.

- Paper must be stored at room temperature.

Dye-Sublimation Printers

Dye-sublimation printers produce photo-quality images for graphic printing. See Figure 2 for an example of a dye-sublimation printer. This type of printer uses solid sheets of ink that change directly from solid to gas in a process called sublimating. The print head passes over a sheet of cyan, magenta, yellow, and a clear overcoat (CMYO). There is a pass for each color.

Dye-sublimation printers have the following advantages:

- Printers produce high-quality images.

- Overcoat layer reduces smearing and increases moisture resistance.

Dye-sublimation printers have the following disadvantages:

- Media can be expensive.

- Printers are better for color than for grayscale (black and white).

In photography, both dye-sublimation printers and small color ink-jet printers provide quality prints.

Refer to
Figure
in online course

7.2   Describe the installation and configuration process for printers

When you purchase a printer, the installation and configuration information is usually supplied by the manufacturer. An installation CD that includes drivers, manuals, and diagnostic software is included with the printer. The same tools might also be available as downloads from the manufacturer's website.

After completing this section, you will meet these objectives:

- Describe how to set up a printer.

- Explain how to power and connect the device using a local or network port.

- Describe how to install and update the device driver, firmware, and RAM.

- Identify configuration options and default settings.

- Describe how to optimize printer performance.

- Describe how to print a test page.

- Describe how to share a printer.

Refer to
Figure
in online course

7.2.1   Describe how to set up a printer

Although all types of printers are somewhat different to connect and configure, there are procedures that should be applied to all printers. After the printer has been unpacked and placed in position, connect it to the computer, network, or print server and plug it into an electrical outlet. Remove all packing materials, such as plastic inserts and tape, from the toner or ink cartridge. Install the toner or ink cartridge in the printer. Insert the paper, labels, or envelopes into the paper tray and attach the paper tray to the printer.

Refer to
Figure
in online course

7.2.2   Explain how to power and connect the device using a local or network port

Now that the printer has been unpacked and placed in position, you must connect it to the computer, network, or print server and plug it into an electrical outlet.

A printer can be connected and used as a local or network printer. A local printer is connected directly to a computer port, such as a USB, parallel, or serial port. The local computer manages and sends the print jobs to the printer. Local printers can be shared over the network with other users. A network printer is connected to a network using a wireless or an Ethernet connection. The network printer allows multiple users to send documents to the printer over the network.

After determining if the printer will be a local or a network printer, connect the appropriate data cable to the communication port on the back of the printer. If the printer has a USB, FireWire, or parallel port, connect the corresponding cable to the printer port. Connect the other end of the data cable to the corresponding port on the back of the computer. If you are installing a network printer, connect the network cable to the network port.

After the data cable has been properly connected, attach the power cable to the printer. Connect the other end of the power cable to an available electrical outlet.

Warning

Never plug a printer into a UPS. The power surge that occurs when the printer is turned on damages the UPS unit.

Refer to **Figure** in online course

7.2.3 Describe how to install and update the device driver, firmware, and RAM

After you have connected the power and data cables to the printer, the operating system might discover the printer and attempt to install a driver. If you have a driver disc from the manufacturer, use this driver. The driver that is included with the printer is usually more current than the drivers used by the operating system. Figure 1 shows the Add Printer wizard, which can also be used to install the new printer.

Printer Driver

Printer drivers are software programs that enable the computer and the printer to communicate with each other. Drivers also provide an interface for the user to configure printer options. Every printer model has a unique driver. Printer manufacturers frequently update drivers to increase the performance of the printer, to add options, or to fix problems. You can download new printer drivers from the manufacturer's website.

Step 1: Find Out If a Newer Driver Is Available

Go to the printer manufacturer's website. Most manufacturers' websites have a link from the main page to a page that offers drivers and support. Make sure the driver is compatible with the computer that you are updating.

Step 2: Download the Driver

Download the printer driver files to your computer. Most driver files come in a compressed or "zipped" format. Download the file to a folder and uncompress or "unzip" the contents. Save instructions or documentation to a separate folder on your computer.

Step 3: Install the Downloaded Driver

Install the downloaded driver automatically or manually. Most printer drivers have a setup file that automatically searches the system for older drivers and replaces them with the new one. If no setup file is available, follow the directions that are supplied by the manufacturer.

Step 4: Test the New Printer Driver

Run multiple tests to make sure the printer works properly. Use a variety of applications to print different types of documents. Change and test each printer option.

Firmware

Firmware is a set of instructions stored on the printer. The firmware controls how the printer operates. The procedure to upgrade firmware is very similar to the procedure for installing printer drivers.

Printer Memory

Adding printer memory to a printer can improve printing speed and allow the printer to handle more complex print jobs. All printers have at least some amount of memory inside. Generally, the more memory a printer has, the more efficiently it operates. Figure 2 is a generic list of steps to follow to upgrade printer memory.

Consult the printer documentation for memory requirements:

- *Memory specifications*– Some printer manufacturers use standard types of memory and other manufacturers use proprietary memory. Check the documentation for the type of memory, the speed of the memory, and the capacity of memory.

- *Memory population and availability*– Some printers have multiple memory slots. To find out how many memory slots are used and how many are available, you might need to open a compartment on the printer to check memory population.

Refer to
Figure
in online course

7.2.4 Identify configuration options and default settings

Each printer might have different configurations and default options. Check the printer documentation for information about configurations and default settings.

Here are some common configurations that are available for printers:

- Paper type – standard, draft, gloss, or photo

- Print quality – draft, normal, photo, or automatic

- Color printing – multiple colors used

- Black-and-white printing – only black ink used

- Grayscale printing – color image printed using only black ink in different shades

- Paper size – standard paper sizes or envelopes and business cards

- Paper orientation – landscape or portrait

- Print layout – normal, banner, booklet, or poster

- Duplex – normal or two-sided printing

Refer to
Figure
in online course

7.2.5 Describe how to optimize printer performance

With printers, most optimization is completed through the software supplied with the drivers.

In the software, there are tools available to optimize performance:

- *Print spool settings*– Cancel or pause current print jobs in the printer queue

- *Color calibration*– Adjust settings to match the colors on the screen to the colors on the printed sheet

- *Paper orientation*– Select landscape or portrait image layout

Refer to
Figure
in online course

7.2.6 Describe how to print a test page

After installing a printer, you should print a test page to verify that the printer is operating properly. The test page confirms that the driver software is installed and working correctly, and that the printer and computer are communicating.

Print a Test Page

To manually print a test page in Windows XP, use the following path:

Start > Printers and Faxes to display the Printers and Faxes menu.

To manually print a test page in Windows Vista, use the following path:

Start > Printers to display the Printers and Faxes menu.

In the Printers and Faxes menu, right-click the desired printer and follow this path:

Properties > General Tab > Print Test Page

A dialog box opens, asking if the page printed correctly. If the page did not print, built-in help files assist you in troubleshooting the problem.

Print from an Application

You can also test a printer by printing a test page from an application such as Notepad or Word-Pad. To access Notepad in Windows XP, use the following path:

Start > All Programs > Accessories > Notepad

To access Notepad in Windows Vista, use the following path:

Start > All Programs > Accessories > Notepad

In the blank document that opens, type some text. Print the document using the following path:

File > Print

Test a Printer

You can also print from the command line to test the printer. Printing from the command line is limited to ASCII files only, such as .txt and .bat files. To send a file to the printer from the command line in Windows XP, use this path:

Start > Run

To send a file to the printer from the command line in Windows Vista, use this path:

Start > Start Search

In the Run box, type **cmd** and then click **OK**.

At the command line prompt, enter the following command:

Print thefile.txt

Test the Printer from the Printer Panel

Most printers have a front panel with controls to allow you to generate test pages. This method of printing enables you to verify the printer operation separately from the network or computer. Consult the printer manufacturer's website or documentation to learn how to print a test page from the front panel of the printer.

Refer to
Figure
in online course

7.2.7 Describe how to share a printer

Printer sharing enables multiple users or clients to access a printer that they are not directly connected to. Figure 1 shows several computers with different operating systems, all connected to the same shared printer. This arrangement reduces the expense on a network, because fewer printers are required.

Setting up printer sharing is simple with Windows XP and Windows Vista. The following steps enable a computer to share a printer:

1. In Windows XP, click **Start > Printers and Faxes**. In Windows Vista, click **Start > Control Panel > Printers**.

2. Right-click the printer and choose **Properties**.

3. Select the **Share** tab.

4. Click the **Share this printer** radio button, as shown in Figure 2.

5. Keep or change the share name.

6. Click **Apply**.

All of the computers that use the shared printer must have the correct drivers installed. Drivers for other operating systems can be installed on the print server.

To connect to the printer from another computer on the network in Windows XP, choose **Start > Printers and Faxes > Add Printer**. In Windows Vista, choose **Start > Control Panel > Printers > Add Printer**. The Add Printer Wizard appears. Follow the steps using the wizard.

Refer to
Figure
in online course

7.3 Describe the types of scanners currently available

As a computer technician, you might be required to purchase, repair, or maintain a scanner. The customer might request you to perform the following tasks:

- Select a scanner.

- Install and configure a scanner.

- Troubleshoot a scanner.

Figure 1 shows some of the different types of scanners.

After completing this section, you will meet the following objectives:

- Describe scanner types, resolution, and interfaces.

- Describe all-in-one devices.

- Describe flatbed scanners.

- Describe handheld scanners.

- Describe drum scanners.

- Compare costs of different types of scanners.

Refer to
Figure
in online course

7.3.1 Describe scanner types, resolution, and interfaces

Scanners convert printed data or images into an electronic data format that a computer can store or process as required. After an image has been scanned, it can be saved, modified, and even e-mailed. Although most scanners perform the same operation, different types of scanners are available, as shown in Figure 1. Click on each type of scanner to learn more information.

As with printers, the features, quality, and speed of the different types of scanners vary. Scanners typically create an RGB image that can be converted into common image formats such as JPEG, TIFF, BMP, and PNG. An RGB image has three channels: red, green, and blue. RGB channels generally follow the color receptors of the human eye and are used in computer displays and image scanners.

Some scanners have the ability to create text documents using optical character recognition (OCR) software. OCR software converts a scanned printed page into text that can be edited with a word processor. The resolution of a scanner is measured in dots per inch (dpi). Like printers, the higher the dpi, the better the quality of the image.

To allow communication of data, the scanner and computer must have compatible interfaces. The interfaces and cables used for printers are typically the same as the interfaces and cables used for scanners, as shown in Figure 2.

Refer to
Figure
in online course

7.3.2 Describe all-in-one devices

An all-in-one device combines the functionality of multiple devices into one physical piece of hardware. The devices may include media card readers and hard drives for storage. All-in-one devices generally include these functions:

- Scanner
- Printer
- Copier
- Fax

All-in-one devices are typically used in home-office environments or where space is limited. These devices are often used with a computer but can operate alone to copy and fax documents.

Refer to
Figure
in online course

7.3.3 Describe flatbed scanners

Flatbed scanners are often used to scan books and photographs for archiving. An electronic image is acquired by placing the book or photograph face down on the glass. The scanner head, consisting of an array of image sensors, lies beneath the glass and moves along the item, capturing the image.

Sheet feeders can be used with flatbed scanners to scan multiple images. A sheet feeder is a device that can be attached to some flatbed scanners to hold multiple sheets and feed them into the scanner, one at a time. This feature allows for faster scanning; however, the image quality is usually not as good as a flatbed scanner that does not use a sheet feeder.

Refer to
Figure
in online course

7.3.4 Describe handheld scanners

A handheld scanner is small and portable. It is difficult to smoothly scan an image using a handheld scanner. To scan an item, carefully pass the scanner head across the item that you want to scan. As with a flatbed scanner, digital images are made from the images collected by the handheld scanner.

When you want to scan an item larger than the head of the handheld scanner, you must make more than one pass to capture the full image. It may be difficult to recreate the original image digitally when it is scanned in more than one pass. The images must be put back together to form a single image of the item that was scanned.

Refer to **Figure** in online course

7.3.5 Describe drum scanners

Drum scanners produce a high-quality transfer of an image. Drum scanners are usually used commercially but are being replaced by lower-priced, high-quality flatbed scanners. Many drum scanners are still in use for high-end reproductions, such as archiving photographs in museums.

To scan an image using a drum scanner, you attach the image to a revolving drum or load it into a supporting canister. The drum is rotated at high speed across optical scanners. The optical scanners move slowly across the drum surface until the entire image is captured. The captured image is then reproduced by the computer as a digital image file.

Refer to **Figure** in online course

7.4 Describe the installation and configuration process for scanners

When you purchase a scanner, the installation and configuration information is usually supplied by the manufacturer. An installation CD that includes drivers, manuals, and diagnostic software is included with the scanner. The same tools might also be available as downloads from the manufacturer's website.

After completing this section, you will meet the following objectives:

- Explain how to power and connect a scanner.
- Describe how to install and update the device driver.
- Identify configuration options and default settings.

Refer to **Figure** in online course

7.4.1 Explain how to power and connect a scanner

Like printers, scanners can connect to a computer using the USB, FireWire, network, or parallel port interface. Some scanners can connect using a SCSI interface.

Scanners that are built into an all-in-one device are plugged directly into an AC wall outlet. Other types of scanners acquire power through the USB or FireWire connector.

After unpacking the scanner, connect the appropriate power and data cables. Use the scanner documentation as your guide, or check the manufacturer's website for instructions.

Refer to **Figure** in online course

7.4.2 Describe how to install and update the device driver

After you have connected and started the scanner, the computer operating system might be able to discover the scanner through the PnP process. If the scanner is discovered, the operating system might automatically install a driver.

After you set up a scanner, install the driver software that the manufacturer includes with the scanner. This driver is usually more current than the drivers on your computer. It might also provide more functionality than the basic driver from Windows.

As with a printer, you might want to install drivers from the manufacturer's website to gain additional functionality, diagnostic tools, and troubleshooting utilities. Download software from the manufacturer's website and follow any directions provided to install the software and utilities for your scanner. Some scanning software automatically downloads and installs updated software, drivers, or firmware. Follow the directions provided by the update utility to install these files.

Install All-in-One Device and Software

Install an all-in-one device, and then find, download, and update the driver and the software for the all-in-one device.

Refer to **Lab Activity** for this chapter

Refer to **Figure** in online course

7.4.3 Identify configuration options and default settings

Scanners have configuration options and default settings that differ between model types and manufacturers.

A scanner might come with a basic graphic editing software package for editing photographs and other images. Editing software packages might include OCR software that allows text in a scanned image to be manipulated as text.

These are some of the configurations that might be available on a scanner:

- Color, grayscale, or black-and-white scanning
- One-touch scanning into your choice of software
- Quality and resolution choices
- Sheet feeders

Color calibration between devices is important so that you see true representations of color. To calibrate a scanner, scan a graphic that contains specific colors. A calibration application installed on the computer compares the output of the scanner against the known colors of the sample graphic on the display. The software adjusts the color of the scanner accordingly. When your scanner, monitor, and printer treat the same colors in the same way, the image you print matches the image you scan.

Refer to **Figure** in online course

7.5 Identify and apply common preventive maintenance techniques for printers and scanners

Printers and scanners have many moving parts that can wear out over time or through extended use. They must be maintained regularly to operate correctly.

Moving parts can be affected by dust and other air particles. Clean printers and scanners regularly to avoid downtime, loss of productivity, and high repair costs.

After completing this section, you will meet the following objectives:

- Describe printer maintenance.
- Describe scanner maintenance.

Refer to **Figure** in online course

7.5.1 Describe printer maintenance

Printers have many moving parts and require a higher level of maintenance than most other electronic devices. Impurities are produced by the printer and collect on the internal components. Over time, if the impurities are not removed, the printer can malfunction. The maintenance schedule for a printer can be found in the manual or on the manufacturer's website.

Caution

Be sure to unplug the printer from the electrical source before beginning any type of maintenance.

Most printers come with printer monitoring and diagnostic software from the manufacturer that can help you maintain the printer. Observe the guidelines from the manufacturer for cleaning the following printer and scanner components:

- Printer roller surfaces
- Printer and scanner paper-handling mechanisms

The type and quality of paper and ink used can affect the life of the printer:

- *Paper selection–* High-quality paper can help to ensure that the printer operates efficiently and for a long time. Many types of printer paper are available, including inkjet and laser. The printer manufacturer might recommend the type of paper to use for best results. Some papers, especially photo paper and transparencies, have a right and wrong side. Load the paper according to the manufacturer's instructions.
- *Ink selection–* The manufacturer recommends the brand and type of ink to use. If the wrong type of ink is installed, the printer might not work or the print quality might deteriorate. You should avoid refilling the ink cartridges because the ink can leak.

7.5.2 Describe scanner maintenance

The scanner surface should be kept clean. If the glass becomes dirty, consult the manufacturer's user manual for cleaning recommendations. To prevent liquid from leaking into the scanner case, do not spray glass cleaner directly on the device. Dampen a cloth with the cleaner, and then apply the cleaner gently to the glass.

If the inside of the glass becomes dirty, check the manual for instructions on how to open the unit or remove the glass from the scanner. If possible, thoroughly clean both sides of the glass, and replace the glass as it was originally set in the scanner. When the scanner is not in use, keep the lid closed. Put handheld scanners in a safe place. Also, never lay anything heavy on a scanner because you can damage the casing or internal parts.

7.6 Troubleshoot printers and scanners

With printer and scanner problems, a technician must be able to determine if the problem exists with the device, cable connection, or the computer that it is attached to. Follow the steps outlined in this section to accurately identify, repair, and document the problem.

After completing this section, you will meet these objectives:

- Review the troubleshooting process.
- Identify common problems and solutions.

7.6.1 Review the troubleshooting process

Printer problems can result from a combination of hardware, software, and network issues. Computer technicians must be able to analyze the problem and determine the cause of the error to repair the printer. This process is called troubleshooting.

The first step in the troubleshooting process is to identify the problem. Figure 1 is a list of open-ended and closed-ended questions to ask the customer.

After you have talked to the customer, you can establish a theory of probable causes. Figure 2 is a list of some common probable causes for printer problems.

After you have developed some theories about what is wrong, test your theories to determine the cause of the problem. Figure 3 is a list of quick procedures that can determine the exact cause of the problem or even correct the problem. If a quick procedure does correct the problem, you can go to step 5 to verify full system functionality. If a quick procedure does not correct the problem, you might need to research the problem further to establish the exact cause.

After you have determined the exact cause of the problem, establish a plan of action to resolve the problem and implement the solution. Figure 4 shows sources of information to gather additional information to resolve an issue.

After you have corrected the problem, verify full functionality and, if applicable, implement preventive measures. Figure 5 is a list of the steps to verify the solution.

In the final step of the troubleshooting process, you must document your findings, actions, and outcomes. Figure 6 is a list of the tasks required to document the problem and the solution.

Refer to
Figure
in online course

7.6.2 Identify common problems and solutions

Printer or scanner problems can be attributed to hardware, software, networks, or some combination of the three. You will resolve some types of printer and scanner problems more often than others. Figure 1 is a chart of common printer and scanner problems and solutions.

Summary

In this chapter, various types of printers and scanners were discussed. You learned that there are many different types and sizes of printers and scanners, each with different capabilities, speeds, and uses. You also learned that both printers and scanners can be connected directly to computers, as well as shared across a network. The chapter also introduced the different types of cables and interfaces available to connect a printer or scanner. The following concepts from this chapter are important to remember:

- Some printers and scanners have low output and are adequate for home use, whereas other printers and scanners have high output and are designed for commercial use.

- Printers can have different speeds and quality of print.

- Older printers and scanners use parallel cables and ports. Newer printers and scanners typically use USB or FireWire cables and connectors.

- Larger printers and scanners might also have an NIC port to connect to a network.

- Newer printers and scanners are PnP. The computer automatically installs the necessary drivers.

- If the device drivers are not automatically installed by the computer, you must supply the drivers on a CD or download them from the manufacturer's website.

- Most optimization is done through software drivers and utilities.

- After you have set up the printer or scanner, you can share the device with other users on the network. This arrangement is cost-efficient because there is no need for every user to have a printer or scanner.

- A good preventive maintenance program extends the life of the printer and scanner and keeps them performing well.

- Troubleshooting printer and scanner problems requires the technician to identify, repair, and document the problem.

- Troubleshooting steps include: identify the problem, establish a theory of probable causes, determine an exact cause, implement a solution, verify solution and full system functionality, and document findings.

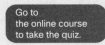
Go to the online course to take the quiz.

Chapter 7 Quiz

Take the chapter quiz to test your knowledge.

Your Chapter Notes

Fundamental Networks

Introduction

This chapter provides an overview of network principles, standards, and purposes. The following types of networks will be discussed in this chapter:

- Local Area Network (LAN)
- Wide Area Network (WAN)
- Wireless LAN (WLAN)

The different types of network topologies, protocols, and logical models as well as the hardware needed to create a network will also be discussed in this chapter. Configuration, troubleshooting, and preventive maintenance will be covered. You will also learn about network software, communication methods, and hardware relationships.

After completing this chapter, you will meet these objectives:

- Explain the principles of networking.
- Describe types of networks.
- Describe basic networking concepts and technologies.
- Describe the physical components of a network.
- Describe LAN topologies and architectures.
- Identify standards organizations.
- Identify Ethernet standards.
- Explain OSI and TCP/IP data models.
- Describe how to configure a NIC and a modem.
- Identify names, purposes, and characteristics of other technologies used to establish connectivity.
- Identify and apply common preventive maintenance techniques used for networks.
- Troubleshoot a network.

Refer to
Figure
in online course

8.1 Explain the principles of networking

Networks are systems that are formed by links. Websites that allow individuals to link to each other's pages are called social networking sites. A set of related ideas can be called a conceptual network. The connections you have with all your friends can be called your personal network.

People use the following networks every day:

- Mail delivery system

- Telephone system
- Public transportation system
- Corporate computer network
- The Internet

Computers can be linked by networks to share data and resources. A network can be as simple as two computers connected by a single cable or as complex as hundreds of computers connected to devices that control the flow of information. Converged data networks can include general purpose computers, such as PCs and servers, as well as devices with more specific functions, including printers, phones, televisions, and game consoles.

All data, voice, video, and converged networks share information and use various methods to direct how this information flows. The information on the network goes from one place to another, sometimes via different paths, to arrive at the appropriate destination.

The public transportation system is similar to a data network. The cars, trucks, and other vehicles are like the messages that travel within the network. Each driver defines a starting point (source) and an ending point (destination). Within this system, there are rules such as stop signs and traffic lights that control the flow from the source to the destination.

After completing this section, you will meet these objectives:

- Define computer networks.
- Explain the benefits of networking.

Refer to
Figure
in online course

8.1.1 Define computer networks

A computer data network is a collection of hosts connected by networking devices. A host is any device that sends and receives information on the network. Peripherals are devices that are connected to hosts. Some devices can serve either as hosts or peripherals. For example, a printer connected to your laptop that is on a network is acting as a peripheral. If the printer is connected directly to a networking device, such as a hub, switch, or router, it is acting as a host.

Computer networks are used globally in businesses, homes, schools, and government agencies. Many of the networks are connected to each other through the Internet.

Many different types of devices can connect to a network:

- Desktop computers
- Laptop computers
- Printers
- Scanners
- PDAs
- Smartphones
- File and print servers

A network can share many different types of resources:

- Services, such as printing or scanning

- Storage space on removable devices, such as hard drives or optical drives

- Applications, such as databases

You can use networks to access information stored on other computers, print documents using shared printers, and synchronize the calendar between your computer and your Smartphone.

Network devices link together using a variety of connections:

- *Copper cabling–* Uses electrical signals to transmit data between devices

- *Fiber-optic cabling–* Uses glass or plastic wire, also called fiber, to carry information as light pulses

- *Wireless connection–* Uses radio signals, infrared technology, or satellite transmissions

Refer to **Figure** in online course

8.1.2 Explain the benefits of networking

The benefits of networking computers and other devices include lower costs and increased productivity. With networks, resources can be shared, which results in less duplication and corruption of data.

Fewer Peripherals Needed

Figure 1 shows that many devices can be connected on a network. Each computer on the network does not need to have its own printer, scanner, or backup device. Multiple printers can be set up in a central location and shared among the network users. All network users send print jobs to a central print server that manages the print requests. The print server can distribute print jobs over multiple printers or queue jobs that require a specific printer.

Increased Communication Capabilities

Networks provide several different collaboration tools that can be used to communicate between network users. Online collaboration tools include e-mail, forums and chats, voice and video, and instant messaging. With these tools, users can communicate with friends, family, and colleagues.

Avoid File Duplication and Corruption

A server manages network resources. Servers store data and share it with users on a network. Confidential or sensitive data can be protected and shared with the users who have permission to access that data. Document tracking software can be used to prevent users from overwriting files or changing files that others are accessing at the same time.

Lower Cost Licensing

Application licensing can be expensive for individual computers. Many software vendors offer site licenses for networks, which can dramatically reduce the cost of software. The site license allows a group of people or an entire organization to use the application for a single fee.

Centralized Administration

Centralized administration reduces the number of people needed to manage the devices and data on the network, reducing time and cost to the company. Individual network users do not need to manage their own data and devices. One administrator can control the data, devices, and permissions of users on the network. Backing up data is easier because the data is stored in a central location.

Conserve Resources

Data processing can be distributed across many computers to prevent one computer from becoming overloaded with processing tasks.

Refer to
Interactive Graphic
in online course.

Refer to
Figure
in online course

Advantages and Disadvantages of Networking
Complete the network matching activity in Figure 2.

8.2 Describe types of networks

Data networks continue to evolve in complexity, use, and design. To communicate about networks, different types of networks are given different descriptive names. A computer network is identified by the following specific characteristics:

- The area it serves

- How data is stored

- How resources are managed

- How the network is organized

- Type of networking devices used

- Type of media used to connect the devices

After completing this section, you will meet these objectives:

- Describe a LAN.

- Describe a WAN.

- Describe a WLAN.

- Explain peer-to-peer networks.

- Explain client/server networks.

Refer to
Figure
in online course

8.2.1 Describe a LAN

A LAN is a group of interconnected devices that is under the same administrative control. In the past, LANs were considered to be small networks that existed in a single physical location. Although LANs can be as small as a single local network installed in a home or small office, over time, the definition of LANs has evolved to include interconnected local networks consisting of many hundreds of devices, installed in multiple buildings and locations.

The important thing to remember is that all of the local networks within a LAN are under one administrative control group that governs the security and access control policies that are in force on the network. In this context, the word Local refers to local consistent control rather than being physically close to each other. Devices in a LAN might be physically close, but this is not a requirement.

Refer to
Figure
in online course

8.2.2 Describe a WAN

A WAN is a network that connects LANs in geographically separated locations. The most common example of a WAN is the Internet. The Internet is a large WAN that is composed of millions of interconnected LANs. Telecommunications service providers are used to interconnect these LANs at different locations.

Refer to
Figure
in online course

8.2.3 Describe a WLAN

In a traditional LAN, devices are connected together using copper cabling. In some environments, installing copper cabling might not be practical, desirable, or even possible. In these situations, wireless devices are used to transmit and receive data using radio waves. These networks are called wireless LANs, or WLANs. As with LANs, on a WLAN you can share resources, such as files and printers, and access the Internet.

In a WLAN, wireless devices connect to access points within a specified area, as shown in Figure 1. Access points are typically connected to the network using copper cabling. Instead of providing copper cabling to every network host, only the wireless access point is connected to the network with copper cabling. The range (radius of coverage) for typical WLAN systems varies from under 30m (98.4 ft.) indoors to much greater distances outdoors, depending on the technology used.

Refer to
Interactive Graphic
in online course.

Network Types
Complete the network type matching activity in Figure 2.

Refer to
Figure
in online course

8.2.4 Explain peer-to-peer networks

In a peer-to-peer network, there are no dedicated servers or hierarchy among the computers. In this type of network, each device has equivalent capabilities and responsibilities. Individual users are responsible for their own resources and can decide which data and devices to share. Because individual users are responsible for the resources on their own computers, the network has no central point of control or administration.

Peer-to-peer networks work best in environments with ten or fewer computers. Because individual users are in control of their own computers, there is no need to hire a dedicated network administrator.

Peer-to-peer networks have several disadvantages:

- There is no centralized network administration, which makes it difficult to determine who controls resources on the network.

- There is no centralized security. Each computer must use separate security measures for data protection.

- The network becomes more complex and difficult to manage as the number of computers on the network increases.

- There might be no centralized data storage. Separate data backups must be maintained. This responsibility falls on the individual users.

Peer-to-peer networks still exist inside larger networks today. Even on a large client network, users can still share resources directly with other users without using a network server. In your home, if you have more than one computer, you can set up a peer-to-peer network. You can share files with other computers, send messages between computers, and print documents to a shared printer.

Refer to
Figure
in online course

8.2.5 Explain client/server networks

In a client/server network, the client requests information or services from the server. The server provides the requested information or service to the client. Servers on a client/server network commonly perform some of the processing work for client machines, for example, sorting through a database before delivering only the records requested by the client.

One example of a client/server network is a corporate environment in which employees use a company e-mail server to send, receive, and store e-mail. The e-mail client on an employee computer issues a request to the e-mail server for any unread e-mail. The server responds by sending the requested e-mail to the client.

In a client/server model, network administrators maintain the servers. The network administrator implements data backups and security measures. The network administrator also controls user access to the network resources. All of the data on the network is stored on a centralized file server. A centralized print server manages shared printers on the network. Each user must provide an authorized username and password to gain access to network resources that each person is permitted to use.

A workgroup is a collection of workstations and servers on a LAN that are designed to communicate and exchange data with one another. Each workstation controls the user accounts, security information, and access to data and resources for that computer.

A domain is a group of computers and electronic devices with a common set of rules and procedures administered as a unit. A domain does not refer to a single location or specific type of network configuration. The computers in a domain are a logical grouping of connected computers that can be located in different locations in the world. A specialized server called a domain controller manages all security-related aspects of users and network resources, centralizing security and administration.

For data protection, an administrator performs a routine backup of all the files on the servers. If a computer crashes, or data is lost, the administrator can easily recover the data from a recent backup.

Refer to **Figure** in online course

8.3 Describe basic networking concepts and technologies

As a computer technician, you will be required to configure and troubleshoot computers on a network. To effectively configure a computer on the network, you should understand IP addressing, protocols, and other network concepts.

After completing this section, you will meet these objectives:

- Explain bandwidth and data transmission.
- Describe IP addressing.
- Define DHCP.
- Describe Internet protocols and applications.
- Define ICMP.

Refer to **Figure** in online course

8.3.1 Explain bandwidth and data transmission

Bandwidth is the amount of data that can be transmitted within a fixed time period. When data is sent over a computer network, it is broken up into small chunks called packets. Each packet contains headers. A header is information added to each packet that contains the source and destination of the packet. A header also contains information that describes how to put all of the packets back together again at the destination. The size of the bandwidth determines the amount of information that can be transmitted.

Bandwidth is measured in bits per second and is usually denoted by any of the following units of measure:

- *bps*– bits per second
- *kbps*– kilobits per second

- *Mbps*– megabits per second

Note

1 byte is equal to 8 bits, and is abbreviated with a capital letter B. 1 MBps is approximately 8 Mbps.

Figure 1 shows how bandwidth on a network can be compared to a highway. In the highway example, the cars and trucks represent the data. The number of lanes on the highway represents the amount of cars that could travel on the highway at the same time. An eight-lane highway can handle four times the number of cars that a two-lane highway can hold.

The amount of time it takes data to travel from source to destination is called latency. Like a car traveling across town that encounters stop lights or detours, data is delayed by network devices and cable length. Network devices add latency when processing and forwarding data. When surfing the Web or downloading a file, latency does not normally cause problems. Time critical applications, such as Internet telephone calls, video, and gaming, can be significantly affected by latency.

The data that is transmitted over the network can flow using one of three modes: simplex, half-duplex, or full-duplex.

Simplex

Simplex, also called unidirectional, is a single, one-way transmission. An example of simplex transmission is the signal that is sent from a TV station to your home TV.

Half-Duplex

When data flows in one direction at a time, it is known as half-duplex. With half-duplex, the channel of communications allows alternating transmission in two directions, but not in both directions simultaneously. Two-way radios, such as police or emergency communications mobile radios, work with half-duplex transmissions. When you press the button on the microphone to transmit, you cannot hear the person on the other end. If people at both ends try to talk at the same time, neither transmission gets through.

Full-Duplex

When data flows in both directions at the same time, it is known as full-duplex. Although the data flows in both directions, the bandwidth is measured in only one direction. A network cable with 100 Mbps in full-duplex mode has a bandwidth of 100 Mbps.

A telephone conversation is an example of full-duplex communication. Both people can talk and be heard at the same time.

Full-duplex networking technology increases network performance because data can be sent and received at the same time. Broadband technology allows multiple signals to travel on the same wire simultaneously. Broadband technologies, such as digital subscriber line (DSL) and cable, operate in full-duplex mode. With a DSL connection, for example, users can download data to the computer and talk on the telephone at the same time.

Refer to
Figure
in online course

8.3.2 Describe IP addressing

An IP address is a number that is used to identify a device on the network. Each device on a network must have a unique IP address to communicate with other network devices. As noted earlier, a host is a device that sends or receives information on the network. Network devices are devices that move data across the network, including hubs, switches, and routers. On a LAN, each host and network device must have an IP address within the same network to be able to communicate with each other.

A person's name and fingerprints usually do not change. They provide a label or address for the physical aspect of the person – the body. A person's mailing address, on the other hand, relates to where the person lives or picks up mail. This address can change. On a host, the Media Access Control (MAC) address (explained below) is assigned to the host NIC and is known as the physical address. The physical address remains the same regardless of where the host is placed on the network in the same way that fingerprints remain with the person regardless of where the person goes.

The IP address is similar to the mailing address of a person. It is known as a logical address because it is logically assigned based on the host location. The IP address, or network address, is based on the local network and is assigned to each host by a network administrator. This process is similar to the local government assigning a street address based on the logical description of the city or village and neighborhood.

An IP address consists of a series of 32 binary bits (ones and zeros). It is very difficult for humans to read a binary IP address. For this reason, the 32 bits are grouped into four 8-bit bytes called octets. An IP address, even in this grouped format, is hard for humans to read, write, and remember; therefore, each octet is presented as its decimal value, separated by a decimal point or period. This format is referred to as dotted-decimal notation. When a host is configured with an IP address, it is entered as a dotted decimal number, such as 192.168.1.5. Imagine if you had to enter the 32-bit binary equivalent of this:

11000000101010000000000100000101. If just one bit were mistyped, the address would be different and the host might not be able to communicate on the network.

The logical 32-bit IP address is hierarchical and is composed of two parts. The first part identifies the network, and the second part identifies a host on that network. Both parts are required in an IP address. As an example, if a host has IP address 192.168.18.57, the first three octets, 192.168.18, identify the network portion of the address, and the last octet, 57 identifies the host. This is known as hierarchical addressing, because the network portion indicates the network on which each unique host address is located. Routers only need to know how to reach each network and not the location of each individual host.

IP addresses are divided into the following five classes:

- *Class A–* Large networks, implemented by large companies and some countries

- *Class B–* Medium-sized networks, implemented by universities

- *Class C–* Small networks, implemented by ISPs for customer subscriptions

- *Class D–* Special use for multicasting

- *Class E–* Used for experimental testing

Subnet Mask

The subnet mask indicates the network portion of an IP address. Like the IP address, the subnet mask is a dotted decimal number. Usually all hosts within a LAN use the same subnet mask. Figure 1 shows the default subnet masks for usable IP addresses that are mapped to the first three classes of IP addresses:

- *255.0.0.0–* Class A, which indicates that the first octet of the IP address is the network portion

- *255.255.0.0*– Class B, which indicates that the first two octets of the IP address is the network portion

- *255.255.255.0*– Class C, which indicates that the first three octets of the IP address is the network portion

If an organization owns one Class B network but needs to provide IP addresses for four LANs, the organization must subdivide the Class B address into four smaller parts. Subnetting is a logical division of a network. It provides the means to divide a network, and the subnet mask specifies how it is subdivided. An experienced network administrator typically performs subnetting. After the subnetting scheme has been created, the proper IP addresses and subnet masks can be configured on the hosts in the four LANs. These skills are taught in the Cisco Networking Academy courses related to CCNA-level networking skills.

Manual Configuration

In a network with a small number of hosts, it is easy to manually configure each device with the proper IP address. A network administrator who understands IP addressing should assign the addresses and should know how to choose a valid address for a particular network. The IP address that is entered is unique for each host within the same network or subnet.

To manually enter an IP address on a host, go to the TCP/IP settings in the Properties window for the NIC. The NIC enables a computer to connect to a network using a MAC address. Whereas the IP address is a logical address that is defined by the network administrator, a MAC address is "burned-in" or permanently programmed into the NIC when it is manufactured. The IP address of a NIC can be changed, but the MAC address never changes.

The main difference between an IP address and a MAC address is that the MAC address delivers frames on the LAN, while an IP address transports frames outside the LAN. A frame is a data packet that, along with address information, is added to the beginning and end of the packet before transmission over the network. After a frame is delivered to the destination LAN, the MAC address delivers the frame to the end host on that LAN.

If more than a few computers comprise the LAN, manually configuring IP addresses for every host on the network can be time-consuming and prone to errors. In this case, the use of a Dynamic Host Configuration Protocol (DHCP) server would automatically assign IP addresses and greatly simplify the addressing process.

Refer to
Worksheet
for this chapter

Refer to
Figure
in online course

Identify IP Address Classes
Print and complete this worksheet.

8.3.3 Define DHCP

DHCP is a software utility used to dynamically assign IP addresses to network devices. This dynamic process eliminates the need for manually assigning IP addresses. A DHCP server can be set up and the hosts can be configured to automatically obtain an IP address. When a computer is set to obtain an IP address automatically, all of the other IP addressing configuration boxes are dimmed, as shown in Figure 1.

The server maintains a list of IP addresses to assign and manages the process so that every device on the network receives a unique IP address. Each address is held for a predetermined amount of time. When the time expires, the DHCP server can use this address for any computer that joins the network.

This is the IP address configuration information that a DHCP server can assign to hosts:

- IP address

- Subnet mask

- Default gateway

- Optional values, such as a Domain Name System (DNS) server address

The DHCP server receives a request from a host. The server then selects IP address information from a set of predefined addresses that are stored in a database. When the IP address information is selected, the DHCP server offers these values to the requesting host on the network. If the host accepts the offer, the DHCP server leases the IP address for a specific period of time.

Using a DHCP server simplifies the administration of a network because the software keeps track of IP addresses. Automatically configuring TCP/IP also reduces the possibility of assigning duplicate or invalid IP addresses. Before a computer on the network can take advantage of the DHCP server services, the computer must be able to identify the server on the local network. A computer can be configured to accept an IP address from a DHCP server by clicking the "Obtain an IP address automatically" option in the NIC configuration window, as shown in Figure 2. The DHCP settings are configured the same when using either a wired or wireless NIC.

If your computer cannot communicate with the DHCP server to obtain an IP address, the Windows operating system automatically assigns a private IP address. If your computer is assigned an IP address in the range of 169.254.0.0 to 169.254.255.255, your computer can only communicate with other computers in the same range. An example of when these private addresses would be useful is in a classroom lab where you want to prevent access outside of your network. This operating system feature is called Automatic Private IP Addressing (APIPA). APIPA continually requests an IP address at five-minute intervals from a DHCP server for your computer. To access a DNS server, a computer uses the IP address configured in the DNS settings of the NIC in the computer.

NAT

Since private addresses are not allowed on the Internet, a process is needed for translating private IP addresses into public IP addresses to allow local clients to communicate over the Internet. The process used to convert private IP addresses to public IP addresses is called Network Address Translation (NAT). By using NAT, a router is able to translate many internal IP addresses to the same public address.

8.3.4 Describe Internet protocols and applications

A protocol is a set of rules. Internet protocols are sets of rules governing communication within and between computers on a network. Protocol specifications define the format of the messages that are exchanged. A letter sent through the postal system also uses protocols. Part of the protocol specifies the position on the envelope that the delivery address needs to be written. If the delivery address is written in the wrong place, the letter cannot be delivered.

Timing is crucial to network operation. Protocols require messages to arrive within certain time intervals so that computers do not wait indefinitely for messages that might have been lost. Therefore, systems maintain one or more timers during transmission of data. Protocols also initiate alternative actions if the network does not meet the timing rules. Many protocols consist of a suite of other protocols that are stacked in layers. These layers depend on the operation of the other layers in the suite to function properly.

These are the main functions of protocols:

- Identifying errors

- Compressing the data

- Deciding how data is to be sent

- Addressing data

- Deciding how to announce sent and received data

Although there are many other protocols, Figure 1 summarizes some of the more common protocols used on networks and the Internet.

To understand how networks and the Internet work, you must be familiar with the commonly used protocols. These protocols are used to browse the web, send and receive e-mail, and transfer data files. You will encounter other protocols as your experience in IT grows, but they are not used as often as the common protocols described here.

In Figure 2, click the protocol names to learn more about each one.

The more you understand about each of these protocols, the more you will understand how networks and the Internet work.

Refer to
Interactive Graphic
in online course.

Refer to
Figure
in online course

Network Protocols Activity
Complete the matching activity in Figure 3.

8.3.5 Define ICMP

Internet Control Message Protocol (ICMP) is used by devices on a network to send control and error messages to computers and servers. There are several different uses for ICMP, such as announcing network errors, announcing network congestion, and troubleshooting.

Packet Internet Groper (Ping) is commonly used to test connections between computers. Ping is a simple but highly useful command line utility used to determine whether a specific IP address is accessible. The command line options that can be used with the ping command are shown in Figure 1.

You can ping the IP address to test IP connectivity. Ping works by sending an ICMP echo request to a destination computer or other network device. The receiving device then sends back an ICMP echo reply message to confirm connectivity. Four ICMP echo requests (pings) are sent to the destination computer. If it is reachable, the destination computer responds with four ICMP echo replies.

The percentage of successful replies can help you to determine the reliability and accessibility of the destination computer.

You can also use ping to find the IP address of a host when the name is known. If you ping the name of a website, for example, cisco.com, as shown in Figure 2, the IP address of the server displays.

Other ICMP messages are used to report undelivered packets, data on an IP network that includes source and destination IP addresses, and whether a device is too busy to handle the packet. Data, in the form of a packet, arrives at a router, which is a networking device that forwards data packets across networks toward their destinations. If the router does not know where to send the packet, the router deletes it. The router then sends an ICMP message back to the sending computer informing it that the data was deleted. When a router becomes very busy, it might send a different ICMP message to the sending computer indicating that it should slow down due to congestion on the network.

Refer to
Figure
in online course

8.4 Describe the physical components of a network

Many devices can be used in a network to provide connectivity. The device you use depends on how many devices you are connecting, the type of connections that they use, and the speed at which the devices operate. These are the most common devices on a network:

- Computers

- Hubs

- Switches

- Routers

- Wireless access points

The physical components of a network are needed to move data between these devices. The characteristics of the media determine where and how the components are used. These are the most common media used on networks:

- Twisted-pair

- Fiber-optic cabling

- Radio waves

After completing this section, you will meet these objectives:

- Identify names, purposes, and characteristics of network devices.

- Identify names, purposes, and characteristics of common network cables.

Refer to
Figure
in online course

8.4.1 Identify names, purposes, and characteristics of network devices

To make data transmission more extensible and efficient than a simple peer-to-peer network, network designers use specialized network devices, such as hubs, switches, routers, and wireless access points, to send data between devices.

Hubs

Hubs, shown in Figure 1, are devices that extend the range of a network by receiving data on one port, and then regenerating the data and sending it out to all other ports. This process means that all traffic from a device connected to the hub is sent to all the other devices connected to the hub every time the hub transmits data. This causes a great amount of network traffic. Hubs are also called concentrators, because they serve as a central connection point for a LAN.

Bridges and Switches

Files are broken up into small pieces of data, called packets, before they are transmitted over a network. This process allows for error checking and easier retransmission if the packet is lost or corrupted. Address information is added to the beginning and to the end of packets before they are transmitted. The packet, along with the address information, is called a frame.

LANs are often divided into sections called segments, similar to the way a company is divided into departments. The boundaries of segments can be defined using a bridge. A bridge is a device used to filter network traffic between LAN segments. Bridges keep a record of all the devices on each segment to which the bridge is connected. When the bridge receives a frame, the destination address is examined by the bridge to determine if the frame is to be sent to a different segment or dropped. The bridge also helps to improve the flow of data by keeping frames confined to only the segment to which the frame belongs.

Switches, shown in Figure 2, are sometimes called multiport bridges. A typical bridge has two ports, linking two segments of the same network. A switch has several ports, depending on how many network segments are to be linked. A switch is a more sophisticated device than a bridge. A switch maintains a table of the MAC addresses for computers that are connected to each port. When a frame arrives at a port, the switch compares the address information in the frame to its MAC address table. The switch then determines which port to use to forward the frame.

Routers

Whereas a switch connects segments of a network, routers, shown in Figure 3, are devices that connect entire networks to each other. Switches use MAC addresses to forward a frame within a single network. Routers use IP addresses to forward frames to other networks. A router can be a computer with special network software installed, or a router can be a device built by network equipment manufacturers. Routers contain tables of IP addresses along with optimal destination routes to other networks.

Wireless Access Points

Wireless access points, shown in Figure 4, provide network access to wireless devices such as laptops and PDAs. The wireless access point uses radio waves to communicate with radios in computers, PDAs, and other wireless access points. An access point has a limited range of coverage. Large networks require several access points to provide adequate wireless coverage.

Multipurpose Devices

There are network devices that perform more than one function. It is more convenient to purchase and configure one device that serves all of your needs than to purchase a separate device for each function. This is especially true for the home user. In your home, you would purchase a multipurpose device instead of a switch, a router, and a wireless access point. The Linksys 300N, shown in Figure 5, is an example of a multipurpose device.

Refer to
Figure
in online course

8.4.2 Identify names, purposes, and characteristics of common network cables

Until recently, cables were the only medium used to connect devices on networks. A wide variety of networking cables are available. Coaxial and twisted-pair cables use copper to transmit data.

Fiber-optic cables use glass or plastic to transmit data. These cables differ in bandwidth, size, and cost. You need to know what type of cable to use in different situations to install the correct cables for the job. You also need to be able to troubleshoot and repair problems that you encounter.

Twisted-Pair

Twisted-pair is a type of copper cabling that is used for telephone communications and most Ethernet networks. A pair of wires forms a circuit that can transmit data. The pair is twisted to provide protection against crosstalk, which is the noise generated by adjacent pairs of wires in the cable. Pairs of copper wires are encased in color-coded plastic insulation and twisted together. An outer jacket protects the bundles of twisted pairs.

When electricity flows through a copper wire, a magnetic field is created around the wire. A circuit has two wires, and in a circuit, the two wires have oppositely-charged magnetic fields. When the two wires of the circuit are next to each other, the magnetic fields cancel each other out. This is called the cancellation effect. Without the cancellation effect, your network communications become slow due to the interference caused by the magnetic fields.

There are two basic types of twisted-pair cables:

- *Unshielded twisted-pair (UTP)*– Cable that has two or four pairs of wires. This type of cable relies solely on the cancellation effect produced by the twisted-wire pairs that limits signal degradation caused by electromagnetic interface (EMI) and radio frequency interference (RFI). UTP is the most commonly used cabling in networks. UTP cables have a range of 100 m (328 ft).

- *Shielded twisted-pair (STP)*– Each pair of wires is wrapped in metallic foil to better shield the wires from noise. Four pairs of wires are then wrapped in an overall metallic braid or foil. STP reduces electrical noise from within the cable. It also reduces EMI and RFI from outside the cable.

Although STP prevents interference better than UTP, STP is more expensive because of extra shielding, and more difficult to install because of the thickness. In addition, the metallic shielding must be grounded at both ends. If improperly grounded, the shield acts like an antenna picking up unwanted signals. STP is primarily used outside North America.

Category Rating

UTP comes in several categories that are based on two factors:

- Number of wires in the cable

- Number of twists in those wires

Category 3 is the wiring used for telephone systems and for Ethernet LAN at 10 Mbps. Category 3 has four pairs of wires. Category 3 telephone cable is usually terminated into an RJ-11 connector.

Category 5 and Category 5e have four pairs of wires with a transmission rate of 100 Mbps. Category 5 and 5e are the most common network cables used. Category 5e has more twists per foot than Category 5 wiring. These extra twists further prevent interference from outside sources and the other wires within the cable.

Some Category 6 cables use a plastic divider to separate the pairs of wires, which prevents interference. The pairs also have more twists than Category 5e cable. A twisted pair cable is shown in Figure 1. Category 5, 5e, and 6 cables terminate into an RJ-45 connector. An RJ-11 telephone connector has six pins and an RJ-45 connector has eight pins, as shown in Figure 2.

Coaxial Cable

Coaxial cable is a copper-cored cable surrounded by a heavy shielding. Coaxial cable is used to connect computers in a network. There are several types of coaxial cable:

- *Thicknet or 10BASE5–* Coax cable used in networks and operated at 10 Mbps with a maximum length of 500 m (1640.4 ft)

- *Thinnet 10BASE2–* Coax cable used in networks and operated at 10 Mbps with a maximum length of 185 m (607 ft)

- *RG-59–* Most commonly used for cable television in the U.S.

- *RG-6–* Higher quality cable than RG-59, with more bandwidth and less susceptibility to interference

A coaxial cable is shown in Figure 3.

Fiber-Optic Cable

An optical fiber is a glass or plastic conductor that transmits information using light. Fiber-optic cable, shown in Figure 4, has one or more optical fibers enclosed in a sheath or jacket. Because it is made of glass, fiber-optic cable is not affected by EMI or RFI. All signals are converted to light pulses to enter the cable, and converted back into electrical signals when they leave it. This means that fiber-optic cable can deliver signals that are clearer, can go farther, and have greater bandwidth than cable made of copper or other metals.

Fiber-optic cable can reach distances of several miles or kilometers before the signal needs to be regenerated. Fiber-optic cable is usually more expensive to use than copper cable, and the connectors are more costly and harder to assemble. Common connectors for fiber-optic networks are SC, ST, and LC. These three types of fiber-optic connectors are half-duplex, which allows data to flow in only one direction. Therefore, two cables are needed.

These are the two types of glass fiber-optic cable:

- *Multimode–* Cable that has a thicker core than single-mode cable. It is easier to make, can use simpler light sources (LEDs), and works well over distances of a few kilometers or less.

- *Single-mode–* Cable that has a very thin core. It is harder to make, uses lasers as a light source, and can transmit signals dozens of kilometers with ease.

Refer to **Packet Tracer Activity** for this chapter

Refer to **Figure** in online course

Cabling a Simple Network

Develop an understanding of the basic functions of Packet Tracer.

Create a simple network using two hosts.

Observe the importance of using the correct cable type to connect PCs.

8.5 Describe LAN topologies and architectures

Most of the computers that you work on will be part of a network. Topologies and architectures are building blocks for designing a computer network. While you might not build a computer network, you need to understand how they are designed to work on computers that are part of a network.

There are two types of LAN topologies: physical and logical. A physical topology, shown in Figure 1, is the physical layout of the components on the network. A logical topology, shown in Figure 2, determines how the hosts communicate across a medium, such as a cable or the airwaves. Topologies are commonly represented as network diagrams.

A LAN architecture is built around a topology. A LAN architecture comprises all the components that make up the structure of a communications system. These components include the hardware, software, protocols, and sequence of operations.

After completing this section, you will meet these objectives:

- Describe LAN topologies.

- Describe LAN architectures.

Refer to
Figure
in online course

8.5.1 Describe LAN topologies

A physical topology defines the way in which computers, printers, and other devices are connected to a network. A logical topology describes how the hosts access the medium and communicate on the network. The type of topology determines the capabilities of the network, such as ease of setup, speed, and cable lengths.

Physical Topologies

Figure 1 shows the common LAN physical topologies:

- Bus

- Ring

- Star

- Hierarchical or extended star

- Mesh

Bus Topology

In the bus topology, each computer connects to a common cable. The cable connects one computer to the next, like a bus line going through a city. The cable has a small cap installed at the end, called a terminator. The terminator prevents signals from bouncing back and causing network errors.

Ring Topology

In a ring topology, hosts are connected in a physical ring or circle. Because the ring topology has no beginning or end, the cable does not need to be terminated. A specially-formatted frame, called a token, travels around the ring, stopping at each host. If a host wants to transmit data, the host adds the data and the destination address to the frame. The frame then continues around the ring until the frame stops at the host with the destination address. The destination host takes the data out of the frame.

Star Topology

The star topology has a central connection point, which is normally a device such as a hub, switch, or router. Each host on a network has a cable segment that attaches the host directly to the central connection point. The advantage of a star topology is that it is easy to troubleshoot. Each host is connected to the central device with its own wire. If there is a problem with that cable, only that host is affected. The rest of the network remains operational.

Hierarchical or Extended Star Topology

A hierarchical or extended star topology is a star network with an additional networking device connected to the main networking device. Typically, a network cable connects to one hub, and then several other hubs connect to the first hub. Larger networks, such as those of corporations or universities, use the hierarchical star topology.

Mesh Topology

The mesh topology connects all devices to each other. When every device is connected to every other device, a failure of any cable does not affect the network. The mesh topology is used in WANs that interconnect LANs.

Logical Topologies

The two most common types of logical topologies are broadcast and token passing.

In a broadcast topology, each host addresses either data to a particular host or to all hosts connected on a network. There is no order that the hosts must follow to use the network – it is first come, first served for transmitting data on the network.

Token passing controls network access by passing an electronic token sequentially to each host. When a host receives the token, it can send data on the network. If the host has no data to send, it passes the token to the next host, and the process repeats itself.

Refer to **Figure** in online course

8.5.2 Describe LAN architectures

LAN architecture describes both the physical and logical topologies used in a network. Figure 1 shows the three most common LAN architectures.

Ethernet

The Ethernet architecture is based on the IEEE 802.3 standard. The IEEE 802.3 standard specifies that a network use the Carrier Sense Multiple Access with Collision Detection (CSMA/CD) access control method. In CSMA/CD, hosts access the network using the first come, first served broadcast topology method to transmit data.

Ethernet uses a logical bus or broadcast topology and either a bus or star physical topology. As networks expand, most Ethernet networks are implemented using an extended star or hierarchical star topology. Standard transfer rates are 10 Mbps and 100 Mbps, but new standards outline Gigabit Ethernet, which is capable of attaining speeds up to 1000 Mbps (1 Gbps).

Token Ring

IBM originally developed Token Ring as a reliable network architecture based on the token-passing access control method. Token Ring is often integrated with IBM mainframe systems. Token Ring is used with computers and mainframes.

Token Ring is an example of an architecture in which the physical topology is different from its logical topology. The Token Ring topology is referred to as a star-wired ring because the outer appearance of the network design is a star. The computers connect to a central hub, called a multistation access unit (MSAU). Inside the device, however, the wiring forms a circular data path, creating a logical ring. The logical ring is created by the token traveling out of an MSAU port to a computer. If the computer does not have any data to send, the token is sent back to the MSAU port and then out the next port to the next computer. This process continues for all computers and therefore resembles a physical ring.

FDDI

Fiber distributed data interface (FDDI) is a type of Token Ring network. The implementation and topology of FDDI differs from the IBM Token Ring LAN architecture. FDDI is often used to connect several buildings in an office complex or on a university campus.

FDDI runs on fiber-optic cable. FDDI combines high-speed performance with the advantages of the token-passing ring topology. FDDI runs at 100 Mbps on a dual-ring topology. The outer ring is called the primary ring, and the inner ring is called the secondary ring.

Normally, traffic flows only on the primary ring. If the primary ring fails, the data automatically flows onto the secondary ring in the opposite direction.

An FDDI dual ring supports a maximum of 500 computers per ring. The total distance of each length of the cable ring is 100 km (62 mi). A repeater, which is a device that regenerates signals, is required every 2 km (1.2 mi). In recent years, many Token Ring networks have been replaced by faster Ethernet networks.

Refer to
Figure
in online course

8.6 Identify standards organizations

Several worldwide standards organizations are responsible for setting networking standards. Standards are used by manufacturers as a basis for developing technology, especially communications and networking technologies. Standardizing technology ensures that the devices you use will be compatible with other devices using the same technology. The standards groups create, examine, and update standards. These standards are applied to the development of technology to meet the demands for higher bandwidth, efficient communication, and reliable service.

Click each of the standards in Figure 1 to learn more information.

Refer to
Figure
in online course

8.7 Identify Ethernet standards

Ethernet protocols describe the rules that control how communication occurs on an Ethernet network. To ensure that all Ethernet devices are compatible with each other, the IEEE developed standards for manufacturers and programmers to follow when developing Ethernet devices.

After completing this section, you will meet these objectives:

- Explain cabled Ethernet standards.
- Explain wireless Ethernet standards.

Refer to
Figure
in online course

8.7.1 Explain cabled Ethernet standards

IEEE 802.3

The Ethernet architecture is based on the IEEE 802.3 standard. The IEEE 802.3 standard specifies that a network implement the CSMA/CD access control method.

In CSMA/CD, all end stations "listen" to the network wire for clearance to send data. This process is similar to waiting to hear a dial tone on a phone before dialing a number. When the end station detects that no other host is transmitting, the end station attempts to send data. If no other station sends any data at the same time, this transmission arrives at the destination computer with no problems. If another end station observed the same clear signal and transmitted at the same time, a collision occurs on the network media.

The first station that detects the collision, or the doubling of voltage, sends out a jam signal that tells all stations to stop transmitting and to run a backoff algorithm. A backoff algorithm calculates random times in which the end station will start to try network transmission again. This random time is typically in one or two milliseconds (ms), or thousandths of a second. This sequence occurs every time there is a collision on the network and can reduce Ethernet transmission by up to 40 percent.

Ethernet Technologies

The IEEE 802.3 standard defines several physical implementations that support Ethernet. Some of the common implementations are described here.

Ethernet

10BASE-T is an Ethernet technology that uses a star topology. 10BASE-T is a popular Ethernet architecture whose features are indicated in its name:

- The ten (10) represents a speed of 10 Mbps.

- BASE represents baseband transmission. In baseband transmission, the entire bandwidth of a cable is used for one type of signal.

- The T represents twisted-pair copper cabling.

10BASE-T

There are many advantages to using 10BASE-T:

- Installation of cable is inexpensive compared to fiber-optic installation.

- Cables are thin, flexible, and easier to install than coaxial cabling.

- Equipment and cables are easy to upgrade.

There are also disadvantages to using 10BASE-T:

- The maximum length for a 10BASE-T segment is only 100 m (328 ft).

- Cables are susceptible to EMI.

Fast Ethernet

The high bandwidth demands of many modern applications, such as live video conferencing and streaming audio, have created a need for higher data-transfer speeds. Many networks require more bandwidth than 10 Mbps Ethernet.

100BASE-TX is much faster than 10BASE-T and has a theoretical bandwidth of 100 Mbps.

100BASE-TX

There are many advantages to using 100BASE-TX:

- At 100 Mbps, transfer rates of 100BASE-TX are ten times that of 10BASE-T.

- 100BASE-X uses twisted-pair cabling, which is inexpensive and easy to install.

There are also disadvantages to using 100BASE-TX:

- The maximum length for a 100BASE-TX segment is only 100 m (328 ft).

- Cables are susceptible to EMI.

1000BASE -T is commonly known as Gigabit Ethernet. Gigabit Ethernet is a LAN architecture.

1000BASE-T

There are many advantages to using 1000BASE-T:

- The 1000BASE-T architecture supports data transfer rates of 1 Gbps. At 1 Gbps, it is ten times faster than Fast Ethernet, and 100 times faster than Ethernet. This increased speed makes it possible to implement bandwidth-intensive applications, such as live video.

- The 1000BASE-T architecture has interoperability with 10BASE-T and 100BASE-TX.

There are also disadvantages to using 1000BASE-T:

- The maximum length for a 1000BASE-T segment is only 100 m (328 ft).

- It is susceptible to interference.

- Gigabit NICs and switches are expensive.

- Additional equipment is required.

10BASE-FL, 100BASE-FX, 1000BASE-SX, and LX are fiber-optic Ethernet technologies.

Refer to
Figure
in online course

8.7.2 Explain wireless Ethernet standards

IEEE 802.11 is the standard that specifies connectivity for wireless networks. IEEE 802.11, or Wi-Fi, refers to a collective group of standards – 802.11a, 802.11b, 802.11g, and 802.11n. These protocols specify the frequencies, speeds, and other capabilities of the different Wi-Fi standards.

802.11a

Devices conforming to the 802.11a standard allow WLANs to achieve data rates as high as 54 Mbps. IEEE 802.11a devices operate in the 5 GHz radio frequency range and within a maximum range of 45.7 m (150 ft).

802.11b

802.11b operates in the 2.4 GHz frequency range with a maximum theoretical data rate of 11 Mbps. These devices operate within a maximum range of 91 m (300 ft).

802.11g

IEEE 802.11g provides the same theoretical maximum speed as 802.11a, which is 54 Mbps, but operates in the same 2.4 GHz spectrum as 802.11b. Unlike 802.11a, 802.11g is backward-compatible with 802.11b. 802.11g also has a maximum range of 91 m (300 ft).

802.11n

802.11n is a newer wireless standard that has a theoretical bandwidth of 540 Mbps and operates in either the 2.4 GHz or 5 GHz frequency range with a maximum range of 250 m (984 ft).

Refer to **Figure** in online course

8.8   Explain OSI and TCP/IP data models

An architectural model is a common frame of reference for explaining Internet communications and developing communication protocols. It separates the functions of protocols into manageable layers. Each layer performs a specific function in the process of communicating over a network.

The TCP/IP model was created by researchers in the U.S. Department of Defense (DoD). The TCP/IP model is a tool used to help explain the TCP/IP suite of protocols, which is the dominant standard for transporting data across networks. This model has four layers, as shown in Figure 1.

In the early 1980s, the International Standards Organization (ISO) developed the Open Systems Interconnect (OSI) model, which was defined in ISO standard 7498-1, to standardize the way devices communicate on a network. This model has seven layers, as shown in Figure 1. This model was a major step forward toward ensuring that there would be interoperability between network devices.

After completing this section, you will meet these objectives:

- Define the TCP/IP model.
- Define the OSI model.
- Compare OSI and TCP/IP.

Refer to **Figure** in online course

8.8.1   Define the TCP/IP model

The TCP/IP reference model provides a common frame of reference for the development of the protocols used on the Internet. It consists of layers that perform functions necessary to prepare data for transmission over a network. The chart in Figure 1 shows the four layers of the TCP/IP model.

A message begins at the top layer, the Application Layer, and moves down the TCP/IP layers to the bottom layer, the Network Access Layer. Header information is added to the message as it moves down through each layer and is then transmitted. After reaching the destination, the message travels back up through each layer of the TCP/IP model. The header information that was added to the message is stripped away as the message moves up through the layers toward its destination.

Application Layer Protocols

Application Layer protocols provide network services to user applications such as web browsers and e-mail programs. Explore some of the more common Internet protocols in Figure 2, to learn more about the protocols that operate in the Application Layer.

Transport Layer Protocols

Transport Layer protocols provide end-to-end management of the data. One of the functions of these protocols is to divide the data into manageable segments for easier transport across the network. Explore each of the protocols in Figure 3, to learn more about the protocols that operate in the Transport Layer.

Internet Layer Protocols

Internet Layer protocols operate in the third layer from the top in the TCP/IP model. These protocols provide connectivity between hosts in the network. Explore each of the protocols in Figure 4, to learn more about the protocols that operate in the Internet Layer.

Network Access Layer Protocols

Network Access Layer protocols describe the standards that hosts use to access the physical media. The IEEE 802.3 Ethernet standards and technologies, such as CSMA/CD and 10BASE-T, are defined in this layer.

Refer to
Figure
in online course

8.8.2 Define the OSI model

The OSI model is an industry-standard framework that is used to divide network communications into seven distinct layers. Although other models exist, most network vendors today build their products using this framework.

A system that implements protocol behavior consisting of a series of these layers is known as a protocol stack. Protocol stacks can be implemented either in hardware or software, or a combination of both. Typically, only the lower layers are implemented in hardware, and the higher layers are implemented in software.

Each layer is responsible for part of the processing to prepare data for transmission on the network. The chart in Figure 1 shows what each layer of the OSI model does.

In the OSI model, when data is transferred, it is said to virtually travel down the OSI model layers of the sending computer, and up the OSI model layers of the receiving computer.

When a user wants to send data, such as an e-mail, the encapsulation process starts at the Application Layer. The Application Layer is responsible for providing network access to applications. Information flows through the top three layers and is considered to be data when it gets down to the Transport Layer.

At the Transport Layer, the data is broken down into more manageable segments, or Transport Layer protocol data units (PDUs), for orderly transport across the network. A PDU describes data as it moves from one layer of the OSI model to another. The Transport Layer PDU also contains information such as port numbers, sequence numbers, and acknowledgement numbers, which is used for reliable data transport.

At the Network Layer, each segment from the Transport Layer becomes a packet. The packet contains logical addressing and other Layer 3 control information.

At the Data Link Layer, each packet from the Network Layer becomes a frame. The frame contains physical address and error correction information.

At the Physical Layer, the frame becomes bits. These bits are transmitted one at a time across the network medium.

At the receiving computer, the de-encapsulation process reverses the process of encapsulation. The bits arrive at the Physical Layer of the OSI model of the receiving computer. The process of virtually traveling up the OSI model of the receiving computer brings the data to the Application Layer, where an e-mail program displays the e-mail.

Note

Mnemonics can help you remember the seven layers of the OSI. Some examples include: "All People Seem To Need Data Processing" and "Please Do Not Throw Sausage Pizza Away".

Refer to
Figure
in online course

8.8.3 Compare OSI and TCP/IP

The OSI model and the TCP/IP model are both reference models used to describe the data communication process. The TCP/IP model is used specifically for the TCP/IP suite of protocols, and the OSI model is used for the development of standard communication for equipment and applications from different vendors.

The TCP/IP model performs the same process as the OSI model, but uses four layers instead of seven. The chart in Figure 1 shows how the layers of the two models compare.

Refer to
Interactive Graphic
in online course.

OSI Model
Complete the OSI model matching activity in Figure 2.

Refer to
Figure
in online course

8.9 Describe how to configure a NIC and a modem

A NIC is required to connect to the Internet. The NIC may come preinstalled, or you might have to purchase one on your own. In rare cases, you might need to update the driver. You can use the driver disc that comes with the motherboard or adapter card, or you can supply a driver that you downloaded from the manufacturer.

After the NIC and the driver have been installed, you can connect the computer to the network.

In addition to installing a NIC, you might also need to install a modem to connect to the Internet.

After completing this section, you will meet these objectives:

- Install or update a NIC driver.
- Attach the computer to an existing network.
- Describe the installation of a modem.

Refer to
Figure
in online course

8.9.1 Install or update a NIC driver

Sometimes a manufacturer publishes new driver software for a NIC. A new driver might enhance the functionality of the NIC, or it might be needed for operating system compatibility.

When installing a new driver, disable virus protection software to ensure that the driver installs correctly. Some virus scanners detect a driver update as a possible virus attack. Install only one driver at a time; otherwise, some updating processes might conflict.

A best practice is to close all applications that are running so that they are not using any files associated with the driver update. Before updating a driver, you should visit the website of the manufacturer. In many cases, you can download a self-extracting executable driver file that automatically installs or updates the driver. Alternatively, you can click the **Update Driver** button in the toolbar of the Device Manager.

The "+" next to the Network adapters category allows you to expand the category and show the network adapters installed in your system. To view and change the properties of the adapter, or update the driver, expand the category and double-click the specific adapter. In the adapter properties window, select the **Driver** tab.

Note

Sometimes the driver installation process prompts you to reboot the computer.

Checking wireless adapter properties for Windows XP

Click the network icon in the system tray > **Properties** > **Configure** > **Advanced**, as shown in Figure 1.

Checking wireless adapter properties for Windows Vista

Click the network icon in the system tray > **Network and Sharing Center** > **Manage wireless networks** > **Adapter properties** > if prompted for permission click **Continue** > **Configure** > **Advanced**, as shown in Figure 2.

Uninstall a NIC Driver

If a new NIC driver does not perform as expected after it has been installed, the driver can be uninstalled, or rolled back, to the previous driver. Double-click the adapter in the Device Manager. In the Adapter Properties window, select the **Driver** tab and click **Roll Back Driver**. If no driver was installed before the update, this option is not available. In that case, you must find a driver for the device and install it manually if the operating system could not find a suitable driver for the NIC.

Internet Search for NIC Drivers
Print and complete this worksheet.

Refer to
Worksheet
for this chapter

Refer to
Figure
in online course

8.9.2 Attach computer to existing network

Now that the NIC drivers are installed, you are ready to connect to the network. Plug a network cable, also called an Ethernet patch or straight-through cable, into the network port on the computer. Plug the other end into the network device or wall jack.

After connecting the network cable, look at the LEDs, or link lights, next to the Ethernet port on the NIC to see if there is any activity. Figure 1 shows the link lights on a NIC. If there is no activity, this might indicate a faulty cable, a faulty hub port, or even a faulty NIC. You might have to replace one or more of these devices to correct the problem.

After you have confirmed that the computer is connected to the network and the link lights on the NIC indicate a working connection, the computer needs an IP address. Most networks are set up so that the computer receives an IP address automatically from a local DHCP server. If the computer does not have an IP address, you must enter a unique IP address in the TCP/IP properties of the NIC.

Every NIC must be configured with the following information:

- *Protocols–* The same protocol must be implemented between any two computers that communicate on the same network.

- *IP address–* This address is configurable and must be unique to each device. The IP address can be manually configured or automatically assigned by DHCP.

- *MAC address–* Each device has a unique MAC address. The MAC address is assigned by the manufacturer and cannot be changed.

After the computer is connected to the network, test connectivity with the **ping** command. Use the **ipconfig** command, shown in Figure 2, to find out what your IP address is. Ping your own IP address to make sure that your NIC is working properly, as shown in Figure 3. After you have determined that your NIC is working, ping your default gateway or another computer on your network. A default gateway allows a host to communicate outside of your network. If you can ping other devices on your own network and your default gateway, you have connectivity and the NIC is working. If any of these pings fail, you need to troubleshoot the network connection, the NIC, and IP address settings.

Telnet, as well as ping and tracert, can be used to verify connectivity. Telnet is a protocol that provides remote access to servers and networking devices. Telnet specifies how to create and terminate a session to a remote computer or device. It also provides the syntax and order of the commands that can be issued during a session. It can be used to make configuration changes to a remote device, such as a router or switch. With the correct permissions, users can start and stop processes, and even shut down the remote device.

To support Telnet client connections, the connected device runs a service called Telnet, as shown in Figure 4. Most operating systems include a Telnet client. On a Microsoft Windows PC, Telnet can be run from the command prompt. Telnet supports user authentication, but it does not support the transport of encrypted data. All data exchanged during a Telnet session is transported as plain text across the network. The data can be intercepted and easily understood, including the username and password used to authenticate the device.

Refer to
Lab Activity
for this chapter

Configure an Ethernet NIC to use DHCP in Windows XP
Configure an Ethernet NIC to use DHCP to obtain an IP address, test connectivity and establish a telnet connection between 2 computers.

Refer to
Lab Activity
for this chapter

Configure an Ethernet NIC to use DHCP in Windows Vista
Configure an Ethernet NIC to use DHCP to obtain an IP address, test connectivity and establish a telnet connection between 2 computers.

Refer to **Packet Tracer Activity** for this chapter

Adding Computers to an Existing Network
Add computers to an existing network.
Configure the computers to use DHCP.
Observe the use of DHCP on the network.

Refer to
Figure
in online course

8.9.3 Describe the installation of a modem

A modem is an electronic device that transfers data between one computer and another using analog signals over a telephone line. Examples of modems are shown in Figure 1. The modem converts digital data to analog signals for transmission. The modem at the receiving end reconverts the analog signals back to digital data to be interpreted by the computer. The process of converting analog signals to digital and back again is called modulation/demodulation. Modem-based transmission is very accurate, despite the fact that telephone lines can be noisy due to clicks, static, and other problems.

An internal modem plugs into an expansion slot on the motherboard. To configure a modem, jumpers might have to be set to select the IRQ and I/O addresses. No configuration is needed for a plug-and-play modem, which can only be installed on a motherboard that supports plug-and-play. A modem using a serial port that is not yet in use must be configured. Additionally, the software drivers that come with the modem must be installed for the modem to work properly. Drivers for modems are installed the same way drivers are installed for NICs.

External modems connect to a computer through the serial and USB ports.

When computers use the public telephone system to communicate, it is called Dialup Networking (DUN). Modems communicate with each other using audio tone signals. This means that modems are able to duplicate the dialing characteristics of a telephone. DUN creates a Point-to-Point Protocol (PPP) connection between two computers over a phone line.

After the line connection has been established, a "handshaking sequence" takes place between the two modems and the computers. The handshaking sequence is a series of short communications that occur between the two systems. This is done to establish the readiness of the two modems and computers to engage in data exchange. Dialup modems send data over the serial telephone line in the form of an analog signal. Because the analog signals change gradually and continuously, they can be drawn as waves. In this system, the digital signals are represented by 1s and 0s. The digital signals must be converted to a waveform to travel across telephone lines. They are converted back to the digital form, 1s and 0s, by the receiving modem so that the receiving computer can process the data.

AT Commands

All modems require software to control the communication session. Most modem software uses the Hayes-compatible command set. The Hayes command set is based on a group of instructions that always begin with a set of attention characters (AT), followed by the command characters. These are known as AT commands. The AT command set is shown in Figure 2.

The AT commands are modem control commands. The AT command set is used to issue dial, hang up, reset, and other instructions to the modem. Most user manuals that come with a modem contain a complete listing of the AT command set.

The standard Hayes-compatible code to dial is ATDxxxxxxx. There are usually no spaces in an AT string. If a space is inserted, most modems ignore it. The "x" signifies the number dialed. There are seven digits for a local call and 11 digits for a long-distance call. A "W" indicates that the modem waits for an outside line, if necessary, to establish a tone before proceeding. Sometimes, a "T" is added to signify tone dialing, or a "P" is added to signify pulse dialing.

Refer to
Figure
in online course

8.10 Identify names, purposes, and characteristics of other technologies used to establish connectivity

There are many ways to connect to the Internet. Phone, cable, satellite, and private telecommunications companies offer Internet connections for businesses and home use.

In the 1990s, the Internet was typically used for data transfer. Transmission speeds were slow compared to the high-speed connections that are available today. Most Internet connections were analog modems that used the "plain old telephone service" (POTS) to send and receive data. In recent years, many businesses and home users have switched to high-speed Internet connections. The additional bandwidth allows for transmission of voice and video as well as data.

You should understand how users connect to the Internet and the advantages and disadvantages of different connection types.

After completing this section, you will meet these objectives:

- Describe telephone technologies.
- Define power line communication.
- Define broadband.
- Define VoIP.

Refer to
Figure
in online course

8.10.1 Describe telephone technologies

Several WAN solutions are available for connecting between sites or to the Internet. WAN connection services provide different speeds and levels of service. Before committing to any type of Internet connection, research all available services to determine the best solution to match the needs of your customer.

Analog Telephone

This technology uses standard voice telephone lines. This type of service uses a modem to place a telephone call to another modem at a remote site, such as an Internet service provider. There are two major disadvantages of using the phone line with an analog modem. The first is that the telephone line cannot be used for voice calls while the modem is in use. The second is the limited bandwidth provided by analog phone service. The maximum bandwidth using an analog modem is 56 Kbps, but in reality, it is usually much lower than that. An analog modem is not a good solution for the demands of busy networks.

Integrated Services Digital Network (ISDN)

The next advancement in WAN service is ISDN. ISDN is a standard for sending voice, video, and data over normal telephone wires. ISDN technology uses the telephone wires as an analog telephone service. However, ISDN uses digital technology to carry the data. Because it uses digital technology, ISDN provides higher quality voice and higher speed data transfer than traditional analog telephone service.

ISDN digital connections offer three services: Basic Rate Interface (BRI), Primary Rate Interface (PRI), and Broadband ISDN (BISDN). ISDN uses two different types of communications channels. The "B" channel carries the information, which might be data, voice, or video. The "D" channel is usually used for controlling and signaling, but can be used for data.

Click the names of the types of ISDN in Figure 1 to learn more.

Digital Subscriber Line (DSL)

DSL is an always-on technology. "Always-on" means that there is no need to dial up each time to connect to the Internet. DSL uses the existing copper telephone lines to provide high-speed digital data communication between end users and telephone companies. Unlike ISDN, where the digital data communications replaces the analog voice communications, DSL shares the telephone wire with analog signals.

The telephone company limits the bandwidth of the analog voice on the lines. This limit allows the DSL to place digital data on the phone wire in the unused portion of the bandwidth. This sharing of the phone wire allows voice calls to be placed while DSL is connecting to the Internet.

There are two major considerations when selecting DSL. DSL has distance limitations. The phone lines used with DSL were designed to carry analog information. Therefore, the length that the digital signal can be sent is limited and cannot pass through any form of multiplexer used with analog phone lines. The other consideration is that the voice information and the data carried by DSL must be separated at the customer site. A device called a splitter separates the connection to the phones and the connection to the local network devices.

Asymmetric Digital Subscriber Line (ADSL)

ADSL is currently the most commonly used DSL technology. ADSL has different bandwidth capabilities in each direction. ADSL has a fast downstream speed – typically 1.5 Mbps. Downstream is the process of transferring data from the server to the end user. This is beneficial to users who are downloading large amounts of data. The high-speed upload rate of ADSL is slower. ADSL does not perform well when hosting a web server or FTP server, both of which involve upload-intensive Internet activities.

Click the types of DSL in Figure 2 to learn more.

Refer to
Figure
in online course

8.10.2   Define power line communication

Power line communication (PLC) is a communication method that uses power distribution wires (local electric grid) to send and receive data.

PLC is known by other names:

- Power Line Networking (PLN)

- Mains Communication

- Power Line Telecoms (PLT)

With PLC, an electric company can superimpose an analog signal over the standard 50 or 60 Hz AC that travels in power lines. The analog signal can carry voice and data signals.

PLC might be available in areas where other high-speed connections are not. PLC is faster than an analog modem and might cost much less than other high-speed connection types. As this technology matures, it will become more common to find and might increase in speed.

You can use PLC to network computers within your home instead of installing network cabling or wireless technology. PLC connections can be used anywhere there is an electrical outlet. You can control lighting and appliances using PLC without installing control wiring.

Refer to
Figure
in online course

8.10.3   Define broadband

Broadband is a technique used to transmit and receive multiple signals using multiple frequencies over one cable. For example, the cable used to bring cable television to your home can carry computer network transmissions at the same time. Because the two transmission types use different frequencies, they do not interfere with each other.

Broadband is a signaling method that uses a wide range of frequencies that can be further divided into channels. In networking, the term broadband describes communication methods that transmit two or more signals at the same time. Sending two or more signals simultaneously increases the rate of transmission. Some common broadband network connections include cable, DSL, ISDN, and satellite. Figure 1 shows equipment used to connect to or transmit broadband signals.

Bluetooth

Bluetooth is a wireless technology that enables devices to communicate over short distances. A Bluetooth device can connect up to seven other Bluetooth devices to create a Wireless Personal

Area Network (WPAN). This technical specification is described by the IEEE 802.15.1 standard. Bluetooth devices are capable of handling voice and data. Refer to Figure 2 for common Bluetooth characteristics.

Bluetooth devices are divided into three classifications:

- Class 1 has a range of approximately 100 m (330 ft)

- Class 2 has a range of approximately 10 m (33 ft)

- Class 3 has a range of approximately 1 m (3 ft)

Bluetooth devices operate in the 2.4 to 2.485 GHz radio frequency range, which is in the Industrial, Scientific, and Medical (ISM) band. The Bluetooth standard incorporates Adaptive Frequency Hopping (AFH). AFH allows signals to "hop" around using different frequencies within the Bluetooth range, thereby reducing the chance of interference when multiple Bluetooth devices are present.

Cellular

Cellular technology enables the transfer of voice, video, and data. With a cellular WAN adapter installed, a laptop user can access the Internet over the cellular network. Refer to Figure 3 for a comparison of different cellular WAN characteristics.

Although slower than DSL and cable connections, cellular WANs are still fast enough to be classified as a high-speed connection. Cellular networks use one or more of the following technologies:

- *Global System for Mobile communications (GSM)*– Standard used by the worldwide cellular network

- *General Packet Radio Service (GPRS)*– Data service for users of GSM

- *Quad-band*– Allows a cellular phone to operate on all four GSM frequencies: 850 MHz, 900 MHz, 1800 MHz, and 1900 MHz

- *Short Message Service (SMS)*– Data service used to send and receive text messages

- *Multimedia Messaging Service (MMS)*– Data service used to send and receive text messages and can include multimedia content

- *Enhanced Data Rates for GSM Evolution (EDGE)*– Provides increased data rates and improved data reliability

- *Evolution-Data Optimized (EV-DO)*– Provides fast download rates

- *High Speed Downlink Packet Access (HSDPA)*– Provides enhanced G3 access speed

Cable

A cable modem connects your computer to the cable company using the same coaxial cable that connects to your cable television (CATV). You can plug your computer directly into the cable modem, or you can connect a router, switch, hub, or multipurpose network device so that multiple computers can share the connection to the Internet.

DSL

With DSL, the voice and data signals are carried on different frequencies on the copper telephone wires. A filter is used to prevent DSL signals from interfering with phone signals. Plug the filter into a phone jack, and plug the phone into the filter.

The DSL modem does not require a filter. The DSL modem is not affected by the frequencies of the telephone. Like a cable modem, a DSL modem can connect directly to your computer, or it can be connected to a networking device to share the Internet connection with multiple computers.

ISDN

ISDN is another example of broadband. ISDN uses multiple channels and can carry different types of services; therefore, it is considered a type of broadband. ISDN can carry voice, video, and data.

Satellite

Broadband satellite is an alternative for customers who cannot get cable or DSL connections. A satellite connection does not require a phone line or cable, but uses a satellite dish for two-way communication. Download speeds are typically up to 500 Kbps; uploads are closer to 56 Kbps. It takes time for the signal from the satellite dish to relay to your ISP through the satellite orbiting the Earth.

People who live in rural areas often use satellite broadband because they need a faster connection than dialup, and no other broadband connection is available.

Fiber Broadband

Fiber broadband provides faster connection speeds and bandwidth than cable modems, DSL, or ISDN. Fiber broadband can deliver a multitude of digital information such as telephone, video, data, and advanced features like video conferencing. A single fiber pair can carry millions of phone calls, as compared to a single copper pair, which can carry six phone calls.

Refer to **Worksheet** for this chapter

Refer to **Figure** in online course

Answer Broadband Questions
Print and complete this worksheet.

8.10.4 Define VoIP

VoIP is a method to carry telephone calls over the data networks and Internet. VoIP converts the analog signals of our voices into digital information that is transported in IP packets.

VoIP can also use an existing IP network to provide access to the Public Switched Telephone Network (PSTN). When using VoIP to connect to the PSTN, you might be dependent on an Internet connection. This can be a disadvantage if the Internet connection experiences an interruption in service. When a service interruption occurs, the user cannot make phone calls.

Refer to **Figure** in online course

8.10.5 Define VPN

A Virtual Private Network (VPN) is a private network that uses a public network, like the Internet, to connect remote sites or users together. A VPN uses dedicated secure connections routed through the Internet from the company private network to the remote user. When connected to the company private network, users become part of that network and have access to all services and resources as if they were physically connected to the LAN.

Remote-access users must install the VPN client on their computers to form a secure connection with the company private network. The VPN client software encrypts data before sending it over the Internet to the VPN gateway at the company private network. VPN gateways establish, manage, and control VPN connections, also known as VPN tunnels. A basic VPN connection is shown in the figure.

Refer to **Figure** in online course

8.11 Identify and apply common preventive maintenance techniques used for networks

There are common preventive maintenance techniques that should continually be performed for a network to operate properly. In an organization, if there is one malfunctioning computer, generally only one user is affected. But if the network is malfunctioning, many or all users are unable to work.

One of the biggest problems with network devices, especially in the server room, is heat. Network devices, such as computers, hubs, and switches, do not perform well when overheated. Often, excess heat is generated by accumulated dust and dirty air filters. When dust gathers in and on network devices, it impedes the proper flow of cool air and sometimes even clogs fans. It is important to keep network rooms clean and change air filters often. It is also a good idea to have replacement filters available for prompt maintenance.

Preventive maintenance involves checking the various components of a network for wear. Check the condition of network cables because they are often moved, unplugged, and kicked. Many network problems can be traced to a faulty cable. You should replace any cables that have exposed wires, are badly twisted, or are bent.

Label your cables. This practice saves troubleshooting time later. Refer to wiring diagrams, and always follow your company's cable labeling guidelines.

Counterfeiting and the IT Industry

A critical aspect of preventive maintenance that is sometimes overlooked is the issue of counterfeiting. Counterfeit products are often called fakes. They can be hardware, software, and documentation that bear a trademark or logo without the trademark owner's knowledge or consent. These include products that do not originate from authorized manufacturers or are produced without the approval of a trademark owner.

Counterfeit products are often made with cheaper materials and with little or no quality control, and can cause problems in your network. These products might also have invalid warranty and software licenses, no support entitlement, or incorrect initial settings. In addition, counterfeit equipment often fails health and safety compliance testing. The counterfeit product might be cheaper to buy initially, but might be more expensive to maintain. A counterfeit product can create risk to a network and can even be a potential health and safety hazard.

To minimize the risk of purchasing counterfeit products, it is recommended that customers purchase only from the manufacturer's authorized partners, or directly from the manufacturer. When products are not purchased through authorized channels, the manufacturer cannot guarantee the source, quality or authenticity of those products. When the equipment you are buying is mission critical, quality and authenticity should always be your most important consideration.

Refer to
Figure
in online course

8.12 Troubleshoot a network

Network issues can be simple or complex. To assess how complicated the problem is, you should determine how many computers on the network are experiencing the problem.

If there is a problem with one computer on the network, start the troubleshooting process at that computer. If there is a problem with all computers on the network, start the troubleshooting process in the network room where all computers are connected. As a technician, you should develop a logical and consistent method for diagnosing network problems by eliminating one problem at a time.

Follow the steps outlined in this section to accurately identify, repair, and document the problem. The troubleshooting process is shown in Figure 1.

Counterfeiting is a serious issue in troubleshooting as well as in preventive maintenance. Network problems could be related to counterfeit components. To help ensure that you are getting authentic products, Figure 2 shows the points to consider when placing orders or requesting quotes.

Counterfeit products not only pose network, health and safety risks, but the trafficking in counterfeit networking equipment is also a crime that carries serious penalties. In 2008, a former owner of a computer company was sentenced to 30 months in prison and ordered to pay a large sum in restitution as a result of his conviction for trafficking in counterfeit computer components. This type of case serves as an important reminder to customers about the risk of purchasing outside the manufacturer's authorized sales and distribution channels.

The cosmetic differences between an authentic networking product and a counterfeit can be extremely subtle. There are also performance differentiators between authentic products and counterfeits. Many manufacturers have teams that are staffed with engineers well-versed in these differentiators.

After completing this section, you will meet these objectives:

- Review the troubleshooting process.
- Identify common network problems and solutions.

Refer to
Figure
in online course

8.12.1 Review the troubleshooting process

Network problems can result from a combination of hardware, software, and connectivity issues. Computer technicians must be able to analyze the problem and determine the cause of the error to repair the network issue. This process is called troubleshooting.

The first step in the troubleshooting process is to identify the problem. Figure 1 is a list of open-ended and closed-ended questions to ask the customer.

After you have talked to the customer, you can establish a theory of probable causes. Figure 2 is a list of some common probable causes for network problems.

After you have developed some theories about what is wrong, test your theories to determine the cause of the problem. Figure 3 is a list of quick procedures that can determine the exact cause of the problem or even correct the problem. If a quick procedure does correct the problem, you can go to step 5 to verify full system functionality. If a quick procedure does not correct the problem, you might need to research the problem further to establish the exact cause.

After you have determined the exact cause of the problem, establish a plan of action to resolve the problem and implement the solution. Figure 4 shows sources of information to gather additional information to resolve an issue.

After you have corrected the problem, verify full functionality and, if applicable, implement preventive measures. Figure 5 is a list of the steps to verify the solution.

In the final step of the troubleshooting process, you must document your findings, actions and outcomes. Figure 6 is a list of the tasks required to document the problem and the solution.

Refer to
Figure
in online course

Refer to
Worksheet
for this chapter

Refer to
Figure
in online course

8.12.2 Identify common network problems and solutions

Network problems can be attributed to hardware, software, connectivity issues, or some combination of the three. You will resolve some types of network problems more often than others. Figure 1 is a chart of common network problems and solutions.

Diagnose a Network Problem

Print and complete this worksheet.

Summary

This chapter introduced you to the fundamentals of networking, the benefits of having a network, and the ways to connect computers to a network. The different aspects of troubleshooting a network were discussed with examples of how to analyze and implement simple solutions. The following concepts from this chapter are important to remember:

- A computer network is composed of two or more computers that share data and resources.

- A LAN refers to a group of interconnected computers that are under the same administrative control.

- A WAN is a network that connects LANs in geographically separated locations.

- In a peer-to-peer network, devices are connected directly to each other. A peer-to-peer network is easy to install, and no additional equipment or dedicated administrator is required. Users control their own resources, and a network works best with a small number of computers. A client/server network uses a dedicated system that functions as the server. The server responds to requests made by users or clients connected to the network.

- A LAN uses a direct connection from one computer to another. It is suitable for a small area, such as in a home, building, or school. A WAN uses point-to-point or point-to-multipoint, serial communications lines to communicate over greater distances. A WLAN uses wireless technology to connect devices together.

- The network topology defines the way in which computers, printers, and other devices are connected. Physical topology describes the layout of the wire and devices, as well as the paths used by data transmissions. Logical topology is the path that signals travel from one point to another. Topologies include bus, star, ring, and mesh.

- Networking devices are used to connect computers and peripheral devices so that they can communicate. These include hubs, bridges, switches, routers, and multipurpose devices. The type of device implemented depends on the type of network.

- Networking media can be defined as the means by which signals, or data, are sent from one computer to another. Signals can be transmitted either by cable or wireless means. The media types discussed were coaxial, twisted-pair, fiber-optic cabling, and radio frequencies.

- Ethernet architecture is now the most popular type of LAN architecture. Architecture refers to the overall structure of a computer or communications system. It determines the capabilities and limitations of the system. The Ethernet architecture is based on the IEEE 802.3 standard. The IEEE 802.3 standard specifies that a network implement the CSMA/CD access control method.

- The OSI reference model is an industry-standard framework that is used to divide the functions of networking into seven distinct layers. These layers include Application, Presentation, Session, Transport, Network, Data Link, and Physical. It is important to understand the purpose of each layer.

- The TCP/IP suite of protocols has become the dominant standard for the Internet. TCP/IP represents a set of public standards that specify how packets of information are exchanged between computers over one or more networks.

- A NIC is a device that plugs into a motherboard and provides ports for the network cable connections. It is the computer interface with the LAN.

- A modem is an electronic device that is used for computer communications through telephone lines. It allows data transfer between one computer and another. The modem converts byte-oriented data to serial bit streams. All modems require software to control the communication session. The set of commands that most modem software uses is known as the Hayes-compatible command set.

- The three transmission methods to sending signals over data channels are simplex, half-duplex, and full-duplex. Full-duplex networking technology increases performance because data can be sent and received at the same time. DSL, two-way cable modem, and other broadband technologies operate in full-duplex mode.

- Network devices and media, such as computer components, must be maintained. It is important to clean equipment regularly and use a proactive approach to prevent problems. Repair or replace broken equipment to prevent downtime.

- When troubleshooting network problems, listen to what your customer tells you so that you can formulate open-ended and closed-ended questions that will help you determine where to begin fixing the problem. Verify obvious issues and try quick solutions before escalating the troubleshooting process.

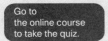

Chapter 8 Quiz

Take the chapter quiz to test your knowledge.

Your Chapter Notes

Fundamental Security

Introduction

Technicians need to understand computer and network security. Failure to implement proper security procedures can have an impact on users, computers, and the general public. Private information, company secrets, financial data, computer equipment, and items of national security are placed at risk if proper security procedures are not followed.

After completing this chapter, you will meet these objectives:

- Explain why security is important.
- Describe security threats.
- Identify security procedures.
- Identify common preventive maintenance techniques for security.
- Troubleshoot security.

Refer to **Figure** in online course

9.1 Explain why security is important

Computer and network security help to keep data and equipment functioning and provide access only to appropriate people. Everyone in an organization should give high priority to security because everyone can be affected by a lapse in security.

Refer to **Figure** in online course

Theft, loss, network intrusion, and physical damage are some of the ways a network or computer can be harmed. Damage or loss of equipment can mean a loss of productivity. Repairing and replacing equipment can cost the company time and money. Unauthorized use of a network can expose confidential information and reduce network resources.

An attack that intentionally degrades the performance of a computer or network can also harm the production of an organization. Poorly implemented security measures to wireless network devices demonstrate that physical connectivity is not necessary for unauthorized access by intruders.

The primary responsibilities of a technician include data and network security. A customer or an organization might depend on you to ensure that their data and computer equipment are secure. You might perform tasks that are more sensitive than those assigned to the average employee. You might repair, adjust, and install equipment. You will need to know how to configure settings to keep the network secure but still keep it available to those who need to access it. You must ensure that software patches and updates are applied, anti-virus software is installed, and anti-spyware software is used. You can also be asked to instruct users how to maintain good security practices with computer equipment.

Refer to **Worksheet** for this chapter

Security Attacks
Print and complete this activity.

9.2 Describe security threats

To successfully protect computers and the network, a technician must understand both types of threats to computer security:

- *Physical–* Events or attacks that steal, damage, or destroy equipment, such as servers, switches, and wiring

- *Data–* Events or attacks that remove, corrupt, deny access, allow access, or steal information

Threats to security can come from the inside or outside of an organization, and the level of potential damage can vary greatly:

- *Internal–* Employees have access to data, equipment, and the network
  - Malicious threats are when an employee intends to cause damage.
  - Accidental threats are when the user damages data or equipment unintentionally.
- *External–* Users outside of an organization that do not have authorized access to the network or resources
  - Unstructured – Attackers use available resources, such as passwords or scripts, to gain access and run programs designed to vandalize.
  - Structured – Attackers use code to access operating systems and software.

Physical loss or damage to equipment can be expensive, and data loss can be detrimental to your business and reputation. Threats against data are constantly changing as attackers find new ways to gain entry and commit their crimes.

After completing this section, you will meet these objectives:

- Define viruses, worms, and Trojans.

- Explain web security.

- Define adware, spyware, and grayware.

- Explain Denial of Service (DoS).

- Describe spam and popup windows.

- Explain social engineering.

- Explain TCP/IP attacks.

- Explain hardware deconstruction and recycling.

Refer to
Figure
in online course

9.2.1 Define viruses, worms, and Trojans

Computer viruses are deliberately created and sent out by attackers. A virus is attached to small pieces of computer code, software, or documents. The virus executes when the software is run on a computer. If the virus is spread to other computers, those computers could continue to spread the virus.

Refer to
Figure
in online course

A virus is a program written with malicious intent and sent out by attackers. The virus is transferred to another computer through e-mail, file transfers, and instant messaging. The virus hides by attaching itself to a file on the computer. When the file is accessed, the virus executes and infects the computer. A virus has the potential to corrupt or even delete files on your computer, use your e-mail to spread itself to other computers, or even erase your entire hard drive.

Some viruses can be exceptionally dangerous. The most damaging type of virus is used to record keystrokes. These viruses can be used by attackers to harvest sensitive information, such as passwords and credit card numbers. Viruses might even alter or destroy information on a computer. Stealth viruses can infect a computer and lay dormant until summoned by the attacker.

A worm is a self-replicating program that is harmful to networks. A worm uses the network to duplicate its code to the hosts on a network, often without any user intervention. It is different from a virus because a worm does not need to attach to a program to infect a host. Even if the worm does not damage data or applications on the hosts it infects, it is harmful to networks because it consumes bandwidth.

A Trojan is technically a worm. The Trojan does not need to be attached to other software. Instead, a Trojan threat is hidden in software that appears to do one thing, and yet behind the scenes it does another. Trojans are often disguised as useful software. The Trojan program can reproduce like a virus and spread to other computers. Computer data damage and production loss could be significant. A technician might be needed to perform the repairs, and employees might lose or have to replace data. An infected computer could be sending critical data to competitors, while at the same time infecting other computers on the network.

Virus protection software, known as anti-virus software, is software designed specifically to detect, disable, and remove viruses, worms, and Trojans before they infect a computer. Anti-virus software becomes outdated quickly, however, and it is the responsibility of the technician to apply the most recent updates, patches, and virus definitions as part of a regular maintenance schedule. Many organizations establish a written security policy stating that employees are not permitted to install any software that is not provided by the company. Organizations also make employees aware of the dangers of opening e-mail attachments that may contain a virus or a worm.

Third-Party Anti-Virus Software
Print and complete this worksheet.

9.2.2 Explain web security

Web security is important because so many people visit the World Wide Web every day. Some of the features that make the web useful and entertaining can also make it harmful to a computer.

Tools that are used to make web pages more powerful and versatile, as shown in Figure 1, can also make computers more vulnerable to attacks. These are some examples of web tools:

- *ActiveX–* Technology created by Microsoft to control interactivity on web pages. If ActiveX is on a page, an applet or small program has to be downloaded to gain access to the full functionality.

- *Java–* Programming language that allows applets to run within a web browser. Examples of applets include a calculator or a counter.

- *JavaScript–* Programming language developed to interact with HTML source code to allow interactive websites. Examples include a rotating banner or a popup window.

Attackers might use any of these tools to install a program on a computer. To prevent against these attacks, most browsers have settings that force the computer user to authorize the downloading or use of ActiveX, Java, or JavaScript, as shown in Figure 2.

9.2.3 Define adware, spyware, and grayware

Adware, spyware, and grayware are usually installed on a computer without the knowledge of the user. These programs collect information stored on the computer, change the computer configuration, or open extra windows on the computer without the user's consent.

Refer to
Figure
in online course

Adware is a software program that displays advertising on your computer. Adware is usually distributed with downloaded software. Most often, adware is displayed in a popup window. Adware popup windows are sometimes difficult to control and will open new windows faster than users can close them.

Grayware or malware is a file or program other then a virus that is potentially harmful. Many grayware attacks are phishing attacks that try to persuade the reader to unknowingly provide attackers with access to personal information. As you fill out an online form, the data is sent to the attacker. Grayware can be removed using spyware and adware removal tools.

Spyware, a type of grayware, is similar to adware. It is distributed without any user intervention or knowledge. Once installed, the spyware monitors activity on the computer. The spyware then sends this information to the organization responsible for launching the spyware.

Phishing is a form of social engineering where the attacker pretends to represent a legitimate outside organization, such as a bank. A potential victim is contacted via e-mail. The attacker might ask for verification of information, such as a password or username, to supposedly prevent some terrible consequence from occurring.

Note

There is rarely a need to give out sensitive personal or financial information online. Be suspicious. Use the postal service to share sensitive information.

Refer to
Interactive Graphic
in online course.

Adware, Spyware, and Phishing
Matching activity for adware, spyware, and phishing

9.2.4 Explain Denial of Service

DoS is a form of attack that prevents users from accessing normal services, such as e-mail and a web server, because the system is busy responding to abnormally large amounts of requests. DoS works by sending enough requests for a system resource that the requested service is overloaded and ceases to operate.

Common DoS attacks include the following:

- Ping of death – A series of repeated, larger than normal pings that crash the receiving computer

- E-mail bomb – A large quantity of bulk e-mail that overwhelms the e-mail server preventing users from accessing it

Distributed DoS (DDoS) is another form of attack that uses many infected computers, called zombies, to launch an attack. With DDoS, the intent is to obstruct or overwhelm access to the targeted server. Zombie computers located at different geographical locations make it difficult to trace the origin of the attack.

Refer to
Figure
in online course

9.2.5 Describe spam and popup windows

Spam, also known as junk mail, is unsolicited e-mail, as shown in Figure 1. In most cases, spam is used as a method of advertising. However, spam can be used to send harmful links or deceptive content, as shown in Figure 2.

When used as an attack method, spam can include links to an infected website or an attachment that could infect a computer. These links or attachments can result in lots of windows designed to capture your attention and lead you to advertising sites. These windows are called popups. As shown in Figure 2, uncontrolled popup windows can quickly cover the user's screen and prevent any work from getting done.

Many anti-virus and e-mail software programs automatically detect and remove spam from an e-mail inbox. Some spam still might get through, so look for some of the more common indications:

- No subject line
- Incomplete return address
- Computer generated e-mail
- Return e-mail not sent by the user

Refer to **Figure** in online course

9.2.6 Explain social engineering

A social engineer is a person who is able to gain access to equipment or a network by tricking people into providing the necessary access information. Often, the social engineer gains the confidence of an employee and convinces the employee to divulge username and password information.

A social engineer might pose as a technician to try to gain entry into a facility, as shown in Figure 1. When inside, the social engineer might look over shoulders to gather information, seek out papers on desks with passwords and phone extensions, or obtain a company directory with e-mail addresses.

Here are some basic precautions to help protect against social engineering:

- Never give out your password.
- Always ask for the ID of unknown persons.
- Restrict access of unexpected visitors.
- Escort all visitors.
- Never post your password in your work area.
- Lock your computer when you leave your desk.
- Do not let anyone follow you through a door that requires an access card.

Refer to **Figure** in online course

9.2.7 Explain TCP/IP attacks

TCP/IP is the protocol suite that is used to control all of the communications on the Internet. Unfortunately, TCP/IP can also make a network vulnerable to attackers.

Some of the most common attacks:

- *SYN flood*– Randomly opens TCP ports, tying up the network equipment or computer with a large amount of false requests, causing sessions to be denied to others
- *DoS*– Sends abnormally large amounts of requests to a system preventing access to the services
- *DDoS*– Uses "zombies" to make tracing the origin of the DoS attack difficult to locate
- *Spoofing*– Gains access to resources on devices by pretending to be a trusted computer
- *Man-in-the-middle*– Intercepts or inserts false information in traffic between two hosts
- *Replay*– Uses network sniffers to extract usernames and passwords to be used at a later date to gain access

- *DNS poisoning–* Changes the DNS records on a system to point to false servers where the data is recorded

Refer to **Figure** in online course

9.2.8 Explain data wiping, hard drive destruction and recycling

Hardware destruction is the process of removing sensitive data from hardware and software before recycling or discarding. Hard drives should be fully erased to prevent the possibility of recovery using specialized software. Three methods are commonly used to either destroy or recycle data and hard drives:

- Data wiping
- Hard drive destruction
- Hard drive recycling

Data Wiping

Data wiping, also known as secure erase, is a procedure performed to permanently delete data from a hard drive. Data wiping is often performed on hard drives containing sensitive data such as financial information. It is not enough to delete files or even format the drive. Use a third-party tool to overwrite data multiple times, rendering the data unusable. It is important to remember that data wiping is irreversible, and the data can never be recovered.

Hard Drive Destruction

Companies with sensitive data should always establish clear policies for hard drive disposal. It is important to be aware that formatting and reinstalling an operating system on a computer does not ensure that information cannot be recovered. Destroying the hard drive is the best option for companies with sensitive data. To fully ensure that data cannot be recovered from a hard drive, you should carefully shatter the platters with a hammer and safely dispose of the pieces.

Other storage media, such as CDs and floppy disks, must also be destroyed. Use a shredding machine that is designed to destroy this type of media.

Hard Drive Recycling

Hard drives that do not contain sensitive data should be reused in other computers. The drive can be reformatted, and a new operating system can be installed. If the drive is not needed, it can be sold or donated.

Refer to **Figure** in online course

9.3 Identify security procedures

A security plan should be used to determine what will be done in a critical situation. Security plan policies should be constantly updated to reflect the latest threats to a network. A security plan with clear security procedures is the basis for a technician to follow. Security plans should be reviewed on a yearly basis.

Part of the process of ensuring security is to conduct tests to determine areas where security is weak. Testing should be done on a regular basis. New threats are released daily. Regular testing provides details of any possible weaknesses in the current security plan that should be addressed.

There are multiple layers of security in a network, including physical, wireless, and data. Each layer is subject to security attacks. The technician needs to understand how to implement security procedures to protect equipment and data.

After completing this section, you will meet these objectives:

- Explain what is required in a basic local security policy.

- Explain the tasks required to protect physical equipment.

- Describe ways to protect data.

- Describe wireless security techniques.

Refer to **Figure** in online course

9.3.1 Explain what is required in a basic local security policy

A security policy should describe how a company addresses security issues, as shown in Figure 1. Though local security policies may vary between organizations, there are questions all organizations should ask:

- What assets require protection?

- What are the possible threats?

- What to do in the event of a security breach?

When creating a security policy, some key areas to observe are shown in Figure 2. The scope of the policy and the consequences of non-compliance should be clearly described. Security policies should be reviewed regularly and updated as necessary. You should keep a revision history to track all policy changes. Security is the responsibility of every person within the company. All employees, including non-computer users, must be trained to understand the security policy and notified of any security policy updates.

Password guidelines are an important component of a security policy. Passwords should be required to have a minimum length and include uppercase and lowercase letters combined with numbers and symbols. It is common for a security policy to require users to change their passwords on a regular basis and govern the number of password attempts before an account is temporarily locked out.

You should also define employee access to data in a security policy. The policy should protect highly sensitive data from public access, while ensuring employees can still perform their job tasks. Data can be classified from public to top secret, and can have several different levels between them. Public information can be seen by anyone and has no security requirements. Public information cannot be used maliciously to hurt a company or an individual. However, top secret information needs the most security, because the data exposure can be extremely detrimental to a government, a company, or an individual.

Refer to **Figure** in online course

9.3.2 Explain the tasks required to protect physical equipment

Physical security is as important as data security. When a computer is taken, the data is also stolen.

There are several methods of physically protecting computer equipment, as shown in Figures 1 and 2:

- Control access to facilities.

- Use cable locks with equipment.

- Keep telecommunication rooms locked.

- Fit equipment with security screws.

- Use security cages around equipment.

- Label and install sensors, such as Radio Frequency Identification (RFID) tags, on equipment.

- Install physical alarms triggered by motion-detection sensors.

- Use webcams with motion-detection and surveillance software.

For access to facilities, there are several means of protection:

- Card keys that store user data, including level of access

- Biometric sensors that identify physical characteristics of the user, such as fingerprints or retinas

- Posted security guard

- Sensors, such as RFID tags, to monitor equipment

One form of hardware security is the Trusted Platform Module (TPM). The TPM is a specialized chip installed on the motherboard of a computer to be used for hardware and software authentication. The TPM stores information specific to the host system, such as encryption keys, digital certificates, and passwords. Applications that use encryption can make use of the TPM chip to secure things like user authentication information, software license protection, and encrypted files, folders, and disks. Integrating hardware security, such as TPM with software security, results in a much safer computer system than using software security alone.

Refer to
Figure
in online course

9.3.3 Describe ways to protect data

The value of physical equipment is often far less than the value of the data it contains. The loss of sensitive data to a company's competitors or to criminals can be costly. Such losses can result in a lack of confidence in the company and the dismissal of computer technicians in charge of computer security. To protect data, several methods of security protection can be implemented.

Password Protection

Password protection can prevent unauthorized access to content, as shown in Figure 1. Attackers can gain access to unprotected computer data. All computers should be password protected. Two levels of password protection are recommended:

- *BIOS*– Prevents the operating system from booting, and prevents BIOS settings from being changed without the appropriate password

- *Login*– Prevents unauthorized access to the local computer and the network

Network logins provide a means of logging activity on the network and either preventing or allowing access to resources. This makes it possible to determine which resources are being accessed. Usually, the system administrator defines a naming convention for the usernames when creating network logins. A common example of a username is the first initial of the person's first name and then the entire last name. You should keep the username naming convention simple so that people do not have a hard time remembering it. Usernames, like passwords, are an important piece of information and should not be revealed. Default usernames should be changed so that hackers do not know either part of the username and password combination.

When assigning passwords, the level of password control should match the level of protection required. A good security policy should be strictly enforced and include, but not be limited to, the following rules:

- Passwords should expire after a specific period of time.

- Passwords should contain a mixture of letters and numbers so that they cannot easily be broken.

- Password standards should prevent users from writing down passwords and exposing them to public view.

- Rules about password expiration and lockout should be defined. Lockout rules apply when an unsuccessful attempt has been made to access the system or when a specific change has been detected in the system configuration.

To simplify the process of administrating security, it is common to assign users to groups, and then to assign groups to resources. This allows the access capability of users on a network to be changed easily by assigning or removing the user from various groups. This is useful when setting up temporary accounts for visiting workers or consultants, giving you the ability to limit access to resources.

To prevent unauthorized users from accessing local computers and network resources, lock your workstation, laptop, or server when you are not present.

Data Encryption

Encrypting data uses codes and ciphers. Traffic between resources and computers on the network can be protected from attackers monitoring or recording transactions by implementing encryption. It might not be possible to decipher captured data in time to make any use of it.

A VPN uses encryption to protect data. A VPN connection allows remote users to safely access resources as if their computer is physically attached to the local network.

Software Firewall

Data being transported on a network is called traffic. A software firewall is a program that runs on a computer to allow or deny traffic between the computer and the network to which it is connected. Every communication using TCP/IP is associated with a port number. HTTPS, for instance, uses port 443 by default. A software firewall, as shown in Figure 2, is capable of protecting a computer from intrusion through the ports. The user can control the type of data sent to a computer by selecting which ports will be open and which will be secured. You must create exceptions to allow certain traffic or applications to connect to the computer. Firewalls can block incoming and outgoing network connections unless exceptions are defined to open and close the ports required by a program.

Data Backups

Data backup procedures should be included in a security plan. Data can be lost or damaged in circumstances such as theft, equipment failure, or a disaster such as a fire or flood. Backing up data is one of the most effective ways of protecting against data loss. Here are some considerations for data backups:

- *Frequency of backups*– Backups can take a long time. Sometimes it is easier to make a full backup monthly or weekly, and then do frequent partial backups of any data that has changed since the last full backup. However, spreading the backups over many recordings increases the amount of time needed to restore the data.

- *Storage of backups*– Backups should be transported to an approved offsite storage location for extra security. The current backup media is transported to the offsite location on a daily, weekly, or monthly rotation, as required by the local organization.

- *Security of backups*– Backups can be protected with passwords. These passwords would have to be entered before the data on the backup media could be restored.

Smart Card Security

A smart card is a small plastic card, about the size of a credit card, with a small chip embedded in it. The chip is an intelligent data carrier, capable of processing, storing, and safeguarding thousands of bytes of data. Smart cards store private information such as bank account numbers, personal identification, medical records, and digital signatures. Smart cards provide authentication and encryption to keep data safe.

Biometric Security

Biometric security compares physical characteristics against stored profiles to authenticate people. A profile is a data file containing known characteristics of an individual such as a fingerprint or a handprint. In theory, biometric security is more secure than security measures such as passwords or smart cards, because passwords can be discovered and smart cards can be stolen. Common biometric devices available include fingerprint readers, handprint readers, iris scanners, and face recognition devices.

Figure 3 shows biometric devices and smart cards.

File System Security

All file systems keep track of resources, but only file systems with journals can log access by user, date, and time. A comparison of the two file systems is shown in Figure 4. The FAT32 file system, which is used in some versions of Windows, lacks both journaling and encryption capabilities. As a result, situations that require good security are usually deployed using a file system such as NTFS, which is part of Windows 2000 and Windows XP. If increased security is needed, it is possible to run certain utilities, such as CONVERT, to upgrade a FAT32 file system to NTFS. The conversion process is not reversible. It is important to clearly define your goals before making the transition.

Refer to
Figure
in online course

9.3.4 Describe wireless security techniques

Because traffic flows through radio waves in wireless networks, it is easy for attackers to monitor and attack data without having to physically connect to a network. Attackers gain access to a network by being within range of an unprotected wireless network. A technician needs to know how to configure access points and wireless NICs to an appropriate level of security.

When installing wireless services, you should apply wireless security techniques immediately to prevent unwanted access to the network, as shown in Figure 1. Wireless access points should be configured with basic security settings that are compatible with the existing network security. The following items are basic security settings that can be configured on a wireless router or access point:

- *Service Set Identifier (SSID)*– The name of the wireless network. A wireless router or access point broadcasts the SSID by default so that wireless devices can detect the wireless network.

Manually enter the SSID on wireless devices to connect to the wireless network when the SSID broadcast has been disabled on the wireless router or access point.

■ *MAC Address Filtering*– A technique used to deploy device-level security on a wireless LAN. Because every wireless device has a unique MAC address, wireless routers and access points can prevent wireless devices from connecting to the wireless network if the devices do not have authorized MAC addresses. Enable MAC address filtering, and list each wireless device MAC address to enforce MAC address filtering.

An attacker can access data as it travels over the radio signal. A wireless encryption system can be used to prevent unwanted capture and use of data by encoding the information that is sent. Both ends of every link must use the same encryption standard. The following items are wireless encryption and authentication technologies:

■ *Wired Equivalent Privacy (WEP)*– The first generation security standard for wireless. Attackers quickly discovered that WEP encryption was easy to break. The encryption keys used to encode the messages could be detected by monitoring programs. Once the keys were obtained, messages could be easily decoded.

■ *Wi-Fi Protected Access (WPA)*– An improved version of WEP. It was created as a temporary solution until the 802.11i (a security layer for wireless systems) was fully implemented. Now that 802.11i has been ratified, WPA2 has been released. It covers the entire 802.11i standard. WPA uses much stronger encryption than WEP encryption.

■ *Wi-Fi Protected Access 2 (WPA2)*– An improved version of WPA. This protocol was released to introduce higher levels of security than WPA. WPA2 supports robust encryption providing government grade security. WPA2 can be enabled in two versions: Personal (password authentication) and Enterprise (server authentication).

■ *Lightweight Extensible Authentication Protocol (LEAP), also called EAP-Cisco*– A wireless security protocol created by Cisco to address the weaknesses in WEP and WPA. LEAP is a good choice when using Cisco equipment in conjunction with operating systems like Windows and Linux.

Refer to
Figure
in online course

Wireless Transport Layer Security (WTLS) is a security layer used in mobile devices that employ the Wireless Applications Protocol (WAP). Mobile devices do not have a great deal of spare bandwidth to devote to security protocols. WTLS was designed to provide security for WAP devices in a bandwidth-efficient manner.

Refer to **Packet Tracer Activity** for this chapter

Connecting Wireless PCs to a Linksys WRT300N
Configure basic wireless settings on a PC.
Configure basic security on the Linksys WRT300N.
Verify full connectivity.

9.4 Identify common preventive maintenance techniques for security

Security strategies are constantly changing, as are the technologies used to secure equipment and data. New exploits are discovered daily. Attackers are constantly searching for new methods to use in an attack. Software manufacturers have to regularly create and issue new patches to fix flaws and vulnerabilities in products. If a computer is left unprotected by a technician, an attacker can easily gain access. Unprotected computers on the Internet can become infected within a few minutes.

Because of the constantly changing security threats, technicians should understand how to install patches and updates. They should also be able to recognize when new updates and patches are available. Some manufacturers release updates on the same day every month, but also send out critical updates when necessary. Other manufacturers provide automatic update services that patch the software every time the computer is turned on, or e-mail notifications when a new patch or update is released.

After completing this section, you will meet these objectives:

- Explain how to update signature files for anti-virus and anti-spyware software.

- Explain how to install operating system service packs and security patches.

Refer to **Figure** in online course

9.4.1   Explain how to update signature files for anti-virus and anti-spyware software

Threats to security from viruses and worms are always present. Attackers constantly look for new ways to infiltrate computers and networks. Because new viruses are always being developed, security software must be continually updated. This process can be performed automatically, but a technician should know how to manually update any type of protection software and all customer application programs.

Click on each step in the figure for more information.

Virus, spyware, and adware detection programs look for patterns in the programming code of the software in a computer. These patterns are determined by analyzing viruses that are intercepted on the Internet and on LANs. These code patterns are called signatures. The publishers of protection software compile the signatures into virus definition tables. To update signature files for anti-virus and spyware software, first check to see if the signature files are the most recent files. This can be done by navigating to the About option of the protection software, or by launching the update tool for the protection software. If the signature files are out of date, update them manually with the Update Now option on most protection software.

You should always retrieve the signature files from the manufacturer's website to make sure the update is authentic and not corrupted by viruses. This can put great demand on the manufacturer's website, especially when new viruses are released. To avoid creating too much traffic at a single website, some manufacturers distribute their signature files for download to multiple download sites. These download sites are called mirrors.

Caution
When downloading the signature files from a mirror, ensure that the mirror site is a legitimate site. Always link to the mirror site from the manufacturer's website.

Refer to **Figure** in online course

9.4.2   Explain how to install operating system service packs and security patches

Viruses and worms can be difficult to remove from a computer. Software tools are required to remove viruses and repair the computer code that the virus has modified. These software tools are provided by operating system manufacturers and security software companies. Make sure that you download these tools from a legitimate site.

Refer to **Figure** in online course

Patches are code updates that manufacturers provide to prevent a newly discovered virus or worm from making a successful attack. From time to time, manufacturers combine patches and upgrades into a comprehensive update application called a service pack. Many infamous and devastating virus attacks could have been much less severe if more users had downloaded and installed the latest service pack.

The Windows operating system routinely checks the Windows Update website for high-priority updates that can help protect a computer from the latest security threat. These updates can include security updates, critical updates, and service packs. Depending on the setting you choose, Windows automatically downloads and installs any high-priority updates that your computer needs, or notifies you as these updates become available.

Updates must be installed, not just downloaded. If you use the Automatic setting, you can schedule the time and day. Otherwise, new updates are installed at 3 a.m. by default. If your computer is turned off during a scheduled update, updates are installed the next time you start your computer. You can also choose to have Windows notify you when a new update is available and install the update yourself.

Follow the steps in Figure 1 to update the operating system with a service pack or security patch.

Refer to
Worksheet
for this chapter

Operating System Updates
Print and complete this worksheet.

9.5 Troubleshoot security

The troubleshooting process is used to help resolve security issues. These problems range from simple, such as preventing someone from watching over your shoulder, to more complex problems, such as manually removing infected files. Use the troubleshooting steps as a guideline to help you diagnose and repair problems.

After completing this section, you will meet these objectives:

- Review the troubleshooting process.

- Identify common problems and solutions.

Refer to
Figure
in online course

9.5.1 Review the troubleshooting process

Computer technicians must be able to analyze a security threat and determine the appropriate method to protect assets and repair damage. This process is called troubleshooting.

The first step in the troubleshooting process is to identify the problem. Figure 1 is a list of open-ended and closed-ended questions to ask the customer.

After you have talked to the customer, you can establish a theory of probable causes. Figure 2 is a list of some common probable causes for security problems.

After you have developed some theories about what is wrong, test your theories to determine the cause of the problem. Figure 3 is a list of quick procedures that can determine the exact cause of the problem or even correct the problem. If a quick procedure does correct the problem, you can go to step 5 to verify full system functionality. If a quick procedure does not correct the problem, you might need to research the problem further to establish the exact cause.

After you have determined the exact cause of the problem, establish a plan of action to resolve the problem and implement the solution. Figure 4 shows sources of information to gather additional information to resolve an issue.

After you have corrected the problem, verify full functionality and, if applicable, implement preventive measures. Figure 5 is a list of the steps to verify the solution.

In the final step of the troubleshooting process, you must document your findings, actions, and outcomes. Figure 6 is a list of the tasks required to document the problem and the solution.

Refer to
Figure
in online course

9.5.2 Identify common problems and solutions

Computer problems can be attributed to hardware, software, connectivity issues, or some combination of the three. You will resolve some types of computer problems more often than others. Figure 1 is a chart of common security problems and solutions.

Refer to
Figure
in online course

The worksheet is designed to reinforce your communication skills to verify information from the customer.

Refer to
Worksheet
for this chapter

Gather Information from the Customer
Print and complete this worksheet.

Summary

This chapter discussed computer security and why it is important to protect computer equipment, networks, and data. Threats, procedures, and preventive maintenance relating to data and physical security were described to help you keep computer equipment and data safe. Security protects computers, network equipment, and data from loss and physical danger. The following are some of the important concepts to remember from this chapter:

- Security threats can come from inside or outside of an organization.
- Viruses and worms are common threats that attack data.
- Develop and maintain a security plan to protect both data and physical equipment from loss.
- Keep operating systems and applications up to date and secure with patches and service packs.

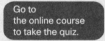
Go to the online course to take the quiz.

Chapter 9 Quiz

Take the chapter quiz to test your knowledge.

Your Chapter Notes

Communication Skills

Introduction

What is the relationship between communication skills and troubleshooting? As a computer technician, you will not only fix computers but will also interact with people. In fact, troubleshooting is as much about communicating with the customer as it is about knowing how to fix a computer. In this chapter, you will learn to use good communication skills as confidently as you use a screwdriver.

After completing this chapter, you will meet these objectives:

- Explain the relationship between communication and troubleshooting.
- Describe good communication skills and professional behavior.
- Explain ethics and legal aspects of working with computer technology.
- Describe the call center environment and technician responsibilities.

10.1 Explain the relationship between communication and troubleshooting

Refer to **Figure** in online course

Think of a time when you had to call a repair person to get something fixed. Did it feel like an emergency to you? Did you appreciate it when the repair person was sympathetic and responsive? Perhaps you had a bad experience with a repair person. Are you likely to call that same person to fix a problem again?

Refer to **Figure** in online course

Good communication skills enhance a technician's troubleshooting skills. Both of these skill sets take time and experience to develop well. As your hardware, software, and OS knowledge increases, your ability to quickly determine a problem and find a solution will improve. The same principle applies to developing communication skills. The more you practice good communication skills, the more effective you will become when working with customers. A knowledgeable technician who uses good communication skills will always be in demand in the job market.

To troubleshoot a computer, you need to learn the details of the problem from the customer. Most people who need a computer problem fixed are probably feeling some stress. If you establish a good rapport with the customer, the customer might relax a bit. A relaxed customer is more likely to be able to provide the information that you need to determine the source of the problem and then fix it.

Speaking directly with the customer is usually the first step in resolving the computer problem. As a technician, you also have access to several communication and research tools. All of these resources can be used to help gather information for the troubleshooting process.

Refer to **Worksheet** for this chapter

Technician Resources

Print and complete this worksheet.

10.2 Describe good communication skills and professional behavior

Whether you are talking with a customer on the phone or in person, it is important to communicate well and to represent yourself professionally. Your professionalism and good communication skills enhance your creditability with the customer.

Your body language can be seen by your customer. A customer can hear your sighs and sense that you are sneering, even over the phone. Conversely, customers can also sense that you are smiling when you are speaking with them on the phone. Many call-center technicians use a mirror at their desk to monitor their facial expressions.

Successful technicians control their own reactions and emotions from one customer call to the next. A good rule for all technicians to follow is that a new customer call means a fresh start. Never carry your frustration from one call to the next.

After completing this section, you will meet these objectives:

- Determine the computer problem of the customer.
- Display professional behavior with the customer.
- Focus the customer on the problem during the call.
- Use proper Netiquette.
- Implement time and stress management techniques.
- Observe Service Level Agreements (SLAs).
- Follow business policies.

Refer to
Figure
in online course

10.2.1 Determine the computer problem of the customer

One of the first tasks of the technician is to determine the type of computer problem that the customer is experiencing.

Remember these three rules at the beginning of your conversation:

- *Know–* Call your customer by name.
- *Relate–* Use brief communication to create a one-to-one connection between you and your customer.
- *Understand–* Determine the customer's level of knowledge about the computer to know how to effectively communicate with the customer.

To accomplish this, practice active listening skills. Allow the customer to tell the whole story. During the time that the customer is explaining the problem, occasionally interject some small word or phrase, such as "I understand", "Yes", "I see", or "Okay". This behavior lets the customer know that you are there and that you are listening.

However, a technician should not interrupt the customer to ask a question or make a statement. This is rude, disrespectful, and creates tension. Many times in a conversation, you might find yourself thinking of what to say before the other person finishes talking. When you do this, you are not really listening. Instead, try listening carefully when other people speak, and let them finish their thoughts.

After you have listened to the customer explain the whole problem, clarify what the customer has said. This helps convince the customer that you have heard and understand the situation. A good practice for clarification is to paraphrase the customer's explanation by beginning with the words "Let me see if I understand what you have told me...". This is a very effective tool that shows the customer that you have listened and that you are concerned with the issues.

After you have assured the customer that you understand the problem, you will probably have to ask some follow-up questions. Make sure that these questions are pertinent. Do not ask questions that the customer has already answered while describing the problem. Doing this only irritates the customer and shows that you were not listening.

Follow-up questions should be targeted, closed-ended questions based on the information that you have already gathered. Closed-ended questions should focus on obtaining specific information. The customer should be able to answer with a simple "yes" or "no" or with a factual response such as, "Windows XP Pro". Use all of the information that you have gathered from the customer to continue filling out the work order.

Refer to **Figure** in online course

10.2.2 Display professional behavior with the customer

When dealing with customers, it is necessary to be professional in all aspects of your role. You must handle customers with respect and prompt attention. When on a telephone, make sure that you know how to place a customer on hold, as well as how to transfer a customer without losing the call. It is important how you conduct the call, and your job is to help the customer focus on and communicate the problem so that you can solve it.

Refer to **Figure** in online course

Be positive when communicating with the customer. Tell the customer what you can do. Do not focus on what you cannot do. Be prepared to explain alternative ways that you can help them, such as e-mailing information, faxing step-by-step instructions, or using remote control software to solve the problem. Customers will quickly sense whether you are interested in helping them.

Figure 1 outlines the process to follow before you put a customer on hold. First, let the customer finish speaking. Then, explain that you have to put the customer on hold, and ask the customer for permission to do so. When the customer agrees to be put on hold, thank the customer. Tell your customer that you will be away only a few minutes and explain what you will be doing during that time.

Figure 2 outlines the process for transferring a call. Follow the same process for a call transfer as you would when placing a customer on hold. Let the customer finish talking and then explain that you have to transfer the call. When the customer agrees to be transferred, tell the customer the phone number that you are transferring the customer to. You should also tell the new technician your name, the name of the customer that you are transferring, and the related ticket number.

When dealing with customers, it is sometimes easier to explain what you should not do. Observe the following list of things that you should not do when communicating with a customer:

- Avoid minimizing customer problems.
- Avoid using jargon, abbreviations, acronyms, and slang.
- Avoid a negative attitude or tone of voice.
- Avoid arguing with customers or becoming defensive.
- Avoid culturally insensitive remarks.
- Avoid being judgmental, insulting, or calling the customer names.
- Avoid distractions or interruptions when talking with customers.
- Avoid taking personal calls when talking with customers.
- Avoid talking to co-workers about unrelated subjects when talking with the customer.

- Avoid unnecessary holds and abrupt holds.

- Avoid transfers without explaining the purpose of the transfer and getting customer consent.

- Avoid negative remarks about other technicians to the customer.

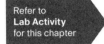

Class Discussion
Demonstrate or discuss positive ways to say negative things.

10.2.3 Focus the customer on the problem during the call

Part of your job is to focus the customer during the phone call. When you focus the customer on the problem, it allows you to control the call. This makes the best use of your time and the customer's time on troubleshooting the problem. Do not take any comments personally, and do not retaliate with any comments or criticism. If you stay calm with the customer, finding a solution to the problem will remain the focal point of the call.

Just as there are many different computer problems, there are many different types of customers, as shown in Figure 1. The list of problem-customer types below is not comprehensive and often a customer can display a combination of traits. Try to recognize which traits your customer exhibits. Recognizing these traits can help you manage the call accordingly.

Talkative Customer

A talkative customer discusses everything except the problem on the call. The customer often uses the call as an opportunity to socialize. It can be difficult to get a talkative customer to focus on the problem.

Rude Customer

A rude customer complains during the call and often makes negative comments about the product, the service, and the technician. This type of customer is sometimes abusive and uncooperative and gets aggravated very easily.

Angry Customer

An angry customer talks loudly during the call and often tries to speak when the technician is talking. Angry customers are usually frustrated that they have a problem and upset that they have to call somebody to fix it.

Knowledgeable Customer

A knowledgeable customer wants to speak with a technician that is equally experienced in computers. This type of customer usually tries to control the call and does not want to speak with a level-one technician.

Inexperienced Customer

An inexperienced customer has difficulty describing the problem. These customers are usually not able to follow directions correctly and not able to communicate the errors that they encounter.

Refer to
Lab Activity
for this chapter

Class Discussion
Identify and discuss managing difficult customers.

Refer to
Figure
in online course

10.2.4 Use proper netiquette

Have you read a blog where two or three members have stopped discussing the issue and are simply insulting each other? These are called "flame wars" and they occur in blogs and e-mail threads. Have you ever wondered if they would actually say those things to each other in person? Perhaps you have received an e-mail that had no greeting or was written entirely in capital letters. How did this make you feel while you were reading it?

As a technician, you should be professional in all communications with customers. For e-mail and text communications, there is a set of personal and business etiquette rules called Netiquette.

In addition to the e-mail and text Netiquette, there are general rules that apply to all of your online interactions with customers and coworkers:

- Remember that you are dealing with people.
- Adhere to the same standards of behavior that you follow in real life.
- Know where you are in cyberspace.
- Respect other people's time and bandwidth.
- Share expert knowledge.
- Do not engage in "flame wars" online.
- Respect other people's privacy.
- Be forgiving of other people's mistakes.

The list above is not comprehensive. What other general rules about online communications can you think of?

Refer to
Figure
in online course

10.2.5 Implement time and stress management techniques

As a technician, you are a very busy person. It is important for your own well-being to use proper time and stress management techniques.

Workstation Ergonomics

The ergonomics of your work area can help you do your job or make it more difficult. Because you spend a major portion of your day at your workstation, make sure that the desk layout works well, as shown in Figure 1. Have your headset and phone in a position that is both easy to reach and easy to use. Your chair should be adjusted to a height that is comfortable. Adjust your computer screen to a comfortable angle so that you do not have to tilt your head up or down to see it. Make sure your keyboard and mouse are also in a position that is comfortable for you. You should not have to bend your wrist to type. If possible, try to minimize external distractions such as noise.

Time Management

For time management, it is important to prioritize your activities. Make sure that you carefully follow the business policy of your company. The company policy might state that you must take "down" calls first, even though they might be harder to solve. A "down" call usually means that a server is not working and the entire office or company is waiting for the problem to be resolved to resume business.

If you have to call back a customer, make sure that you do it as close to the callback time as possible. Keep a list of callback customers and check them off one at a time as you complete these calls. Doing this ensures that you do not forget a customer.

When working with many customers, do not give favorite customers faster or better service. When reviewing the call boards, do not take only the easy customer calls. See Figure 2 for a sample customer call board. Do not take the call of another technician, unless you have permission to do so.

Stress Management

For stress management, take a moment to compose yourself between customer calls. Every call should be independent of each other, and you should not carry any frustrations from one call to the next.

You might have to do some physical activity to relieve stress. You should stand up and take a short walk. Do a few simple stretch movements or squeeze a tension ball. Take a break if you can, and try to relax. You will then be ready to answer the next customer call effectively.

Figure 3 shows ways to relax. Can you think of any other appropriate activities that might relieve stress at work?

Refer to **Figure** in online course

10.2.6 Observe Service Level Agreements

When dealing with customers, it is important to adhere to that customer's SLA. An SLA is a contract that defines expectations between an organization and the service vendor to provide an agreed upon level of support. As an employee of the service company, your job is to honor the SLA that you have with the customer. Take a closer look at some of the standard sections found in an SLA by moving over the circles in Figure 1.

An SLA is typically a legal agreement that contains the responsibilities and liabilities of all parties involved. Some of the contents of an SLA usually include the following:

- Response time guarantees (often based on type of call and level of service agreement)
- Equipment and software that is supported
- Where service is provided
- Preventive maintenance
- Diagnostics
- Part availability (equivalent parts)
- Cost and penalties
- Time of service availability (for example, 24x7; Monday to Friday, 8 a.m. to 5 p.m. EST; and so on)

There might be exceptions to the SLA. Make sure to follow your company business rules in detail. Some of the exceptions might include the ability of the customer to upgrade the level of service, or to escalate to management for review. Escalation to management should be reserved for special situations. For example, a long-standing customer or a customer from a very large company might have a problem that falls outside the parameters stated in their SLA. In these cases, your management might choose to support the customer for customer-relation reasons.

Can you think of any other circumstances in which it might be a good idea to escalate a call to management?

Refer to **Figure** in online course

10.2.7 Follow business policies

As a technician, you should be aware of all business policies related to customer calls. You would not want to make a promise to a customer that you cannot keep. You should also have a good understanding of all rules governing employees.

Customer Call Rules

The following rules are examples of the specific rules a call center might have to handle customer calls:

- Maximum time on call (example: 15 minutes)
- Maximum call time in queue (example: three minutes)
- Number of calls per day (example: minimum of 30)
- Passing calls on to other technicians (example: only when absolutely necessary and not without that technician's permission)
- What you can and cannot promise to the customer (see that customer's SLA for details)
- When to follow SLA and when to escalate to management

Call Center Employee Rules

There are also other rules to cover general daily activities of employees:

- Arrive at your workstation on time and early enough to become prepared, usually about 15 to 20 minutes before the first call.
- Do not exceed the allowed number and length of breaks.
- Do not take a break or go to lunch if there is a call on the board.
- Do not take a break or go to lunch at the same time as other technicians (stagger breaks among technicians).
- Do not leave an ongoing call to take a break, go to lunch, or go to a personal appointment.
- Make sure that another technician is available if you have to leave.
- Contact the customer if you are going to be late for an appointment.
- If no other technician is available, check with the customer to see if you can call back later, possibly in the morning.
- Do not show favoritism to certain customers.
- Do not take another technician's calls without permission.
- Do not talk negatively about the capabilities of another technician.

Customer Satisfaction

The following rules should be followed by all employees to ensure customer satisfaction:

- Set and meet a reasonable timeline for the call or appointment and communicate this to the customer.

- Communicate service expectations to the customer as early as possible.

- Communicate the repair status with the customer, including explanations for any delays.

- Offer different repair or replacement options to the customer, if applicable.

- Give the customer proper documentation on all services provided.

- Follow up with the customer at a later date to verify satisfaction.

Refer to
Figure
in online course

10.3 Explain ethics and legal aspects of working with computer technology

When you are working with customers and their equipment, there are some general ethical customs and legal rules that you should observe. Often, these customs and rules overlap.

Ethical Customs

You should always have respect for your customers, as well as for their property. Property includes any information or data that might be accessible. Such information or data includes any of the following items:

- E-mails

- Phone lists

- Records or data on the computer

- Hard copies of files, information, or data left on desk

Before accessing a computer account, including the administrator account, you should get the permission of the customer. From the troubleshooting process, you might have gathered some private information, such as usernames and passwords. If you document this type of private information, you must keep it confidential. Divulging any customer information to anyone else is not only unethical, but might be illegal. Legal details of customer information are usually covered under the SLA.

Do not send unsolicited messages to a customer. Do not send unsolicited mass mailings or chain letters to customers. Never send forged or anonymous e-mails. All of these activities are considered unethical and, in certain circumstances, might be considered illegal.

Legal Rules

Several computer-related activities are not only unethical but are illegal. Be aware that this is not an exhaustive list:

Refer to
Figure
in online course

- Do not make any changes to system software or hardware configurations without customer permission.

- Do not access a customer's or co-worker's accounts, private files, or e-mail messages without permission.

- Do not install, copy, or share digital content (including software, music, text, images, and video) in violation of copyright and software agreements or applicable federal and state law.

- Do not use a customer's company IT resources for commercial purposes.

- Do not make a customer's IT resources available to unauthorized users.

- Keep sensitive customer information confidential.

- Do not knowingly use a customer's company resources for illegal activities. Criminal or illegal use includes obscenity, child pornography, threats, harassment, copyright infringement, university trademark infringement, defamation, theft, identity theft, and unauthorized access.

Do you know the copyright and trademark laws in your state or country?

Class Discussion

Discuss privacy issues.

> Refer to
> **Lab Activity**
> for this chapter

10.4 Describe call center environment and technician responsibilities

A call center environment is usually very professional and fast-paced. It is a help desk system where customers call in and are placed on a callboard. Available technicians take the customer calls. A technician must supply the level of support that is outlined in the customer's SLA.

After completing this section, you will meet these objectives:

- Describe the call center environment.

- Describe level-one technician responsibilities.

- Describe level-two technician responsibilities.

> Refer to
> **Figure**
> in online course

10.4.1 Describe the call center environment

A call center might exist within a company and offer service to the employees of that company as well as to the customers of that company's products. Alternatively, a call center might be an independent business that sells computer support as a service to outside customers. In either case, a call center is a busy, fast-paced work environment, often operating 24 hours a day.

Call centers tend to have a large number of cubicles. As shown in Figure 1, each cubicle has a chair, at least one computer, a phone, and a headset. The technicians working at these cubicles have varied levels of experience in computers, and some have specialties in certain types of computers, software, or operating systems.

All of the computers in a call center have help desk software. The technicians use this software to manage many of their job functions. Figure 2 shows some of the features of help desk software.

Your call center will have its own business policies regarding call priority. Figure 3 provides a sample chart of how calls can be named, defined, and prioritized.

> Refer to
> **Figure**
> in online course

10.4.2 Describe level-one technician responsibilities

Call centers sometimes have different names for level-one technicians. These technicians might be known as level-one analysts, dispatchers, or incident screeners. Regardless of the title, the level-one technician's responsibilities are fairly similar from one call center to the next.

The primary responsibility of a level-one technician is to gather pertinent information from the customer. The technician has to document all information in the ticket or work order. The information that the level-one technician must obtain is shown in Figure 1.

Some problems are very simple to resolve, and a level-one technician can usually take care of these without escalating the work order to a level-two technician.

Often, a problem requires the expertise of a level-two technician. In these cases, the level-one technician must be able to translate a customer's problem description into a succinct sentence or two that is entered into the work order. This translation is important so that other technicians can quickly understand the situation without having to ask the customer the same questions again. Figure 2 shows how a customer might describe some of the most common problems and how a technician should document those problems.

Refer to
Figure
in online course

10.4.3 Describe level-two technician responsibilities

As with level-one technicians, call centers sometimes have different names for level-two technicians. These technicians might be known as product specialists or technical-support personnel. The level-two technician's responsibilities are generally the same from one call center to the next.

The level-two technician is usually more knowledgeable than the level-one technician about technology, or has been working for the company for a longer period of time. When a problem cannot be resolved within ten minutes, the level-one technician prepares an escalated work order, as shown in Figure 1. The level-two technician receives the escalated work order with the description of the problem. They then call the customer back to ask any additional questions and resolve the problem.

The following list of guidelines details when to escalate a problem to a more experienced technician. These are generic guidelines. You should follow your company's business policy for problem escalation.

- Escalate problems that require opening the computer case.

- Escalate problems that require installation of applications, operating systems, or drivers.

- Escalate problems that will take a long time to walk a customer through - like CMOS changes.

- Escalate down calls. The entire network is down, and a more experienced technician might be able to resolve the issue faster.

Refer to
Figure
in online course

Problems that require opening up the computer needs a level-two technician. Level-two technicians can also use remote diagnostic software to connect to the customer's computer to update drivers and software, access the operating system, check the BIOS, and gather other diagnostic information to solve the problem.

Summary

In this chapter, you learned about the relationship between communication skills and troubleshooting skills. You have learned that these two skills need to be combined to make you a successful technician. You also learned about the legal aspects and ethics of dealing with computer technology and the property of the customer.

The following concepts from this chapter are important to remember:

- To be a successful technician, you must practice good communication skills with customers and co-workers. These skills are as important as technical expertise.

- You should always conduct yourself in a professional manner with your customers and co-workers. Professional behavior increases customer confidence and enhances your credibility. You should also learn to recognize the classic signs of a difficult customer and learn what to do and what not to do when you are on a call with this customer.

- There are a few techniques that you can use to keep a difficult customer focused on the problem during a call. Primarily, you must remain calm and ask pertinent questions in an appropriate fashion. These techniques keep you in control of the call.

- There is a right way and a wrong way to put a customer on hold, or transfer a customer to another technician. Learn and use the right way every time. Doing either of these operations incorrectly can cause serious damage to your company's relationship with its customers.

- Netiquette is a list of rules to use whenever you communicate through e-mail, text messaging, instant messaging, or blogs. This is another area where doing things the wrong way can cause damage to your company's relationship with its customers.

- You must understand and comply with your customer's SLA. If the problem falls outside the parameters of the SLA, you need to find positive ways of telling the customer what you can do to help, and not what you cannot do. In special circumstances, you might decide to escalate the work order to management.

- In addition to the SLA, you must follow the business policies of the company. These policies include how your company prioritizes calls, how and when to escalate a call to management, and when you are allowed to take breaks and lunch.

- A computer technician's job is stressful. You rarely meet a customer who is having a good day. You can alleviate some of the stress by setting up your workstation in the most ergonomically beneficial way possible. You should practice time and stress management techniques every day.

- There are ethical and legal aspects of working in computer technology. You should be aware of your company's policies and practices. In addition, you might need to familiarize yourself with your state or country's trademark and copyright laws.

- The call center is a fast-paced environment. Level-one technicians and level-two technicians each have specific responsibilities. These responsibilities might vary slightly from one call center to another.

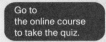
Go to
the online course
to take the quiz.

Chapter 10 Quiz

Take the chapter quiz to test your knowledge.

Your Chapter Notes

Advanced Personal Computers

Introduction

In your career as a technician, you may have to determine if a component for a customer's computer should be upgraded or replaced. It is important that you develop advanced skills in installation procedures, troubleshooting techniques, and diagnostic methods for computers. This chapter discusses the importance of component compatibility across hardware and software. It also covers the need for adequate system resources to efficiently run the customer's hardware and software.

After completing this chapter, you will meet these objectives:

- Give an overview of field, remote, and bench technician jobs.
- Explain safe lab procedures and tool use.
- Describe situations requiring replacement of computer components.
- Upgrade and configure personal computer components and peripherals.
- Identify and apply common preventive maintenance techniques for personal computer components.
- Troubleshoot computer components and peripherals.

Refer to
Figure
in online course

11.1 Give an overview of field, remote, and bench technician jobs

Your experience working with computers and earning a technical certification can help you become qualified for employment as any of the following:

Refer to
Figure
in online course

- Field technician
- Remote technician
- Bench technician

Technicians in different computer careers work in different environments. The skills required by each career can be very similar. The degree to which different skills are needed vary from one job to the next. When you train to become a computer technician, you are expected to develop the following skills:

- Building and upgrading computers
- Performing installations
- Installing, configuring, and optimizing software
- Performing preventive maintenance
- Troubleshooting and repairing computers
- Communicating clearly with the customer

- Documenting customer feedback and the steps involved in finding the solution to a problem

Field technicians, shown in Figure 1, work in various conditions and businesses. You might work for one company and only repair that company's assets. Alternatively, you may work for a company that provides onsite computer equipment repair for a variety of companies and customers. In either of these situations, you need both excellent troubleshooting skills and customer service skills, because you are in regular contact with customers and work on a wide variety of hardware and software.

If you are a remote technician, you might work at a help desk answering calls or e-mails from customers who have computer problems, as shown in Figure 2. You create work orders and communicate with the customer to try to diagnose and repair the problem.

Good communication skills are valuable because the customer must clearly understand your questions and instructions. Some help desks use software to connect directly to a customer's computer to fix the problem. As a remote technician, you may work on a team of help desk technicians for an organization or from home.

As a bench technician, you typically would not work directly with customers. Bench technicians are often hired to perform computer warranty service in a central depot or work facility, as shown in Figure 3.

Refer to Worksheet for this chapter

Job Opportunities
Gather information for jobs in the computer service and repair field.

11.2   Explain safe lab procedures and tool use

Safety should always be your priority on a job or in the lab. As a computer technician, you should be aware of the many workplace hazards, and you should take the necessary precautions to avoid them.

Practice safety in the lab so that it becomes part of your regular routine. Follow all safety procedures and use the correct tools for the job. This policy will help prevent personal injury and damage to equipment.

To accomplish a safe working environment, it is better to be proactive rather than reactive. Figure 1 gives a list of safety rules to help you maintain a safe working environment.

After completing this section, you will meet these objectives:

- Review safe working environments and procedures.

- Review names, purposes, characteristics, and safe and appropriate use of tools.

- Identify potential safety hazards and implement proper safety procedures for computer components.

- Describe environmental issues.

Refer to Figure in online course

11.2.1   Review safe working environments and procedures

Workplace safety is necessary to ensure that you, and everyone near you, stay unharmed. In any situation, you should always follow these basic rules:

- Use antistatic mats and pads to reduce the chance of ESD damaging your equipment.

- Store hazardous or toxic materials in a secured cabinet.

- Keep the floor clear of anything that might trip someone.

- Clean work areas on a regular basis.

You should use caution when you move computer equipment from one place to another. Make sure that customers follow the safety rules in your work area. You may need to explain these rules and assure customers that the rules are there to protect them.

Follow local codes and government rules whenever you dispose of such things as batteries, solvents, computers, and monitors. Failing to do so may result in a fine. Many countries have agencies to enforce safety standards and ensure safe working conditions for employees. What are some of the documents that describe work safety codes and standards in your country?

Refer to **Figure** in online course

11.2.2 Review names, purposes, characteristics, and safe and appropriate use of tools

A computer technician needs proper tools to work safely and prevent damage to the computer equipment. As shown in Figure 1, a technician uses many tools to diagnose and repair computer problems:

- Straight-head screwdriver, large and small

- Phillips-head screwdriver, large and small

- Tweezers or part retriever

- Needle-nosed pliers

- Wire cutters

- Chip extractor

- Hex wrench set

- Torx screwdriver

- Nut driver, large and small

- Three-claw component holder

- Digital multimeter

- Wrap plugs

- Small mirror

- Small dust brush

- Soft, lint-free cloth

- Cable ties

- Scissors

- Small flashlight

- Electrical tape

- Pencil or pen

- Compressed air

Various specialty tools, such as Torx bits, antistatic bags and gloves, and integrated circuit pullers, can be used to repair and maintain computers. Always avoid magnetized tools, such as screwdrivers with magnetic heads, or tools that use extension magnets to retrieve small metal objects that are out of reach. Using magnetic tools can cause loss of data on hard drives and floppy disks. Magnetic tools can also induce current, which can damage internal computer components. Additionally, there are specialized testing devices used to diagnose computer and cable problems:

- *Multimeter–* A device that measures AC/DC voltage, electric current, and other cable and electrical characteristics, as shown in Figure 2.

- *Power supply tester–* A device that checks whether the computer power supply is working properly. A simple power supply tester might just have indicator lights, while more advanced versions show the amount of voltage and amperage.

- *Cable tester–* A device that checks for wiring shorts or faults, such as wires connected to the wrong pin.

- *Loopback plug–* A device that connects to a computer, hub, switch, or router port to perform a diagnostic procedure called a loopback test. In a loopback test, a signal is transmitted through a circuit and then returned to the sending device to test the integrity of the data transmission.

ESD is one of the biggest concerns for computer technicians when working in many environments. The tools you use and even your own body can store thousands of volts of electricity. Walking across a carpet or a rug and touching a computer component before grounding yourself can severely damage the component.

Antistatic devices help control static electricity. Use antistatic devices to prevent damage to sensitive components. Before you touch a computer component, be sure to ground yourself by touching a grounded computer chassis or mat. These are some antistatic devices:

- *Antistatic wrist strap–* A device that keeps the technician and the computer at the same potential (level of electric charge) to prevent electrostatic discharge from damaging components.

- *Antistatic mat–* A device that grounds the computer frame.

- *Antistatic bag–* A device that keeps sensitive computer components safe when not installed inside a computer.

- *Cleaning products–* Products that maintain components without creating a buildup of static electricity.

Refer to
Figure
in online course

Caution

Do not wear an antistatic wrist strap when working with high-voltage circuits, such as those found in monitors and printers. Do not open monitors unless you are properly trained.

Refer to
Lab Activity
for this chapter

Using a Multimeter and a Power Supply Tester
Learn how to use and handle a multimeter and a power supply tester.

Refer to
Lab Activity
for this chapter

Testing UTP Cables using a Loopback Plug and a Cable Meter
Use a loopback plug and a cable meter to test an Ethernet cable.

11.2.3 Identify potential safety hazards and implement proper safety procedures for computer components

Most internal computer components use low-voltage electricity. Some components, however, operate with high voltage and can be dangerous if you do not follow safety precautions. The following dangerous, high-voltage computer components should only be serviced by authorized personnel:

- Power supplies
- Display monitors
- Laser printers

Power Supplies

The cost to repair a power supply can sometimes equal the cost of a new power supply. For this reason, most broken or used power supplies are replaced. Only experienced certified technicians should service power supplies.

Display Monitors

The internal electronic parts of a display monitor cannot be repaired, but they can be replaced. Monitors, especially CRT monitors, operate using high voltages. Only a certified electronic technician should service them.

Laser Printers

Laser printers can be very expensive. It is more cost effective to fix broken printers by repairing or replacing broken parts. Laser printers use high voltages and may have very hot surfaces inside. Use caution when servicing laser printers.

Refer to **Figure** in online course

11.2.4 Describe environmental issues

The hazardous materials found in computer components must be disposed of in specific ways so that they do not pollute the environment. A computer recycling warehouse is a place where discarded computer equipment can be taken apart. Computer parts that are still usable can be recycled for repairing other equipment. Figure 1 shows a computer recycling warehouse.

Recycling warehouses must obey the codes and regulations for the disposal of each type of computer part. Before parts are recycled, they are separated into groups. CRT monitors contain as much as 4 to 5 lbs (1.6 to 2.3 kg) of lead, a dangerous element. Much of the lead is inside cathode ray tubes. Other materials inside computer equipment are also dangerous:

- Mercury
- Cadmium
- Hexavalent chromium

Batteries are used to power laptop computers, digital cameras, camcorders, and remote-control toys. Batteries may contain some of these toxic materials:

- Nickel cadmium (Ni-Cd)

- Nickel metal hydride (Ni-MH)

- Lithium ion (Li-ion)

- Lead (Pb)

Discarding Components

Many organizations have policies that define disposal methods for the hazardous components found in electronic equipment. These methods typically include programs to reuse, recycle, or exchange.

You may need to dispose of computer components because they have become outdated, or you may need additional functionality. In addition to recycling parts, you can donate them to other people or organizations. Some businesses exchange used computer equipment for partial payment of new equipment.

Refer to
Figure
in online course

11.3 Describe situations requiring replacement of computer components

Situations that require the replacement of computer components include the repair of broken parts or an upgrade for functionality.

After completing this section, you will meet these objectives:

- Select a case and power supply.

- Select a motherboard.

- Select a CPU and cooling system.

- Select RAM.

- Select adapter cards.

- Select storage devices and hard drives.

- Select input and output devices.

Refer to
Figure
in online course

11.3.1 Select a case and power supply

You should determine the customer's needs before making any purchases or performing upgrades. Ask your customer what devices will be connected to the computer both internally and externally. The computer case must be able to accommodate the size and shape of the power supply.

The computer case holds the power supply, motherboard, memory, and other components. When purchasing a new computer case and power supply separately, you should ensure that all of the components will fit into the new case and that the power supply is powerful enough to operate all of the components. Many times a case comes with a power supply inside. You still need to verify that the power supply provides enough power to operate all the components that will be installed in the case.

Power supplies convert AC input to DC output voltages. Power supplies typically provide voltages of 3.3, 5, and 12 V, and are measured in wattage. It is recommended that the power supply has approximately 25 percent more wattage than all the attached components require. Determine the total wattage required by adding together the wattage for each component in the computer. If the wattage is not listed on a component, calculate it by multiplying the voltage and amperage of the component. If the component requires different levels of wattage, use the higher required wattage.

After determining the wattage required for the power supply, ensure that the power supply has the required connectors for all of the components.

Refer to
Figure
in online course

11.3.2 Select a motherboard

New motherboards often have new features or standards that may be incompatible with older components. When you select a replacement motherboard, make sure that it supports the CPU, RAM, video adapter, and other adapter cards. The socket and chipset on the motherboard must be compatible with the CPU. The motherboard must also accommodate the existing heat sink/fan assembly. Pay particular attention to the number and type of expansion slots. Do they match the existing adapter cards? The existing power supply must have connections that fit the new motherboard. Finally, the new motherboard must physically fit into the current computer case.

Different motherboards use different chipsets. A chipset consists of integrated circuits, which allows the CPU to communicate and interact with the other components of the computer. The chipset establishes how much memory can be added to a motherboard and the type of connectors on the motherboard. When building a computer, choose a chipset that provides the capabilities that you need. For example, you can purchase a motherboard with a chipset that enables multiple USB ports, eSATA connections, surround sound, or basic video.

Motherboards have different types of CPU sockets and CPU slots that are determined by the chipset. This socket or slot provides the connection point and the electrical interface for the CPU. The CPU package must match the motherboard socket type or CPU slot type. A CPU package contains the CPU, connection points, and materials that surround the CPU and dissipate heat.

Data travels from one part of a computer to another through a collection of wires known as the bus. The bus has two parts. The data portion of the bus, known as the data bus, carries data between components of a computer. The address portion of the bus, known as the address bus, carries the memory addresses of the locations where data is read or written by the CPU.

The bus size refers to the width of the bus. The bus size determines how much data can be transmitted at one time. A 32-bit bus transmits 32 bits of data at one time from the processor to RAM or to other motherboard components, while a 64-bit bus transmits 64 bits of data at one time. The speed at which data travels through the bus is determined by the clock speed, measured in MHz.

PCI expansion slots connect to a parallel bus, which sends multiple bits over multiple wires simultaneously. PCI expansion slots are being replaced with PCIe expansion slots that connect to a serial bus, which sends one bit at a time at a faster rate. When building a computer, choose a motherboard that has slots to meet your current and future needs. For example, if you are building a computer for advanced gaming that needs dual graphics cards, you might choose a motherboard with dual PCIe slots.

Motherboards have expansion slots, which provide a connection point on the motherboard where a circuit board can be attached to add new capabilities to the computer. Expansion slots are used to add a variety of capabilities, such as video adapters, TV tuner cards, video capture cards, and NICs.

Refer to
Figure
in online course

11.3.3 Select the CPU and heat sink/fan assembly

Replace the CPU when it fails or is no longer adequate for the current applications. For example, you may have a customer who has purchased an advanced graphics application, as shown in Figure 1. The application might run poorly because it requires a faster processor than the current CPU.

Before you buy a CPU, make sure that it is compatible with the existing motherboard:

- The new CPU must use the same socket type or slot type and chip set.

- The BIOS must support the new CPU.

- The new CPU may require a different heat sink/fan assembly.

Manufacturers' websites are a good resource to investigate the compatibility between CPUs and other devices. When upgrading the CPU, make sure the correct voltage is maintained. A Voltage Regulator Module (VRM) is integrated into the motherboard. The voltage setting for the CPU can be configured with jumpers, switches located on the motherboard, or settings in the BIOS. Figure 2 shows two similar CPUs that use different sockets. Figure 3 shows common AMD socket types and the processors supported. Figure 4 shows common Intel socket types and the processors supported.

Multi-core processors have two or more processors on the same integrated circuit. By integrating the processors on the same chip, a very fast connection is created between them. Multi-core processors execute instructions more quickly and have increased data throughput than single-core processors. Instructions can be distributed to all of the processors at the same time. With multi-core processors, RAM is shared between the processors because the cores reside on the same chip. A multi-core processor is recommended for applications such as video editing, gaming, and photo manipulation.

High power consumption creates more heat in the computer case. Multi-core processors conserve power and produce less heat than multiple single-core processors, thus increasing performance and efficiency.

Processors have areas of fast memory designed to increase the speed and performance of the processor. When this area of memory is located inside the processor, it is the primary, or Level 1 (L1), cache. Cache memory external to the processor is Level 2 (L2) cache. Starting with the Pentium Pro and later processors, the L2 cache was included in the processor architecture. After the L2 cache was added to the processor, the extra cache installed on the motherboard was named Level 3 (L3). These CPU caches are much faster than the main memory. With multi-core processors, the L3 cache contains duplicate instructions found in the L1 and L2 caches.

The speed of a processor is measured in gigahertz (GHz). A maximum speed rating refers to the maximum speed at which a processor can function without errors. Two primary factors can limit the speed of a processor:

- The processor chip is a collection of transistors interconnected by wires. There are delays created by the transmission of data flowing through the transistors and wires.

- As the transistors change state, from on to off or off to on, small amounts of electricity are released. The amount of heat generated increases as the speed of the processor increases. When the processor becomes too hot, it will begin to produce errors.

The Front Side Bus (FSB) is the path between the CPU and the various components, such as the chip set, expansion cards, and RAM. Data can travel in both directions across the FSB. The frequency of the bus is measured in megahertz (MHz). The frequency at which a CPU operates is determined by applying a clock multiplier to the FSB speed. For example, a processor running at 3200 MHz might be using a 400 MHz FSB. 3200 MHz divided by 400 MHz is 8. In this example, the CPU is 8 times faster than the FSB.

Processors are further classified as 32 bit and 64 bit. The primary difference is the number of instructions that can be handled by the processor at one time. A 64-bit processor processes more instructions per clock cycle than a 32-bit processor. A 64-bit processor can also support much more memory than a 32-bit processor. To utilize the 64-bit processor capabilities, ensure that the operating system installed supports a 64-bit processor and applications are compatible.

One of the most expensive and sensitive components in the computer case is the CPU. The CPU can become very hot. Many CPUs require a heat sink, combined with a fan for cooling. A heat sink is a piece of copper or aluminum that sits between the processor and the CPU fan. The heat sink absorbs the heat from the processor and then the fan disperses the heat. When choosing a heat sink or fan, there are several factors to consider:

- *Socket type–* The heat sink or fan type must match the socket type of the motherboard.

- *Motherboard physical specifications–* The heat sink or fan must not interfere with any components attached to the motherboard.

- *Case size–* The heat sink or fan must fit within the case.

- *Physical environment–* The heat sink or fan must be able to disperse enough heat to keep the CPU cool in warm environments.

The CPU is not the only component in a computer case that can be adversely affected by heat. A computer has many internal components that generate heat while the computer is running. Case fans should be installed to move cooler air into the case while moving heat out of the computer case. When choosing case fans, there are several factors to consider:

- *Case size–* Larger cases often require larger fans because smaller fans cannot create enough air flow.

- *Fan speed–* Larger fans spin more slowly than smaller fans, which reduce fan noise.

- *Number of components in the case–* Multiple components in a computer create additional heat, which requires more fans, larger fans, or faster fans.

- *Physical environment–* The case fans must be able to disperse enough heat to keep the interior of the case cool.

- *Number of mounting places available–* Different cases have different numbers of mounting places for fans.

- *Location of mounting places available–* Different cases have different locations for mounting fans.

- *Electrical connections–* Some case fans are connected directly to the motherboard while others are connected directly to the power supply.

Note

The direction of air flow created by all the fans in the case must work together to bring the cooler air in while moving the hotter air out. Installing a fan backwards or using fans with the incorrect size or speed for the case can cause the air flows to work against each other.

Refer to **Figure** in online course

11.3.4 Select RAM

New RAM may be needed when an application locks up or the computer displays frequent error messages. To determine if the problem is the RAM, replace the old RAM module as shown in Figure 1. Restart the computer to see if the application runs properly.

Note

To close a stalled application, press **Ctrl-Alt-Del** to open the Task Manager. In the window, select the application. Click **End Task** to close it, as shown in Figure 2.

When selecting new RAM, you must ensure that it is compatible with the current motherboard. It must also be the same type of RAM as installed in the computer. The speed of the new RAM must be the same or faster than the existing RAM. It may help to take the original memory module with you when you shop for the replacement RAM.

Refer to
Figure
in online course

11.3.5 Select adapter cards

Adapter cards, also called expansion cards, are designed for a specific task and add extra functionality to a computer. Figure 1 shows some of the adapter cards available. Before you purchase an adapter card, you should be able to answer the following questions:

- Is there an open expansion slot?

- Is the adapter card compatible with the open slot?

- What are the customer's current and future needs?

- What are the possible configuration options?

- What are the reasons for the best choice?

If the motherboard does not have a compatible expansion slot, an external device may be an option. Other factors that affect the selection process include cost, warranty, brand name, and availability.

Graphics Cards

The type of graphics card installed has a big impact on the overall performance of a computer. The programs and tasks that the graphics card may need to support could be RAM intensive, CPU intensive, or both. There are several factors to consider when purchasing a new graphics card:

- Slot type

- Port types

- Amount and speed of Video RAM (VRAM)

- Graphics Processor Unit (GPU)

- Maximum resolution

- Frames per second

A computer system must have the slots, RAM, and CPU to support the full functionality of an upgraded graphics card to receive all of the benefits of the card. Choose the correct graphics card based on your customer's current and future needs. For example, if a customer wants to play 3D games, the graphics card must meet or exceed the minimum requirements for any game they wish to play.

Sound Cards

The type of sound card installed will determine the sound quality of your computer. There are several factors to consider when purchasing a new sound card:

- Slot type

- Digital Signal Processor (DSP)

- Sample rate

- Port and connection types

- Hardware decoders

- Signal-to-noise ratio

A computer system must have quality speakers and a subwoofer to support the full functionality of an upgraded sound card to receive all of the benefits of the card. Choose the correct sound card based on your customer's current and future needs. For example, if a customer wants to hear a specific type of surround sound, the sound card must have the correct hardware decoder to reproduce it. Also the customer can get improved sound accuracy with a sound card that has a higher sample rate.

Storage Controllers

A storage controller is a chip that can be integrated into the motherboard or on an expansion card. Storage controllers allow for the expansion of internal and external drives for a computer system. The drives can be connected internally using IDE, SCSI, or SATA connectors. External drives can be connected using SCSI or eSATA connectors. Storage controllers, such as RAID controllers, can also provide fault tolerance or increased speed. There are several factors to consider when purchasing a new storage controller card:

- Slot type

- Drive type

- Connector quantity

- Connector location

- Card size

- Controller card RAM

- Controller card processor

- RAID types

The amount of data and the level of data protection needed for the customer will influence the type of storage controller required. Choose the correct storage controller based on your customer's current and future needs. For example, if a customer wants to implement RAID 5, a RAID storage controller with at least three drives is needed.

Input/Output Cards (I/O)

Installing an I/O card in a computer is a fast and easy way to add I/O ports. There are several factors to consider when purchasing an I/O card:

- Slot type

- I/O port type

- I/O port quantity

- Additional power requirements

FireWire, USB, parallel, and serial ports are some of the most common ports to install on a computer. Choose the correct I/O card based on your customer's current and future needs. For example, if a customer wants to add an internal card reader, a USB I/O card with an internal USB connection is needed.

NICs

Customers upgrade their NICs to get faster speeds, more bandwidth, and better access. There are several factors to consider when purchasing a NIC:

- Slot type

- Speed

- Connector type

- Connection type

- Standards compatibility

- Wake on LAN

Wired and wireless NICs should be selected based on your customer's current and future needs. For example, if a customer wants to connect to a wireless N network, a wireless NIC that is compatible with the 802.11n standard is needed to operate at the full speed provided by 802.11n.

Capture Cards

A capture card imports video into a computer and records it on a hard drive. The addition of a capture card with a TV tuner allows you to view and record television programming. There are several factors to consider when purchasing a capture card:

- Slot type

- Resolution and frame rate

- I/O ports

- Format standards

The computer system must have enough CPU processing power, adequate RAM, and a high-speed storage system to support the capture, recording, and editing demands of the customer. Choose the correct capture card based on your customer's current and future needs. For example, if a customer wants to record one program while watching another, either multiple capture cards or a capture card with dual TV tuners must be installed.

Refer to
Figure
in online course

11.3.6 Select storage devices and hard drives

You may need to replace a storage device when it no longer meets your customer's needs or it fails. The signs that a storage device is failing might include:

- Unusual noises

- Unusual vibrations

- Error messages

- Corrupt data or applications

Floppy Disk Drive (FDD)

While FDDs still have some limited uses, they have been largely superseded by USB flash drives, external hard drives, CDs, DVDs, and memory cards. If an existing FDD fails, replace it with one of the newer storage devices.

Media Readers

A media reader is a device that reads and writes to different types of media cards, for example, those found in a digital camera, smartphone, or MP3 player. When replacing a media reader, ensure that it supports the type of cards used and the storage capacity of the cards to be read. There are several factors to consider when purchasing a new media reader:

- Internal or external

- Type of connector used

- Type of media cards supported

Choose the correct media reader based on your customer's current and future needs. For example, if a customer needs to use multiple types of media cards, a multiple format media reader is needed.

Hard Drives

A hard drive stores data on magnetic platters. There are several different types and sizes of hard drives. Hard drives use different connection types. Figure 1 shows PATA, SATA, and SCSI connectors. There are several factors to consider when purchasing a new hard drive:

- Adding or replacing

- Internal or external

- Case location

- System compatibility

- Heat generation

- Noise generation

- Power requirements

PATA hard drives use a 40-pin / 80-conductor cable or a 40-pin / 40-conductor cable. Choose the PATA hard drive if your customer's system is a legacy system or does not support SATA.

SATA and eSATA hard drives use a 7-pin / 4-conductor cable. Although SATA and eSATA cables are similar, they are not interchangeable. SATA drives are internal. eSATA drives are external. Choose a SATA or eSATA hard drive if your customer needs a much higher data-transfer rate than PATA and the system supports SATA or eSATA.

SCSI hard drives use a 50-pin, 68-pin, or 80-pin connector. Up to 15 SCSI drives can be connected to a SCSI drive controller. A typical use for SCSI drives is to run a server or to implement RAID. SCSI devices are typically connected in a series, forming a chain that is commonly called a daisy chain, as shown in Figure 2. Figure 3 shows the different types of SCSIs.

Solid State Drives

A Solid State Drive (SSD) uses static RAM instead of magnetic platters to store data. SSDs are considered to be reliable because they have no moving parts. There are several factors to consider when purchasing an SSD:

- Cost

- Adding or replacing

- Internal or external

- Case location

- System compatibility

- Power requirements

- Speed

- Capacity

Choose an SSD if your customer needs to do any of the following:

- Connect to any interface used by traditional hard drives

- Operate in extreme environments

- Use less power

- Produce less heat

- Reduce startup time

Optical Drives

An optical drive uses a laser to read and write data to and from optical media. There are several factors to consider when purchasing an optical drive:

- Interface type

- Reading capabilities

- Writing capabilities

- Formats

A CD-ROM drive can only read CDs. A CD-RW can read and write to CDs. Choose a CD-RW if your customer needs to read and write to CDs.

A DVD-ROM drive can only read DVDs and CDs. A DVD-RW can read and write to DVDs and CDs. DVDs hold significantly more data than CDs. Choose a DVD-RW if your customer needs to read and write to DVDs and CDs.

A Blu-ray reader (BD-R) can only read Blu-ray discs, DVDs, and CDs. A Blu-ray writer (BD-RE) can read and write to Blu-ray discs and DVDs. Blu-ray discs hold significantly more data than DVDs. Choose a BD-RE drive if your customer needs to read and write to Blu-ray discs.

External Storage

This type of storage connects to an external port such as a USB, IEEE 1394, SCSI, or eSATA. External flash drives, sometimes called thumb drives, that connect to a USB port are a type of removable storage. There are several factors to consider when purchasing external storage:

- Port type

- Storage capacity

- Speed

- Portability

- Power requirements

External storage offers portability and convenience when working with multiple computers. Choose the correct type of external storage for your customer's needs. For example, if your customer needs to transfer a small amount of data, such as a single presentation, an external flash drive is a good choice. If your customer needs to back up or transfer large amounts of data, choose an external hard drive.

Refer to **Figure** in online course

11.3.7 Select input and output devices

An input device can be any piece of equipment that transfers information into a computer:

- Mouse
- Keyboard
- Scanner
- Camera
- Process-control sensor
- MIDI interface
- Microphone

An output device transfers information to the outside of the computer:

- Display monitor
- Projector
- Printer
- Process-control equipment
- Speaker

To select input and output devices, you should first find out what the customer wants. Next, you should select the hardware and software by researching the Internet for possible solutions. After you determine which input or output device the customer needs, you must determine how to connect it to the computer. Figure 1 shows common input and output port symbols.

Technicians should have a good understanding of several types of interfaces:

- *USB 1.1*– Transfers data at a maximum speed of 12 Mbps
- *USB 2.0*– Transfers data at a maximum speed of 480 Mbps
- *FireWire (IEEE 1394)*– Transfers data at 100, 200, or 400 Mbps and IEEE 1394b at 800 Mbps
- *Parallel (IEEE 1284)*– Transfers data at a maximum speed of 3 MBps
- *Serial (RS-232)*– Early versions were limited to 20 Kbps, but newer versions can reach transfer rates of 1.5 Mbps

Refer to
Worksheet
for this chapter

Refer to
Figure
in online course

■ *SCSI (Ultra-320 SCSI)–* Connects as many as 15 devices with a transfer rate of 320 MBps

Research Computer Components

Gather information about the components you will need to upgrade your customer's computer.

11.4   Upgrade and configure personal computer components and peripherals

Computer systems need periodic upgrades for various reasons:

■ User requirements change

■ Upgraded software packages require new hardware

■ New hardware offers enhanced performance

Changes to the computer may cause you to upgrade or replace components and peripherals. You should research the effectiveness and cost for both upgrading and replacing.

After completing this section, you will meet these objectives:

■ Upgrade and configure a motherboard.

■ Upgrade and configure a CPU and a heat sink/fan assembly.

■ Upgrade and configure RAM.

■ Upgrade and configure BIOS.

■ Upgrade and configure storage devices and hard drives.

■ Upgrade and configure input and output devices.

Refer to
Figure
in online course

11.4.1   Upgrade and configure a motherboard

To upgrade or replace a motherboard, you may have to replace several other components, such as the CPU, heat sink/fan assembly, and RAM.

A new motherboard must fit into the old computer case. The power supply must also be compatible for the new motherboard and be able to support all new computer components.

You should begin the upgrade by moving the CPU and heat sink/fan assembly to the new motherboard. These are much easier to work with when they are outside of the case. You should work on an antistatic mat and wear a wrist strap to avoid damaging the CPU. Remember to use thermal compound between the CPU and the heat sink. If the new motherboard requires a different CPU and RAM, install them at this time.

CPU Installation

Different CPU architectures are installed in four common socket connection designs:

■ Single-Edge Connector (SEC)

■ Low-Insertion Force (LIF)

■ Zero-Insertion Force (ZIF)

■ Land Grid Array (LGA) socket

SEC and LIF sockets are no longer commonly used. Consult the motherboard manual for instructions on how to install the CPU.

Jumper Settings

Jumpers are upright gold pins on the motherboard. Each grouping of two or more pins is called a jumper block. A motherboard might use a Dual In-line Package (DIP) switch instead of jumpers. Both methods are used to complete electrical circuits which provide a variety of options supported by the motherboard. The motherboard manual indicates which pins should be connected or not connected to accommodate the various options:

- CPU voltage
- CPU speed
- Bus speed
- Cache size and type
- Flash BIOS enabled
- Clear CMOS
- Size of system memory

CMOS Battery Installation

A CMOS battery might need to be replaced after a few years. Make sure the new battery matches the model required by the motherboard.

Follow these instructions for CMOS battery installation:

Step 1.   Gently slide aside, or raise, the thin metal clips to remove the old battery.

Step 2.   Line up positive and negative poles to the correct orientation.

Step 3.   Gently slide aside, or raise, the thin metal clips to insert the new battery.

Motherboard Installation

When it is time to remove and replace the old motherboard, remove the cables from the motherboard that attach to the case LEDs and buttons. They may have the same labels, but there may be minor differences. Make the appropriate notes in your journal to know where and how everything is connected before you start the upgrade.

Note how the motherboard secures to the case. Some mounting screws provide support, and some may provide an important grounding connection between the motherboard and chassis. In particular, you should pay attention to screws and standoffs that are non-metallic, because these may be insulators. Replacing insulating screws and supports with metal hardware that conducts electricity might damage electrical components.

Before installing the new motherboard into the computer case, examine the I/O shield located at the back of the computer case. Replace the old I/O shield if the new motherboard has different I/O ports or if the ports are in different locations.

Make sure that you use the correct screws. Do not swap threaded screws with self-tapping metal screws; they will damage the threaded screw holes and may not be secure. Make sure that threaded screws are the correct length and have the same number of threads per inch. If the thread is correct, they will fit easily. You may make a screw fit by using force, but you will damage the threaded hole and it will not hold the motherboard securely. Using the wrong screw can also produce metal shavings that can cause short circuits.

Note

It does not matter if you replace a screw made for a slotted screwdriver with one made for a Phillips-head screwdriver, as long as the threaded part of the screw is the same length and has the same number of threads.

Next you should connect the power supply cables. If the ATX power connectors are not the same size (some have more pins than others), you may need to use an adapter. Connect the cables for the case LEDs and buttons. Refer to the motherboard manual for the layout of these connections. The connectors are not keyed, so it is possible to connect the wire backwards. Polarized connectors usually have a small arrow or plus sign adjacent to indicate which conductor should attach to the positive pin. The polarized connectors include the power and reset switch, the hard disk drive LED, and the power LED.

Follow these instructions for front panel connections:

Step 1.   Align the connector with the correct pins on the motherboard.

Step 2.   Press down gently until the connector is fully seated.

Note

If an LED or button does not work, the wire to the motherboard is probably connected improperly.

After the new motherboard is in place and cabled, you should install and secure all expansion cards.

It is now time to check your work. Make sure there are no loose parts or leftover wires. Connect a keyboard, mouse, monitor, and power. If any problem is detected, shut the power supply off immediately.

An expansion card can have the same functionality that is integrated into the motherboard. In this case, you may need to disable the onboard functions in the system BIOS. Use the documentation that came with the motherboard to learn what BIOS adjustments may be required.

BIOS Updates

The firmware encoded in the motherboard EEPROM chip may need to be updated so that the motherboard can support added hardware. Updating the firmware can be risky. Before updating motherboard firmware, record the manufacturer of the BIOS, the motherboard, and the motherboard model. You will need this information when you go to the motherboard manufacturer's site to get the correct software. Only update the firmware if there are problems with system hardware or to add functionality to the system.

Advanced BIOS Settings

Some computer manufacturers limit the advanced options in the BIOS to reduce errors resulting from incorrectly configuring BIOS settings. The advanced chipset features in the BIOS may allow overclocking the processor. Overclocking is changing the settings of a component so that it runs at a higher speed than its original specification. Overclocking should be done with caution as it will void the CPU warranty and might damage the system. The default settings found in the advanced BIOS settings menu usually do not need to be changed.

Refer to
Lab Activity
for this chapter

Install a NIC in Windows XP

Install a NIC, verify NIC operation, manually configure an IP address, and set the NIC to use DHCP.

Refer to
Lab Activity
for this chapter

Install a NIC in Windows Vista

Install a NIC, verify NIC operation, manually configure an IP address, and set the NIC to use DHCP.

Refer to
Figure
in online course

11.4.2 Upgrade and configure a CPU and a heat sink/fan assembly

One way to increase the apparent power of a computer is to increase the processing speed. You can often do this by upgrading the CPU. However, there are some requirements that you must meet:

- The new CPU must fit into the existing CPU socket.

- The new CPU must be compatible with the motherboard chip set.

- The new CPU must operate with the existing motherboard and power supply.

- The new CPU must operate with the existing RAM. The RAM may need to be upgraded or expanded to take advantage of the faster CPU.

If the motherboard is older, you may not be able to find a compatible CPU. In that case, you would replace the motherboard.

Caution

Always work on an antistatic mat and wear a wrist strap when installing and removing CPUs. Place a CPU on the antistatic mat until you are ready to use it. Store CPUs in antistatic packaging.

To change the CPU, you should remove the existing CPU by releasing it from the socket using the zero insertion force lever. Different sockets have slightly different mechanisms, but all serve to lock the CPU in place after it is correctly oriented in the socket.

Insert the new CPU into place. Do not force the CPU into its socket or use excessive force to close the locking bars. Excessive force may damage the CPU or its socket. If you encounter resistance, make sure that you have aligned the CPU properly. Most have a pattern of pins that will fit only one way:

- *SEC socket*– Align the notches on the CPU to the keys in the SEC socket.

- *LIF or ZIF socket*– Align the CPU so that the connection 1 indicator is lined up with pin 1 on the CPU socket.

- *LGA socket*– Align the CPU so that the two notches on the CPU will fit into the two socket extensions.

If there is a question, examine the new CPU to ensure it is physically similar to the old one. The new CPU may require a different heat sink/fan assembly. The heat sink/fan assembly must physically fit the CPU and be compatible with the CPU socket. The heat sink/fan assembly must also be adequate to remove the heat of the faster CPU.

The following steps outline how to install the heat sink/fan assembly:

Step 1.	Align the heat sink/fan assembly retainers with the holes on the motherboard.
Step 2.	Place the heat sink/fan assembly onto the CPU socket, being careful not to pinch the CPU fan wires.
Step 3.	Tighten the heat sink/fan assembly retainers to secure the assembly in place.
Step 4.	Connect the heat sink/fan assembly power cable to the header on the motherboard.

Caution

You must apply thermal compound between the new CPU and the heat sink/fan assembly.

With some types of BIOS, you can view thermal settings to determine if there are any problems with the CPU and the heat sink/fan assembly. Third-party software applications can report CPU temperature information in an easy-to-read format. Refer to the motherboard or CPU user documentation to determine if the chip is operating in the correct temperature range. Some CPU and case fans turn on and off automatically, depending on the CPU temperature and the internal case temperature. The temperatures are measured through thermal probes built into the fan assembly or internal circuitry in the CPU.

The following steps outline how to install extra case fans:

Step 1.   Align the fan so that it faces the correct direction to either draw air in or blow air out.

Step 2.   Mount the fan using the predrilled holes in the case. Mount the fan at the bottom of the case to draw air into the case or at the top of the case to direct hot air out of the case.

Step 3.   Connect the fan to the power supply or the motherboard, depending on the case fan plug type.

Refer to
Figure
in online course

11.4.3 Upgrade and configure RAM

Increasing the amount of system RAM almost always improves overall system performance. Prior to upgrading or replacing the RAM, there are some questions you must answer:

- What type of RAM does the motherboard currently use?
- Can the RAM be installed one module at a time, or should it be grouped into matching banks?
- Are there any available RAM slots?
- Does the new RAM chip match the speed, latency, type, and voltage of the existing RAM?

Caution

When working with system RAM, work on an antistatic mat and wear a wrist strap. Place the RAM on the mat until you are ready to install it. Store RAM in antistatic packaging.

Remove the existing RAM by freeing retaining clips that secure it. Pull it from the socket. Current DIMMs pull straight out and insert straight down. Earlier SIMMs were inserted at an angle to lock into place.

When inserting the new RAM, make sure the notches in the RAM and RAM slot on the motherboard align properly. Press down firmly and lock the RAM into place with the retaining clips.

Caution

Make sure to insert the memory module completely into the socket. RAM can cause serious damage to the motherboard if it is incorrectly aligned and shorts the main system bus.

The system discovers the newly installed RAM if it is compatible and installed correctly. If the BIOS does not indicate the presence of the correct amount of RAM, check to make sure that the RAM is compatible with the motherboard and is correctly installed.

Refer to
Lab Activity
for this chapter

Install Additional RAM in Windows XP

Install additional RAM into the computer.

Refer to
Lab Activity
for this chapter

Install Additional RAM in Windows Vista

Install additional RAM into the computer.

Refer to **Figure** in online course

11.4.4 Upgrade and configure BIOS

Motherboard manufacturers periodically release updates for their BIOS. The release notes, such as those shown in Figure 1, describe the upgrade to the product, compatibility improvements, and the known bugs that have been addressed. Some newer devices only operate properly with an updated BIOS.

Early computer BIOS information was contained in ROM chips. To upgrade the BIOS information, the ROM chip had to be replaced, which was not always possible. Modern BIOS chips are EEPROM, or flash memory, which can be upgraded by the user without opening the computer case. This process is called "flashing the BIOS".

To view the current BIOS settings on your computer, you must enter the BIOS setup program, as shown in Figure 2. Press the setup sequence keys while the computer is performing the POST. Depending on the computer, the setup key may be the F1, F2, or the Delete key. Watch the text on the screen or consult the motherboard manual to find the setup key or combination of keys.

The first part of the boot process displays a message that tells you which key to press to enter the setup, or BIOS mode. There are a variety of settings in the BIOS that should not be altered by anyone unfamiliar with this procedure. If you are unsure, it is best not to change any BIOS setting unless you research the problem in depth.

To download a new BIOS, consult the manufacturer's website and follow the recommended installation procedures, as shown in Figure 3. Installing BIOS software online may involve downloading a new BIOS file, copying or extracting files to removable media, and then booting from the removable media. An installation program prompts the user for information to complete the process.

Although it is still common to flash the BIOS through a command prompt, several motherboard manufacturers provide software on their websites that allow a user to flash the BIOS from within Windows. The procedure varies from manufacturer to manufacturer.

Caution
An improperly installed or aborted BIOS update can cause the computer to become unusable.

Refer to **Lab Activity** for this chapter

BIOS File Search
Identify the current BIOS version, and then search for BIOS update files.

11.4.5 Upgrade and configure storage devices and hard drives

Instead of purchasing a new computer to get increased access speed and storage space, you may consider adding another hard drive. There are several reasons for installing an additional drive:

- To install a second operating system
- To provide additional storage space
- To provide a faster hard drive
- To hold the system swap file
- To provide a backup for the original hard drive
- To increase fault tolerance

There are several things to consider before adding a new hard drive. When two hard drives are connected to the same data cable, one drive must be jumpered as the master drive and the other drive must be jumpered as the slave drive. This allows the computer to communicate with both drives individually. As shown in Figure 1, jumpers are usually located on the back of the hard drive and can configure a hard drive to be a standalone drive, a master drive, or a slave drive.

Some drives can be jumpered to auto-detect. Refer to the hard drive diagram or manual for correct jumper settings. If the new drive is PATA and is on the same data cable, one of the drives must be set as the master drive and the other must be set as the slave drive. Each SATA hard drive has its own data cable; therefore, there is no master-slave relationship between drives. Any new partitions or drive letter assignments should be well-planned. The boot order in BIOS may need to be adjusted.

RAID can provide fault tolerance when connecting multiple hard drives, as shown in Figure 2. RAID requires two or more hard drives. You can install RAID using hardware or software. Hardware installations are usually more dependable, but are more expensive. Software installations are created and managed by an operating system, such as Windows Server 2008. It is important to understand the cost, performance, and reliability of each RAID array configuration.

After selecting the appropriate hard drive for the computer, follow these general guidelines during installation:

Step 1.   Place the hard drive in an empty drive bay and tighten the screws to secure the hard drive.

Step 2.   Configure the PATA hard drive as master, slave, or auto-detect. If you have a SCSI hard drive, set the ID number and terminate the SCSI chain if necessary.

Step 3.   Attach the power cable and the data cable to the hard drive. Ensure that pin one of the PATA data cable is properly aligned.

Step 4.   Attach the other end of the data cable to the motherboard or hard drive controller.

When the second hard drive has been installed, you will need to partition the drive. Windows Disk Management utility can be used to partition the second hard drive:

Start > Run > type **diskmgmt.msc > OK**

In Windows Vista, use the following path:

Start > Start Search > type **diskmgmt.msc > Enter > Continue**

Another type of storage device you might need to install is a media reader. External media readers can be attached to a FireWire or USB port on the computer. The internal media reader requires an empty 5.25-inch or 3.5-inch drive bay. To install the internal media reader, use the following steps.

Step 1.   Place the media reader in an empty external drive bay and tighten the screws to secure the media reader.

Step 2.   Connect the media reader data cable to an unused USB connector on the motherboard.

Refer to
Lab Activity
for this chapter

Install, Configure, and Partition a Second Hard Drive in Windows XP
Change the boot order, install a second hard drive, create partitions, and map drive letters to partitions.

Refer to
Lab Activity
for this chapter

Install, Configure, and Partition a Second Hard Drive in Windows Vista
Change the boot order, install a second hard drive, create partitions, and map drive letters to partitions.

Refer to
Figure
in online course

11.4.6 Upgrade and configure input and output devices

If an input or output device stops operating, you may have to replace the device. Some customers may wish to upgrade their input or output devices to increase performance and productivity.

An ergonomic keyboard, shown in Figure 1, may be more comfortable to use. Sometimes a reconfiguration is necessary to enable a user to perform special tasks, such as typing in a second language with additional characters. Finally, replacing or reconfiguring an input or output device may make it easier to accommodate users with disabilities.

Sometimes it is not possible to perform an upgrade using the existing expansion slots or sockets. In this case, you may be able to accomplish the upgrade using a USB connection. If the computer does not have an extra USB connection, you must install a USB adapter card or purchase a USB hub, as shown in Figure 2.

After obtaining new hardware, you may have to install new drivers. You can usually do this by using the installation media. If you do not have media, you can obtain updated drivers from the website of the manufacturer.

Note
A signed driver is a driver that has passed the Windows hardware quality lab test and has been given a driver signature by Microsoft. Installing an unsigned driver can cause system instability, error messages, and boot problems. During hardware installation, if an unsigned driver is detected, you will be asked to stop or continue installation of this driver.

Refer to
Figure
in online course

11.5 Identify and apply common preventive maintenance techniques for personal computer components

To keep computers working properly, you must maintain them by performing preventive maintenance. Preventive maintenance can extend the life of the components, protect data, and improve computer performance.

After completing this section, you will meet these objectives:

- Clean internal components.
- Clean the case.
- Inspect computer components.

Refer to
Figure
in online course

11.5.1 Clean internal components

One important part of computer preventive maintenance is to keep the system clean. The amount of dust in the environment and the habits of the user determine how often to clean the computer components. Most of your cleaning is to prevent the accumulation of dust.

To remove dust, do not use a vacuum cleaner. Vacuum cleaners can generate static and can damage or loosen components and jumpers. Instead, you should use compressed air to blow the dust away. If you use compressed air from a can, keep the can upright to prevent the fluid from leaking onto computer components. Always follow the instructions and warnings on the compressed air can.

Regular cleaning also gives you a chance to inspect components for loose screws and connectors. There are several parts inside the computer case that you should keep as clean as possible:

- Heat sink/fan assembly
- RAM
- Adapter cards
- Motherboard
- Case fan
- Power supply
- Internal drives

Caution

When you clean a fan with compressed air, hold the fan blades in place. This prevents over-spinning the rotor or moving the fan in the wrong direction.

Refer to
Figure
in online course

11.5.2 Clean the case

Dust or dirt on the outside of a computer can travel through cooling fans and loose computer case covers. Dirt can also enter a computer through missing expansion slot covers, as shown in Figure 1. If dust accumulates inside the computer, it can prevent the flow of air and affect cooling.

Use a cloth or a duster to clean the outside of the computer case. If you use a cleaning product, do not spray it directly on the case. Instead, put a small amount onto a cleaning a cloth or a duster and wipe the outside of the case.

While cleaning the case, you should look for and correct things that might cause a problem later:

- Missing expansion slot covers that let dust, dirt, or living pests into the computer
- Loose or missing screws that secure adapter cards
- Missing or tangled cables that can pull free from the case

Refer to
Figure
in online course

11.5.3 Inspect computer components

The best method of keeping a computer in good condition is to examine the computer on a regular schedule. Cleaning provides a good opportunity to make this inspection. You should have a checklist of components to inspect:

- *CPU and cooling system–* Examine the CPU and cooling system for dust buildup. Make sure that the fan can spin freely. Check that the fan power cable is secure, as shown in Figure 1. Check the fan while the power is on to see the fan turn. Inspect the CPU to be sure that it is seated securely in the socket. Make sure that the heat sink is properly attached. To avoid damage, do not remove the CPU for cleaning.

- *RAM connections–* The RAM chips should be seated securely in the RAM slots. Figure 2 shows that sometimes the retaining clips can loosen. Reseat them, if necessary. Use compressed air to remove any dust.

- *Storage devices–* Inspect all storage devices, including the hard drives, floppy drive, optical drives, and tape drive. All cables should be firmly connected. Check for loose, missing, or incorrectly set jumpers, as shown in Figure 3. A drive should not produce rattling, knocking, or grinding sounds. Read the manufacturer's manual to learn how to clean optical drive and tape heads by using cotton swabs and compressed air. Clean floppy drives with a drive cleaning kit.

- *Adapter cards–* Adapter cards should be seated properly in their expansion slots. Loose cards, as shown in Figure 4, can cause short circuits. Secure adapter cards with the retaining screw to avoid having the cards come loose in their expansion slots. Use compressed air to remove any dirt or dust on the adapter cards or the expansion slots.

Note

If a video adapter is used in an expansion slot, the integrated video adapter from the motherboard might be disabled. To disable an integrated video adapter, you might need to change the settings in the CMOS. If you connect a monitor to a disabled adapter, the monitor will not display video.

These are some common computer items to inspect:

- *Power devices–* Inspect power strips, surge suppressors (surge protectors), and UPS devices. Make sure that there is proper and unobstructed ventilation. Replace the power strip if it does not work properly.

- *Loose screws–* Loose screws can cause problems if they are not immediately fixed or removed. A loose screw in the case may later cause a short circuit or roll into a position where the screw is hard to remove.

- *Keyboard and mouse–* Use compressed air or a small vacuum cleaner to clean the keyboard, mouse, and mouse sensor.

- *Cables–* Examine all cable connections. Look for broken and bent pins. Ensure that all connector retaining screws are finger-tight. Make sure cables are not crimped, pinched, or severely bent.

Refer to **Figure** in online course

11.6 Troubleshoot computer components and peripherals

The troubleshooting process helps resolve problems with the computer or peripherals. These problems range from simple, such as updating a drive, to more complex problems, such as installing a CPU. Use the troubleshooting steps as a guideline to help you diagnose and repair problems.

After completing this section, you will meet these objectives:

- Review the troubleshooting process.

- Identify common problems and solutions.

- Apply troubleshooting skills.

Refer to **Figure** in online course

11.6.1 Review the troubleshooting process

Computer technicians must be able to diagnose and repair computer hardware problems. This process is called troubleshooting.

The first step in the troubleshooting process is to identify the problem. Figure 1 is a list of open-ended and closed-ended questions to ask the customer.

After you have talked to the customer, you can establish a theory of probable causes. Figure 2 is a list of some common probable causes for hardware problems.

After you have developed some theories about what is wrong, test your theories to determine the cause of the problem. Figure 3 is a list of quick procedures that can determine the exact cause of the problem or even correct the problem. If a quick procedure does correct the problem, you can go to step 5 to verify full system functionality. If a quick procedure does not correct the problem, you might need to research the problem further to establish the exact cause.

After you have determined the exact cause of the problem, establish a plan of action to resolve the problem and implement the solution. Figure 4 shows sources of information to gather additional information to resolve an issue.

After you have corrected the problem, verify full functionality and, if applicable, implement preventive measures. Figure 5 is a list of the steps to verify the solution.

In the final step of the troubleshooting process, you must document your findings, actions, and outcomes. Figure 6 is a list of the tasks required to document the problem and the solution.

Refer to
Figure
in online course

11.6.2 Identify common problems and solutions

Computer problems can be attributed to hardware, software, networks, or some combination of the three. You will resolve some types of problems more often than others. Hardware problems include:

Storage Device Problems

Storage device problems are often related to loose or incorrect cable connections, incorrect drive and media formats, and incorrect jumper and CMOS settings, as shown in Figure 1.

Motherboard and Internal Component Problems

Often these problems are caused by incorrect or loose cables, failed components, incorrect drivers, and corrupted updates, as shown in Figure 2.

Power Supply Problems

Power problems are often caused by a faulty power supply, loose connections, and inadequate wattage, as shown in Figure 3.

CPU Problems and Memory Problems

Processor and memory problems are often caused by incorrect installations, bad CMOS settings, inadequate cooling and ventilation, and compatibility issues, as shown in Figure 4.

Refer to
Figure
in online course

11.6.3 Apply troubleshooting skills

Now that you understand the troubleshooting process, it is time to apply your listening and diagnostic skills.

Refer to
Figure
in online course

The first lab is designed to test your troubleshooting skills with hardware problems. You will troubleshoot and fix a computer that does not boot.

The second lab is designed to reinforce your communication and troubleshooting skills. In this lab, you will perform the following steps:

- Receive the work order

- Talk the customer through various steps to try and resolve the problem

- Document the problem and the resolution

The third lab is designed to reinforce your skills with PC hardware problems. You will troubleshoot and repair a computer that has more than one problem.

Refer to
Lab Activity
for this chapter

Repair Boot Problem

Troubleshoot and repair a computer that does not boot.

Refer to
Lab Activity
for this chapter

Remote Technician: Repair Boot Problem

Gather data from the customer, and then instruct the customer on how to fix a computer that does not boot.

Refer to
Lab Activity
for this chapter

Troubleshooting Hardware Problems in Windows XP

Diagnose the cause of various hardware problems and fix them.

Refer to
Lab Activity
for this chapter

Troubleshooting Hardware Problems in Windows Vista

Diagnose the cause of various hardware problems and fix them.

Summary

In this chapter, you learned about advanced computer diagnosis and repair, and how to consider upgrades and select components. This chapter also presented some detailed troubleshooting techniques to help you locate and resolve problems, and present your findings to the customer.

- You learned about the roles of the field, remote, and bench technicians and the job possibilities that are available to those who enter the workforce with some knowledge of advanced troubleshooting skills.

- You are able to explain and perform safe lab procedures and tool use. You can describe basic electrical safety, especially as it applies to monitors and laser printers. You understand the purpose and enforcement of worker safety standards.

- You know the safe disposal procedures for various types of computer batteries and types of hardware, such as monitors.

- You can advise customers of ways to protect their computers by using good preventive maintenance practices.

- You can describe ways to clean the external components of a computer, including the monitor, case, printer, and peripherals. You can describe how to clean internal components of a computer, such as the motherboard, CPU and cooling system, RAM, and adapter cards.

- You can advise customers when it is best to upgrade a computer and components and when it is best to buy new products.

- You can explain the steps involved in adding and configuring a second hard drive. You can describe the steps involved in updating various computer components, such as cases, power supplies, the CPU and cooling system, RAM, hard drives, and adapter cards.

- You can demonstrate the use of open- and closed-ended questions that are appropriate for a level-two technician to determine the problem.

- You can describe the troubleshooting steps, including gathering data from the customer, verifying obvious issues, trying quick solutions first, evaluating problems, and implementing solutions until the problem is fixed.

- You understand the role of the level-two technician, and how to build on the troubleshooting efforts of a level-one technician.

Chapter 11 Quiz

Go to
the online course
to take the quiz.

Take the chapter quiz to test your knowledge.

Your Chapter Notes

Advanced Operating Systems

Introduction

The installation, configuration, and optimization of operating systems are examined in greater detail in this chapter.

Various brands of operating systems are available on the market today, including Microsoft Windows, Apple Mac OS, UNIX, and Linux. A technician must consider the current computer system when selecting an operating system. Additionally, there are several versions or distributions of an operating system. Some versions of Microsoft Windows include Windows 2000 Professional, Windows XP Home Edition, Windows XP Professional, Windows Media Center, Windows Vista Home Basic, Windows Vista Business, and Windows Vista Premium.

Each of these operating systems offers many of the same features with a similar interface. However, some functions necessary for specific customer needs may not be available in all of them. You must be able to compare and contrast operating systems to find the best one based on your customer's needs.

After completing this chapter, you will meet these objectives:

- Select the appropriate operating system based on customer needs.
- Install, configure, and optimize an operating system.
- Describe how to upgrade operating systems.
- Describe preventive maintenance procedures for operating systems.
- Troubleshoot operating systems.

Refer to **Figure** in online course

12.1 Select the appropriate operating system based on customer needs

There are many operating systems to choose from, each with features that should be considered when consulting with a customer. When selecting an operating system for a customer, you should select hardware that meets or exceeds the minimum requirements for equipment called for by the operating system.

In this chapter, Windows XP Professional is used to describe the functions of an operating system. At some point during your career, you will likely upgrade or repair a computer with a Windows operating system.

After completing this section, you will meet these objectives:

- Describe operating systems.
- Describe network operating systems.

Refer to
Figure
in online course

12.1.1   Describe operating systems

An operating system is the interface between the user and the computer. Without an operating system, the user would not be able to interact with the hardware or software on the computer. An operating system provides the following operational and organizational capabilities:

- Provides a bridge between the hardware and applications

- Creates a file system to store data

- Manages applications

- Interprets user commands

Operating systems have minimum requirements for hardware. Figure 1 shows the minimum hardware requirements for several operating systems.

Refer to
Figure
in online course

12.1.2   Describe network operating systems

A NOS is an operating system that contains additional features to increase functionality and manageability in a networked environment. The following are examples of network operating systems:

- Windows 2000 Server

- Windows 2003 Server

- UNIX

- Linux

- Novell NetWare

- Mac OS X

The NOS is designed to provide network resources to clients:

- Server applications, such as shared databases

- Centralized data storage

- Directory services that provide a centralized repository of user accounts and resources on the network, such as Active Directory

- Network print queue

- Network access and security

- Redundant storage systems, such as RAID and backups

Network operating systems provide several protocols designed to perform network functions. These protocols are controlled by code on the network servers. As shown in Figure1, protocols used by network operating systems provide services such as web browsing, file transfer, e-mail, name resolution, and automatic IP addressing.

Refer to
Interactive Graphic
in online course.

Refer to
Figure
in online course

Network Protocols

Complete the network protocol matching activity in Figure 2.

12.1.3 Windows OS directory structures

There are many different versions of each Windows OS. During installation, the Windows setup program creates directories that have specific purposes. There are directories designed to store the system files, user files, and program files, among others. When files of the same type are saved to a certain location, it is easy for users to find needed data.

User File Locations

By default, Windows stores most of the files created by the user in the folder **C:\Documents and Settings**_User_name_**\My Documents**.

The My Documents folder contains folders for music, videos, websites, and pictures, among others. Many programs also store specific user data here. All users of a single computer have their own My Documents folder containing each user's favorites, cookies, and desktop items.

System File Locations

When the Windows operating system is installed, all of the files that are used to run the computer are located in the folder **C:\WINNT\system32** for Windows 2000 and **C:\Windows\system32** for Windows XP and Windows Vista.

Fonts

The Fonts folder contains all of the fonts that have been installed in the computer. Fonts come in several formats, including TrueType, OpenType, Composite, and PostScript. Font typefaces are the fonts that you can choose from within programs. Some examples of font typefaces are Arial, Times New Roman, and Courier.

The Fonts folder can be accessed through the Control Panel. Fonts can be installed using the **File > Install New Font** menu. All of the installed fonts are located in **C:\Windows\Fonts**.

Temporary Files

The Temporary Files folder contains files created by the operating system and programs that are needed for a short period of time. For example, temporary files might be created while an application is being installed to make more RAM available for other applications.

Temporary files are found in the folder **C:\Documents and Settings**_User_name_**\Local Settings\Temp**.

Program Files

The Program Files folder is used by most application installation programs to install software. Programs are usually installed in the folder **C:\Program Files**.

Offline Files and Folders

With Windows 2000, a new feature to help mobile users be more productive was introduced. Offline Files and Folders allows you to select shared files and folders from the network to be stored on your computer. These files are available after the computer is disconnected from the network. When you reconnect to the network, the changes that you have made offline are automatically applied to the original files on the network.

To set up your computer to use offline files and folders, follow these steps:

Step 1.   Select **Start > My Computer > C: drive**.

Step 2.   Select **Tools > Folder Options > Offline Files**.

Step 3.   Check the **Enable Offline Files** checkbox.

To make a file or folder available to you offline, follow these steps:

Step 1.   Select **Start > My Computer**.

Step 2.   Open a network drive.

Step 3.   Select the shared network files or folders to make available offline.

Step 4.   Select **File > Make Available Offline**.

To view a list of all of the shared, offline network files, follow these steps:

Step 1.   Select **Tools > Folder Options**.

Step 2.   Select **Offline Files > View Files**.

Refer to
Figure
in online course

12.2 Install, configure, and optimize an operating system

Most operating systems are easy to install. After the computer starts, the Windows XP installation media displays a wizard to guide you through the installation process with a series of questions. After the answers to the questions are provided, the installation wizard completes the installation automatically. In this section, you will perform a custom installation of Windows XP.

After completing this section, you will meet these objectives:

- Compare and contrast a default installation and a custom installation.

- Install Windows XP using a custom installation.

- Create, view, and manage disks, directories, and files.

- Identify procedures and utilities used to optimize the performance of operating systems.

- Identify procedures and utilities used to optimize the performance of browsers.

- Describe the installation, use, and configuration of e-mail software.

- Set the screen resolution and update the video driver.

- Describe the installation of a second operating system.

Refer to
Figure
in online course

12.2.1 Compare and contrast a default installation and a custom installation

The default installation of Windows XP is sufficient for most computers used in a home or small office network. A custom installation of Windows XP is typically used in a larger network.

Default Installation

A default installation requires minimal user interaction. You are prompted to provide information for the specific computer and the owner or user.

Custom Installation

In Windows XP, the custom installation is very similar to the default installation. There are only two screens that offer a custom selection during setup. The first screen is to customize the regional settings, and the second screen is to customize the network settings. A technician or a user with technical experience often performs the custom installation. In a custom installation, the wizard prompts the user for detailed performance information to ensure that the operating system is customized to meet the preferences or requirements of the individual user or the network administrator of a company. You can perform a custom Windows XP installation on more than one computer on a network by using an answer file that contains predefined settings and answers to the questions that are asked by the wizard during setup.

The technician can automate and customize a Windows XP installation to include the following features:

- Productivity applications, such as Microsoft Office
- Custom applications
- Support for multiple languages
- OS Deployment Feature Pack using Microsoft Systems Management Server (SMS)
- Hardware device drivers

Refer to
Figure
in online course

12.2.2 Install Windows XP using a custom installation

The default installation of Windows XP is sufficient for most computers used in a home or small office environment. A custom installation of Windows XP can save time and provide a consistent configuration of the operating system across computers on a large network. There are several different types of custom installations of Windows XP:

- An Unattended installation from a network distribution point uses an answer file.
- An Image-based installation using Sysprep and a disk-imaging program copies an image of the operating system directly to the hard drive with no user intervention.
- A Remote installation using Remote Installation Services (RIS) downloads the installation across the network. This installation can be requested by the user or forced onto the computer by the administrator.
- An OS Deployment Feature Pack using Microsoft SMS dramatically simplifies deployment of an operating system across the organization.

Unattended Installation in Windows XP

The unattended installation using an unattend.txt answer file is the easiest custom installation method to perform on a network. An answer file can be created using an application called setup-mgr.exe located within the deploy.cab file on the Windows XP media.

Figure 1 shows an example of an answer file. After you have answered all of the questions, the unattend.txt file is copied to the distribution shared folder on a server. At this point, you can do one of two things:

- Run the unattended.bat file on the client machine. This prepares the hard drive and automatically installs the operating system from the server over the network.

- Create a boot disk that boots up the computer and connects to the distribution share on the server. Run the batch file to install the operating system over the network.

Unattended Installation in Windows Vista

To customize a standard Windows Vista installation, the System Image Manager (SIM) is used to create the setup answer file. The Windows SIM allows you to perform the following operations:

- Create an unattended answer file.

- Update an unattended answer file.

- Add packages such as applications or drivers to an unattended answer file.

- Validate an unattended answer file.

The Windows SIM is part of the Windows Automated Installation Kit (AIK) and can be downloaded from the Microsoft website.

Image-based Installation

When performing image-based installations, begin by completely configuring one computer to an operational state. Next, run Sysprep to prepare the system for imaging. A third-party drive imaging application prepares an image of the completed computer, which can be burned onto a CD or DVD. This image can then be copied onto computers with compatible Hardware Access Layers (HALs) to complete the installation of multiple computers. After the image has been copied, you can boot up the computer, but you may have to configure some settings, such as the computer name and domain membership.

Remote Installation

With RIS, the process is very much like an image-based installation, except you do not use a drive imaging utility. You can use RIS to remotely set up new Microsoft Windows computers by using an RIS network shared folder as the source of the Windows operating system files. You can install operating systems on remote boot-enabled client computers. User computers that are connected to the network can be started by using a remote boot disk or network adapter capable of booting the computer. The client then logs on with valid user account credentials.

RIS is designed to be used in a relatively small network and should not be used over low-speed links of a WAN. Microsoft SMS allows a network administrator to manage large numbers of computers on a network. SMS can be used to manage updates, provide remote control, and perform inventory management. An optional feature is operating system deployment, which requires the installation of the SMS OS Deployment Feature Pack on the Windows 2003 server. SMS allows the installation of a large number of client computers across an entire network concurrently.

Refer to
Lab Activity
for this chapter

Refer to
Lab Activity
for this chapter

Refer to
Figure
in online course

Advanced Installation of Windows XP

Install a Windows XP operating system by using an answer file for automation.

Advanced Installation of Windows Vista

Install a Windows Vista operating system by using an answer file for automation.

12.2.3 Create, view, and manage disks, directories, and files

Within the operating system, disks and directories are locations where data is stored and organized. The file system used by the operating system determines additional factors that affect storage such as partition size, cluster size, and security features.

Disk Structure

A hard disk is divided into specific areas called partitions. Partitions are formatted so that they can store information. The Disk Management utility displays information and performs services such as partitioning and formatting disks in Windows. Figure 1 shows the Disk Management utility used in Windows XP.

There are several types of partitions on a hard drive:

- *Primary partition–* This is usually the first partition. A primary partition cannot be subdivided into smaller sections. There can be up to four partitions per hard drive.

- *Active partition–* This partition is used by the operating system to boot the computer. Only one primary partition can be marked active.

- *Extended partition–* This partition normally uses the remaining free space on a hard drive or takes the place of a primary partition. There can be only one extended partition per hard drive, and it can be subdivided into smaller sections called logical drives.

Note

At any given time, you can only designate one partition as the active partition. The operating system uses the active partition to boot up the system. The active partition must be a primary partition.

In most cases, the C: drive is the active partition and contains the boot and system files. Some users create additional partitions to organize files or to be able to dual-boot the computer.

There are several ways to access the Disk Management utility in Windows XP:

- Select **Start** > right-click **My Computer** > **Manage**.

- Select **Disk Management**.

- Select **Start** > **Settings** > **Control Panel** > **Administrative Tools** > **Computer Management**.

- Select **Disk Management**.

There are several ways to access the Disk Management utility in Windows Vista:

- Select **Start** > right-click **My Computer** > **Manage**.

- Select **Disk Management**.

- Select **Start** > **Settings** > **Control Panel** > **Administrative Tools** > **Computer Management** > **Continue**.

■ Select **Disk Management**.

In Windows, letters are used to name the drives. A Windows computer can have up to 26 physical and logical drives because there are 26 letters in the English alphabet. Drives A and B are reserved for floppy disk drives, and drive C is reserved for the primary, active partition. Therefore, the maximum number of additional drives is 23.

With the NTFS file system, a drive can be mapped to an empty folder on a volume and is referred to as a mounted drive. Mounted drives are assigned drive paths instead of letters and are displayed as a drive icon in Windows Explorer. Use a mounted drive to configure more than 26 drives on your computer or when you need additional storage space on a volume.

To mount a volume in Windows:

Step 1.	Select **Start > Control Panel > Administrative Tools > Computer Management**.
Step 2.	Click **Disk Management** in the left pane.
Step 3.	Right-click the partition or volume to be mounted.
Step 4.	Click **Change Drive Letter and Paths**.
Step 5.	Click **Add**.
Step 6.	Click **Mount in the following empty NTFS folder**.
Step 7.	Create an empty folder, type the path to an empty folder, or browse to an empty folder on an NTFS volume and click **OK**.
Step 8.	Close **Computer Management**.

Drive Status

The Disk Management utility displays the status of each disk, as shown in Figure 2. The hard drives in the computer will display one of the following conditions:

■ *Foreign–* A dynamic disk that has been moved to a computer from another computer running Windows 2000 or Windows XP

■ *Healthy–* A volume that is functioning properly

■ *Initializing–* A basic disk that is being converted into a dynamic disk

■ *Missing–* A dynamic disk that is corrupted, turned off, or disconnected

■ *Not Initialized–* A disk that does not contain a valid signature

■ *Online–* A basic or dynamic disk that is accessible and shows no problems

■ *Online (Errors)–* I/O errors that are detected on a dynamic disk

■ *Offline–* A dynamic disk that is corrupted or unavailable

■ *Unreadable–* A basic or dynamic disk that has experienced hardware failure, corruption, or I/O errors

Other drive status indicators might be displayed when using drives other than hard drives:

■ *Audio CD–* An audio CD that is in the optical drive

■ *No Media–* An optical or removable drive that is empty

File System

Partitions are formatted with a file system. The three file systems available in Windows XP are FAT (FAT16), FAT32, and NTFS. FAT32 and NTFS are compared in Figure 3. NTFS has greater stability and security features.

For example, Windows does not display the file extension, but this practice can cause security problems. Virus writers are able to distribute executable files disguised as a non-executable file. To avoid this security breach, you should always show file extensions by doing the following:

Select **Start > Control Panel > Folder Options > View**, and uncheck the **Hide extensions for known file types** check box, as shown in Figure 4.

Note

Saving files to the root directory of the C: drive can cause organizational problems with data. It is a best practice to store data in folders created on the C: drive.

Refer to **Lab Activity** for this chapter

Create a Partition in Windows XP
Create a FAT32 formatted partition on a disk, convert the partition to NTFS, and identify the differences between the FAT32 format and the NTFS format.

Refer to **Figure** in online course

Create a Partition in Windows Vista
Create a FAT32 formatted partition on a disk, convert the partition to NTFS, and identify the differences between the FAT32 format and the NTFS format.

Refer to **Lab Activity** for this chapter

12.2.4 Identify procedures and utilities used to optimize the performance of operating systems

Several procedures and tools are available to optimize the performance of an operating system. The concepts may be the same across operating systems, but the optimization methods and procedures are different. For example, while virtual memory performs the same function on a Windows 98 and Windows XP operating system, the path to find and set virtual memory settings is different.

System Tools

To maintain and optimize an operating system, you can access various tools within Windows. Some of these tools include disk error checking, which can scan the hard drive for file structure errors, and hard drive defragmentation, which can consolidate files for faster access. Figure 1 shows the hard drive management tools.

Disk Error-Checking Tool

The Windows operating system uses CHKDSK from within the GUI or at the command line to detect and repair disk errors.

To check a drive for errors using the GUI, follow these steps:

1. Double-click **My Computer**.

2. Right-click the drive that you want to check.

3. On the Tools tab, under Error-checking, click **Check Now**.

4. Under Check disk options, select the **Scan for and attempt recovery of bad sectors** check box.

> **Note**
>
> The **Scan for and attempt recovery of bad sectors** option will automatically fix file system errors as well as check the disk for bad sectors and recover any data from sectors that are found to be bad. Any data that is recovered is saved to files in the root directory of the disk.

The CLI version of the utility has four options to check a drive for errors:

- *chkdsk–* Displays a status report of the drive

- *chkdsk /f–* Fixes errors on the disk

- *chkdsk /r–* Recovers readable information from bad sectors

- *chkdsk /x–* Dismounts the volume if necessary

CHKDSK makes multiple passes over the disk, checking for specific criteria:

- *Phase 1: Checking Files–* CHKDSK examines each file record in the Master File Table (MFT) for consistency. By the end of this phase, used and available space on the volume have been identified.

- *Phase 2: Checking Indexes–* CHKDSK examines the MFT to ensure that every file and directory is referenced by at least one entry. Finally, CHKDSK checks that the time stamps and file sizes are correct in the directory listings.

- *Phase 3: Checking Security Descriptors–* CHKDSK examines the security descriptors for file or directory ownership information and NTFS permissions.

- *Phases 4 and 5: Checking Sectors–* If the /r option is used, CHKDSK makes two more passes looking for sectors that have physical damage.

Disk Defragmenter

To help optimize the files on the hard drive, Windows operating systems provide a defragmentation utility. As files are accessed and stored on a hard drive, the files change from being contiguous on the disk to being scattered across the disk. This can cause the operating system to slow down. The hard drive has to search several areas on the hard drive platter to find the entire file. For one file, the effect of the process is minimal. When this occurs for thousands of files, however, the process will physically slow down the reading and writing of a file to a hard drive.

To defragment a drive in Windows XP, double-click **My Computer** on the desktop. Right-click the drive that you want to optimize. Choose **Properties**. On the **Tools** tab, click **Defragment Now**.

To defragment a drive in Windows Vista, double-click **Computer** on the desktop. Right-click the drive that you want to optimize. Choose **Properties**. In the **Tools** tab, click **Defragment Now**.

System Information

Administrators can use the System Information tool, as shown in Figure 2, to collect and display information about local and remote computers. The System Information tool quickly finds information about software, drivers, hardware configurations, and computer components. The information can be used by support personnel to diagnose and troubleshoot a computer.

To access the System Information tool, use the following path:

Start > All Programs > Accessories > System Tools > System Information

It may be necessary to send a file containing all of the information about a computer to another technician or help desk. To export a System Information file, click **File > Export**, type the name of the file, choose a location, and click **Save**.

The System Information tool in Windows XP also provides quick access to many other tools:

- *Net Diagnostics*– This tool runs a variety of network tests to troubleshoot network-related problems.

- *System Restore*– This tool creates or loads a restore point for restoring the computer's system files and settings.

- *File Signature Verification Utility*– This tool checks for system files that are not digitally signed.

- *DirectX Diagnostic Tool*– This tool reports detailed information about the DirectX components that are installed on your computer.

- *Dr Watson*– This tool debugs Windows to help diagnose program errors.

To view the information from a remote computer, follow these steps:

Step 1.	Choose **View > Remote Computer**.
Step 2.	Choose **Remote Computer on the Network**.
Step 3.	Type the name of the computer that you want to view and click **OK**.

Remote Desktop Protocol

The Remote Desktop Protocol allows you to use an application such as Remote Desktop or Remote Assistance to connect to another computer. These applications allow you to view the screen and control the computer's mouse and keyboard as though you were local to that computer. The Remote Desktop Protocol is also used to operate computers that are connected to the network but do not have a monitor, mouse, or keyboard.

To access the Remote Desktop program, use the following path:

Start > All Programs > Accessories >Remote Desktop Connection

Remote Assistance uses the Remote Desktop Protocol to allow another user to connect to your computer, see your computer screen, and chat over a network. With your permission, the remote user can control your computer.

To access the Remote Assistance program in Windows XP, use the following path:

Start > Help and Support > Invite a friend to connect to your computer with Remote Assistance > Invite someone to help you

In Windows Vista, use the following path:

Start > Help and Support > Use Windows Remote Assistance to get help from a friend or offer help > Invite someone you trust to help you

An e-mail invitation must be sent to another user to allow them to connect and control your computer. After the recipient has received the invitation, the recipient can see your desktop and help you.

Virtual Memory

Virtual memory, shown in Figure 3, allows the CPU to address more memory than is installed in the computer. This is done so that every application can address the same amount of memory. Virtual memory is a swap or page file that is constantly read in and out of RAM. Typically, you should let Windows manage the size of the swap file. The only setting that you should change is the location of the swap file. You must be a member of the administrator group to make this change.

To access virtual memory settings in Windows XP, use the following path:

Start > Control Panel > System > Advanced tab > Performance, click Settings button > Advanced tab

To access virtual memory settings in Windows Vista, use the following path:

Start > Control Panel > System > Advanced system settings > Continue > Advanced tab > Performance, click Settings button > Advanced tab

Administrative Tools

Windows contains many tools that are used to manage permissions and users or configure computer components and services. You must possess administrator rights to access administrative tools. These are some of the most common administrative tools:

- *Event Viewer–* This tool logs a history of events regarding applications, security, and the system.

- *Computer Management–* This tool allows you to access administrative areas such as System Tools, Storage, and Services and Applications.

- *Services–* This tool allows you to manage all of the services on local and remote computers.

- *Performance Monitor–* This tool displays and logs real-time information about the processors, disks, memory, and network usage for the computer.

Services

Services are a type of application that runs in the background to achieve a specific goal or wait for a request. Only necessary services should be started to reduce unnecessary security risks. See Figure 4 for some of the services available on a computer. Four settings, or states, can be used to control the services:

- Automatic

- Manual

- Disabled

- Stopped

If a service, such as DHCP or Automatic Updates, is set to automatic, it will start up when the PC starts. Manual services, such as the support of an UPS, need to be manually configured to work. Some services may be stopped or disabled for troubleshooting purposes, such as turning off the print spooler when there are printer problems.

Device Manager

The Device Manager, shown in Figure 5, allows you to view all of the settings for devices in a computer such as the IRQ, I/O address, and the DMA settings. It can also be used to diagnose and resolve device conflicts. From the Device Manager, you can view details about the installed driver version. You can also perform the following functions:

- Update a driver

- Roll back a driver

- Uninstall a driver

- Disable a device

The Device Manager uses special icons to indicate a problem with a specific device:

- A red X appears on the icon of devices that have been disabled.

- An exclamation point inside a yellow triangle appears on the icon of devices that do not have properly installed drivers or do not respond.

Task Manager

The Task Manager, shown in Figure 6, allows you to view information about applications that are currently running. From the Task Manager, you can perform many functions:

- Close any applications that have stopped responding.

- Start a new task.

- Monitor the performance of the CPU.

- Monitor the performance of the virtual memory.

- View all processes that are currently running.

- View information about network connections.

There are five tabs within the Task Manager:

- *Applications*– This tab shows all of the applications that are running. From this tab, you can create, switch to, or end tasks using the buttons at the bottom of this tab.

- *Processes*– This tab shows all of the processes that are running. A process is any set of instructions running on the computer that were started by a user, a program, or the operating system. From this tab, you can end processes or set process priorities.

- *Performance*– This tab shows the CPU and page file usage of the computer.

- *Networking*– This tab shows the usage of all network adapters in the computer.

- *Users*– This tab shows all users that are logged on the computer. From this tab, you can disconnect remote users or log off local users.

Be careful when ending processes. Ending a process will cause the program to end immediately without saving any information. Ending a process that Windows has initiated may prevent the system from running correctly. Be careful when changing the priority of processes. If you change the priority of a process, the change might adversely affect the performance of the computer.

System Monitor

The System Monitor, shown in Figure 7, is part of the Performance Console and displays real-time information about the processors, disks, memory, and network usage of the computer. You can easily summarize these activities through histograms, graphs, and reports.

You must have administrative privileges to access the Performance Monitor console. To view the Performance Monitor console in Windows XP, use the following path:

Start > Control Panel > Administrative Tools > Performance

To view the Performance Monitor console in Windows Vista, use the following path:

Start > Control Panel > Administrative Tools > Reliability and Performance Monitor > Continue

The data that the System Monitor displays is used to help you understand how the workload of the computer affects system resources such as the CPU, memory, and network. Use the System Monitor to display detailed data about the resources that you are using when performing specific tasks or multiple tasks. The data that you collect helps you to determine when an upgrade might be necessary. The System Monitor shows how configuration changes or system tuning affects the computer. For example, use the System Monitor to determine whether a newly installed program needs more RAM in the computer.

Regional and Language Options

You can change many of the standards and formats for numbers, currencies, dates, and time by using the Regional and Language Options settings. These settings also allow you to change the primary language or install an additional language. To access the Regional and Language Options settings, use the following path:

Start > Control Panel > Regional and Language Options

Temporary Files

Almost every program uses temporary files, which are usually automatically deleted when the application or the operating system is finished using them. However, some of the temporary files must be deleted manually. Since temporary files take up hard drive space that could be used for other files, it is a good idea to check and delete as necessary every two or three months. Temporary files are usually located in the following locations in Windows XP:

- C:\Temp
- C:\Tmp
- C:\Windows\Temp
- C:\Windows\Tmp
- C:\Documents and Settings\%USERPROFILE%\Local Settings\Temp

Temporary files are usually located in the following locations in Windows Vista:

- C:\Windows\Temp
- C:\Users\%USERPROFILE%\AppData\Local\Temp

Note

In the paths above, %USERPROFILE% is an environment variable set by the operating system with the name of the user that is currently logged on to the computer. Environment variables are used by the operating system, applications, and software installation programs. To see the environment variables that are configured on your Windows XP computer, use the following path:
Start > Control Panel > System > Advanced > Environment Variables

Refer to
Lab Activity
for this chapter

Customize Settings in Windows XP

This lab is comprised of five parts.
Part 1: Customize Virtual Memory settings, customize the Startup Folder and RunOnce Key in the Registry, and change the default Windows Update option.
Part 2: Examine the results after using Disk Check and Disk Defragmenter on a hard drive.
Part 3: Examine regional and language settings and explore how to manage processes in Task Manager.

Part 4: Manage and monitor Windows XP system performance.

Part 5: Remotely connect to a computer, examine device drivers, and provide remote assistance.

Refer to
Lab Activity
for this chapter

Customize Settings in Windows Vista

This lab is comprised of five parts.

Part 1: Customize Virtual Memory settings, customize the Startup Folder and RunOnce Key in the Registry, and change the default Windows Update option.

Part 2: Examine the results after using Disk Check and Disk Defragmenter on a hard drive.

Part 3: Examine regional and language settings and explore how to manage processes in Task Manager.

Part 4: Manage and monitor Windows Vista system performance.

Part 5: Remotely connect to a computer, examine device drivers, and provide remote assistance.

Refer to
Figure
in online course

12.2.5 Identify procedures and utilities used to optimize the performance of browsers

Web browsers and e-mail applications are typically the applications used the most on a computer. Optimizing the web browsers and the e-mail application should increase the performance of the computer.

Refer to
Figure
in online course

The Microsoft browser, Internet Explorer (IE), has general settings for changing the homepage and browser appearance settings. Additional settings allow you to view or delete the information saved by the browser:

- History

- Temporary files

- Cookies

- Passwords

- Web-form information

Note

Cookies are information transmitted between a web browser and a web server with the purpose of tracking user information to customize the page delivered to the user.

To access the settings in IE, open an IE browser window and select **Tools > Internet Options**.

Caching, or storing, Internet files is a feature of the web browser that is used to speed up the process of accessing previously visited websites. The file-storing tool in IE downloads copies of the images or the HTML files of sites you have visited to the hard disk. When you revisit the website, the site opens more quickly because the files are in the local disk cache and do not need to be downloaded again.

Cached files in the web browser can become outdated or may be very large. These IE settings allow you to configure how often the cache is refreshed:

- Every visit to the page

- Every time you start IE

- Automatically

- Never

To access the cache settings in Windows XP, open an IE browser window and choose **Tools > Internet Options**. In the **Temporary Internet Files** area, click **Settings**. Click the tabs in Figure 1 to explore other IE configuration options.

To access the cache settings in Windows Vista, open an IE browser window and choose **Tools > Internet Options**. In the **Browsing History** area, click **Settings**.

Refer to
Lab Activity
for this chapter

Install an Alternate Browser
Install the Mozilla Firefox Web Browser in Windows.

12.2.6 Describe installation, use, and configuration of e-mail software

E-mail software may be installed as part of a web browser or as a standalone application. Outlook Express is an e-mail tool that is a component of the Microsoft Windows operating system. To configure Outlook Express, you must provide information about your e-mail account, as shown in Figure 1.

You should have the following information available when installing e-mail accounts into the e-mail client software:

- Display name
- E-mail address
- Type of incoming mail server, such as POP3 or IMAP
- Incoming mail server name
- Outgoing mail server name
- Username
- Account password

The protocols used in e-mail include the following:

- *Post Office Protocol version 3 (POP3)*– This protocol retrieves e-mails from a remote server over TCP/IP. It does not leave a copy of the e-mail on the server; however, some implementations allow users to specify that mail be saved for some period of time.

- *Internet Message Access Protocol (IMAP)*– This protocol allows local e-mail clients to retrieve e-mail from a server. Typically leaves a copy of the e-mail on the server until you move the e-mail to a personal folder in your e-mail application. IMAP synchronizes e-mail folders between the server and client.

- *Simple Mail Transfer Protocol (SMTP)*– This protocol transmits e-mails across a TCP/IP network. It is the e-mail format for text that only uses ASCII encoding.

- *Multipurpose Internet Mail Extensions (MIME)*– This protocol extends the e-mail format to include text in ASCII standard, as well as other formats such as pictures and word processor documents. Normally used in conjunction with SMTP.

Refer to
Figure
in online course

Additional features are available with e-mail software:

- Automatic handling rules for e-mails
- Different e-mail coding, such as HTML, plain text, or rich text
- Newsgroups

Refer to
Interactive Graphic
in online course.

E-mail Protocols

Complete the e-mail protocol matching activity in Figure 2.

12.2.7 Set screen resolution and update video driver

After the operating system is installed, you can set the screen resolution to meet the requirements of your customer. If the screen resolution is not set properly, you may get unexpected display results from different video cards and monitors. The unexpected results could include a Windows desktop that does not take up the full area of the screen, or a blank screen if the resolution is set too high.

When using an LCD screen, the resolution should be set to native mode, or native resolution. Native mode is the screen resolution that is the same as the number of pixels that the monitor has. If you move from the native mode, the monitor does not produce the best picture. See Figure 1 for the screen resolution settings on a Windows XP computer.

You can change the screen settings in Windows XP in the Settings tab of the Display Properties control panel applet:

■ *Screen resolution–* This setting determines the number of pixels. A higher number of pixels displays a better resolution and picture.

■ *Refresh rate–* This setting determines how often the image in the screen is redrawn. Refresh rate is expressed in Hertz (Hz). The higher the refresh rate, the more steady the screen image.

■ *Display colors–* This setting determines the number of colors visible on the screen at once. The more bits, the greater the number of colors. The following is a list of color depths:
  ■ 256 colors - 8-bit color
  ■ 65,536 colors - 16-bit color (High Color)
  ■ 16 million colors - 24-bit color (True Color)
  ■ 16 million colors - 24-bit (True Color plus an 8-bit alpha channel for color blending)

You can change the screen settings in Windows Vista in the Display Settings link of the Personalization control panel applet.

When troubleshooting a display problem, check that the driver is fully compatible with the graphics card. Windows may install a default driver that works, but may not provide all of the available options for best viewing and performance. See Figure 2 for the Hardware Update Wizard in Windows XP. Perform the following steps to update the video adapter driver:

Step 1. Download the most recent driver from the manufacturer website.

Step 2. Disable anti-virus software.

Step 3. Install the new driver.

Step 4. Restart the computer.

Step 5. Verify that your anti-virus software is functioning.

Caution

Disabling the anti-virus software leaves your computer vulnerable to viruses.

You may encounter problems when you install or reinstall a video driver. For example, after updating the video adapter driver, you are unable to view the screen when you restart the computer. To investigate the problem and restore the settings in Windows XP, reboot the computer. During the boot phase, press the **F8** key. Enter the boot options when prompted and select **Enable VGA**

Mode to use a 640 x 480 resolution. After the operating system is loaded, you can then select **Roll Back Driver** from the **Properties** of the graphics card. You should then do some research to determine any possible issues with the driver that you tried to install.

To investigate the problem and restore the settings in Windows Vista, reboot the computer. During the boot phase, press the **F8** key. Enter the boot options when prompted and select **Enable low-resolution video** to use a 640 x 480 resolution. After the operating system is loaded, you can then select **Roll Back Driver** from the **Properties** of the graphics card.

12.2.8 Describe installation of a second operating system

Refer to **Figure** in online course

You can have multiple operating systems on a single computer. Some software applications may require the most recent version of an operating system, while other software applications require an older version. There is a dual-boot process for multiple operating systems on a computer. When the boot.ini file determines that more than one operating system is present during the boot process, you are prompted to choose the operating system that you want to load. See Figure 1 for a sample boot.ini file.

To create a dual-boot system in Microsoft Windows, you typically must have more than one hard drive, or the hard drive must contain more than one partition.

You should install the oldest operating system on the primary partition or the hard drive marked as the active partition first. You should then install the second operating system on the second partition or hard drive. The boot files are automatically installed in the active partition.

The boot.ini File

During the installation, the boot.ini file is created on the active partition to allow the selection of the operating system to boot on startup. The boot.ini file can be edited to change the order of the operating systems. You can also edit the file for the length of time an operating system selection can be made during the boot phase. Typically, the default time to select an operating system is 30 seconds. This always delays the boot time of the computer by 30 seconds, unless the user intervenes to select a particular operating system. In the boot.ini file, the boot time should be changed to 5 or 10 seconds to boot up the computer faster.

To edit the boot.ini file in Windows XP, right-click **My Computer > Properties > Advanced Tab**. In the **Startup and Recovery** area, select **Settings**. Click **Edit**.

To edit the boot configuration data in Windows Vista, use the bcdedit.exe command-line tool, as shown in Figure 2. To access the bcdedit.exe tool, use the following path:

Select **Start > All Programs > Accessories >** right-click **Command Prompt > Run as administrator > Continue >** type **bcdedit.exe**.

12.2.9 Windows CLI commands

Refer to **Figure** in online course

When troubleshooting problems with the operating system, you may need to use CLI commands and options to perform tasks. This may be necessary when Windows will not start or from within Windows at a command line. The figure describes the most common CLI commands, how to use them, and what they do.

MSCONFIG

The MSCONFIG command brings up the System Configuration Utility that performs diagnostic procedures on the Windows startup files. You must be logged on with Administrator permissions to complete the troubleshooting procedure. MSCONFIG should be used when the computer boots but will not load the Windows operating system correctly. To troubleshoot the Windows operating system with MSCONFIG, follow these steps:

1. Start Windows using only the basic drivers and services.

2. Select **Start > Run > General > Diagnostic startup – load basic devices and services only > OK**.

3. Restart the computer.

If the problem still exists after restarting, you will need to investigate other possible causes such as a missing or corrupted file, a corrupted registry, or a virus infection.

If the computer restarted successfully with basic drivers and services, open the System Configuration Utility and follow these steps:

1. Select **General > Selective Startup**.

2. Uncheck all items under **Selective Startup**.

3. Check only the first item under **Selective Startup**.

4. Restart the computer.

5. If the computer starts successfully, select one more item under **Selective Startup**.

6. Restart the computer.

7. Repeat steps 5 and 6 until the problem is identified.

8. After the problem has been identified, click the tab of the last item you selected under **Selective Startup**.

Use the same process of elimination to determine which item is causing the problem. You must research the problem and implement fixes until the problem is solved.

SFC

The System File Checker (SFC) allows you to check all of the protected system files, such as krnl386.exe, and replace them with known good versions if they have become corrupted or deleted. If you receive a notice from Windows or suspect that a file has been altered, replaced, or corrupted, use the command **sfc /scannow** at the command line to initiate the system file checker. The SFC replaces any bad files with known good versions. You might be asked for the original installation media if Windows is unable to retrieve a copy from its cache of original files.

12.3 Describe how to upgrade operating systems

Refer to
Figure
in online course

An operating system must be upgraded periodically to remain compatible with the latest hardware and software. When newer versions of an operating system are released, support for older operating systems is eventually withdrawn.

New hardware products are continually coming on the market. The new design of the products often requires that the latest operating system be installed to operate correctly. While this may be expensive, you gain enhanced functionality through new features and support for newer hardware.

A Windows XP upgrade can be performed from a CD or over a network. You should ensure that the new operating system is compatible with the computer. Microsoft provides a utility called the Upgrade Advisor to scan the system for incompatibility issues before upgrading to newer Windows operating systems. You can download the Upgrade Advisor from the Microsoft Windows website free of charge. After the Upgrade Advisor is finished, a report is produced to inform you of any problems. Incompatibility in hardware is the most common reason for failure in the upgrade process.

Not all older Windows operating systems are upgradeable to the newer versions, as described in the following list:

- Windows 98, Windows 98 SE, and Windows Me can be upgraded to Windows XP Home or Windows XP Professional.

- Windows NT workstation 4.0 with Service Pack 6 and Windows 2000 Professional can be upgraded only to Windows XP Professional.

- Windows 3.1 and Windows 95 cannot be upgraded to Windows XP.

- Windows 2000 or earlier cannot be upgraded to Windows Vista.

Note

Remember to back up all data prior to beginning the upgrade.

Refer to
Figure
in online course

12.4   Describe preventive maintenance procedures for operating systems

Preventive maintenance for an operating system includes automating tasks to perform scheduled updates. It also includes installing service packs that help keep the system up-to-date and compatible with new software and hardware.

If a driver or system becomes corrupted, you can use restore points to restore the system to a previous state. However, restore points cannot recover lost data.

After completing this section, you will meet these objectives:

- Schedule automatic tasks and updates.

- Set restore points.

Refer to
Figure
in online course

12.4.1   Schedule automatic tasks and updates

You can automate tasks in Windows XP using the Scheduled Tasks utility. The Scheduled Tasks utility monitors selected, user-defined criteria and then executes the tasks when the criteria have been met.

GUI Scheduled Tasks

Some of the common tasks that are automated using the Scheduled Tasks utility include the following:

- Disk cleanup

- Backup

- Disk defragmenter

- Starting other applications

To open the Scheduled Tasks wizard in Windows XP, select **Start > All Programs >Accessories > System Tools > Scheduled Tasks**. Double-click **Add Scheduled Task** as shown in Figure 1.

To open the Scheduled Tasks wizard in Windows Vista, select **Start > All Programs >Accessories > System Tools > Task Scheduler > Continue**. Select **Create Basic Task** or **Create Task** as shown in Figure 2.

CLI Scheduled Tasks

The Scheduled Tasks utility is a Windows-based GUI utility. You can also use the **at** command in the command line utility to automatically schedule a command, a script file, or an application to run at a specific date and time. To use the **at** command, you must be logged in as a member of the Administrators group.

To learn more about the **at** command in Windows XP, choose **Start > Run**. At the CLI prompt, type **cmd**, and then press **Enter**. At the command prompt, type **at/?**.

To learn more about the **at** command in Windows Vista, choose **Start**. At the **Start Search**, type **cmd**, and then press **Enter**. At the command prompt, type **at/?** and press **Enter**.

Windows Automatic Updates

You should use one of the following methods to configure updates for the Windows XP operating system:

Refer to
Figure
in online course

- Automatic (need to specify a date and time)

- Download updates for me, but let me choose when to install them

- Notify me but don't automatically download or install them

- Turn off Automatic Updates

The Automatic Updates screen, shown in Figure 3, is found in the Control Panel.

Refer to
Lab Activity
for this chapter

Schedule Task Using GUI and "at" Command in Windows XP
Schedule a task using the Windows XP GUI and schedule a task in a cmd window using the at command.

Refer to
Lab Activity
for this chapter

Schedule Task Using GUI and "at" Command in Windows Vista
Schedule a task using the Windows Vista GUI and schedule a task in a cmd window using the **at** command.

12.4.2 Set restore points

Restore points return the operating system to a predefined point in time. In some cases, the installation of an application or a hardware driver can cause instability or create unexpected changes to the computer. Uninstalling the application or hardware driver normally corrects the problem. If uninstalling does not solve the problem, you should try to restore the computer to an earlier time when the system worked properly.

Refer to
Figure
in online course

To open the System Restore utility, select **Start > All Programs > Accessories > System Tools > System Restore**.

Windows XP can create restore points in the following scenarios:

- When an install or upgrade takes place

- Every 24 hours, if the computer is running

- Manually, at any time

The restore points contain information about the system and registry settings that are used by Windows operating systems. System restore does not back up personal data files nor recover personal files that have been corrupted or deleted. To back up data, you should use a dedicated backup system, such as a tape drive, CDs, or a USB storage device.

Refer to
Lab Activity
for this chapter

Restore Points in Windows XP

Create a restore point and return your computer back to that point in time.

Refer to
Lab Activity
for this chapter

Restore Points in Windows Vista

Create a restore point and return your computer back to that point in time.

12.5 Troubleshoot operating systems

The troubleshooting process helps resolve problems with the operating system. These problems range from simple, such as a driver that does not operate properly, to complex, such as a system that locks up. Use the troubleshooting steps as a guideline to help you diagnose and repair problems.

After completing this section, you will meet these objectives:

- Review the troubleshooting process.

- Identify common problems and solutions.

- Apply troubleshooting skills.

Refer to
Figure
in online course

12.5.1 Review the troubleshooting process

Operating system problems can result from a combination of hardware, software, and network issues. Computer technicians must be able to analyze the problem and determine the cause of the error to repair the computer. This process is called troubleshooting.

The first step in the troubleshooting process is to identify the problem. Figure 1 is a list of open-ended and closed-ended questions to ask the customer.

After you have talked to the customer, you can establish a theory of probable causes. Figure 2 is a list of some common probable causes for operating system problems.

After you have developed some theories about what is wrong, test your theories to determine the cause of the problem. Figure 3 is a list of quick procedures that can determine the exact cause of the problem or even correct the problem. If a quick procedure does correct the problem, you can go to step 5 to verify full system functionality. If a quick procedure does not correct the problem, you may need to research the problem further to establish the exact cause.

After you have determined the exact cause of the problem, establish a plan of action to resolve the problem and implement the solution. Figure 4 shows sources of information to gather additional information to resolve an issue.

After you have corrected the problem, verify full functionality and, if applicable, implement preventive measures. Figure 5 is a list of the steps to verify the solution.

In the final step of the troubleshooting process, you must document your findings, actions, and outcomes. Figure 6 is a list of the tasks required to document the problem and the solution.

Refer to
Figure
in online course

12.5.2 Identify common problems and solutions

Computer problems can be attributed to hardware, software, networks, or some combination of the three. You will resolve some types of computer problems more often than others. A stop error is a hardware or software malfunction that causes the system to lock up. This type of error is known as the Blue Screen of Death (BSOD) and appears when the system is unable to recover from an error. The BSOD is usually caused by device driver errors.

The Event Log and other diagnostic utilities are available to research a stop error or BSOD error. To prevent these types of errors, verify that the hardware and software drivers are compatible. In addition, install the latest patches and updates for Windows. When the system locks up during startup, the computer can automatically reboot. The reboot is caused by the auto restart function in Windows and makes it difficult to see the error message.

The auto restart function can be disabled in the Advanced Startup Options menu. Figures 1 and 2 are charts of common operating system problems and solutions.

Refer to
Figure
in online course

12.5.3 Apply troubleshooting skills

Now that you understand the troubleshooting process, it is time to apply your listening and diagnostic skills.

Refer to
Figure
in online course

The first lab is designed to reinforce your skills with the operating system. You will check restore points before and after using Windows Update.

The second lab is designed to reinforce your communication and troubleshooting skills. In this lab, you will perform the following steps:

- Receive the work order
- Take the customer through various steps to try and resolve the problem
- Document the problem and the resolution

The third lab is designed to reinforce your skills with operating system problems. You will troubleshoot and repair a computer that has more than one problem.

Refer to
Lab Activity
for this chapter

Fix Operating System Problem
Troubleshoot and fix a computer that does not connect to the network.

Refer to
Lab Activity
for this chapter

Remote Technician: Fix an Operating System Problem
Gather data from the customer, instruct the customer on how to fix a computer that does not connect to the network, and document the customer's problem.

Refer to
Lab Activity
for this chapter

Troubleshooting Operating System Problems in Windows XP
Diagnose the causes of various operating system problems and solve the problems.

Refer to
Lab Activity
for this chapter

Troubleshooting Operating System Problems in Windows Vista
Diagnose the causes of various operating system problems and solve the problems.

Summary

This chapter discussed how to select an operating system based on the needs of the customer. You have learned the differences between operating systems and network operating systems. The labs have helped you become familiar with Windows, creating partitions, customizing virtual memory, and scheduling tasks. You have also learned some optimization tips for operating systems, as well as how to troubleshoot a computer problem from the perspective of a level-two technician. The following concepts discussed in this chapter will be useful to you when selecting and installing an operating system:

- Ensure that you fully understand the technology needs of the customer.

- Know the differences between common operating systems.

- Match the customer needs to the proper technologies.

- Know the different methods to install an operating system.

- Know how to upgrade different operating systems.

- Understand how preventive maintenance can stop problems before they start.

- Know which preventive maintenance procedures are appropriate for the customer.

- Know how to troubleshoot operating system problems.

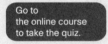

Go to
the online course
to take the quiz.

Chapter 12 Quiz

Take the chapter quiz to test your knowledge.

Your Chapter Notes

Advanced Laptops and Portable Devices

Introduction

With the increase in demand for mobility, the popularity of laptops and portable devices will continue to grow. During the course of your career, you will be expected to know how to configure, repair, and maintain these devices. The knowledge you acquire about desktop computers will help you service laptops and portable devices. However, there are important differences between the two technologies.

To facilitate mobility, laptops and portable devices use wireless technologies more than desktops. All laptops use batteries when they are disconnected from a power source. Docking stations are commonly used to connect a laptop to peripheral devices. As a computer technician, you will be required to configure, optimize, and troubleshoot these docking stations and accessories, as well as the laptop or portable device that they accompany. Many laptop components are proprietary, so some manufacturers require that you complete specialized certification training to perform laptop repairs.

Servicing laptops can be very challenging. Mastering the skills necessary to work on laptops is important to your career advancement.

After completing this chapter, you will meet these objectives:

- Describe wireless communication methods for laptops and portable devices.
- Describe repairs for laptops and portable devices.
- Select laptop components.
- Describe preventive maintenance procedures for laptops.
- Describe how to troubleshoot a laptop.

Refer to **Figure** in online course

13.1 Describe wireless communication methods for laptops and portable devices

Wireless devices give people the freedom to work, learn, play, and communicate wherever they want. People using wireless-capable devices do not need to be tied to a physical location to send and receive voice, video, and data communications. As a result, wireless facilities, such as Internet cafes, are opening in many countries. College campuses use wireless networks to allow students to sign up for classes, watch lectures, and submit assignments in areas where physical connections to the network are unavailable. This trend toward wireless communications will continue to grow as more people use wireless devices.

After completing this section, you will meet these objectives:

- Describe Bluetooth technology.
- Describe infrared technology.

- Describe cellular WAN technology.

- Describe Wi-Fi technology.

- Describe satellite technology.

Refer to
Figure
in online course

13.1.1 Describe Bluetooth technology

Bluetooth is a wireless technology that enables devices to communicate over short distances. A Bluetooth device can connect up to seven other Bluetooth devices to create a Wireless Personal Area Network (WPAN). This technical specification is described by the Institute of Electrical and Electronics Engineers (IEEE) 802.15.1 standard. Bluetooth devices are capable of handling voice, music, videos, and data and are ideally suited for connecting the following devices:

- Laptops

- Printers

- Cameras

- PDAs

- Cell phones

- Hands-free headsets

Refer to Figure 1 for common Bluetooth characteristics.

The distance of a Bluetooth Personal Area Network (PAN) is limited by the amount of power used by the devices in the PAN. Bluetooth devices are broken into three classifications as shown in Figure 2. The most common Bluetooth network is Class 2, which has a range of approximately 33 feet (10 m).

Bluetooth devices operate in the 2.4 to 2.485 GHz radio frequency range, which is in the Industrial, Scientific, and Medical (ISM) band. This band often does not require a license if approved equipment is used. The Bluetooth standard incorporates Adaptive Frequency Hopping (AFH). AFH allows signals to "hop" around using different frequencies within the Bluetooth range, thereby reducing the chance of interference when multiple Bluetooth devices are present. AFH also allows the device to learn frequencies that are already in use and to choose a different subset of frequencies hopping.

Security measures are included in the Bluetooth standard. The first time that a Bluetooth device connects, the device is authenticated using a Personal Identification Number (PIN). Bluetooth supports both 128-bit encryption and PIN authentication.

Refer to
Figure
in online course

13.1.2 Describe infrared technology

Infrared (IR) wireless technology is a low-power, short-range wireless technology. IR transmits data using LEDs and receives data using photodiodes.

IR wireless networks are globally unregulated. However, the Infrared Data Association (IrDA) defines the specifications for IR wireless communication. Refer to Figure 1 for common IR characteristics.

There are four types of IR networks:

- *Line of sight–* The signal is transmitted only if there is a clear, unobstructed view between devices.

- *Scatter–* The signal is bounced off ceilings and walls.

- *Reflective–* The signal is sent to an optical transceiver and is redirected to the receiving device.

- *Broadband optical telepoint–* The transmission can handle high-quality multimedia requirements.

Infrared networks are ideal for connecting laptops to the following types of devices that are in close proximity:

- Multimedia projector

- PDA

- Printer

- Remote control

- Wireless mouse

- Wireless keyboard

The setup and configuration of IR devices is quite simple. Many IR devices connect to the USB port on a laptop or desktop computer. When the computer detects the new device, Windows XP installs the appropriate drivers, as shown in Figure 2. The installation is similar to setting up a local area network connection.

IR is a practical, short-range connection solution, but it has some limitations:

- IR light cannot penetrate ceilings or walls.

- IR signals are susceptible to interference and dilution by strong light sources, such as florescent lighting.

- Scatter IR devices are able to connect without the line of sight, but data transfer rates are lower and distances are shorter.

- IR distances should be 3 feet (1 m) or less when used for computer communications.

Refer to **Figure** in online course

13.1.3 Describe cellular WAN technology

Originally, cellular networks were designed for voice communication only. Cellular technology has been evolving and now enables the transfer of voice, video, and data simultaneously. It also enables the use of laptops and portable devices remotely. With a cellular WAN adapter installed, a laptop user is able to travel and access the Internet. Refer to Figure 1 for common cellular WAN characteristics.

Although slower than DSL and cable connections, cellular WANs are still fast enough to be classified as a high-speed connection. To connect a laptop to a cellular WAN, you should install an adapter that is designed to work with cellular networks. A cellular adapter needs to support some or all of the following:

- *Global System for Mobile Communications (GSM)–* Worldwide cellular network

- *General Packet Radio Service (GPRS)–* Data service for users of GSM

- *Quad-band–* Allows a cellular phone to operate on all four GSM frequencies: 850 MHz, 900 MHz, 1800 MHz, and 1900 MHz

- *Short Message Service (SMS)–* Text messages

- *Multimedia Messaging Service (MMS)–* Multimedia messages

- *Enhanced Data Rates for GSM Evolution (EDGE)–* Provides increased data rates and improved data reliability

- *Evolution-Data Optimized (EV-DO)–* Faster download rates

- *High Speed Downlink Packet Access (HSDPA)–* Provides enhanced G3 access speed

Connecting to a cellular WAN is a simple process. Cellular WAN cards, as shown in Figure 2, are Plug and Play (PnP). These cards plug in to the PC Card slot or are built in to the laptop.

The speed at which cellular WAN devices communicate has increased with each generation of cellular technology. Refer to Figure 3 for a comparison of the characteristics of each generation of cellular WAN.

Refer to **Figure** in online course

13.1.4   Describe Wi-Fi technology

The wireless technology Wi-Fi is based on IEEE 802.11 networking standards and specifications. The number 802.11 denotes a set of standards that are specified in the IEEE 802.11 documentation. Hence, the terms 802.11 and Wi-Fi are interchangeable. Figure 1 shows some characteristics of Wi-Fi.

There are currently four major 802.11 standards:

- 802.11a

- 802.11b

- 802.11g

- 802.11n

Technicians often refer to Wi-Fi standards by just the final letters. For example, a technician may refer to an 802.11b wireless router as simply a "b" router.

The 802.11g standard was released in 2003. The 802.11n standard was released in draft form in 2006 and ratified in 2009.

The 802.11b, 802.11g, and 802.11n standards use the 2.4 GHz frequency band. The 2.4 GHz frequency band is unregulated and heavily used. The large amount of traffic can cause wireless signals in the 2.4 GHz range to be interfered with by other 2.4 GHz wireless devices. For this reason, the 802.11a standard was designed to use the 5.0 GHz frequency band. As a result, 802.11a is only compatible with the 802.11n standard because it also supports the 5.0 GHz frequency. See Figure 2 for data rate and range information.

Security is a major concern for wireless networks. Anyone within the coverage area of a wireless router can potentially gain access to the network. These precautions should be taken for security purposes:

- Never send login or password information using clear, unencrypted text.

- Use a VPN connection when possible.

- Enable security on home networks.

- Use Wi-Fi Protected Access (WPA) security.

Wi-Fi Protected Access standards (WPA, WPA2) are used to secure Wi-Fi networks. WPA uses a sophisticated encryption and authentication technology to protect data flow between Wi-Fi devices. WPA uses a 128-bit encryption key and should be enabled on all wireless devices. WPA was introduced to replace WEP, which had known security issues.

Refer to
Figure
in online course

13.1.5 Describe satellite technology

Satellite service is ideal for rural or remote users who require high-speed, broadband access in areas where no other high-speed services are available. However, because of the higher initial cost and relatively slower speeds, high-speed satellite network connections are recommended only if a cable or DSL connection is unavailable. Refer to Figure 1 for common satellite characteristics.

Refer to
Figure
in online course

Satellite Internet connections use two-way data channels. One channel is used for uploading and another for downloading. Both download and upload can be accomplished using a satellite connection. In some cases, a telephone line and modem are used for the upload. Download speeds are typically in the 500 Kbps range, while uploads are around 50 Kbps, making this an asymmetrical connection similar to DSL. Satellite connections are slower than cable or DSL connections but faster than telephone modem connections. Connecting by satellite has some advantages:

- Two-way, high-speed Internet access, available in rural and remote areas
- Quick file downloads
- Satellite dish can be used for TV access

Proper placement, installation, and configuration of a satellite system are important for the system to work effectively. Even if you point the satellite dish toward the equator where most satellites orbit the Earth, obstructions and adverse weather can still interfere with signal reception.

Specific equipment is needed to set up a satellite connection:

- 24-inch (610 mm) satellite dish
- Modem for uplink and downlink
- Coaxial cable and connectors

Refer to
Interactive Graphic
in online course.

Wireless Technologies
Complete the wireless technology matching activity in Figure 2.

13.2 Describe repairs for laptops and portable devices

When a laptop or portable device begins to malfunction, what should you do? Some parts of a laptop, typically called Customer Replaceable Units (CRUs), can be replaced by the customer. CRUs include such components as the laptop battery and RAM. Parts that should not be replaced by the customer are called Field Replaceable Units (FRUs). FRUs include such components as the laptop motherboard, LCD display, and keyboard. In many cases, the device may need to be returned to the place of purchase, a certified service center, or even to the manufacturer.

Refer to
Figure
in online course

A repair center can provide service on laptops made by different manufacturers, or a repair center may specialize in a specific brand and be considered an authorized dealer for warranty work and repair. The following are common repairs performed at local repair centers:

- Hardware and software diagnostics

- Data transfer and recovery

- Hard drive installation and upgrades

- RAM installation and upgrades

- Keyboard and fan replacement

- Internal laptop cleaning

- LCD screen repair

- LCD inverter and backlight repair

Most repairs to LCD displays must be performed in a repair center. The repairs include replacing the LCD screen, the backlight that shines through the screen to illuminate the display, and the inverter that produces the high voltage required by the backlight. If the backlight has failed, the screen is only visible when looking at it from an angle.

If no local services are available, you may be required to send the laptop to a regional repair center or to the manufacturer. If the laptop damage is severe or requires specialized software and tools, the manufacturer can decide to replace the laptop instead of attempting a repair.

Caution

Before attempting to repair a laptop or portable device, check the warranty to see if repairs during the warranty period must be done at an authorized service center to avoid invalidating the warranty. If you repair a laptop yourself, you should always back up the data and disconnect the device from the power source.

Refer to **Worksheet** for this chapter

Investigating Repair Centers
Investigate the services provided by a computer repair center.

13.3 Select laptop components

Laptop components need to be replaced for a variety of reasons. The original part may be worn, damaged, or faulty. You may want additional functionality, such as a wireless PC card that supports new standards. You may want to improve performance by adding memory. When implementing any of these changes, make sure that all new components are physically and electrically compatible with the existing components and operating system.

It is always a good idea to purchase components from a reputable source and research the warranty information. Components generally fall into two categories: retail packaged or Original Equipment Manufacturer (OEM). Retail packaged, or retail box, components usually come with documentation, a full warranty, cables, mounting hardware, drivers, and software.

OEM components are usually sold without packaging. OEM components require the user to locate documentation, software, drivers, and any additional hardware that may be needed. OEM components are usually less expensive and offer a shorter warranty period than similar retail packaged components. Using OEM components can result in substantial savings when upgrades are performed in bulk on many laptops and additional support is not needed.

After completing this section, you will meet these objectives:

- Select batteries.

- Select a docking station or port replicator.

- Select storage devices.

- Select additional RAM.

Refer to **Figure** in online course

13.3.1 Select batteries

How do you know when you need a new laptop battery? The signs may not always be apparent, but some are obvious:

Refer to **Figure** in online course

- The laptop shuts off immediately when AC power is removed.

- The battery is leaking.

- The battery overheats.

- The battery does not hold a charge.

If you experience problems that you suspect are battery related, exchange the battery with a known, good battery that is compatible with the laptop. If a replacement battery cannot be located, take the battery to an authorized repair center for testing.

A replacement battery must meet or exceed the specifications of the laptop manufacturer. New batteries must use the same form factor as the original battery. Voltages, power ratings, and AC adapters must also meet manufacturer specifications.

Note

Always follow the instructions provided by the manufacturer when charging a new battery. The laptop can be used during an initial charge, but do not unplug the AC adapter. Ni-Cad and NiMH rechargeable batteries should occasionally be discharged completely to remove the charge memory. When the battery is completely discharged, it should then be charged to maximum capacity.

Caution

Handle batteries with care. Batteries can explode if they are shorted, mishandled, or improperly charged. Be sure that the battery charger is designed for the chemistry, size, and voltage of your battery. Batteries are considered toxic waste, and must be disposed of according to local laws.

Refer to **Worksheet** for this chapter

Laptop Batteries
Use the Internet, a newspaper, or a local store to gather information and record the specifications for a laptop battery.

13.3.2 Select a docking station or port replicator

Docking stations and port replicators increase the number of ports available to a laptop. A port replicator may contain a SCSI port, a networking port, PS/2 ports, USB ports, and a game port. A docking station has the same ports as a port replicator, but adds the ability to connect to PCI cards, additional hard drives, optical drives, and floppy drives. Docking stations make it convenient to connect a laptop to an office network and peripherals. A laptop connected to a docking station has the same capabilities as a desktop computer. Figure 1 shows several docking stations and port replicators that support the same laptop.

Refer to **Figure** in online course

Docking stations and port replicators offer several connection options:

- Ethernet (RJ-45)

- Modem (RJ-11)

- S-Video, TV out

- USB 2.0 port

- External monitor

- Parallel port

- High-speed serial port

- IEEE 1394 port

- Stereo headphone output

- Stereo microphone input

- Docking port

Some docking stations connect to a laptop using a docking station port that is located on the bottom of the laptop, as shown in Figure 2. Other docking stations are designed to plug directly into a USB port of the laptop. Most laptops can be docked when in use or while shut off. The addition of new devices when docking can be handled by using PnP technology that recognizes and configures the newly added components, or by having a separate hardware profile for the docked and undocked state.

Many docking stations and port replicators are proprietary and only work with particular laptops. Before buying a docking station or port replicator, check the laptop documentation or the website of the manufacturer, to determine the appropriate make and model for the laptop.

Refer to
Worksheet
for this chapter

Docking Station

Use the Internet, a newspaper, or a local store to gather information and record the specifications for a laptop docking station.

13.3.3 Select storage devices

Storage devices are CRUs, unless a warranty requires technical assistance. There are several options when adding, replacing, or upgrading a storage device for a laptop:

Refer to
Figure
in online course

- External USB hard drive

- FireWire hard drive

- BD/DVD/CD burner

The form factor of an internal hard drive storage device is smaller for a laptop than for a desktop computer. Like desktop computers, traditional laptop hard drives are magnetic. Magnetic hard drives have drive motors designed to spin magnetic platters, which are read by movable drive heads. In contrast, SSDs do not have moving parts. Because there are no drive motors and moving parts, the SSD uses less energy than the magnetic hard drive. Flash memory chips manage all storage on an SSD, which results in faster access to data, higher reliability, and reduced power usage.

An external USB hard drive connects to a laptop using the USB port. Another type of external drive is the IEEE 1394 external hard drive that connects to the FireWire port. A laptop automatically detects when an external hard drive is plugged into a USB or FireWire port.

DVD-RW and CD-RW drives are optical drives that read and write data to and from CDs or DVDs. A Blu-ray-R drive is an optical drive that reads and writes data to and from Blu-ray Discs (BDs). This is a convenient method of creating backups and archiving data. The two most common types of writable CDs, DVDs, and BDs are writable (R) and rewritable (RW/RE).

Before purchasing a new internal or external storage device, check the laptop documentation or the website of the manufacturer for compatibility requirements. Documentation often contains Frequently Asked Questions (FAQs) that may be helpful. It is also important to research known laptop component issues on the Internet.

On most laptops, the internal hard drive and the internal optical drive are connected behind a cover on the underside of the case. However, on some laptops, the keyboard must be removed to access these drives. It is important to note that Blu-ray, DVD, and CD drives may not be interchangeable in the laptop.

To confirm the currently installed storage device, check the POST screen or BIOS. If installing a second hard drive or an optical drive to the laptop, confirm proper installation in the Device Manager window:

Use the following path in Windows XP:

Start > Control Panel > System > Hardware tab **> Device Manage.**

Use the following path in Windows Vista:

Start > Control Panel > System > Device Manage.

Research DVD Drives
Use the Internet, a newspaper, or a local store to gather information about a DVD rewritable drive for a laptop.

13.3.4 Select additional RAM

Additional RAM improves laptop performance by decreasing the number of times the operating system reads and writes data to the hard drive swap file. Additional RAM also helps the operating system to run multiple applications more efficiently.

Graphic processing in laptops is usually performed by the CPU and often requires extra RAM to store the video while the CPU decodes it for viewing. New applications, such as video sharing and video editing, demand increased performance from laptops. Installing expansion RAM can help increase laptop performance.

The make and model of the laptop determines the type of RAM chip needed. It is important to select the correct memory type that is physically compatible with the laptop. Most desktop computers use memory that fits into a DIMM slot. Most laptops use a smaller profile memory chip that is called Small Outline DIMM (SODIMM). SODIMMs are smaller than DIMMs, so they are ideal for use in laptops, printers, and other devices where conserving space is desirable. When replacing or adding memory, determine if the laptop has available slots to add memory, and that the laptop supports the quantity and type of memory to be added, as shown in Figure 1.

Before purchasing and installing additional RAM, consult the laptop documentation or the website of the manufacturer for form-factor specifications. Use the documentation to find where to install RAM on the laptop. On most laptops, RAM is inserted into slots behind a cover on the underside of the case, as shown in Figure 2. However, on some laptops, the keyboard must be removed to access the RAM slots.

Caution
Before installing RAM, remove the battery and unplug the computer from the electrical outlet to avoid electrical damage.

To confirm the currently installed amount of RAM, check the POST screen, BIOS, or System Properties window. Figure 3 shows where the amount of RAM can be found in the System Properties window:

Start > Control Panel > System > General Tab.

Laptop RAM

Use the Internet, a newspaper, or a local store to gather information about expansion memory for a laptop.

Refer to
Worksheet
for this chapter

13.4   Describe preventive maintenance procedures for laptops

Preventive maintenance should be scheduled at regular intervals to keep laptops running properly. Because laptops are portable, they are more likely than desktop computers to be exposed to these harmful materials and situations:

- Dirt and contamination
- Spills
- Wear and tear
- Drops
- Excessive heat or cold
- Excessive moisture

Properly managing data files and folders can ensure data integrity.

After completing this section, you will meet these objectives:

- Describe how to schedule and perform maintenance for laptops.
- Explain how to manage data version control between desktops and laptops.

Refer to
Figure
in online course

13.4.1   Describe how to schedule and perform maintenance for laptops

Proper care and maintenance can help laptop components run more efficiently and extend the life of the equipment.

An effective preventive maintenance program must include a routine schedule for maintenance. Most organizations will have a preventive maintenance schedule in place. If a schedule does not exist, work with the manager to create one. The most effective preventive maintenance programs require a set of routines to be conducted monthly, but still allow for maintenance to be performed when usage demands it.

The preventive maintenance schedule for a laptop may include practices that are unique to a particular organization, but should also include these standard procedures:

- Cleaning
- Hard drive maintenance
- Software updates

To keep a laptop clean, be proactive, not reactive. Keep fluids and food away from the laptop. Close the laptop when it is not in use. When cleaning a laptop, never use harsh cleaners or solutions that contain ammonia. Nonabrasive materials, as shown in Figure 1, are recommended for cleaning a laptop:

- Compressed air

- Mild cleaning solution

- Cotton swabs

- Soft, lint-free cleaning cloth

Caution

Before you clean a laptop, disconnect it from all power sources.

Routine maintenance includes the monthly cleaning of these laptop components:

- Exterior case

- Cooling vents

- I/O ports

- Display

- Keyboard

Note

If it is obvious that the laptop needs to be cleaned, clean it. Do not wait for the next scheduled maintenance.

The operating system, application files, and documents should also be maintained. The hard drive can become disorganized as files are opened, saved, and deleted. The computer can have reduced performance if the operating system is searching through fragmented files. Windows has two programs that are designed to clean the hard drive and increase hard drive performance:

- Disk Cleanup

- Disk Defragmenter

Disk Cleanup is used to scan a hard drive for files that are not needed, such as temporary files and cached Internet sites. Other files that are saved, deleted, or modified, are fragmented across various locations on the hard drive. Disk Defragmenter places files in adjacent clusters for faster access.

To run Disk Cleanup in Windows XP [Figure 2]:

1. Click the **Start** button.

2. Select **All Programs > Accessories > System Tools**.

3. Select **Disk Cleanup**.

4. The files available for deletion are listed. Check the check box next to the file to mark the file for deletion, and then click **OK**.

To run Disk Cleanup in Windows Vista:

1. Select the hard drive that you want to clean.

2. Right-click and choose **Properties**.

3. On the General tab, click **Disk Cleanup**.

4. Choose which files to clean up, **My files only** or **Files from all users on this computer**.

5. The files available for deletion are listed. Check the check box next to the file to mark the file for deletion, and then click **OK**.

To run Disk Defragmenter in Windows XP and Windows Vista [Figure 3]:

1. Select the hard drive that you want to clean.

2. Right-click and choose **Properties**.

3. On the Tools tab, click **Defragment Now**. In Windows Vista, you must click **Continue**. The length of time to complete the defragmentation varies according to the amount of hard drive fragmentation.

Note

It may be necessary to close all programs running in the background before running Disk Defragmenter.

Refer to
Figure
in online course

13.4.2 Explain how to manage data version control between desktops and laptops

It is important to manage your data files and folders properly. Restoration and recovery procedures, as well as backups, are more successful if the data is organized.

Windows XP has a default location, sometimes available as an icon on the desktop, called My Documents. You can use My Documents to create a folder structure and store files.

When moving files from a laptop to a desktop computer, start by creating a similar folder structure in both locations. Files can be transferred over a network, with an optical disc, or with a portable drive.

You should be careful that data copied from one computer does not inadvertently overwrite data on the other computer. When you are copying a file to a destination folder, you might encounter a **Confirm File Replace** message, as shown in Figure 1. This message indicates that Windows XP has stopped the copying process until you choose whether to replace the file. If you are unsure, click **No**. To determine which file to keep, compare the dates and file size. You may also open the files to view their content.

Note

No operating system allows files with the same name to exist in the same folder.

Caution

Be careful not to **cut** a file from its original location when you need to **copy** it.

Refer to
Figure
in online course

13.5 Describe how to troubleshoot a laptop

The troubleshooting process helps resolve problems with the laptop or peripherals. These problems range from simple, such as updating a drive, to more complex problems, such as installing RAM. Use the troubleshooting steps as a guideline to help you diagnose and repair problems.

After completing this section, you will meet these objectives:

- Review the troubleshooting process.
- Identify common problems and solutions.
- Apply troubleshooting skills.

Refer to
Figure
in online course

13.5.1 Review the troubleshooting process

Computer technicians must be able to analyze the problem and determine the cause of the error to repair a laptop. This process is called troubleshooting.

The first step in the troubleshooting process is to identify the problem. Figure 1 is a list of open-ended and closed-ended questions to ask the customer.

After you have talked to the customer, you can establish a theory of probable causes. Figure 2 is a list of some common probable causes for laptop problems.

After you have developed some theories about what is wrong, test your theories to determine the cause of the problem. Figure 3 is a list of quick procedures that can determine the exact cause of the problem or even correct the problem. If a quick procedure does correct the problem, you can go to step 5 to verify full system functionality. If a quick procedure does not correct the problem, you may need to research the problem further to establish the exact cause.

After you have determined the exact cause of the problem, establish a plan of action to resolve the problem and implement the solution. Figure 4 shows sources of information to gather additional information to resolve an issue.

After you have corrected the problem, you will need to verify full functionality and, if applicable, implement preventive measures. Figure 5 is a list of the steps to verify the solution.

In the final step of the troubleshooting process, you must document your findings, actions, and solutions. Figure 6 is a list of the tasks required to document the problem and the solution.

Refer to
Figure
in online course

13.5.2 Identify common problems and solutions

Laptop problems can be attributed to hardware, software, networks, or some combination of the three. You will resolve some types of laptop problems more often than others.

If you need to replace laptop components, make sure that you have the correct replacement component and tools recommended by the manufacturer. Some components are hot-swappable, which means that they can be removed and replaced while the computer is on.

Note

Each laptop manufacturer uses unique hardware installation and removal procedures. Check the laptop manual for specific installation information and follow safe installation and ESD precautions.

Caution

Always disconnect power and remove the battery before installing or removing laptop components that are not hot-swappable.

For proper re-assembly, remember these disassembly recommendations:

- Document screw locations
- Organize parts
- Refer to manufacturer documentation
- Use appropriate hand tools

Figure 1 is a chart of common laptop LCD screen problems and solutions. Before replacing laptop screen parts, make sure you understand the steps involved and the skills required for the installation.

Figure 2 is a chart of common storage device and RAM problems and solutions. Most replacement steps for storage devices and memory follow a generic installation process.

Hard Drive Replacement Steps

1. On the bottom of the laptop, remove the screw that holds the hard drive in place.
2. Slide the assembly outward. Remove the hard drive assembly.
3. Remove the hard drive faceplate from the hard drive.
4. Attach the hard drive faceplate to the new hard drive.
5. Slide the hard drive into the hard drive bay.
6. On the bottom of the laptop, install the screw that holds the hard drive in place.

Expansion Memory Replacement Steps

Laptop expansion memory is also called SODIMM. Remove the existing SODIMM if there are no available slots for the new SODIMM:

1. Remove the screw to expose the SODIMM.
2. Press outward on the clips that hold the sides of the SODIMM.
3. Lift up to loosen the SODIMM from the slot and remove the SODIMM.
4. Align the notch at a 45-degree angle.
5. Gently press down until the clips lock.
6. Replace the cover and install the screw.

Optical Drive Replacement Steps

1. Press the button to open the drive and remove any media in the drive. Close the tray.
2. Slide the latch to release the lever that secures the drive.
3. Pull on the lever to expose the drive. Remove the drive.

4. Insert the drive securely.

5. Push the lever inward.

Figure 3 is a chart of common power and input device problems and solutions. Most replacement steps for a laptop battery follow a generic installation process.

Battery Replacement Steps

1. Move the battery lock to the unlocked position.

2. Hold the release lever in the unlock position and remove the battery.

3. Insert the new battery.

4. Make sure that both battery levers are locked.

Figure 4 is a chart of common ventilation, CPU, sound, and expansion card problems and solutions. All PC expansion cards, including ExpressCards, are inserted and removed using similar steps.

PC Expansion Card Replacement Steps

1. Press the top eject button to release the PC expansion card.

2. Press the blue button inward.

3. Insert the PC expansion card into the express slot.

Caution

On some laptops, the PC Card, optical drive, and USB devices are hot-swappable. However, the internal hard drive, RAM, and battery are not hot-swappable.

<table>
<tr><td>Refer to
Figure
in online course</td></tr>
</table>

Hot-Swappable Device Removal Steps

1. Click the Safely Remove Hardware icon in the Windows system tray to ensure that the device is not in use.

2. Click the device that you want to remove. A message window appears when it is safe to remove the device.

3. Remove the hot-swappable device from the laptop.

13.5.3 Apply troubleshooting skills

Now that you understand the troubleshooting process, it is time to apply your listening and diagnostic skills.

<table>
<tr><td>Refer to
Figure
in online course</td></tr>
</table>

The worksheets are designed to reinforce your troubleshooting and communication skills to verify information from the customer.

The optional lab is designed to test your troubleshooting skills with laptop hardware and software problems. You will troubleshoot and repair a laptop that has more than one problem.

Refer to
Worksheet
for this chapter

Verify Work Order Information
Verify information that a level-one tech has documented in a work order.

Refer to
Worksheet
for this chapter

Investigating Support Websites and Repair Companies
Investigate the services provided by a local laptop repair company or a laptop manufacturer support website.

Refer to
Lab Activity
for this chapter

Troubleshooting Laptop Problems in Windows XP
Diagnose, solve, and document various laptop problems.

Refer to
Lab Activity
for this chapter

Troubleshooting Laptop Problems in Windows Vista
Diagnose, solve, and document various laptop problems.

Summary

This chapter has described components of laptops and portable devices. Here are some important concepts contained in this chapter:

- Bluetooth creates a small wireless PAN for connected cell phones, printers, and laptops.

- An IR network uses infrared light to create short-range networks that are primarily used to control input devices and mobile devices.

- A cellular WAN allows you to use your cell phone and laptop for voice and data communications.

- The most popular wireless technology is Wi-Fi. There are four major Wi-Fi releases, each with different speed and bandwidth ratings: IEEE 802.11 a, b, g, and n.

- Satellite networks are faster than modems, but slower than DSL and cable networks. Satellite networks are primarily used in remote locations.

- A CRU is a component that a user can easily install without technical training.

- An FRU is a component that a trained service technician may install at a remote location.

- Most repairs can be done at customers' sites or at any local repair center. However, there are occasions when a laptop must be sent directly to the manufacturer for repairs.

- Professional technicians follow preventive maintenance schedules to keep their equipment at optimal performance levels.

- Laptops are more susceptible to contamination and damage. A well-maintained laptop will reduce repair costs.

- A docking station allows a laptop to easily connect to peripheral devices similar to those found on desktop computers. A port replicator can be added to a laptop if the user needs more I/O ports.

- Know how to troubleshoot laptop problems.

Chapter 13 Quiz

Go to
the online course
to take the quiz.

Take the chapter quiz to test your knowledge.

Your Chapter Notes

Advanced Printers and Scanners

Introduction

This chapter explores the functionality of printers and scanners. You will learn how to maintain, install, and repair these devices in both local and network configurations. The chapter discusses safety hazards, configuration procedures, preventive maintenance, and printer and scanner sharing.

After completing this chapter, you will meet these objectives:

- Describe potential safety hazards and safety procedures associated with printers and scanners.
- Install and configure a local printer and scanner.
- Describe how to share a printer and a scanner on a network.
- Upgrade and configure printers and scanners.
- Describe printer and scanner preventive maintenance techniques.
- Troubleshoot printers and scanners.

14.1 Describe potential safety hazards and safety procedures associated with printers and scanners

Refer to **Figure** in online course

You must always follow safety procedures when working on any computer. There are also rules that you must follow as you work with printers and scanners. These rules keep you and the equipment safe.

The first rule of safety concerns moving large pieces of equipment. Always lift equipment by using the strength in your legs and knees, not your back. Wear appropriate work clothes and shoes. Do not wear loose jewelry or baggy clothes when servicing computer equipment.

Printers, scanners, and all-in-one devices that connect to AC outlets can become hot while in use. If you plan to perform any services on equipment, you should turn it off and allow it to cool before beginning any repairs on internal components. Print heads on dot matrix printers may become very hot when in use. The fuser assembly on a laser printer can also become hot.

Some printers retain a large amount of voltage even after you disconnect them from a power source. Only qualified technicians should perform advanced repairs on laser printers, particularly if the repair involves the corona wire or transfer roller assembly. These areas can retain high voltage, even after the printer has been turned off. Check the service manuals or contact the manufacturer to be sure that you know where these areas are inside the devices.

Printers and scanners can be expensive. If you do not service printers correctly, or install the wrong part, you can damage them beyond repair.

Refer to
Figure
in online course

14.2   Install and configure a local printer and scanner

A local device is one that connects directly to the computer. Before you install a local device, such as a printer or scanner, be sure that you remove all packing material. Take out anything that prevents moving parts from shifting around during shipping. Keep the original packing material in case you need to return the equipment to the manufacturer for warranty repairs.

After completing this section, you will meet these objectives:

- Connect the device to a local port.

- Install and configure the driver and software.

- Configure options and default settings.

- Verify functionality.

Refer to
Figure
in online course

14.2.1   Connect the device to a local port

Depending on the manufacturer, local printers may communicate with computers using serial, parallel, USB, FireWire, or SCSI ports and cables. Click the buttons in Figure 1 to review the characteristics of these ports. Wireless technologies, such as Bluetooth and infrared, are also used to connect these devices.

To connect a printer, attach the appropriate cable to the communication port on the back of the printer. Connect the other end of the cable to the corresponding port on the back of the computer.

Printers can be shared over a network. Connecting a printer to a network requires cabling that is compatible with both the existing network and the network port installed in the printer. Most network printers use an RJ-45 interface to connect to a network.

After the data cable has been properly connected, attach the power cable to the printer. Connect the other end of the power cable to an available electrical outlet. When you turn on the power to the device, the computer tries to determine the correct device driver to install.

Tip

Always check the packaging for cables when you buy a printer or scanner. Many manufacturers keep production costs down by not including a cable with the printer. If you have to buy a cable, be sure that you buy the correct type.

Refer to
Figure
in online course

14.2.2   Install and configure the driver and software

Printer drivers are software programs that make it possible for computers and printers to communicate with each other. Configuration software provides an interface that enables users to set and change printer options. Every printer model has its own type of driver and software configuration software.

When you connect a new printer device to a computer, Windows locates and installs a default driver by using PnP. If Windows cannot find the necessary driver on the computer, it searches the Internet for the driver. Printer manufacturers frequently update drivers to increase the performance of the printer, to add new and improved printer options, and to address general compatibility issues.

Printer Driver Installation

The process of installing and updating a printer driver usually involves the following five steps:

1. Determine the current version of the installed printer driver.

2. Search the Internet to locate the most recent version of the driver.

3. Download the driver. Follow the instructions on the website.

4. Install the driver. When activated, most driver installation programs automatically install the new driver.

5. Test the driver. To test the driver, choose **Start > Settings > Printers and Faxes** in Windows 2000 or **Start > Control Panel > Printers and Faxes** in Windows XP or **Start > Control Panel > Printers** in Windows Vista. Right-click the printer and choose **Properties.** Then choose **Print Test Page.** If the printer does not work, restart the computer and then try again.

The printed test page should contain text that is readable. If the text is unreadable, the problem could be a bad driver program or that the wrong page description language has been used.

Graphics Device Interface (GDI) is a Windows component that manages how graphical images are transmitted to output devices. GDI works by converting images to a bitmap that uses the computer instead of the printer to transfer the images.

Page Description Language (PDL)

A PDL is a type of code that describes the appearance of a document in a language that a printer can understand. The PDL for a page includes the text, graphics, and formatting information. Software applications use PDLs to send What You See Is What You Get (WYSIWYG) images to the printer. The printer translates the PDL file so that whatever is on the computer screen is what is printed. PDLs speed up the printing process by sending large amounts of data at one time. They also manage the computer fonts.

Adobe Systems developed PostScript (PS) to allow fonts or text types to share the same characteristics on the screen as on paper. Hewlett-Packard developed Printer Command Language (PCL) for communication with early inkjet printers. PCL is now an industry standard for nearly all printer types. The figure compares PS with PCL.

Refer to **Figure** in online course

14.2.3 Configure options and default settings

Common printer options that can be configured by the user include media control and printer output.

The following media control options set the way a printer manages media:

- Input paper tray selection

- Output path selection

- Media size and orientation

- Paper weight selection

The following printer output options manage how the ink or toner goes on the media:

- Color management

- Print speed

Some printers have control switches on the printer for users to select options. Other printers use the printer driver options. Two methods of selecting options are the global and per-document methods.

Global Method

The global method refers to printer options that are set to affect all documents. Each time a document is printed, the global options are used, unless overridden by per-document selections.

To change the configuration of a global printer, choose **Start > Control Panel > Printers and Faxes** and right-click the printer. The following examples show how you can manage printer options.

To designate a default printer, choose **Start > Control Panel > Printers and Faxes**. Right-click the printer, and then choose **Set as Default Printer**, as shown in Figure 1.

> **Note**
>
> Depending on the driver installed, **Set as Default Printer** may not appear on the menu. If this happens, double-click the printer to open the Document Status window, and then choose **Printer > Set as Default Printer**.

To limit printing to only black and white, choose **Start > Control Panel > Printer and Faxes**. Right-click the printer, and then choose **Printing Preferences**. Choose the **Color** tab. Check **Print In Grayscale** and choose the **Black Print Cartridge Only** radio button, as shown in Figure 2. Click **OK**.

Per-Document Method

Letters, spreadsheets, and digital images are some of the document types that may require special printer settings. You can change the settings for each document sent to the printer by changing the document print settings.

To change the printer settings, keep the document open and select **File > Page Setup**. The default settings are displayed, as shown in Figure 3. You can alter the colors, print quality, paper direction, and margin size for the document that you are printing without changing the default settings.

Scanner Calibrations

You should calibrate a scanner after installing a driver. Use the bundled software that came with the device to perform this procedure. The default settings can be altered later to meet customer requirements.

Scanner calibrations can include positioning the sensor and using an IT8 target to adjust the color. An IT8 target is a color calibration chart that you use to create profiles for specific devices. A scanner analyzes the target for comparison, while a printer reproduces the target for comparison.

To ensure calibration, compare the printed output of the device to the IT8 target. Adjust the printer color settings to match the IT8 targer. The next time you print or scan an image, the color should match the target.

Printer Calibrations

The calibration of the printer is performed using the print driver software. This process makes sure that the print heads are aligned and can print on special paper. Inkjet print heads are usually fitted to the ink cartridge, which means that you may have to recalibrate the printer each time you change a cartridge.

Refer to
Figure
in online course

14.2.4 Verify functionality

The installation of any device is not complete until you have successfully tested all the functions of your device. These functions might include:

- Print double-sided documents.

- Use different paper trays for different paper sizes.

- Change the settings of a color printer so that it prints in black and white or grayscale.

- Print in draft mode.

- Change a scanner's scan resolution.

- Edit scanned images of saved documents.

- Use an optical character recognition (OCR) application.

Note

Electronic manuals and support websites explain how to clear paper jams, install ink cartridges, and load all types of paper trays.

Printer Test

There are several ways to print a test page:

- Use the Print Test Page option from the printer.

- Use the Print Test Page option from Windows.

- Use the print function of an application.

- Send a file directly to a parallel port printer using the command line.

To test a printer, first print a test page from the printer, and then print from the printer properties in the control panel on the computer. Next, open a document and print from within the application. This ensures that the printer is working properly, the driver software is installed and working, and the printer and computer are communicating.

Scanner Test

Test the scanner by scanning a paper document using the buttons on the device. Next, re-scan the document using the scanner software on the computer. If the scanned, electronic image is the same as the paper document, you have successfully completed the installation.

For an all-in-one device, you should test all of the functions:

- *Fax*– Fax to another known working fax.

- *Copy*– Create a copy of a document.

- *Scan*– Scan a document.

- *Print*– Print a document.

Refer to
Lab Activity
for this chapter

Refer to
Figure
in online course

Install an All-in-one Printer/Scanner
Check the Windows XP Hardware Compatibility List (HCL) for your All-in-one Printer/Scanner, install the all-in-one printer/scanner, upgrade the driver and any associated software, and test the printer and scanner.

14.3   Describe how to share a printer and a scanner on a network

One of the primary reasons that networks were developed was to allow groups of computer users to share peripheral devices. The most common shared device is the printer. Sharing a single printer among a group of users costs much less than buying a printer for each computer.

Low-cost printers usually require a separate print server to allow network connectivity because these printers do not have built-in network interfaces. The computer that is connected to the printer can serve as the print server. Most personal computer operating systems have built-in printer sharing capability.

After you confirm that the printer sharing software is installed, the server must know which printer it is going to share. In the Printers folder for Windows XP, right-click the printer to share, select **Properties**, and click the **Sharing** tab. Select the **Share this printer** option and assign the printer a name.

In the **Network and Sharing Center** window for Windows Vista, scroll down to the **Sharing and Discovery** section and turn on **Printer sharing**. Click **Apply** to make the changes. Right-click the printer to share and select **Properties > Sharing**. Select the **Share this printer** option and assign the printer a name.

After completing this section, you will meet these objectives:

- Describe types of print servers.
- Describe how to install network printer software and drivers on a computer.

Refer to
Figure
in online course

14.3.1   Describe types of print servers

Print servers enable multiple computer users to access a single printer. A print server has three functions. The first is to provide client access to print resources. The second is to administrate print jobs, storing them in a queue until the print device is ready for them, and then feeding or spooling the print information to the printer. The third is to provide feedback to the users. This includes providing notification that a print job is finished, or error messages that something has gone wrong.

As a technician, you must choose the type of print server that best suits the customer's needs. There are three kinds:

- Network print servers
- Dedicated PC print servers
- Computer-shared printers

Network Print Servers

Network print servers allow many users on a network to access a single printer. A network print server can manage network printing through either wired or wireless connections. You should consider the advantages and disadvantages of a dedicated network print server before you install one:

- An advantage of using a network print server is that the server accepts incoming print jobs from computers, and then frees the computers for other tasks. The print server is always available to the users, unlike a printer shared from a user's computer.

- A disadvantage of a network print server is that it may only allow you to print to an all-in-one device. Some printers are not compatible with print servers.

Dedicated PC Print Servers

A dedicated PC print server is a computer dedicated to handling client print jobs in the most efficient manner. Dedicated PC print servers can manage more than one printer at a time. A print server needs to have resources available to meet the requests of print clients:

- *Powerful processor*– Because the PC print server uses its processor to manage and route printing information, it needs to be fast enough to handle all incoming requests.

- *Adequate hard disk space*– A PC print server captures print jobs from clients, places them in a print queue, and sends them to the printer in a timely way. This requires the computer to have enough storage space to hold these jobs until completed.

- *Adequate memory*– The server processor and RAM handle sending print jobs to a printer. If server memory is not large enough to handle an entire print job, the hard drive must send the job, which is much slower.

Computer-shared Printers

A user's computer that has a printer attached can share that printer with other users on the network. Windows makes the process fast and easy. In a home network, it means users can print documents from wherever they are in the house by using a wireless laptop. In a small office network, sharing a printer means one printer can serve many users.

Sharing a printer from a computer also has disadvantages. The computer sharing the printer uses its own resources to manage the print jobs coming to the printer. If a user on the desktop is working at the same time that a user on the network is printing, the desktop user may notice a performance slowdown. In addition, the printer is not available if the user reboots or powers down the computer with a shared printer.

Refer to
Figure
in online course

14.3.2 Describe how to install network printer software and drivers on a computer

Windows allows computer users to share their printers with other users on the network. There are two steps:

Step 1.   Configure the computer attached to the printer to share the printer with other network users.

Step 2.   Configure a user's computer to recognize the shared printer and print to it.

To configure the computer with the printer attached to accept print jobs from other network users, follow these steps for Windows XP:

1. Choose **Start > Control Panel > Printers and Other Hardware > Printers and Faxes**.

2. Select the printer you want to share.

3. The **Printer Task**s box will appear on the left. Select **Share this printer**.

4. The **Printer Properties** dialog box for that printer will display. Select the **Sharing** tab. Select **Share this printer** and enter the desired shared printer name. This is the name of the printer that will be displayed to other users.

5. Verify that sharing has been successful. Return to the **Printers and Faxes** folder and notice that the printer icon now has a hand under it, as shown in Figure 1. This shows that the printer is now a shared resource.

To configure the computer with the printer attached to accept print jobs from other network users, follow these steps for Windows Vista:

1. Choose **Start > Control Panel > Hardware and Sound > Printers**.

2. Right click the printer you want to share and choose **Sharing**.

3. The **Printer Properties** dialog box for that printer will display. Select **Share this printer** and enter the desired shared printer name. This is the name of the printer that will be displayed to other users.

4. Verify that sharing has been successful. Return to the Printers window and notice that the printer now has a share icon under it, as shown in Figure 1. This shows that the printer is now a shared resource.

Other users who can now connect to the shared printer may not have the required drivers installed. These other users may also be using different operating systems than the computer that is hosting the shared printer. Windows can automatically download the correct drivers to these other users. Click the **Additional Drivers** button to select operating systems that the other users may be using. When you close that dialog box by clicking OK, Windows will ask to obtain those additional drivers. If all of the other users are also using the same Windows OS, you do not need to click the **Additional Drivers** button.

Connecting Other Users

Other users on the network can now connect to this printer by following these steps in Windows XP:

1. Choose **Start > Control Panel > Printers and other Hardware > Add a Printer**.

2. The Add Printer wizard appears. Click **Next**.

3. Select **A network printer, or a printer attached to another computer**, as shown in Figure 2. Click **Next**.

4. Type in the name of the printer, or browse for it on the network using the **Next** button. A list of shared printers will appear.

5. After you select the printer, a virtual printer port is created and displayed in the **Add a Printer** window. The required print drivers are downloaded from the print server and installed on the computer. The wizard then finishes the installation.

Other users on the network can now connect to this printer by following these steps in Windows Vista:

1. Choose **Start > Control Panel > Hardware and Sound > Add a Printer**.

2. The Add Printer wizard appears.

3. Select **Add a network, wireless or Bluetooth printer**, as shown in Figure 3.

4. A list of shared printers will appear. If the printer is not listed, select **The printer that I wanted is not listed**.

5. After selecting the printer, click **Next**.

6. A virtual printer port is created and displayed in the **Add a Printer** window. The required print drivers are downloaded from the print server and installed on the computer. The wizard then finishes the installation.

Refer to
Lab Activity
for this chapter

Share the All-in-one Printer/Scanner in Windows XP

Share the Epson printer/scanner, configure the printer on a networked computer, and print a test page from the remote computer.

Refer to
Lab Activity
for this chapter

Share the All-in-one Printer/Scanner in Windows Vista

Share the Epson printer/scanner, configure the printer on a networked computer, and print a test page from the remote computer.

Refer to
Figure
in online course

14.4 Upgrade and configure printers and scanners

Some printers can be expanded to print faster and to accommodate more print jobs by adding hardware. The hardware may include additional paper trays, sheet feeders, network cards, and expansion memory.

Scanners can be optimized to include color correction and resizing.

After completing this section, you will meet these objectives:

- Describe printer upgrades.

- Describe scanner optimization.

Refer to
Figure
in online course

14.4.1 Describe printer upgrades

Upgrading the printer memory increases the printing speed and enhances complex print job performance. All printers have RAM. The more memory a printer has, the more efficiently it works. The added memory helps with tasks such as job buffering, page creation, improved photo printing, and graphics.

Print job buffering is when a print job is captured into the internal printer memory. Buffering allows the computer to continue with other work instead of waiting for the printer to finish. Buffering is a common feature in laser printers and plotters, as well as in advanced inkjet and dot matrix printers.

Printers usually arrive from the factory with enough memory to handle jobs that involve text. However, print jobs involving graphics, and especially photographs, run more efficiently if the printer memory is adequate to store the entire job before it starts. If you receive errors that indicate the printer is out of memory or that there has been a memory overload, you may need more memory.

Installing Printer Memory

The first step in installing additional printer memory is to read the printer manual to determine the following:

- *Memory type*– This denotes the physical type of memory, its speed, and capacity. Some are standard types of memory, whereas others require special or proprietary memory.

- *Memory population and availability*– This denotes the number of memory upgrade slots in use and how many are available. This may require opening a compartment to check RAM.

Printer manufacturers have set procedures for upgrading memory, including the following tasks:

- Removing covers to access the memory area

- Installing or removing memory

- Initializing the printer to recognize the new memory

- Installing updated drivers if needed

Additional Printer Upgrades

These are some of the additional printer upgrades:

- Duplex printing to enable dual-sided printing

- Extra trays to hold more paper

- Specialized tray types for different media

- Network cards to access a wired or wireless network

- Firmware upgrades to add functionality or to fix bugs

Follow the instructions included with the printer when you install or upgrade components. Contact the manufacturer or an authorized service technician for additional information if you have any problems when installing upgrades. Follow all safety procedures outlined by the manufacturer.

Refer to
Figure
in online course

14.4.2 Describe scanner optimization

Scanners work well for most users without any changes to the default settings. There are, however, features that can improve document or image scans depending on user requirements. These are the most common types of scanner options:

Refer to
Figure
in online course

- Resizing

- Sharpening

- Brightening or darkening

- Color correction

- Resolution changes

- Output file format

- Color inversion

Scanning resolution affects the size of the output file. The end use of the image determines the required resolution. If the image is for use on a web publication, you only need low resolution and a small file size. This makes it possible for browsers to load the image quickly. Medium resolution images are normally used for laser prints. In commercial printing, where the quality of the image is very important, a higher resolution is the best setting. Low resolution means a small file size; high resolution means a large file size. Figure 1 shows the settings for resolution and output type.

Scanners may allow you to choose different file formats for the scanned output, as shown in Figure 2.

If a scanner does not produce output in a file format required by the customer, the format can be converted later using software tools. After changing device settings, you should test the changes by making some sample printouts.

Refer to Lab Activity for this chapter

Optimize Scanner Output
Scan a picture at two different levels of DPI.

14.5 Describe printer and scanner preventive maintenance techniques

Preventive maintenance decreases downtime and increases the service life of the components. You should maintain printers and scanners to keep them working properly. A good maintenance program guarantees good quality prints and scans. The printer or scanner manual contains information on how to maintain and clean the equipment.

After completing this section, you will meet these objectives:

- Determine scheduled maintenance according to vendor guidelines.
- Describe a suitable environment for printers and scanners.
- Describe cleaning methods.
- Describe how to check the capacity of ink cartridges and toners.

Refer to Figure in online course

14.5.1 Determine scheduled maintenance according to vendor guidelines

Read the information manuals that come with every new piece of equipment. Follow the recommended maintenance instructions. Also, use the supplies listed by the manufacturer. Less expensive supplies can save money, but may produce poor results, damage the equipment, or void the warranty.

Refer to Figure in online course

When maintenance is completed, reset the counters to allow the next maintenance to be completed at the correct time. On many types of printers, the page count is viewed through the LCD display or a counter located inside the main cover.

Most manufacturers sell maintenance kits for their printers. Figure 1 shows a sample maintenance kit. For laser printers, the kit may contain replacement parts that often break or wear out:

- Fuser assembly
- Transfer rollers
- Separation pads
- Pickup rollers

Each time you install new parts or replace toners and cartridges, do a visual inspection of all the internal components, and perform the following tasks:

- Remove any bits of paper and dust.

- Clean any spilled ink or toner.

- Look for any worn gears, cracked plastic, or broken parts.

Users that do not know how to maintain printing equipment should call a manufacturer-certified technician.

Refer to
Worksheet
for this chapter

Search for Certified Printer Technician Jobs
Use the Internet to gather information about becoming a certified printer technician.

14.5.2 Describe a suitable environment for printers and scanners

Printers and scanners, like all other electrical devices, are affected by temperature, humidity, and electrical interference. Laser printers produce heat and should be operated in well-ventilated areas to prevent overheating. If possible, store all printers and scanners in a cool, dry, dust-free environment.

Keep paper and toner cartridges in their original wrappers. These supplies should also be stored a cool, dry, dust-free environment. High humidity causes paper to absorb moisture from the air. This makes it difficult for the toner to attach to the paper correctly. If the paper and printer are dusty, you may use compressed air to blow away the dust.

Refer to
Figure
in online course

14.5.3 Describe cleaning methods

Always follow the manufacturer's guidelines when cleaning printers and scanners. Information on the manufacturer's website or in the user manual explains the proper cleaning methods.

Caution

Remember to unplug scanners and printers before cleaning to prevent danger from high voltage.

Printer Maintenance

Make sure that you turn off and unplug any printer before performing maintenance. Use a damp cloth to wipe off any dirt, paper dust, and spilled ink on the exterior of the device.

Print heads in an inkjet printer are replaced when the cartridges are replaced. However, sometimes print heads become clogged and require cleaning. Use the utility supplied by the manufacturer to clean the print heads. After you clean them, you should test them. Repeat this process until the test shows a clean and uniform print.

Printers have many moving parts. Over time, the parts collect dust, dirt, and other debris. If not cleaned regularly, the printer may not work well, or could stop working completely. When working with dot matrix printers, clean the roller surfaces with a damp cloth. On inkjet printers, clean the paper-handling machinery with a damp cloth.

Caution

Do not touch the drum of a laser printer while cleaning. You may damage the surface of the drum.

Laser printers do not usually require much maintenance unless they are in a dusty area or they are very old. When cleaning a laser printer, use a specially designed vacuum cleaner to pick up toner particles. Figure 1 shows a vacuum designed for electronic equipment. A standard vacuum cleaner cannot hold the tiny particles of toner and may scatter them about. Use only a vacuum cleaner with HEPA filtration. HEPA filtration catches microscopic particles within the filters.

Choosing the correct paper type for a printer helps the printer last longer and print more efficiently. Several types of paper are available. Each type of paper is clearly labeled with the type of printer for which it is intended. The manufacturer of the printer may also recommend the best type of paper. Check the printer manual.

Information about the brands and types of ink recommended by the manufacturer is also found in the manual. Using the wrong type of ink may cause the printer not to work or may reduce the print quality. To prevent ink leaks, do not refill ink cartridges.

Scanner Maintenance

You should clean scanners regularly to prevent dirt, fingerprints, and other smudges from showing in scanned images. On flatbed scanners, keep the lid closed when the scanner is not in use. This will help to prevent dust build-up and accidental fingertip smudges. If the glass becomes dirty, consult the user guide for the manufacturer's cleaning recommendations. If the manual does not list any recommendations, use a glass cleaner and a soft cloth to protect the glass from scratching. Even very small scratches can be visible on high-resolution scans. If dirt becomes lodged in the scratches, the scratches will become more visible.

If the inside of the glass becomes dirty, check the manual for instructions on how to open the unit or remove the glass from the scanner. If possible, thoroughly clean both sides and replace the glass as it was originally installed in the scanner.

Refer to **Figure** in online course

14.5.4 Describe checking capacity of ink cartridges and toners

When an inkjet printer produces blank pages, the ink cartridges may be empty. Laser printers, however, do not produce blank pages, but do begin to print very poor quality printouts. Most inkjet printers provide a utility that shows ink levels in each cartridge, as shown in Figure 1. Some printers have LCD message screens or LED lights that warn users when ink supplies are low.

A method for checking ink levels is to look at the page counter inside the printer or the printer software to determine how many pages have been printed. Then look at the cartridge label information. The label should show how many pages the cartridge can print. You can then easily estimate how many more pages you can print. For this method to be accurate, each time you replace the cartridge, you must remember to reset the counter. In addition, some printouts use more ink than others do. For example, a letter uses less ink than a photograph.

You can set the printer software to reduce the amount of ink or toner that the printer uses. This setting may be called toner save or draft quality. This setting reduces the print quality of laser and inkjet products, and reduces the time it takes to print a document on an inkjet printer.

Refer to **Figure** in online course

14.6 Troubleshoot printers and scanners

With printer and scanner problems, a technician must be able to determine if the problem exists with the device, cable connection, or the computer to which it is attached. Follow the steps outlined in this section to accurately identify, repair, and document the problem.

After completing this section, you will meet these objectives:

- Review the troubleshooting process.

- Identify common problems and solutions.

- Apply troubleshooting skills.

Refer to
Figure
in online course

14.6.1   Review the troubleshooting process

Printer and scanner problems can result from a combination of hardware, software, and connectivity issues. Computer technicians must be able to analyze the problem and determine the cause of the error to repair the printer and scanner issues.

The first step in the troubleshooting process is to identify the problem. Figure 1 is a list of open-ended and closed-ended questions to ask the customer.

After you have talked to the customer, you can establish a theory of probable causes. Figure 2 is a list of some common probable causes for printer and scanner problems.

After you have developed some theories about what is wrong, test your theories to determine the cause of the problem. Figure 3 is a list of quick procedures that can determine the exact cause of the problem or even correct the problem. If a quick procedure does correct the problem, you can go to step 5 to verify full system functionality. If a quick procedure does not correct the problem, you may need to research the problem further to establish the exact cause.

After you have determined the exact cause of the problem, establish a plan of action to resolve the problem and implement the solution. Figure 4 shows sources of information to gather additional information to resolve an issue.

After you have corrected the problem, you will need to verify full functionality and, if applicable, implement preventive measures. Figure 5 is a list of the steps to verify the solution.

In the final step of the troubleshooting process, you must document your findings, actions, and outcomes. Figure 6 is a list of the tasks required to document the problem and the solution.

Refer to
Figure
in online course

14.6.2   Identify common problems and solutions

Printer and scanner problems can be attributed to hardware, software, networks, or some combination of the three. You will resolve some types of problems more often than others. Figure 1 is a chart of common problems and solutions.

Refer to
Figure
in online course

14.6.3   Apply troubleshooting skills

Now that you understand the troubleshooting process, it is time to apply your listening and diagnostic skills.

Refer to
Figure
in online course

The first lab is designed to reinforce your skill with printers. You will troubleshoot and fix a printer problem.

The second lab is designed to reinforce your communication and troubleshooting skills with printers. In this lab, you will perform the following steps:

- Receive the work order.

- Take the customer through various steps to try and resolve the problem.

- Document the problem and the resolution.

The third lab is designed to reinforce your skills with printer and scanner problems. You will troubleshoot and repair multiple printing problems.

Refer to
Lab Activity
for this chapter

Fix a Printer Problem

Troubleshoot and fix a printer that does not print documents for a user.

Refer to
Lab Activity
for this chapter

Remote Technician: Fix a Printer Problem

Gather data from the customer, and then instruct the customer on how to fix a printer that does not print documents for a user.

Refer to
Lab Activity
for this chapter

Troubleshooting Printer Problems in Windows XP

Diagnose the causes and solve various printer problems.

Refer to
Lab Activity
for this chapter

Troubleshooting Printer Problems in Windows Vista

Diagnose the causes and solve various printer problems.

Summary

This chapter reviewed and discussed information about printers and scanners. The chapter explored hazards and safety procedures associated with printers and scanners. You have learned preventive maintenance methods, and have installed, configured, and upgraded a printer or scanner, both locally and on a network. Here are some other important facts covered in this chapter:

- Always follow safety procedures when working with printers and scanners. Many parts inside printers contain high voltage or become very hot with use.

- Use the device manual and software to install a printer or scanner. After the installation, update the drivers and firmware to fix problems and increase functionality.

- Use the Windows interface to share printers and scanners across the network.

- Consult the customers to determine how best to upgrade and configure printers and scanners to meet their needs.

- Keep printers, scanners, and supplies clean and dry. Keep supplies in their original packaging. Develop a maintenance schedule to clean and check devices on a regular basis.

- Use a sequence of steps to fix a problem. Start with simple tasks before you decide on a course of action. Call a certified printer technician when a problem is too difficult for you to fix.

Go to
the online course
to take the quiz.

Chapter 14 Quiz

Take the chapter quiz to test your knowledge.

Your Chapter Notes

Advanced Networks

Introduction

This chapter focuses on advanced networking topics, including network design, network component upgrades, and e-mail server installations. Basic networking topics, such as safety, network components, and preventive maintenance, are also discussed.

To meet the expectations and needs of your customers and network users, you must be familiar with networking technologies. You must understand the basics of how a network is designed and why some components affect the flow of data on a network. Troubleshooting advanced network situations is also described in this chapter.

After completing this chapter, you will meet these objectives:

- Identify potential safety hazards and implement proper safety procedures related to networks.
- Design a network based on the customer's needs.
- Determine the components for your customer's network.
- Implement the customer's network.
- Upgrade the customer's network.
- Describe installation, configuration, and management of a simple mail server.
- Describe preventive maintenance procedures for networks.
- Troubleshoot the network.

Refer to
Figure
in online course

15.1 Identify potential safety hazards and implement proper safety procedures related to networks

Installing network cables, whether copper or fiber optic, can be dangerous. Often, cables must be pulled through ceilings and walls where there are obstacles and unexpected or toxic materials. You should wear clothing that protects you from these materials. For example, wear long pants, long-sleeved shirts, sturdy shoes that cover your feet, and gloves. Most importantly, wear safety glasses. If possible, ask building management or someone responsible for the building if there are any dangerous materials or obstacles that you need to be aware of before entering the ceiling area.

Be aware of the safety issues when using a ladder:

- Read the labels on the ladder and follow any safety instructions written on it.
- Never stand on the top rung of the ladder. You could easily lose your balance and fall.
- Make sure that people in the area know you will be working there.
- Cordon off the area with caution tape or safety cones.

- When you are using a ladder that leans up against a wall, have someone hold the ladder to keep it steady.

The tools required to install copper and fiber-optic cable may be dangerous to use. Rules should always be followed when working with cables:

- Make sure that the tools you are using are in good working order.

- Pay attention to what you are doing and take your time. Make sure that you do not cut yourself or place anyone in danger.

- Always wear safety glasses when cutting, stripping, or splicing cables of any kind. Tiny fragments can injure your eyes.

- Wear gloves whenever possible and make sure to dispose of any waste properly.

After completing this section, you will meet these objectives:

- Explain fiber-optic safety.

- Explain cable, cable cutters, and cable cutting safety hazards.

Refer to
Figure
in online course

15.1.1 Explain fiber-optic safety

Specific types of tools and chemicals are used when working with fiber-optic cable. These materials must be handled safely.

Chemicals

The solvents and glues used with fiber optics are dangerous. You should handle them with extreme care. Read any instructions and follow them carefully. Also, read the MSDS that accompanies the chemicals to know how to treat someone in an emergency.

Tools

When working with any tool, safety should always be your first priority. Any compromise in safety could result in serious injury or even death. The tools used for working with fiber optics have sharp cutting surfaces that are used to scribe glass. Other tools pinch cables with high pressure to fasten connectors to them. These tools can produce shards of glass that can splinter and fly into the air. You must avoid getting them in your skin, mouth, or eyes.

Harmful Light

Protect your eyes from the harmful light that may be in the fiber-optic strands. The light is a color that humans cannot see. It can damage your eyes before you can feel it. When you use a magnifier to inspect fiber-optic cable and connectors, the light emitted from the fiber could be directed into your eye. When working with fiber, be sure to disconnect the light source. A fiber-optic meter can be used to ensure that the light source has been disconnected.

Glass Shards

The process of cutting and trimming the strands of fiber-optic cables can produce tiny fragments of glass or plastic that can penetrate your eyes or skin and cause severe irritation. The fibers can be extremely difficult to see on your skin because they are clear and small. When working with fiber-optic cabling, the working surface should be a dark mat so that tiny glass or plastic fragments can be seen. The mat should also be resistant to chemical spills.

You should keep the work area clean and neat. Never pick up fiber-optic fragments with your fingers. Use tape to pick up small fragments and dispose of them properly. Use a disposable container, such as a plastic bottle with a screw-on lid, to store fiber fragments. Close the lid tightly before disposing of the container.

Caution

Obtain proper training before you attempt to cut, strip, or splice fiber-optic cable. An experienced technician should supervise you until you become adequately skilled.

Refer to **Figure** in online course

15.1.2 Explain cable, cable cutters, and cable cutting safety hazards

All levels of technicians should know the hazards before working with network cable and equipment.

Copper Cable Hazards

Copper cables can also be dangerous to handle. When you cut copper cable, the small copper strands can puncture your skin or cut you. The small pieces that come off after cutting cables often fly into the air. Remember to always wear safety glasses when cutting any type of cable.

The cutting and crimping tools used to repair or terminate copper cables can be dangerous if not used properly. Read the documentation that comes with the tool. Practice using the tool on scrap cable, and ask an experienced installer for help if you need it.

Refer to **Figure** in online course

15.2 Design a network based on the customer's needs

Building a network requires analysis of the environment and an understanding of networking options. You should interview the customer, as well as any other people involved in the project. It is important to have a general idea about the hardware and software that will be used on the network. You should inquire about future growth of the company and the network.

After completing this section, you will meet these objectives:

- Determine a topology.

- Determine protocols and network applications.

Refer to **Figure** in online course

15.2.1 Determine a topology

Understanding the needs of the customer and determining the general layout of the new network are required to properly determine the network topology. These network decisions need to be discussed with the customer:

- Cable and wireless types

- Expandability
- Number and location of users

The number of users and the estimated amount of future growth determines the initial physical and logical topology of the network. An inspection, called a site survey, should be done early in the project. A site survey is a physical inspection of the building that helps determine a basic logical topology, which is the flow of data and protocols. You should create a checklist to record the needs of your customer:

- The location of users' computers
- The position of network equipment such as switches and routers
- The position of the servers

A floor plan or blueprint is helpful to determine the physical layout of equipment and cables. The physical layout is often based on available space, power, security, and air conditioning. Figure 1 shows different types of network topologies. If a floor plan or blueprint is not available, you should make a drawing of where the network devices will be located, including the location of the server room, the printers, the end stations, and cable runs. This drawing can be used for discussions when the customer makes the final layout decisions.

Refer to **Figure** in online course

15.2.2 Determine protocols and network applications

In the design of a network, you must determine the protocols that are going to be used. Some protocols are proprietary and only work on specific equipment, while other protocols are open standard and work on a variety of equipment. Figure 1 shows details of the various network protocols.

Consider the following when selecting protocols:

- The TCP/IP suite of protocols is required for every device to connect to the Internet. This makes it a preferred protocol for networking.

- NetBEUI is a small, fast protocol that is useful in low security networks. NetBEUI performs well in a small network that is not connected to the Internet. It is easy to install and requires no configuration. However, NetBEUI can cause unnecessary traffic on a large network, so it is not a good choice if there will be network growth.

- IPX/SPX is a protocol used with older versions of Novell Netware. Because of the growth of the Internet, newer versions of Novell Netware use TCP/IP instead of IPX/SPX.

- Apple Macintosh networks have abandoned the AppleTalk protocol for the TCP/IP suite of protocols to ensure connectivity with other TCP/IP networks, most notably the Internet.

When the TCP/IP protocol stack is enabled, other protocols become available on specific ports, as shown in Figure 2. Network software applications use these protocols and ports to perform functions over the Internet or over a network.

Some network software applications include services to host a web page, send e-mail, and transfer files. These services may be provided by a single server or by several servers. Clients use well-known ports for each service. Client requests can be identified by using a specific destination port.

VoIP is a popular example of a network software application. VoIP is a method to carry telephone calls over the data networks and Internet. VoIP converts the analog signals of our voices into digital information that is transported in IP packets. VoIP can also use an existing IP network to provide access to the Public Switched Telephone Network (PSTN).

There are several ways to use VoIP:

- *IP phone*– A device that connects to an IP network using an RJ-45 Ethernet connector or a wireless connection.

- *Analog Telephone Adapter (ATA)*– A device that connects standard analog devices, such as telephones, facsimile machines, or answering machines, to an IP network.

- *IP phone software*– This application connects by using a microphone, speakers, and a sound card to emulate the IP phone functionality.

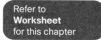

Protocols

Write the name of the protocol and the default port(s) for each protocol definition in the table.

> Refer to **Figure** in online course

15.3   Determine the components for your customer's network

The choice of network topology determines the type of devices, cables, and network interfaces that will be required to construct the network. In addition, an outside connection to an Internet service provider must be set up.

After completing this section, you will meet these objectives:

- Select cable types.

- Select an ISP connection type.

- Select network cards.

- Select the network device.

> Refer to **Figure** in online course

15.3.1   Select cable types

Select the cable type that is the most beneficial and cost effective for the users and services that will connect to the network.

Cable Types

The size of the network determines the type of network cable that will be used. Most networks today are wired using one or more types of twisted-pair copper cable:

- Cat5

- Cat5e

- Cat6

- Cat6A

Cat5 and Cat5e cables look the same, but Cat5e cable is manufactured with a higher standard to allow for higher data transfer rates. Cat6 cable is constructed with even higher standards than Cat5e. Cat6 cable may have a center divider to separate the pairs inside the cable.

The most common type of cable used in a network is Cat5e. Cat5e is suitable for Fast Ethernet up to 330 feet (100 m). Some businesses and homes have installed Cat6 cable so that they are prepared for additional bandwidth requirements in the future. Applications such as video, videoconferencing, and gaming use a large amount of bandwidth.

Cat6A cable carries Ethernet signals at a rate of 10 Gbps. The abbreviation for 10 Gb Ethernet over twisted-pair cable is 10GBase-T, as defined in the IEEE 802.3an-2006 standard. Customers who need high-bandwidth networks can benefit from installing cable that can support Gigabit Ethernet or 10 Gb Ethernet.

New or renovated office buildings often have some type of UTP cabling that connects every office to a central point called the Main Distribution Facility (MDF). The distance limitation of UTP cabling used for data is 330 feet (100 m). Cable runs in excess of this distance limitation need a repeater or hub to extend the connection to the MDF.

Cables that are installed inside the walls and ceilings of buildings must be plenum rated. A plenum cable is one that is safe for installation between a dropped ceiling and the structural ceiling of a building where air circulation takes place. Plenum rated cables are made from a special plastic which retards fire and produces less smoke than other cable types.

Wireless

A wireless solution may be possible in places where cables cannot be installed. Consider an older, historic building where local building codes do not permit structural modifications. In this case, installing cable is not possible and therefore a wireless connection is the only solution.

Cost

When designing a network, cost is a consideration. Installing cables is expensive, but after a one-time expense, a wired network is normally inexpensive to maintain.

Security

A wired network is usually more secure than a wireless network. The cables in a wired network are usually installed in walls and ceilings and therefore not easily accessible. It is easier to gain unauthorized access to the signals on a wireless network than the signals on a wired network. The signals are available to anyone who has a receiver. To make a wireless network as secure as a wired network requires the use of encryption.

Design for the Future

Many organizations install the highest grade of cable that is available. This ensures that the networks are prepared for additional bandwidth requirements in the future. To avoid expensive cable installations later, you and your customer must decide if the cost of installing a higher grade cable is necessary.

Refer to
Figure
in online course

15.3.2 Select an ISP connection type

The ISP that you choose can have a noticeable effect on network service. Some private resellers that connect to a phone company may sell more connections than allowed, which slows the overall speed of the service to customers.

There are three main considerations for an Internet connection:

- Speed
- Reliability
- Availability

POTS

A POTS connection is extremely slow, but it is available wherever there is a telephone. A modem uses the telephone line to transmit and receive data. This method of connection is known as dial-up.

ISDN

ISDN offers faster connection times and has faster speeds than dial-up, and allows multiple devices to share a single telephone line. ISDN is very reliable because it uses POTS lines. ISDN is available in most places where the telephone company supports digital signaling.

DSL

DSL, like ISDN, allows multiple devices to share a single telephone line. DSL speeds are generally higher than ISDN. DSL allows the use of high-bandwidth applications or multiple users to share the same connection to the Internet. In most cases, the copper wires already in your home or business are capable of carrying the signals needed for DSL communication.

There are limitations to DSL technology. DSL service is not available everywhere, and it works better and faster the closer the installation is to the telephone provider's Central Office (CO). Also, DSL is much faster when receiving data over the Internet than it is when sending it. In some cases, the lines that are in place to carry telephone signals do not technically qualify to carry DSL signals.

Cable

A cable Internet connection does not use telephone lines. Cable uses coaxial cable lines originally designed to carry cable television. Like DSL, cable offers high speeds and an always-on connection, which means that even when the connection is not in use, the connection to the Internet is still available. Many cable companies offer telephone service as well.

Because cable television reaches many homes, it is an alternative for people unable to receive DSL service. Theoretically, the bandwidth of cable is higher than DSL, but can be affected by limitations of the cable provider. Most homes that have cable television have the option to install high-speed Internet service.

Satellite

For people who live in rural areas, broadband satellite Internet connections provide a high-speed connection that is always on. A satellite dish is used to transmit and receive signals to and from a satellite that relays these signals back to a service provider.

The cost of installation and the monthly service fees are much higher than those for DSL and cable subscribers. Heavy storm conditions can degrade the quality of the connection between the user and the satellite, or the satellite to the provider, slowing down or even disconnecting the connection.

Cellular

Many types of wireless Internet services are available. The same companies that offer cellular service may offer Internet service. PCMCIA and PCI cards are used to connect a computer to the Internet. The service is not available in all areas.

Service providers may offer wireless Internet service using microwave technology in limited areas. Signals are transmitted directly to an antenna on the roof of the house or building.

Research the connection types that the ISPs offer before selecting an ISP. Check the services available in your area. Compare connection speeds, reliability, and cost before committing to a service agreement.

ISP Connection Types

Determine the best ISP type for your customer.

Refer to **Worksheet** for this chapter

Refer to **Figure** in online course

15.3.3 Select network cards

Every device on a network requires a network interface. There are many types of network interfaces:

- Most network interfaces for desktop computers are either integrated into the motherboard or are an expansion card that fits into an expansion slot.

- Most laptop network interfaces are either integrated into the motherboard or fit into a PC Card or ExpressBus expansion slot.

- USB network adapters plug into any available USB port and can be used with both desktops and laptops.

Before purchasing a NIC, you should research the speed, form factor, and capabilities that the card offers. Check the speed and capabilities of the hub or switch that will be connected to the computer.

Ethernet NICs may be backward-compatible:

- If you have a 10/100 Mbps NIC and a hub that is only 10 Mbps, the NIC will operate at 10 Mbps.

- If you have a 10/100/1000 Mbps NIC and a switch that is only operating at 100 Mbps, the NIC will operate at 100 Mbps.

If you have a gigabit switch, you will most likely need to purchase a gigabit NIC to match speeds. If there are any plans to upgrade the network in the future to Gigabit Ethernet, make sure to purchase NICs that are able to support the speed. Costs can vary greatly, so select NICs that match the needs of your customer.

Wireless NICs are available in many formats with many capabilities. You should select wireless NICs based on the type of wireless network that is installed, as described in these examples:

- 802.11b NICs can be used on 802.11g networks.

- 802.11a can be used only on a network that supports 802.11a.

- 802.11a, 802.11b, and 802.11g NICs can be used on 802.11n networks.

You should know what wireless equipment is in use and what will be installed on the network to ensure compatibility and usability.

Refer to
Figure
in online course

15.3.4 Select the network device

Several types of devices are available to connect components on a network. Select network devices to meet the needs of your customer.

Hubs

A hub is used to share data between multiple devices on a section of the network. The hub may connect to another networking device like a switch or router that connects to other sections of the network. The maximum speed of the network is determined by the speed of the hub.

Hubs are used less often today because of the effectiveness and low cost of switches. Hubs do not segment network traffic, so they decrease the amount of available bandwidth to any device. In addition, because hubs cannot filter data, a lot of unnecessary traffic constantly moves between all the devices connected to it.

One advantage of a hub is that it regenerates the data that passes through it. This means that a hub can also function as a repeater. A hub can extend the reach of a network because it rebuilds the signal, which overcomes the effects of distance.

Switches

In modern networks, switches have replaced hubs as the central point of connectivity. Like a hub, the speed of the switch determines the maximum speed of the network. However, switches filter and segment network traffic by sending data only to the device to which it is sent. This provides higher dedicated bandwidth to each device on the network.

Switches maintain a switching table. The switching table contains a list of all MAC addresses on the network, and a list of which switch port can be used to reach a device with a given MAC address. The switching table records MAC addresses by inspecting the source MAC address of every incoming frame, as well as the port on which the frame arrives. The switch then creates a switching table that maps MAC addresses to outgoing ports. When a frame arrives that is destined for a particular MAC address, the switch uses the switching table to determine which port to use to reach the MAC address. The frame is forwarded from the port to the destination. By sending frames out of only one port to the destination, other ports are not affected.

Routers

Routers connect networks together. On a corporate network, one router port connects to the WAN connection and the other ports connect to the corporate LANs. The router becomes the gateway, or path to the outside, for the LAN. In a home network, the router connects the computers and network devices in the home to the Internet. In this case, the router is a home gateway. The wireless router, shown in Figure 1, serves as a home gateway, wireless access point, and a switch. When the home router provides multiple services, it may be called a multi-function device.

ISP Equipment

When subscribing to an ISP, you should find out what type of equipment is available so that you can select the most appropriate device. Many ISPs offer a discount on equipment that is purchased at the time of installation.

Refer to
Figure
in online course

Some ISPs may rent equipment on a month-to-month basis. This may be more attractive because the ISP supports the equipment if there is a failure, change, or upgrade to the technology. Home users may select to purchase equipment from the ISP because, after a period of time, the initial cost of the equipment will be lower than the cost of renting the equipment.

Refer to
Interactive Graphic
in online course.

Network Devices

Complete the network devices activity in Figure 2.

15.4   Implement the customer's network

Installing and implementing a network can be a complicated task. Even a small home network installation can become difficult and time-consuming. However, careful planning helps ensure an easier and faster installation.

During the installation, there may be some downtime for the existing network. For example, disruptions can be caused by building modifications and network cable installation. The project is not complete until all devices have been installed, configured, and tested.

After completing this section, you will meet these objectives:

- Install and test the customer's network.

- Configure the customer's Internet and network resources.

Refer to
Figure
in online course

15.4.1   Install and test the customer's network

After you have determined the location of all of the network devices, you are ready to install the network cables.

Network Installation Steps

If you are going to install the cable yourself, all of the necessary materials should be available at the site, as well as a blueprint of the network's physical topology.

These steps outline the process for physically creating a network:

Step 1.   To install the cable in ceilings and behind walls, you perform a cable pull. One person pulls the cable, and another feeds the cable through the walls. Make sure to label the ends of every cable. Follow a labeling scheme that is already in place, or follow the guidelines outlined in TIA/EIA 606-A.

Step 2.   After the cables have been terminated at both ends, use a cable tester to make sure that there are no shorts or interference.

Step 3.   Make sure that the network interfaces are properly installed in the desktops, laptops, and network printers. After the network interfaces have been installed, configure the client software and the IP address information on all of the devices.

Step 4.   Install switches and routers in a secured, centralized location. All of the LAN connections terminate in this area. In a home network, you may need to install these devices in separate locations, or you may have only one device.

Step 5.   Install an Ethernet patch cable from the wall connection to each network device. Check to see if you have a link light on all network interfaces and on each network device port that connects to a device.

Step 6.   When all devices are connected and all link lights are functioning, test the network for connectivity. Use the **ipconfig /all** command to view the IP configuration on each workstation. Use the **ping** command to test basic connectivity. You should be able to ping other computers on the network, including the default gateway and remote computers. After you have confirmed basic connectivity, you must configure and test network applications, such as e-mail and an Internet browser.

Refer to
Figure
in online course

15.4.2 Configure the customer's Internet and network resources

After the network has been set up and tested, you should configure a web browser, such as Microsoft Internet Explorer (IE). You can configure browser settings and perform maintenance tasks in the Internet Options dialog box, as shown in Figure 1.

Temporary Internet Files

When an operating system such as Windows XP has been installed, IE is also installed by default. With IE, every time that you visit a website, many files are downloaded to your computer in the Temporary Internet Files folder. Most of these files are image files that represent banners and other components of the website.

Temporary Internet files are stored on your computer so that the browser can load content faster the next time you visit the same website. Depending on the number of websites you visit, the Temporary Internet Files folder can fill up quickly. While this may not be an urgent problem, you should delete the files occasionally. This is especially important after you have entered personal information into the Web browser.

Default Browser

You can confirm which browser Windows uses by default. In Windows XP, choose **Start > Run**, enter a website address, and click **OK**.

In Windows Vista, choose **Start > Start Search**, enter a website address, and click **OK**. The website opens in the browser that is currently set as the default.

If you want IE to be your default browser, start by opening IE. On the toolbar, select **Tools > Internet Options > Programs**. Place a check in the box next to **Tell me if Internet Explorer is not the default web browser**. The next time you click a web link in a program or in a document, you will be asked if you would like to make Internet Explorer your default web browser. This path might vary based on your version of IE.

File Sharing

Users can share resources over the network. You can share a single file, specific folders, or an entire drive, as shown in Figure 2.

To share a file in Windows XP, you should first copy it to a folder. Right-click the folder and select **Sharing and Security**. Next select **Share this folder**. You can identify who has access to the folder and what permissions they have on the objects in the folder. Figure 3 shows the permissions window of a shared folder.

In Windows Vista, right-click the folder and select **Sharing**. Add a user to the folder and then select **Share**.

Permissions define the type of access a user has to a file or folder:

- *Read–* This allows the user to view the file and subfolder names, navigate to subfolders, view data in files, and run program files.

- *Change–* This allows all of the permissions of Read but allows the user to add files and subfolders, change the data in files, and delete subfolders and files.

- *Full Control–* This allows all of the permissions of Change and Read. If the file or folder is in an NTFS partition, Full Control allows you to change permissions on the file or folder, and take ownership of the file or folder.

Windows XP Professional and Windows Vista Business are limited to a maximum of 10 simultaneous file-sharing connections.

Printer Sharing

To share a printer in Windows XP, select **Start > Control Panel > Printers and Faxes**. Right-click the printer icon and select **Sharing**. Click **Share this Printer** and then click **OK**. The printer is now available for other computers to access.

Refer to
Figure
in online course

To access a printer shared by another computer in Windows XP, select **Start > Control Panel > Printers and Faxes**. Click **File > Add Printer**. Use the **Add Printers** wizard to find and install the shared network printer.

To share a printer in Windows Vista, select **Start > Control Panel > Printers**. Right-click the printer icon and select **Sharing > Change sharing options > Continue**. Click **Share this Printer** and then click **OK**. The printer is now available for other computers to access.

To access a printer shared by another computer in Windows Vista, select **Start > Control Panel > Printers**. Click **Add a printer**. Use the **Add Printers** wizard to find and install the shared network printer.

Refer to
Lab Activity
for this chapter

Configure Browser Settings in Windows XP
Configure browser settings in Microsoft Internet Explorer and select Internet Explorer as the default browser.

Refer to
Lab Activity
for this chapter

Configure Browser Settings in Windows Vista
Configure browser settings in Microsoft Internet Explorer and select Internet Explorer as the default browser.

Refer to
Lab Activity
for this chapter

Share a Folder, Share a Printer, and Set Share Permissions in Windows XP
Create and share a folder, share a printer, and set permissions for the shares.

Refer to
Lab Activity
for this chapter

Share a Folder, Share a Printer, and Set Share Permissions in Windows Vista
Create and share a folder, share a printer, and set permissions for the shares.

15.5 Upgrade the customer's network

You must be able to upgrade, install, and configure components when a customer asks for increased speed or new functionality to be added to a network. If your customer is adding additional computers or wireless functionality, you should be able to recommend equipment based on their needs, such as wireless access points and wireless network cards. The equipment that you suggest must work with the existing equipment and cabling, or the existing infrastructure must be up-graded.

After completing this section, you will meet these objectives:

Refer to
Figure
in online course

- Install and configure a wireless NIC.

- Install and configure a wireless router.

- Test a connection.

15.5.1 Install and configure a wireless NIC

To connect to a wireless network, your computer must have a wireless adapter. A wireless adapter is used to communicate with other wireless devices, such as computers, printers, or wireless access points.

Refer to
Figure
in online course

Before purchasing a wireless adapter, make sure that it is compatible with other wireless equipment that is already installed on the network. Also, verify that the wireless adapter is the correct form factor for the customer's computer. A wireless USB adapter can be used with any desktop or laptop computer that has an open USB port.

To install a wireless adapter, such as a wireless NIC in a desktop computer, you must remove the case cover. Install the wireless NIC into an available PCI slot or PCI express slot. Some wireless NICs have an antenna connected to the back of the card. Some antennas are attached with a cable so that they can be positioned for the best signal reception.

After the wireless NIC is installed, configure the device drivers and enter the IP address information. If the wireless NIC is configured with a static IP address, you may need to change the IP address if your computer joins a different network. Therefore, it may be more practical to enable DHCP on your computer to receive IP address information from the DHCP server. After IP addressing is complete, the computer should be able to detect and connect to the wireless LAN.

Wireless NICs may use a wizard to connect to the wireless network. In this case, you would insert the media that comes with the adapter and follow the directions to get connected.

Refer to
Lab Activity
for this chapter

Install a Wireless NIC in Windows XP
Install and configure a wireless NIC.

Refer to
Lab Activity
for this chapter

Install a Wireless NIC in Windows Vista
Install and configure a wireless NIC.

Refer to **Packet
Tracer Activity**
for this chapter

Install a Wireless NIC
Install a Wireless NIC.
Configure the PC to join a wireless network.

15.5.2 Install and configure a wireless router

When installing a wireless network, you can use a wireless access point or a wireless router. A wireless access point only provides connectivity to the network, while a wireless router provides additional features, such as DHCP. The Linksys WRT300N is a multipurpose device that provides both router and access point capabilities. You have to decide where you want to install access points and then configure them. The following steps describe the installation of an access point:

Step 1.   Use a floor plan to find the locations for access points that allow maximum coverage. The best place for a wireless access point is at the center of the area you are covering, with line of sight between the wireless devices and the access point.

Step 2.   Connect the access point to the existing network. The back of the Linksys WRT300N router has five ports. Connect a DSL or cable modem to the port labeled Internet. The switching logic of the device forwards all of the packets through this port when there is communication to and from the Internet and other connected computers. Connect one computer to any of the remaining ports to access the configuration web pages.

Step 3.   Turn on the broadband modem and plug in the power cord to the router. When the modem finishes establishing a connection to the ISP, the router automatically communicates with the modem to receive network information from the ISP that is necessary to gain access to the Internet: IP address, subnet mask, and DNS server addresses. The Internet LED will light up to indicate communication with the modem.

Step 4.   When the router has established communication with the modem, you must configure the router to communicate with the devices on the network. Turn on the computer that is connected to the router. Open a web browser. In the Address field, enter **192.168.1.1.** This is the default address for the Linksys router configuration and management.

Step 5.   A security window prompts you for authentication to access the router configuration screens. The user name field must be left blank. Enter **admin** as the default password. When logged in, the first setup screen opens.

Step 6.   Continue with the setup. There are tabs that have sub-tabs on the setup screen. You must click **Save Settings** at the bottom of each screen after making any changes.

When you use the configuration screens of the 300N router, you can click the help tab to see additional information about a tab. For information beyond what is shown on the help screen, consult the user manual.

After establishing the connection, there are several configurations that can help secure and increase the speed of a wireless network. Some of these configurations are listed below:

- 802.11 protocol selection

- Static IP address configuration

- Service Set Identifier (SSID) setting

- Firmware update

802.11 Protocol Selection

The 802.11 protocol can provide increased throughput based on the wireless network environment. If all wireless devices connect with the same 802.11 standard, maximum speeds can be obtained for that standard. If the access point is configured to accept only one 802.11 standard, devices that do not use that standard will not be able to connect to the access point.

A mixed mode wireless network environment can include 802.11a, 802.11b, 802.11g, and 802.11n. This environment provides easy access for legacy devices that need a wireless connection.

Static IP Address Configuration

Static IP address assignments give better protection against network attacks than DHCP. For example, static IP address assignments allow firewalls to be configured to permit specific traffic or connections between specific devices. There are disadvantages to configuring static IP addresses on large networks. It is more time consuming to assign static IP addresses and more difficult to manage than using DHCP assignments.

SSID Setting

The SSID is the name of the wireless network. The SSID broadcast allows other devices to automatically discover the name of the wireless network. When the SSID broadcast is disabled, you must manually enter the SSID on wireless devices. This provides protection from automatic discovery of the wireless network name.

Firmware Update

Firmware updates can improve performance, fix bugs, or update security features. When updating the firmware, it is vital to follow the manufacturer's instructions. Firmware updates and instructions can be downloaded from the manufacturer's website. Always back up the wireless router configuration files and current firmware before updating.

> Refer to
> **Figure**
> in online course

Note

The access point can stop functioning if the update fails to complete.

> Refer to
> **Lab Activity**
> for this chapter

Configure Wireless Router

Configure and test the wireless settings on the Linksys WRT300N.

15.5.3 Test a connection

It may be difficult to know if your wireless connection is working properly, even when Windows indicates that you are connected. You might be connected to a wireless access point or home gateway, but you might not be connected to the Internet. The easiest way to test for an Internet connection is to open a web browser and see if the Internet is available. To troubleshoot a wireless connection, you can use the Windows GUI or CLI.

Network Connections

To verify a wireless connection using the Windows XP GUI, select **Start > Control Panel > Network Connections**, as shown in Figure 1. Double-click the **Wireless Network Connection** to display the status.

The **Connection Status** screen shown in Figure 2 displays the number of packets that have been sent and received. The packets are the communication between the computer and the network device. The window shows whether or not the computer is connected, along with the speed and duration of the connection.

To display the Address Type, as shown in Figure 3, choose the **Support** tab on the Connection Status screen. The Connection Status information includes either a static address, which is assigned manually, or a dynamic address, which is assigned by a DHCP server. The subnet mask and default gateway are also listed. To access the MAC address and other information about the IP address, click **Details....** If the connection is not functioning correctly, click **Repair** to reset the connection information and attempt to establish a new connection.

To verify a wireless connection using the Windows Vista GUI, select **Start > Control Panel > Network and Sharing Center > Manage Network Connections**. Double-click the **Wireless Network Connection** to display the status.

Click the **Details...** button on the Connection Status screen. The Connection Status information includes either a static address, which is assigned manually, or a dynamic address, which is assigned by a DHCP server. The subnet mask, default gateway, MAC address and other information about the IP address are also listed. If the connection is not functioning correctly, click **Diagnose** to reset the connection information, and attempt to establish a new connection.

Ipconfig

The ipconfig command is a CLI tool used to verify that the connection has a valid IP address. The window displays basic IP address information for network connections. To perform specific tasks, add options to the ipconfig command, as shown in Figure 4.

Ping

Ping is a CLI tool used to test connectivity between devices. You can test your own connection by pinging your computer. To test your computer, ping your NIC. In Windows XP, select **Start > Run > cmd**. At the command prompt, enter **ping localhost**. This command lets you know if your adapter is working properly.

Ping a public IP address outside of your network to check if your WAN connection is working properly. You can find the address for the default gateway by using the ipconfig command.

To test the Internet connection and DNS, ping a popular website. In Windows XP, select **Start > Run > cmd**. At the command prompt, enter **ping** *destination_name*.

The response of the ping command displays the IP address resolution of the domain. The response shows replies from the ping or that the request timed out because there is a problem.

To perform other specific tasks, add options to the ping command, as shown in Figure 5.

Tracert

Tracert is a CLI tool used to trace the route that packets take from your computer to a destination address. In Windows XP, select **Start > Run > cmd**. At the command prompt, enter **tracert**.

The first listing in the window for the tracert result is your default gateway. Each listing after that is the router that packets are traveling through to reach the destination. Tracert shows you where packets are stopping, indicating where the problem is occurring. If there are listings that show problems after the default gateway, it may mean that the problems are with the ISP, the Internet, or the destination server.

Net

The net command is used to manage network computers, servers, and resources like drives and printers. Net commands use the NetBIOS protocol in Windows. These commands are used to start, stop, and configure networking services, as shown in Figure 6.

Nslookup

Nslookup is a CLI tool for testing and troubleshooting DNS servers. The nslookup command queries the DNS server to discover IP addresses or host names.

In Windows XP, select **Start > Run > cmd**. At the command prompt, enter **nslookup** *hostname*. Nslookup returns the IP address for the host name entered. A reverse nslookup command, **nslookup** *IP_address* returns the corresponding host name for the IP address entered.

Refer to
Lab Activity
for this chapter

Test the Wireless NIC in Windows XP

Check the status of your wireless connection, investigate the availability of wireless networks, and test connectivity.

Refer to
Lab Activity
for this chapter

Test the Wireless NIC in Windows Vista

Check the status of your wireless connection, investigate the availability of wireless networks, and test connectivity.

Refer to **Packet
Tracer Activity**
for this chapter

Test a Wireless Connection

Configure a PC to join a wireless network.
Test the wireless connection.

Refer to
Figure
in online course

15.6 Describe installation, configuration, and management of a simple mail server

An e-mail system uses e-mail client software on the users' devices and e-mail server software on one or more e-mail servers. Clients read e-mail from the e-mail server using one of two protocols:

- Post Office Protocol (POP)

- Internet Message Access Protocol (IMAP)

Clients send e-mail to an e-mail server, and e-mail servers forward e-mail to each other, using Simple Mail Transfer Protocol (SMTP).

You need to know how to configure a client computer to accept the correct incoming mail format and also understand the process for setting up a mail server. Configuring the e-mail client software can be done using connection wizards, as shown in Figure 1. The advantages and disadvantages of each e-mail protocol are shown in Figure 2.

SMTP

SMTP sends e-mail from an e-mail client to an e-mail server, or from one e-mail server to another. SMTP has these characteristics:

- Simple, text-based protocol

- Sent over TCP using port 25

- Must be implemented to send e-mail

- Message is sent after recipients are identified and verified

POP

POP is used by an e-mail client to download e-mail from an e-mail server. The most recent version of POP is POP3. POP3 usually uses port 110.

POP3 supports end users that have intermittent connections, such as dial-up. A POP3 user can connect, download e-mail from the server, and then disconnect. The downloaded e-mail no longer resides on the server.

IMAP

IMAP is similar to POP3 but has additional features. Like POP3, IMAP allows you to download e-mail from an e-mail server using an e-mail client. The difference is that IMAP allows the user to organize e-mail on the network e-mail server, and download copies of e-mail. The original e-mail remains on the network e-mail server. IMAP is faster than POP3, but IMAP requires more disk space on the server and more CPU resources. The most recent version of IMAP is IMAP4. IMAP4 is often used in large networks such as a university campus. IMAP usually uses port 143.

E-mail Server

An e-mail server is a computer that can send and receive e-mail on behalf of e-mail clients. These are some common e-mail servers:

- Microsoft Exchange
- Sendmail
- Eudora Internet Mail Server (EIMS)

As shown in Figure 3, there are often wizards and tools available to guide you in setting up an e-mail server. To install and set up an e-mail server, such as Microsoft Exchange, you must first make sure that the network has all of the proper qualifications in place and that it is properly configured. Active directory servers, global catalog servers, and domain name servers (DNS) must all be in place and functioning before Exchange can be installed and work properly. An active directory server is a computer that hosts a database that allows centralized administration over an enterprise network. A global catalog server is a centralized repository that contains information about every domain in an enterprise network.

Exchange must be installed on a domain where every computer runs at least Windows 2000. This is known as native mode. Windows NT domain controllers cannot function in a native environment.

The Active Directory database is organized in a pattern called a schema. One server running Windows 2003 is designated as the Schema Master. This is the only server that can change the way the Active Directory user database is organized. When the network administrator needs to modify the Active Directory structure, the change is made on the Schema Master. Active Directory then automatically copies the update to all the rest of the authentication servers.

E-mail Server Installation

You should test the environment before you install Exchange. To prevent the installation from affecting the daily operation of your network, set up the services required and install Exchange on a dedicated set of servers away from the main network. Keep the installation of Exchange separated from your production network until you are sure that it is functioning properly.

Before you install Exchange, be prepared with the proper equipment and information:

- Fully functional and reliable DNS deployment
- Active Directory domain

- At least one Global Catalog

- Windows 2000 or higher native domain functionality

- Exchange server software

- Windows server support tools

- Schema master server

- High-speed Internet connection

You are ready to install the mail server when all of the qualifications of your network are in place. You will have to add Internet Information Services (IIS) using the Add/Remove Windows Components wizard before initiating the installation of the Exchange server. IIS is a server that has programs used for building and administering website services. After IIS has been installed, Exchange can be installed. Insert the installation CD and begin the New Exchange installation wizard.

The installation wizard will take you through a series of steps to verify that Exchange is ready to be installed. The wizard will check to make sure that IIS is installed, the domain servers are running properly, and the Windows support tools are installed. The setup program will notify you of any problems with the installation environment. Restart the setup program from the beginning after fixing any issues.

Once Exchange is installed, the Microsoft Management Console plug in for Exchange, shown in Figure 4, will provide access to many settings at one convenient location. Make sure to install all updates so that the server will run properly. The Exchange System Manager, which is a console that controls the Exchange deployment, can be used to manage the options of the server.

Use the Active Directory Users and Computer (ADUC) console to configure a user's mailbox. This is also known as making the user mailbox-enabled.

Open the ADUC to create a new user. Fill out the username and password information according to the domain security policy, as shown in Figure 5. The user's mailbox will be created by the Exchange server when the user receives the first e-mail.

Setting up Exchange takes careful planning, including ensuring that the servers, services, and technologies are in place and working correctly on the network. In some cases, during an installation, if there is a failure, you may need to reinstall the operating system and start the Exchange installation from the beginning.

Note

Before planning an e-mail server installation, consult with network professionals, experienced Windows networking experts, or experienced e-mail technicians.

Refer to **Figure** in online course

15.7 Describe preventive maintenance procedures for networks

Preventive maintenance is just as important for the network as it is for the computers on a network. You must check the condition of cables, network devices, servers, and computers to make sure that they are kept clean and are in good working order. You should develop a plan to perform scheduled maintenance and cleaning at regular intervals. This will help you to prevent network downtime and equipment failures.

As part of a regularly scheduled maintenance program, inspect all cabling for breaks. Make sure that cables are labeled correctly and labels are not coming off. Replace any worn or unreadable labels. Check that cable supports are properly installed and no attachment points are coming loose. Cabling can become damaged and worn. You should keep the cabling in good repair to maintain good network performance.

As a technician, you may notice that equipment is failing, damaged, or making unusual sounds. Inform the network administrator if you notice any of these issues, to prevent unnecessary network downtime.

Cables at workstations and printers should be checked carefully. Cables are often moved or kicked when they are underneath desks and can be bent. These conditions can result in loss of bandwidth or connectivity. You should also be proactive in the education of network users. Demonstrate to network users how to properly connect and disconnect cables, as well as how to move them, if necessary.

Refer to
Figure
in online course

15.8 Troubleshoot the network

To begin troubleshooting a network problem, you should first try to locate the source of the problem. Check to see whether a group of users, or only one user, has the problem. If only one user has the problem, begin troubleshooting with that user's computer.

After completing this section, you will meet these objectives:

- Review the troubleshooting process.
- Identify common problems and solutions.
- Apply troubleshooting skills.

Refer to
Figure
in online course

15.8.1 Review the troubleshooting process

Network problems can result from a combination of hardware, software, and connectivity issues. Computer technicians must be able to analyze the problem and determine the cause of the error to repair the network issue. This process is called troubleshooting.

The first step in the troubleshooting process is to identify the problem. Figure 1 is a list of open-ended and closed-ended questions to ask the customer.

After you have talked to the customer, you can establish a theory of probable causes. Figure 2 is a list of some common probable causes for network problems.

After you have developed some theories about what is wrong, test your theories to determine the cause of the problem. Figure 3 is a list of quick procedures that can determine the exact cause of the problem or even correct the problem. If a quick procedure does correct the problem, you can go to step 5 to verify full system functionality. If a quick procedure does not correct the problem, you may need to research the problem further to establish the exact cause.

After you have determined the exact cause of the problem, establish a plan of action to resolve the problem and implement the solution. Figure 4 shows sources of information to gather additional information to resolve an issue.

After you have corrected the problem, you will need to verify full functionality and, if applicable, implement preventive measures. Figure 5 is a list of the steps to verify the solution.

In the final step of the troubleshooting process, you must document your findings, actions, and outcomes. Figure 6 is a list of the tasks required to document the problem and the solution.

Refer to
Figure
in online course

15.8.2 Identify common problems and solutions

Network problems can be attributed to hardware, software, networks, or some combination of the three. You will resolve some types of problems more often than others, while other problems may require more in-depth troubleshooting skills.

Network Connection Problems

These types of connection problems are often related to incorrect TCP/IP configurations, firewall settings, or devices that have stopped working, as shown in Figure 1.

E-mail Failure

Not being able to send or receive e-mail is often caused by incorrect e-mail software settings, firewall settings, and hardware connectivity issues, as shown in Figure 2.

FTP and Secure Internet Connection Problems

File transfer problems between FTP clients and servers are often caused by incorrect IP address and port settings, or security policies. Secure Internet connection problems are often related to incorrect certificate settings and ports blocked by software or hardware, as shown in Figure 3.

Problems Revealed by CLI Commands

Unexpected information reported from CLI commands is often caused by incorrect IP address settings, hardware connection issues, and firewall settings, as shown in Figure 4.

Refer to
Figure
in online course

15.8.3 Apply troubleshooting skills

Now that you understand the troubleshooting process, it is time to apply your listening and diagnostic skills.

Refer to
Figure
in online course

The first lab is designed to reinforce your skills with networks. You will troubleshoot and fix a computer that does not connect to the network.

The second lab is designed to reinforce your communication and troubleshooting skills. In this lab, you will perform the following steps:

- Receive the work order
- Take the customer through various steps to try and resolve the problem
- Document the problem and the resolution

The third lab is designed to test your troubleshooting skills with networking problems. You will troubleshoot and repair a router and computers that have more than one problem.

Refer to
Lab Activity
for this chapter

Fix Network Problem
Troubleshoot and fix a computer that does not connect to the network.

Refer to
Lab Activity
for this chapter

Remote Technician: Fix Network Problem
Gather data from the customer, and then instruct the customer on how to fix a computer that does not connect to the network.

Refer to
Lab Activity
for this chapter

Troubleshooting Network Problems in Windows XP
Diagnose and solve various network problems.

Refer to
Lab Activity
for this chapter

Troubleshooting Network Problems in Windows Vista
Diagnose and solve various network problems.

Summary

The advanced networks chapter discussed the planning, implementation, and upgrading of networks and network components. The following are some of the important concepts to remember from this chapter:

- Many safety hazards are associated with network environments, devices, and media. You should follow proper safety procedures at all times.

- Make network design decisions that will meet the needs and the goals of your customers.

- Select network components that offer the services and capabilities necessary to implement a network based on the needs of the customer.

- Plan network installations based on the needed services and equipment.

- Upgrading a network may involve additional equipment or cabling. Discuss how upgrading can help to enhance the future usability of the network.

- Plan for an e-mail installation before deployment. Consult a specialist to make sure that the installation and configuration of an e-mail server goes smoothly.

- Prevent network problems by developing and implementing a comprehensive preventive maintenance policy.

- Follow a logical methodology to troubleshoot advanced network problems.

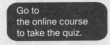

Chapter 15 Quiz

Take the chapter quiz to test your knowledge.

Your Chapter Notes

Advanced Security

Introduction

This chapter reviews the types of attacks that threaten the security of computers and the data contained on them. A technician is responsible for the security of data and computer equipment in an organization. This chapter describes how you can work with customers to ensure that the best possible protection is in place.

Risks to computers and network equipment come from both internal and external sources. Risks include physical threats, such as theft or damage to equipment, and data threats, such as the loss or corruption of data.

After completing this chapter, you will meet these objectives:

- Outline security requirements based on customer needs.
- Select security components based on customer needs.
- Implement customer's security plan.
- Perform preventive maintenance on security.
- Troubleshoot security.

Refer to
Figure
in online course

16.1 Outline security requirements based on customer needs

An organization should strive to achieve the best and most affordable security protection against data loss or damage to software and equipment. Network technicians and the organization's management should work together to develop a security policy that ensures that data and equipment have been protected against all security threats. A security policy includes a comprehensive statement about the level of security required and how this security will be achieved.

You may be involved in developing a security policy for a customer or organization. When creating a security policy, you should ask the following questions to determine security factors:

- Is the computer located at a home or a business?

Home computers are generally more vulnerable to wireless intrusion than business computers. Business computers also have a high threat of network intrusion, because of users abusing their access privileges.

- Is there full-time Internet access?

The longer a computer is connected to the Internet, the greater the chance of attacks from other infected computers. A computer accessing the Internet should be configured with a firewall and antivirus software.

- Is the computer a laptop?

Physical security is an issue with laptop computers. There are measures to secure laptops, such as cable locks.

After completing this section, you will meet these objectives:

- Outline a local security policy.

- Explain when and how to use security hardware.

- Explain when and how to use security application software.

Refer to
Figure
in online course

16.1.1   Outline a local security policy

A security policy is a collection of rules, guidelines, and checklists. Network technicians and managers of an organization work together to develop the rules and guidelines for the security needs of computer equipment. A security policy includes the following elements:

- It defines an acceptable computer usage statement for an organization.

- It dentifies the people permitted to use the computer equipment in an organization.

- It identifies the devices that are permitted to be installed on a network, as well as the conditions of the installation. Modems and wireless access points are examples of hardware that could expose the network to attacks.

- It defines the requirements necessary for data to remain confidential on a network.

- It determines a process for employees to acquire access to equipment and data. This process may require the employee to sign an agreement regarding the company rules. It also lists the consequences for failure to comply.

The security policy should also provide detailed information about the following issues in case of an emergency:

- Steps to take after a breach in security

- Who to contact in an emergency

- Information to share with customers, vendors, and the media

- Secondary locations to use in an evacuation

- Steps to take after an emergency is over, including the priority of services to be restored

Note

A security policy must be enforced and followed by all employees to be effective.

Refer to
Worksheet
for this chapter

Refer to
Figure
in online course

Answer Security Policy Questions

Answer security questions regarding the IT Essentials classroom.

16.1.2   Explain when and how to use security hardware

The security policy should identify hardware and equipment that can be used to prevent theft, vandalism, and data loss. As illustrated in Figure 1, physical security involves four interrelated aspects: access, data, infrastructure, and the physical computer.

Restrict access to premises with the following:

- Fences

- Security hardware

Protect the network infrastructure, such as cabling, telecommunication equipment, and network devices with the following:

- Secured telecommunications rooms

- Wireless detection for unauthorized access points

- Hardware firewalls

- Network management system that detects changes in wiring and patch panels

Protect individual computers with the following:

- Cable locks

- Laptop docking station locks

- Lockable cases

Protect data with hardware that prevents unauthorized access or theft of media with the following:

- Lockable hard drive carriers

- Secure storage and transport of backup media

- USB security dongles

The Right Security Mix

Factors that determine the most effective security equipment to use to secure equipment and data include the following:

- How the equipment is used

- Where the computer equipment is located

- What user access to data is required

For instance, a computer in a busy public place, such as a library, requires additional protection from theft and vandalism. In a busy call center, a server may need to be secured in a locked equipment room.

Where it is necessary to use a laptop computer in a public place, a security dongle, shown in Figure 2, ensures that the system locks if the user and laptop are separated.

Refer to **Figure** in online course

16.1.3 Explain when and how to use security application software

Security applications protect the operating system and software application data.

The following products and software applications can be used to protect network devices:

- *Software firewall*– Filters incoming data and is built into Windows

- *Intrusion Detection Systems (IDS)*– Monitors and reports on changes in program code and unusual network activity

■ *Application and OS patches*– Updates applications and the operating system to repair security weaknesses that are discovered

Software applications are available to protect computers from viruses, spyware, adware, and grayware.

In small offices and homes, computers usually connect directly to the Internet rather than through a protected LAN. This puts computers that are outside of a LAN at high risk for viruses and other attacks. At a minimum, these computers should use firewall, anti-virus, and anti-malware programs. Application software and the operating system should be updated with the latest patches.

The security policy should determine the level of security applications put in place. In developing a policy, management should calculate the cost of data loss versus the expense of security protection and determine which trade-offs are acceptable.

Refer to
Figure
in online course

16.2 Select security components based on customer needs

The security policy helps customers to select the security components necessary to keep equipment and data safe. If there is no security policy, you should discuss security issues with the customer.

Use your past experience as a technician and research the current security products on the market when selecting security components for the customer. The goal is to provide the security system that best matches the customer's needs.

After completing this section, you will meet these objectives:

■ Describe and compare security techniques.

■ Describe and compare access control devices.

■ Describe and compare firewall types.

Refer to
Figure
in online course

16.2.1 Describe and compare security techniques

A technician should determine the appropriate techniques to secure equipment and data for the customer. Depending on the situation, more than one technique may be required.

Passwords

Using secure, encrypted login information for computers with network access should be a minimum requirement in any organization. Malicious software monitors the network and may record plaintext passwords. If passwords are encrypted, attackers would have to decode the encryption to learn the passwords.

Logging and Auditing

Event logging and auditing should be enabled to monitor activity on the network. The network administrator audits the log file of events to investigate network access by unauthorized users.

Wireless Configurations

Wireless connections are especially vulnerable to access by attackers. Wireless clients should be configured to encrypt data.

Security Technologies

Security technologies include hash encoding, symmetric encryption, asymmetric encryption, and Virtual Private Networks (VPNs). Each technology is used for a specific purpose:

- *Hash encoding–* Hash encoding, or hashing, ensures that messages are not corrupted or tampered with during transmission. Hashing uses a mathematical function to create a numeric value that is unique to the data. If even one character is changed, the function output, called the message digest, will not be the same. However, the function is one way. Knowing the message digest does not allow an attacker to recreate the message. This makes it difficult for someone to intercept and change messages. Hash encoding is illustrated in Figure 1. The names of the most popular hashing algorithms are SHA and MD5.

- *Symmetric encryption–* Symmetric encryption requires both sides of an encrypted conversation to use an encryption key to encode and decode the data. The sender and receiver must use identical keys. Symmetric encryption is illustrated in Figure 2. DES and 3DES are examples of symmetric encryption.

- *Asymmetric encryption–* Asymmetric encryption requires two keys, a private key and a public key. The public key can be widely distributed, including e-mailing in clear text or posting on the web. The private key is kept by an individual and must not be disclosed to any other party. These keys can be used in two ways. Public key encryption is used when a single organization needs to receive encrypted text from a number of sources. The public key can be widely distributed and used to encrypt the messages. The intended recipient is the only party to have the private key, which is used to decrypt the messages. In the case of digital signatures, a private key is required for encrypting a message, and a public key is needed to decode the message. This approach allows the receiver to be confident about the source of the message because only a message encrypted using the originator's private key could be decrypted by the public key. Asymmetric encryption using digital signatures is illustrated in Figure 3. RSA is the most popular example of asymmetric encryption.

- *VPN–* A VPN uses secure protocols to encrypt and to secure data as if it was traveling in a private, corporate LAN, even though the data actually travels over any network, for example, the Internet. The secured data pipelines between points in the VPN are called secure tunnels. The process is illustrated in Figure 4. VPN technology often uses IPSec to secure communications between devices.

Refer to
Figure
in online course

16.2.2 Describe and compare access control devices

Computer equipment and data can be secured using overlapping protection techniques to prevent unauthorized access to sensitive data. An example of overlapping protection is using two different techniques to protect an asset. This is known as two-factor security, as shown in Figure 1. When considering a security program, the cost of the implementation has to be balanced against the value of the data or equipment to be protected.

Physical Security

Use security hardware to help prevent security breaches and loss of data or equipment. Physical security access control measures include the following:

- *Lock–* This is the most common device for securing physical areas. If a key is lost, all identically keyed locks must be changed.

- *Conduit–* This is a casing that protects the infrastructure media from damage and unauthorized access.

- *Card key–* This is a tool used to secure physical areas. If a card key is lost or stolen, only the missing card must be deactivated. The card key system is more expensive than security locks.

- *Video equipment–* This records images and sound for monitoring activity. The recorded data must be monitored for problems.

- *Security guard–* This person controls access to the entrance of a facility and monitors the activity inside the facility.

Network equipment should be mounted in secured areas. All cabling should be enclosed in conduits or routed inside walls to prevent unauthorized access or tampering. Network ports that are not in use should be disabled.

Biometric devices, which measure physical information about a user, are ideal for use in highly secure areas. However, for most small organizations, this type of solution would be too expensive.

Data Security

You can protect data by using data security devices to authenticate employee access. Two-factor identification is a method to increase security. Employees must use both a password and a data security device similar to those listed here:

- *Smart card–* This is a device that has the ability to store data safely. The internal memory is an embedded Integrated Circuit Chip (ICC) that connects to a reader either directly, or through a wireless connection. Smart cards are used in many applications worldwide, such as secure ID badges, online authentication devices, and secure credit card payments.

- *Security key fob–* This is a small device that resembles the ornament on a key ring. It has a small radio system that communicates with the computer over a short range. The fobs are small enough to attach to a key rings. The computer must detect the signal from the key fob before it will accept a username and password.

- *Biometric device–* This measures a physical characteristic of the user, such as fingerprints or the patterns of the iris in the eye. The user is granted access if these characteristics match its database and the correct login information is supplied.

Hardware destruction is the process of removing sensitive data from hardware and software when data is no longer needed. Hardware destruction must be performed before recycling or discarding items that store data. Three methods are commonly used to either destroy or recycle data and hard drives:

- Data wiping

- Hard drive destruction

- Hard drive recycling

Refer to
Interactive Graphic
in online course.

The level of security that the customer needs determines which devices are used to keep data and equipment secure, and how the data should be removed or destroyed.

Security Devices

Refer to
Figure
in online course

Complete the security device matching activity in Figure 2.

16.2.3 Describe and compare firewall types

Hardware and software firewalls protect data and equipment on a network from unauthorized access. A firewall should be used in addition to security software.

Hardware and software firewalls have several modes for filtering network data traffic:

- *Packet filter*– This is a set of rules that allows or denies traffic based on criteria such as IP addresses, protocols, or ports used.

- *Proxy firewall*– This is a firewall installed on a proxy server that inspects all traffic and allows or denies packets based on configured rules. A proxy server is a server that is a relay between a client and a destination server on the Internet.

- *Stateful packet inspection*– This is a firewall that keeps track of the state of network connections traveling through the firewall. Packets that are not part of a known connection are dropped.

Hardware Firewall

A hardware firewall is a physical filtering component that inspects data packets from the network before they reach computers and other devices on a network. A hardware firewall is a free-standing unit that does not use the resources of the computers it is protecting, so there is no impact on processing performance.

Software Firewall

A software firewall is an application on a computer that inspects and filters data packets. Windows Firewall is an example of a software firewall that is included in the Windows operating system. A software firewall uses the resources of the computer, resulting in reduced performance for the user.

Consider the items listed in Figure 1 when selecting a firewall.

Note

On a secure network, if computer performance is not an issue, you should enable the internal operating system firewall for additional security. Some applications may not operate properly unless the firewall is configured correctly for them.

Refer to
Worksheet
for this chapter

Refer to
Figure
in online course

Research Firewalls
Use the Internet, a newspaper, or a local store to gather information about hardware and software firewalls.

16.3   Implement customer's security policy

Adding layers of security on a network will make the network more secure, but can be expensive. You must compare the value of the data and equipment to be protected with the cost of protection when implementing the customer's security policy.

After completing this section, you will meet these objectives:

- Configure security settings.

- Describe configuring firewall types.

- Describe protection against malicious software.

Refer to
Figure
in online course

16.3.1   Configure security settings

A network has many different types of security settings. Technicians must configure security settings for folders and files, wireless devices and clients, and hardware and software firewalls.

Permission Levels for Folders and Files

Permission levels are configured to limit individual or group user access to specific data. Both FAT and NTFS allow folder sharing and folder-level permissions for users with network access. Folder permissions are shown in Figure 1. The additional security of file-level permissions is provided with NTFS. File-level permissions are shown in Figure 2.

When configuring network share permissions for a computer that has NTFS, you must create a network share and assign shared permissions to users or groups. Only users and groups with both NTFS permissions and shared permissions can access a network share.

File and network share permissions can be granted to individuals or through membership within a group. If an individual or a group is denied permissions to a network share, this denial overrides any other permissions given. For example, if you deny someone permission to a network share, the user cannot access that share, even if the user is the administrator or part of the administrators group.

Securing a network includes the proper selection and configuration of several different technologies. Some of these technologies, which are shown in Figure 3, are used to configure wireless security. The type of security needed by the network will indicate which security technologies must be enabled and configured in each network device.

Note

All router configurations, in this text, are based on the Linksys WRT300N wireless router. The configuration examples assume you are already logged on to the wireless router.

Wireless Antennae

The gain and signal pattern of the antenna connected to a wireless access point can influence where the signal can be received. Avoid transmitting signals outside of the network area by installing an antenna with a pattern that serves your network users.

Network Device Access Permissions

Many wireless devices built by a specific manufacturer have the same default username and password for accessing the wireless configuration. If left unchanged, unauthorized users can easily log on to the access point and modify the settings. When you first connect to the network device, change the default username and password. Some devices allow you to change both the username and the password, while others only allow you to change the password.

To change the default password, use the following path:

Administration > Management > type the new router password > **Re-enter to confirm > Save Settings**.

Wireless Security Modes

Most wireless access points support several different security modes. The most common ones are:

- *Wired Equivalent Privacy (WEP)*– This encrypts the broadcast data between the wireless access point and the client using a 64-bit or 128-bit encryption key. Figure 4 shows the WEP configuration.

- *Wi-Fi Protected Access (WPA)*– This is an improved version of WEP. It was created as a temporary solution until 802.11i became ratified. Now that 802.11i has been ratified, WPA2 has been released. It covers the entire 802.11i standard. WPA uses much stronger encryption than WEP encryption.

- *Wi-Fi Protected Access 2 (WPA2)*– This is an improved version of WPA. WPA2 supports robust encryption, which provides government-grade security. WPA2 can be enabled with password authentication (Personal) or server authentication (Enterprise).

- *Lightweight Extensible Authentication Protocol (LEAP), also called EAP-Cisco*– This is a wireless security protocol created by Cisco to address the weaknesses in WEP and WPA.

To add wireless security, use the following path:

Wireless > Wireless Security > select a Security Mode > select an Encryption Type > type the **Pre-shared Key >** set **Key Renewal > Save Settings > Continue**.

SSID

A wireless access point broadcasts the SSID by default so that wireless devices can detect the wireless network. You can disable SSID broadcasting on a wireless network to prevent the wireless access point or router from revealing the name of the wireless network.

To disable SSID broadcasting, use the following path:

Wireless > Basic Wireless Setting > select **Disabled** for SSID Broadcast > **Save Settings > Continue**.

Disabling SSID broadcasting can make it more difficult for legitimate clients to find the wireless network. Manually enter the SSID on wireless devices to connect to the wireless network when the SSID broadcast has been disabled on the wireless router or access point. Simply turning off the SSID broadcast is not sufficient to prevent unauthorized clients from connecting to the wireless network. Instead of turning off the SSID broadcast, use stronger encryption such as WPA or WPA2.

MAC Address Filtering

MAC address filtering is a technique used to deploy device-level security on a wireless LAN. Because every wireless client has a unique MAC address, wireless access points can prevent wireless clients from connecting to the wireless network if they do not have authorized MAC addresses. MAC address filtering, as shown in Figure 5, is vulnerable to attack when used alone and should be combined with other security techniques.

To set up a MAC address filter, use the following path:

Wireless > Wireless MAC Filter > select **Enabled**.

Select **Prevent** or **Permit** for the access restriction type.

Select **Wireless Client List >** select the client **> Save to MAC Address Filter List > Add > Save Settings > Continue**.

Add a MAC address for each client that you wish to permit or deny access to the wireless client list.

The MAC address of a wireless NIC can be found by typing **ipconfig /all** at the command prompt. For devices other than computers, the MAC address can usually be found on the label of the device or within the manufacturer's instructions. On wireless networks with a large number of clients, MAC address filtering can become tedious because you must enter each MAC address in the filter.

MAC address filtering is not a strong layer of security. Instead of using MAC address filtering, use stronger encryption techniques such as WPA or WPA2.

Firewalls

A firewall is a device or application installed on a network to protect it from unauthorized users and malicious attacks. A software firewall is software installed on a computer to block specific incoming or outgoing traffic. For example, a firewall that is configured to block outgoing traffic on port 21 will not allow the computer to connect to a standard FTP server. The firewall can be configured to block multiple individual ports, a range of ports, or even traffic specific to an application.

The Linksys WRT300N wireless router is also a hardware firewall. A hardware firewall isolates your network from other networks. A hardware firewall will pass two different types of traffic into your network:

- Traffic that originates from inside your network
- Traffic destined for a port that you have intentionally left open

There are several types of hardware firewall configurations:

- *Packet filter–* This configuration does not allow packets to pass through the firewall, unless they match the established rule set configured in the firewall. Traffic can be filtered based on many attributes, such as source IP address, source port or destination IP address or port, and destination services such as WWW or FTP.

- *Application layer–* This configuration intercepts all packets traveling to or from an application. It prevents all unwanted outside traffic from reaching protected devices.

- *Proxy–* This configuration intercepts all traffic between computers and different networks and uses established rules to determine if data requests should be allowed.

To configure hardware firewall settings on the Linksys WRT300N, use the following path:

Security > Firewall > select **Enable** for SPI Firewall Protection. Then select other Internet filters and web filters required to secure the network. Click **Save Settings > Continue**.

Port Forwarding and Port Triggering

Hardware firewalls are mainly used to block ports to prevent unauthorized access in and out of a LAN. However, there are situations when specific ports must be opened so that certain programs and applications can function properly. Port forwarding is a rule-based method of directing traffic between devices on separate networks. When traffic reaches the router, the router determines if the traffic should be forwarded to a certain device based upon the port number found with the traffic. For example, port numbers are associated with specific services such as FTP, HTTP, HTTPS, and POP3. The rules determine which traffic will be sent onto the LAN. For example, a router might be configured to forward port 80, which is associated with the HTTP protocol. If the router then receives a packet with the destination port of 80, the router will forward this traffic to a web server inside the network.

To add Port Forwarding, use the following path:

Applications & Gaming > Single Port Forwarding > select or enter an **Application Name**. You may need to enter the **External Port** number, **Internet Port** number, and **Protocol** type. Then enter the **IP Address** of the computer that should receive the requests. Click **Enable > Save Settings > Continue**.

Port triggering allows the router to temporarily forward data through inbound ports to a specific device. You can use port triggering to forward data to a computer only when a designated port range is used to make an outbound request.

For example, a video game might use ports 27000 to 27100 for connecting with other players. These are the trigger ports. A chat client might use port 56 for connecting the same players so that they can interact with each other. An example of a port triggering rule is when any gaming traffic uses an outbound port that is within the triggered port range, inbound chat traffic on port 56 will be forwarded to the computer that is being used to play the video game and chat with friends. When the game is over and the triggered ports are no longer in use, port 56 will no longer be allowed to send traffic of any type to this computer.

To add Port Triggering, use the following path:

Applications & Gaming > Port Range Triggering > type the **Application Name**. Enter the **starting and ending port numbers** of the triggered port range, and **starting and ending port numbers** of the forwarded port range. Click **Enable > Save Settings > Continue.**

Configure Wireless Security
Configure and test the wireless settings on the Linksys WRT300N.

Refer to
Lab Activity
for this chapter

Refer to
Figure
in online course

16.3.2 Describe configuring firewall types

A firewall selectively denies traffic to a computer or network segment. Firewalls generally work by opening and closing the ports used by various applications. By opening only the required ports on a firewall, you are implementing a restrictive security policy. Any packet not explicitly permitted is denied. In contrast, a permissive security policy permits access through all ports, except those explicitly denied. In the past, software and hardware were shipped with permissive settings. As users neglected to configure their equipment, the default permissive settings left many devices exposed to attackers. Most devices now ship with settings as restrictive as possible, while still allowing easy setup.

Software Firewalls

Software firewalls can be either an independent application or part of the operating system. There are several third-party software firewalls. There is also a software firewall built into Windows XP, as shown in Figure 1.

Configuring the Windows XP or Windows Vista firewall can be completed in two ways:

- *Automatically–* The user is prompted to **Keep Blocking**, **Unblock**, or **Ask Me Later** for any unsolicited requests. These requests may be from legitimate applications that have not been configured previously or may be from a virus or worm that has infected the system.

- *Manage Security Settings–* The user manually adds the program or ports that are required for the applications in use on the network.

Windows XP

To add a program, select:

Start > Control Panel > Security Center > Windows Firewall > Exceptions > Add Program.

To disable the firewall, select:

Start > Control Panel > Security Center > Windows Firewall.

Windows Vista

To add a program, select:

Start > Control Panel > Security Center > Windows Firewall > Change Settings > Continue > Exceptions > Add Program.

To disable the firewall, select:

Start > Control Panel > Security Center > Windows Firewall > Turn Windows Firewall on or off > Continue > select Off (not recommended) > OK.

The Windows firewall blocks all incoming network connections, except for specific programs and services. For example, the Windows Update service and Internet Explorer are allowed through the firewall by default. An exception, as shown in Figure 2, is a rule that opens a blocked port in the firewall for a specific need. For instance, to allow an FTP connection you must create an exception that will open up port 21. Each different type of connection requires a unique port number to pass data through the firewall.

To add a port exception to the Windows Firewall, select the **Exceptions** tab.

Click **Add port** > type a **Name** > type a **Port number** > select a Protocol. To specify that only certain computers will be affected by the exception, click **Change scope >** Specify the computers **> OK > OK > OK**.

> Refer to
> **Lab Activity**
> for this chapter

Configure Windows XP Firewall

Explore the Windows XP Firewall and configure some advanced settings.

> Refer to
> **Lab Activity**
> for this chapter

Configure Windows Vista Firewall

Explore the Windows Vista Firewall and configure some advanced settings.

> Refer to
> **Figure**
> in online course

16.3.3 Describe protection against malicious software

Malware is malicious software that is installed on a computer without the knowledge or permission of the user. Certain types of attacks, such as those performed by spyware and phishing, collect data about the user that can be used by an attacker to gain confidential information.

You should run virus and spyware scanning programs to detect and clean unwanted software. Many browsers now come equipped with special tools and settings that prevent the operation of several forms of malicious software. It may take several different programs and multiple scans to completely remove all malicious software:

- *Virus protection–* Anti-virus programs typically run automatically in the background and monitor for problems. When a virus is detected, the user is warned and the program attempts to quarantine or delete the virus.

- *Spyware protection–* Anti-spyware programs that scan for keyloggers, which capture your keystrokes, and other malware so that it can be removed from the computer.

- *Adware protection–* Anti-adware programs look for programs that display advertising on your computer.

- *Phishing protection–* Anti-phishing programs block the IP addresses of known phishing websites and warn the user about suspicious websites.

Note

Malicious software may become embedded in the operating system. Special removal tools are available from the operating system manufacturer to clean the operating system.

Refer to
Figure
in online course

16.4 Perform preventive maintenance on security

Several maintenance tasks are necessary to ensure that security is effective. This section covers how to maximize protection by performing updates, backups, reconfiguration of the operating systems, user accounts, and data.

After completing this section, you will meet these objectives:

- Describe the configuration of operation system updates.

- Maintain accounts.

- Explain data backup procedures, access to backups, and securing physical backup media.

Refer to
Figure
in online course

16.4.1 Describe the configuration of operating system updates

An operating system is often the target of attacks in order to gain control of a computer. The compromised computer can then be used to launch attacking e-mails without the knowledge of that computer's user. A computer compromised in this way is called a zombie.

Windows automatically downloads and installs updates to operating systems by default. However, this may not be the best way to update systems. The updates may conflict with the security policy of an organization or may conflict with other settings on a computer. The following options available in Windows give users the ability to control when software is updated:

- *Automatic*– Downloads and installs updates automatically without user intervention

- *Only download updates*– Downloads the updates automatically, but the user is required to install them

- *Notify me*– Notifies the user that updates are available and gives the option to download and install

- *Turn off automatic updates*– Prevents any checking for updates

If the user is on a dial-up network, the Windows Update setting should be configured to notify the user of available updates, or it should be turned off. The dial-up user may want to control the update by selecting a time when the update does not interrupt other network activity or use the limited resources available.

Refer to
Figure
in online course

16.4.2 Maintain accounts

Employees in an organization may require different levels of access to data. For example, a manager and an accountant may be the only employees in an organization with access to the payroll files.

Employees can be grouped by job requirements and given access to files according to group permissions. This process helps manage employee access to the network. Temporary accounts can be set up for employees that need short-term access. Close management of network access can help to limit areas of vulnerability that might allow a virus or malicious software to enter the network.

Terminating Employee Access

When an employee leaves an organization, access to data and hardware on the network should be terminated immediately. If the former employee has stored files in a personal space on a server, eliminate access by disabling the account. If, at a later time, the employee's replacement requires access to the applications and personal storage space, re-enable the account and change the name to the name of the new employee.

Guest Accounts

Temporary employees and guests may need access to the network. For example, many visitors might require access to e-mail, the Internet, and a printer on the network. These resources can be made available to a special account called Guest. When guests are present, they can be assigned to the Guest account. When no guests are present, the account can be disabled until the next guest arrives.

Some guest accounts may require extensive access to resources, as in the case of a consultant or a financial auditor. This type of access should be granted only for the period of time required to complete the work.

Refer to
Figure
in online course

16.4.3 Explain data backup procedures, access to backups, and securing physical backup media

A data backup stores a copy of the information on a computer to removable backup media that can be kept in a safe place. If the computer hardware fails, the data can be restored from the backup to functional hardware.

Data backups should be performed on a regular basis. The most current data backup is usually stored offsite to protect the backup media if anything happens to the main facility. Backup media is often reused to save on media costs. Always follow your organization's media rotation guidelines.

Backup operations for Windows XP can be performed at the command line or from a batch file using the NTBACKUP command. The default parameters for NTBACKUP will be the ones set in the Windows XP backup utility. Any options you want to override must be included in the command line. You cannot restore files from the command line using the NTBACKUP command.

The Windows XP Backup or Restore Utility wizard files have the extension .bkf. A .bkf file can be saved to a hard drive, a DVD, or to any other recordable media. The source location and target drive can be either NTFS or FAT.

The Windows Vista backup files have the extension .zip. Backup data is automatically compressed, and each file has a maximum compressed size of 200 MB. A Windows Vista backup file can be saved to a hard drive, any recordable media, or to another computer or server connected to your network. The backup can only be created from an NTFS partition. The target hard drive must be either NTFS or FAT formatted.

Note

You can manually exclude directories in the Windows XP Backup or Restore Utility wizard. This is not supported in the Windows Vista Backup Files wizard.

You can make a Windows backup manually or schedule how often the backup will take place automatically. To successfully backup and restore data in Windows, the appropriate user rights and permissions are required:

- All users can back up their own files and folders. They can also back up files for which they have the Read permission.

- All users can restore files and folders for which they have the Write permission.

- Members of the Administrators, Backup Operators, and Server Operators (if joined to a domain) can back up and restore all files (regardless of the assigned permissions). By default, members of these groups have the Backup Files and Directories and Restore Files and Directories user rights.

The Windows XP Backup or Restore Utility wizard provides five backup types:

- *Full or Normal*– This backup type copies all selected files and marks each file as having been backed up.

- *Incremental*– This backup type backs up only files that have been created or changed since the last full or incremental backup. Restoring files requires that you have the last full backup set and all incremental backup sets.

- *Differential*– This backup type copies only files that have been created or changed since the last full backup. Restoring files requires that you have the last full and one differential backup.

- *Daily*– This backup type copies all selected files that have been modified the day that the daily backup has been performed.

- *Copy*– This backup type copies all selected files but does not mark them as having been backed up.

To start the Windows XP Backup or Restore Utility wizard, select:

Start > All Programs > Accessories > System Tools > Backup. The Backup or Restore wizard starts. To change the backup setting, select **Advanced Mode > Tools > Options**.

To restore a backed up file in Windows XP, in the Backup or Restore wizard, select:

Next > Restore files and settings > Next > select the backed up file > **Next > Finish**.

To start the Windows Vista Backup Files wizard, select:

Start > All Programs > Maintenance > Backup and Restore Center > Back up files.

To change the backup settings, select **Change settings > Change backup settings > Continue**.

To restore a backed up file in Windows Vista, select:

Start > All Programs > Maintenance > Backup and Restore Center > Restore files.

A combination of backup types, as shown in Figure 1, allow the data to be backed up efficiently. A full backup is a copy of all files on the drive. An incremental backup backs up only those files created or changed since the last normal or incremental backup. It marks files as having been backed up. A differential backup copies files created or changed since the last normal or incremental backup, but it does not mark files as having been backed up. Backing up data can take time, so it is preferable to do backups when the network traffic is low. Other types of backups include daily backup and copy backup, which do not mark the files as having been backed up.

The data backup media is just as important as the data on the computer. You should store the backup media in a climate-controlled offsite storage facility with good physical security. The backups should be readily available for access in case of an emergency.

Refer to
Lab Activity
for this chapter

Data Backup and Recovery in Windows XP
Back up and perform a recovery of data.

Refer to
Lab Activity
for this chapter

Data Backup and Recovery in Windows Vista
Back up and perform a recovery of data.

Refer to
Figure
in online course

16.5 Troubleshoot security

The troubleshooting process is used to help resolve security issues. These problems range from simple, such as creating a backup, to more complex, such as firewall configuration. Use the troubleshooting steps as a guideline to help you diagnose and repair problems.

After completing this section, you will meet these objectives:

- Review the troubleshooting process.
- Identify common problems and solutions.
- Apply troubleshooting skills.

Refer to
Figure
in online course

16.5.1 Review the troubleshooting process

Computer technicians must be able to analyze a security threat and determine the appropriate method to protect assets and repair damage. This process is called troubleshooting.

The first step in the troubleshooting process is to identify the problem. Figure 1 is a list of open-ended and closed-ended questions to ask the customer.

After you have talked to the customer, you can establish a theory of probable causes. Figure 2 is a list of some common probable causes for security problems.

After you have developed some theories about what is wrong, test your theories to determine the cause of the problem. Figure 3 is a list of quick procedures that can determine the exact cause of the problem or even correct the problem. If a quick procedure does correct the problem, you can go to step 5 to verify full system functionality. If a quick procedure does not correct the problem, you may need to research the problem further to establish the exact cause.

After you have determined the exact cause of the problem, establish a plan of action to resolve the problem and implement the solution. Figure 4 shows sources of information to gather additional information to resolve an issue.

After you have corrected the problem, you will need to verify full functionality and, if applicable, implement preventive measures. Figure 5 is a list of the steps to verify the solution.

In the final step of the troubleshooting process, you must document your findings, actions, and outcomes. Figure 6 is a list of the tasks required to document the problem and the solution.

Refer to
Figure
in online course

16.5.2 Identify common problems and solutions

Security problems can be attributed to hardware, software, networks, or some combination of the three. You will resolve some types of security problems more often than others.

Malware Settings

Virus and spyware protection problems are often related to incorrect software settings or configurations, as shown in Figure 1. As a result of these faulty settings, a computer may display one or more of the symptoms caused by malware and boot sector viruses, as shown in Figure 2.

User Accounts and Permissions

Unauthorized access or blocked access is often caused by incorrect user account settings, as shown in Figure 3, and incorrect permissions as shown in Figure 4.

Computer Security

Computer security problems can be caused by incorrect security settings in the BIOS or on the hard drive, as shown in Figure 5.

Firewall and Proxy Settings

Blocked connections to networked resources and the Internet are often related to incorrect firewall and proxy rules, and incorrect port settings, as shown in Figure 6.

Refer to
Figure
in online course

16.5.3 Apply troubleshooting skills

Now that you understand the troubleshooting process, it is time to apply your listening and diagnostic skills.

The first lab is designed to test your troubleshooting skills with security problems. You will troubleshoot and repair a computer with a security problem that is preventing it from connecting to the wireless network.

The second lab is designed to reinforce your communication and troubleshooting skills. In this lab, you will perform the following steps:

- Receive the work order

- Talk the customer through various steps to try and resolve the problem

- Document the problem and the resolution

The third lab is designed to test your troubleshooting skills with security problems. You will troubleshoot and repair a network that has more than one security problem.

Refer to
Lab Activity
for this chapter

Fix a Security Problem

Correct a security issue that is preventing connection to the wireless network.

Refer to
Lab Activity
for this chapter

Remote Technician: Fix a Security Problem

Gather data from the customer, and then instruct the customer on how to fix a computer that does not connect to the network.

Refer to
Lab Activity
for this chapter

Troubleshooting Access Security with Windows XP

Diagnose and solve various access security problems.

Refer to
Lab Activity
for this chapter

Troubleshooting Access Security with Windows Vista

Diagnose and solve various access security problems.

Summary

This chapter discussed computer security and why it is important to protect computer equipment, networks, and data. Threats, procedures, and preventive maintenance relating to data and physical security were described to help you keep computer equipment and data safe. Security protects computers, network equipment, and data from loss and physical danger. The following are some of the important concepts to remember from this chapter:

- Security threats can come from inside or outside of an organization.

- Viruses and worms are common threats that attack data.

- Develop and maintain a security plan to protect both data and physical equipment from loss.

- Keep operating systems and applications up to date and secure with patches and service packs.

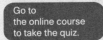

Chapter 16 Quiz

Take the chapter quiz to test your knowledge.

Your Chapter Notes

1000BASE-T
Gigabit Ethernet specification that uses UTP Cat5, 5e, or 6. Each network segment can have a maximum distance of 328 feet (100 m) without a repeater. Also known as 801.3ab.

100BASE-FX
100-Mbps baseband Fast Ethernet that uses multimode fiber-optic. Based on the IEEE 802.3 standard.

100BASE-TX
100-Mbps baseband Fast Ethernet specification that uses two pair of UTP or STP wiring. Based on the IEEE 802.3 standard.

100BASE-X
100-Mbps baseband Fast Ethernet specification that refers to the 100BASE-FX and 100BASE-TX standards for Fast Ethernet over fiber-optic and copper cabling. Based on the IEEE 802.3 standard.

10BASE2
10-Mbps baseband Ethernet that uses coaxial cable that can carry a signal a maximum of 185 meters, also referred to as Thinnet. Based on the IEEE 802.3 standard.

10BASE5
10-Mbps baseband Ethernet that uses coaxial cable that can carry a signal a maximum of 500 meters, also referred to as Thicknet. Based on the IEEE 802.3 standard.

10BASE-FL
10-Mbps baseband Ethernet over fiber-optic which can include an optional asynchronous hub. Based on the IEEE 802.3 standard.

10BASE-T
10-Mbps baseband Ethernet specification that uses two pairs of Category 3, 4, or 5 twisted-pair cabling. One pair of wires is used to receive data and the other pair is used to transmit data. 10BASE-T, which is part of the IEEE 802.3 specification, has a distance limit of approximately 328 feet (100 m) per segment.

AC power connector
Socket that is used to connect the AC power adapter to a computer or docking station.

AC power cord
Cable that transfers electricity from the AC power supply to the computer power supply.

Accelerated Graphics Port (AGP)
High-speed, 32-bit bus technology designed to support the acceleration of 3D computer graphics.

Access Control List (ACL)
List managed by a network administrator that itemizes what a user is permitted to access and the type of access granted.

access point
Device that connects wireless devices to form a wireless network. An access point usually connects to a wired network, and can relay data between wired and wireless devices. Connectivity distances can range from several feet or meters, to several miles or kilometers.

active partition
Partition on a hard disk drive that is set as the bootable partition and usually contains the operating system to be used on the computer. Only one partition on a computer can be set as an active or bootable partition on a hard disk drive.

ActiveX
Applet or small program created by Microsoft to control interactivity on web pages that has to be downloaded to gain access to the full functionality.

adapter card
Expansion card that increases the number of controllers and ports available on a computer.

Address Resolution Protocol (ARP)
Discovers the local address (MAC address) of a station on the network when the IP address is known. End stations as well as routers use ARP to discover local addresses:

-a Switch used with the ARP command that displays the cache.
-d Switch used with the ARP command that deletes an entry from the ARP cache.
-s Switch used with the ARP command that adds a permanent IP-to-MAC address mapping.

administrator
Person who queries the User Registrar to analyze individual subscriber status and to gather data.

Advanced Configuration and Power Interface (ACPI)
Interface that allows the operating system to control power management. Replaces Advanced Power Management (APM).

Advanced Power Management (APM)
Interface that allows the BIOS to control the settings for power management. This has been replaced by the Advanced Configuration and Power Interface (ACPI).

Advanced Technology Extended (ATX) power connector
20-pin or 24-pin internal power supply connector.

Advanced Technology Extended (ATX)
Standard computer case form factor for modern computers.

adware
Software program that displays advertising on a computer, usually distributed with downloaded software.

all-in-one type printer
Multi-functional device designed to provide services such as printing, fax, and copier functions.

alternating current (AC)
Current that changes direction at a uniformly repetitious rate. This type of electricity is typically provided by a utility company and is accessed by wall sockets.

American National Standards Institute (ANSI)
Private, nonprofit organization that administers and coordinates the US voluntary standardization and conformity assessment system. ANSI identifies industrial and public requirements for national consensus standards and coordinates and manages their development, resolves national standards problems, and ensures effective participation in international standardization.

American Standard Code for Information Interchange (ASCII)
8-bit code for character representation (7 bits plus parity).

analog transmission
Signal transmission over wires or through the air in which information is conveyed through the variation of some combination of signal amplitude, frequency, and phase.

answer file
File that contains predefined settings and answers to the questions that are required by the operating system setup wizard.

antistatic bag
Packaging material that protects components from ESD.

antistatic mat
Surface that provides a safe environment for computer components by dissipating ESD.

antistatic wrist strap
Device worn on the wrist to dissipate ESD between a person and electronic equipment.

anti-virus application
Program that is installed on a system to prevent computer viruses from infecting the computer.

AppleTalk
Protocol suite to network Macintosh computers. It is comprised of a comprehensive set of protocols that span the seven layers of the OSI reference model.

application layer
Layer 7 of the OSI reference model. This layer provides services to application

processes such as electronic mail, file transfer, and terminal emulation that are outside of the OSI model. The application layer identifies and establishes the availability of intended communication partners and the resources required to connect with them, synchronizes co-operating applications, and establishes agreement on procedures for error recovery and control of data integrity. Corresponds roughly with the transaction services layer in the Systems Network Architecture (SNA) model. The OSI reference model includes application layer, presentation layer, session layer, transport layer, network layer, data link layer, and physical layer.

Application Programming Interface (API)
A set of tools, routines and protocols used to develop software applications that will be compatible with an operating system.

application software
Program that performs a specific function by accepting input from the user and then manipulating it to achieve a result, known as the output.

arm (Acorn RISC Machine) architecture
Low-power RISC CPU.

Asymmetric DSL (ADSL)
Currently the most common DSL implementation. Speeds vary from 384 kbps to more than 6 Mbps downstream. The upstream speed is typically lower.

asymmetric encryption
Method for encrypting data on a network. Uses a private key for writing messages and a public key to decode the messages. Only the private key needs to be kept secret. Public keys can be distributed openly.

attention (AT) command set
Issues dial, hang up, reset, and other instructions to the modem. It is based on the Hayes command set.

Automatic Private IP Addressing (APIPA)
Operating system feature that enables a computer to assign itself an address if it is unable to contact a DHCP server. The Internet Assigned Numbers Authority (IANA) has reserved private IP addresses in the range of 169.254.0.0 -169.254.255.255 for APIPA.

Automatic Update
Utility to schedule the Windows Update feature to check for critical updates.

auxiliary (AUX) power connector
4-, 6-, or 8-pin connector that supplies extra voltage to the motherboard from the power supply.

backplane
Physical connection between an interface processor or card, the data buses, and the power distribution buses inside a chassis.

backup
Copy of data saved onto alternate media, and should be physically removed from the source data.

backward compatible
Hardware or software systems that can use interfaces and data from earlier versions of the system or with other systems. Also known as backward-compatible or backwards compatible.

bandwidth
Amount of data that can be transmitted within a fixed time period.

base station
Device that attaches a laptop to AC power and to desktop peripherals.

Basic Input/Output System (BIOS)
Program stored in a ROM chip in the computer that provides the basic code to control the computer's hardware and to perform diagnostics on it. The BIOS prepares the computer to load the operating system.

Basic Rate Interface (BRI)
ISDN interface composed of two B channels and one D channel for circuit-switched communication of voice, video, and data. Compare with PRI.

battery latch
Tool used to insert, remove, and secure the laptop battery.

battery status indicator LED
Light that indicates the condition of the laptop battery.

battery
Electrical device that converts chemical energy into electrical energy.

beep code
Audible reporting system for errors that are found by the BIOS during the POST, represented by a series of beeps.

Berg power connector
Keyed connector that supplies power to a floppy drive.

biometric device
Tool that uses sensors, such as a fingerprint or retinal scanner, that identify physical characteristics of the user to allow access to a device or a network.

bit rate
Speed at which bits are transmitted, usually expressed in bits per second (bps).

bit
Smallest unit of data in a computer. A bit can take the value of either 1 or 0. A bit is the binary format in which data is processed by computers.

blackout
Complete loss of AC power.

Blu-ray Disc (BD) drive
Optical device that reads Blu-ray discs.

Blu-ray Disc-recordable (BD-R)
High-density optical media that records HD video and PC data storage one time.

Blu-ray Disc-rewritable (BD-RE)
High-density optical media that records HD video and PC data multiple times.

Blu-ray Disc read-only media (BD-ROM)
High-density optical media that is prerecorded with HD video and PC data.

Bluetooth
Wireless industry standard that uses an unlicensed radio frequency for short-range communication enabling portable devices to communicate over short distances.

boot
To start a computer.

boot record
512-byte file containing a table that describes the partition, the number of bytes per sector, and the number of sectors per cluster.

bootable disk
Troubleshooting tool that allows the computer to boot from a disk when the hard drive will not boot.

bridge
A Data Link layer device that connects and passes frames between two network segments. The frames are filtered and forwarded using MAC addresses.

broadband
Multiple signals using multiple frequencies over one cable.

broadband optical telepoint
Infrared broadband transmission capable of handling high-quality multimedia requirements.

broadband satellite
Network connection using a satellite dish.

brownout
Temporary drop in AC power.

buffer
Storage area used for handling data in transit. Buffers are used in internetworking to compensate for differences in processing speed between network devices. Bursts of data can be stored in buffers until they can be handled by slower processing devices. Sometimes referred to as a packet buffer.

bus topology
Network with each computer connecting on a common cable.

bus
Media through which data is transferred from one part of a computer to another. The bus can be compared to a highway on which data travels within a computer.

byte
A unit of measure that describes the size of a data file, the amount of space on a disk or other storage medium, or the amount of data being sent over a network. One byte consists of 8 bits of data.

C: drive
Generally the label for the first hard drive in a computer system. Drive A and Drive B are reserved for floppy drives. Drive B is rarely used on current computers.

cable modem
Acts like a LAN interface by connecting a computer to the Internet. The cable modem connects a computer to the cable company network through the same coaxial cabling that feeds cable TV (CATV) signals to a television set.

cable tie
Fastener used to bundle cables inside and outside of a computer.

cable
Set of conductors, bundled and sheathed together, made of insulated copper or optical fiber that transport signals and power between electrical devices.

cache
Data storage area that provides high-speed access for the system.

capacitor
An electronic component that contains a charge in an electrical circuit.

Caps lock indicator LED
Light that shows the on/off status of the caps lock.

card key
Identity card with a chip that stores user data, including the level of access.

Category 3
Cable that is primarily used in telephone connections.

Category 5
Cable that contains four pairs of wires, with a maximum data rate of 1 Gbps.

Category 5e
Cable that provides more twists per foot than Category 5 at the same data rate of 1 Gbps.

Category 6
Cable that is enhanced with more twists than Category 5e cable. It contains a plastic divider that separates the pairs of wires to prevent crosstalk.

cellular WAN
Wide area network that has the technology for the use of a cell phone or a laptop for voice and data communications.

Central Processing Unit (CPU)
Interprets and processes software instructions and data. Located on the motherboard, the CPU is a chip contained on a single integrated circuit called the microprocessor. The CPU contains two basic components, a control unit and an Arithmetic/Logic Unit (ALU).

Central Processing Unit (CPU) throttling
A technique used when the processor runs at less than the rated speed to conserve power or produce less heat.

chip
Small slice of silicon or germanium processed to have electrical characteristics so that it can be developed into an electronic component. Also called semiconductor.

chipset
Chips on a motherboard that enable the CPU to communicate and interact with the other components of the computer.

CHKDSK
Command used to check the integrity of files and folders on a hard drive by scanning the disk surface for physical errors.

client/server network
Network in which services are located in a dedicated computer that responds to client, or user, requests.

cluster
Smallest unit of space used for storing data on a disk. Also called file allocation unit.

CMOS battery
Battery that supplies power to maintain basic configuration information, including the real time clock, when the computer is turned off.

CMYK
Display colors: cyan, magenta, yellow, and black.

coaxial cable
Copper-cored cable surrounded by a heavy shielding used to connect computers in a network.

cold boot
To power up a computer from the off position.

color ink jet printer
Type of printer that uses liquid-ink–filled cartridges that spray ink to form an image on the paper.

Comité Consultatif International Téléphonique et Télégraphique (CCITT)
Committee that defines international communications standards. The CCITT defines the standards for sending fax documents and the standards for data transmission over telephone lines.

Command Line Interface (CLI)
Interface, such as a DOS prompt, that requires commands to be entered manually on the command line.

Compact Disc - read only memory (CD-ROM)
Optical storage media for audio and data.

Compact Disc (CD) drive
Optical device that reads compact discs.

Compact Disc-recordable (CD-R)
Optical media that allows data to be recorded but not modified.

Compact Disc-rewritable (CD-RW)
Optical storage media that allows data to be recorded and modified.

Complementary Metal Oxide Semiconductor (CMOS)
Type of semiconductor, or low-power memory firmware, that stores basic configuration information.

Complex Instruction Set Computer (CISC)
Architecture that uses a broad set of instructions, with several choices for almost every

operation. The result is that a programmer can execute precisely the command needed, resulting in fewer instructions steps per operation.

compressed air
Air under pressure in a can that blows dust off of computer components without creating static. Also called canned air.

computer
Electrical machine that can execute a list of instructions and perform calculations based on those instructions.

computer network
Two or more computers connected together by some medium to share data and resources.

computer system
Combination of hardware and software components. Hardware is the physical equipment such as the case, floppy disk drives, keyboards, monitors, cables, speakers, and printers. Software describes the programs that operate the computer system.

computer-aided design (CAD)
Application used for creating architectural, electrical, and mechanical design. More complex forms of CAD include solid modeling and parametric modeling, which allow objects to be created with real-world characteristics.

conduit
Casing that protects the infrastructure media from damage and unauthorized access.

configuration tool
Service management tool or a Element management service tool with a GUI.

connector
Device used to terminate cable.

conventional memory
All memory addresses from 0 to 640 KB.

cookie
Small text file that is stored on the hard disk that allows a website to track the user's association to that site.

copper cable
Cabling that uses copper wires to transmit data. A series of individual copper wires inside the cable form circuits to connect two or more devices.

copy backup
Backs up user-selected files to tape. This backup does not reset the archive bit.

crosstalk
Interfering energy, such as Electro Magnetic Interference (EMI) that is transferred from one circuit to another.

CSMA/CD
Carrier sense multiple access with collision detection is a media-access mechanism wherein devices ready to transmit data first check the communication channel for a carrier. If no carrier is sensed for a specific period of time, a device can transmit. If two devices transmit at once, a collision occurs and is detected by all devices on the communication channel. This collision delays all transmissions on the communication channel for a random length of time. CSMA/CD access is used by Ethernet and IEEE 802.3.

current (I)
Flow of electrons in a conductor that is measured in amperes.

Customer Replaceable Unit (CRU)
Component that customers may install at their location.

cylinder
All the tracks on a hard disk with the same number. Collectively, the same track on all platters of a multi-platter hard drive.

daily backup
Backs up only the files that are modified on the day of the backup. This backup does not reset the archive bit.

data backup
Information on a computer stored on removable backup media that can be kept in a safe place. If the computer hardware fails, the data backup can be restored so that processing can continue.

diagnostic tools
Utilities that monitor the network server.

data transfer rate
Refers to how fast the computer can transfer information into memory.

database
Organized collection of data that can be easily accessed, managed, indexed, searched, and updated.

Data Link Layer
Layer 2 of the OSI reference model. This layer provides reliable transit of data across a physical link. The Data Link Layer is concerned with physical addressing, network topology, line discipline, error notification, ordered delivery of frames, and flow control. The IEEE has divided this layer into two sublayers, the MAC sublayer and the LLC sublayer. The OSI reference model includes Application Layer, Presentation Layer, Session Layer, Transport Layer, Network Layer, Data Link Layer, and Physical Layer.

de-encapsulation
The process of removing encapsulation in a receiving device. As datagrams arrive at the receiving device, the device discards the previous layer headers to analyze the datagram at the current OSI model layer.

default gateway
Route taken so that a computer on one segment can communicate with a computer on another segment.

default installation
Installation that requires minimal user interaction. Also called a typical installation.

default printer
First option that an application uses when the user clicks the printer icon. The default printer can be changed by the user.

DEFRAG
Command that rearranges the data and rewrites all the files on the hard drive to the beginning of the drive, making it easier and faster for the hard drive to retrieve data.

Denial of Service (DoS)
Form of attack that prevents users from accessing normal services, such as e-mail or a web server, because the system is busy responding to abnormally large amounts of requests. DoS works by sending an abundance of requests for a resource to cause the system to overload and cease to operate.

desktop
Metaphor used to portray file systems. A desktop consists of pictures, called icons, which show files, folders, and any resource available to a user in a GUI operating system.

desktop computer
Type of computer designed to fit on top of a desk, usually with the monitor on top of the computer to conserve space. Desktop computers are not mobile like laptop computers.

Device Manager
Application that displays a list of all the hardware that is installed on the system.

diagnostic software
Programs that assist in the troubleshooting process.

diagnostic tools
Utilities that monitor the network server.

Dial-up Networking (DUN)
Using the public telephone system or network to communicate.

differential backup
Backs up all the files that have been created or modified since the last full backup. It does not reset the archive bit.

Digital Audio Tape (DAT)
Tape standard that uses 4 mm digital audiotapes to store data in the Digital Data Storage (DSS) format.

Digital Linear Tape (DLT)
Technology offers high capacity and relatively high-speed tape backup capabilities.

digital multimeter
Tool that combines the functionality of a voltmeter, ohmmeter, and ammeter into one easy measuring device.

digital subscriber line (DSL)
Public network technology that delivers high bandwidth over conventional copper wiring at limited distances. Always-on technology that allows users to connect to the Internet.

Digital Versatile Disc (DVD) drive
Optical device that reads DVDs.

Digital Versatile Disc +/- Recordable (DVD+/-R)
Optical media which can be recorded one time.

Digital Versatile Disc +/- Rewriteable (DVD+/-RW)
Optical media which can be recorded mulitple times.

Digital Versatile Disc Random Access Memory (DVD-RAM)
Optical media which can be recorded mulitple times and allows for data to be modified.

Digital Versatile Disc Read-Only Memory (DVD-ROM)
Optical storage media for audio, video, and data.

Digital Visual Interface (DVI)
Interface that supplies uncompressed digital video to a digital monitor.

Direct Memory Access (DMA)
Method for bypassing the CPU when transferring data from the main memory directly to a device.

direct current (DC)
Current flowing in one direction, as used in a battery.

directory
1) Type of file that organizes other files in a hierarchical structure. 2) Related program and data files organized and grouped together in the DOS file system.3) Place to store data in the Windows file-management system.

disk cleanup
Disk management software that is used to clear space on a hard drive by searching for files that can be safely deleted, such as temporary Internet files.

disk management
System utility used to manage hard drives and partitions, such as initializing disks, creating partitions, and formatting partitions.

disk operating system (DOS)
Collection of programs and commands that control overall computer operations in a disk-based system.

display
Computer output surface and projecting mechanism that shows text and graphic images.

Distributed Denial of Service (DDoS)
A DDoS attack is similar to a DoS attack except that the DDoS originates from multiple coordinated sources by infecting multiple computers with zombie software. The infected computers, called zombies, are then used to carry out the DDoS attack.

DNS poisoning
Changing the DNS records on a system to point to false servers where the data is recorded.

docking connector
Socket used to attach a docking station to the laptop.

docking station
Device that attaches a laptop to AC power and desktop peripherals.

domain
Logical group of computers and electronic devices with a common set of rules and procedures administered as a unit.

Domain Name System (DNS)
System that provides a way to map friendly host names, or URLs, to IP addresses.

dot matrix printer
Printer that operates by impacting the ribbon to place an image on the paper.

dots per inch (dpi)
Measurement of print quality. How the quality of print is measured on a dot matrix printer, and the higher the dpi, the higher the quality of print.

drive bay
Standard-sized area for adding hardware to a computer case. The two most common drive bays are used to house a CD\DVD drive and a floppy drive.

drive letter
Designation that distinguishes the physical or logical drives in Windows.

drive mapping
Process of assigning a letter to a physical or logical drive.

dual core CPU
Two cores inside a single CPU chip. Both cores can be used together to increase speed, or they can be used in two locations at the same time.

dual in-line memory module (DIMM)
Circuit board with a 64-bit data bus that holds memory chips. Memory module with 168 pins. Supports 64-bit data transfers.

dual ring
All the devices on the network connect to two cables and the data travels in both directions. Only one cable is used at a time. In the event of a failure of one ring, data is transmitted on the other ring.

dye-sublimation printer
Printer that uses solid sheets of ink that change from solid to gas, in a process called sublimating. The gas then passes through the paper, where it turns back to a solid. The print head passes over a sheet of cyan, magenta, yellow, and a clear overcoat (CMYO). Also called thermal dye printer.

Dynamic Host Configuration Protocol (DHCP)
Software utility that automatically assigns IP addresses to client devices in a large network.

Dynamic RAM (DRAM)
RAM that stores information in capacitors that must be periodically refreshed. Delays can occur because DRAMs are inaccessible to the processor when refreshing their contents. However, DRAMs are less complex and have greater capacity than SRAMs.

dynamic routing
Routing that adjusts automatically to network topology or traffic changes. Also called adaptive routing.

eject button
Lever that releases an object, such as the button on a floppy drive.

Electrically Erasable Programmable Read-Only Memory (EEPROM)
A special type of PROM that retains its contents without power. Exposing EEPROM to an electrical charge will erase its contents.

Electromagnetic Interference (EMI)
Interference in an electrical circuit that is caused by electromagnetic radiation emitted from an external source.

Electronic Industries Alliance (EIA)
The Electronic Industries Alliance is an alliance of trade organizations that together have developed data transmission standards.

Electronic Industries Association (EIA)
Group that specifies electrical transmission standards. The EIA and TIA have developed numerous well-known communications standards, including EIA/TIA-232 and EIA/TIA-449.

electronic mail (e-mail)
Ability for users to communicate over a computer network. The exchange of computer-stored messages by network communication.

electrophotographic drum
Central part of the laser printer that acquires the toner to be printed on paper.

Electrostatic Discharge (ESD)
Discharge of static electricity from one conductor to another conductor of a different potential.

encapsulation
The wrapping of data within datagrams for transmission across a network.

encryption
Security feature that applies a coding to a file so that only authorized users can view the file.

Encryption File System (EFS)
Microsoft specific file system for encryption.

Enhanced Integrated Drive Electronics (EIDE)
Enhanced version of the standard IDE interface that connects hard disks, CD-ROM drives, and tape drives to a PC.

Erasable Programmable Read-Only Memory (EPROM)
A special type of PROM that retains its contents without power. Ultraviolet light erases the contents of EPROM so that it can be updated.

Ethernet
Baseband LAN specification invented by Xerox Corporation and developed jointly by Xerox, Intel, and Digital Equipment Corporation. Ethernet networks use CSMA/CD and run over a variety of cable types at 10 Mbps or more. Ethernet is similar to the IEEE 802.3 series of standards.

Ethernet port
RJ-45 socket that is used to connect a computer to a cabled local area network.

event
Network message indicating operational irregularities in physical elements of a network or a response to the occurrence of a significant task, typically the completion of a request for information.

Event Viewer
Application that monitors system events, application events, and security events.

exhaust vent
Outlet that expels hot air from the interior of a device or room.

expansion card modem
Modem that is inserted into a motherboard expansion slot (ISA or PCI). Also called an internal modem.

expansion slot
Opening in a computer where a PC card can be inserted to add capabilities to the computer.

ExpressCard
High-throughput, laptop expansion card standard that was developed by the PCMCIA. The ExpressCard expansion slot uses the built-in PCI Express (x1) and/or USB bus of a laptop. ExpressCards have a 26-pin connector and are hot-swappable.

extended memory
Memory above 1 MB.

extended partition
Second partition on the hard drive.

extended-star topology
Star topology that is expanded to include additional networking devices.

external hard drive
Device that connects to the computer to provide additional data storage.

external modem
Modem that connects to the serial port (COM1 or COM2) of most computers. An external modem, such as a cable modem, is typically used for high-speed connections.

Fast Ethernet
Any of a number of 100-Mbps Ethernet specifications. Fast Ethernet offers a speed increase ten times that of the 10BASE-T Ethernet specification, while preserving such qualities as frame format, MAC mechanisms, and MTU. Such similarities allow the use of existing 10BASE-T applications and network management tools on Fast Ethernet networks. Based on an extension to the IEEE 802.3 specification. Compare with Ethernet.

fault tolerance
The ability of a system to continue to function despite an unexpected hardware or software failure.

FDISK
Command used to delete and create partitions on the hard drive:\STATUS Switch that displays partition information when used with the FDISK - command.

Fiber Distributed Data Interface (FDDI)
Type of Token Ring network that is used in larger LANs.

fiber-optic cable
Physical medium capable of conducting modulated light transmission. Compared with other transmission media, fiber-optic cable is more expensive, but is not susceptible to electromagnetic interference, and is capable of higher data rates. This cabling uses glass or plastic wire to carry information as light pulses. The modulated light is carried through the cable to transmit data.

Field-Replaceable Unit (FRU)
Component that a trained service technician may install at a remote location.

file
A block of logically related data that is given a single name and is treated as a single unit.

File Allocation Table (FAT)
Table that the operating system uses to store information about the location of the files stored on a disk. This file is stored in track 0 on the disk.

file extension
Designation that describes the file format or the type of application that created a file.

file management
Hierarchical structure of files, folders, and drives in Windows.

file system
The two file systems available in Windows XP are FAT32 and NTFS. NTFS has greater stability and security features.

File Transfer Protocol (FTP)
Set of rules governing how files are transferred. FTP allows multiple simultaneous connections to remote file systems.

fingerprint reader
Input device that scans fingerprints to authenticate login using biometric identification.

firewall
Router or access server, or several routers or access servers, designated as a buffer between any connected public networks and a private network. A firewall router uses access lists and other methods to ensure the security of the private network.

FireWire
High-speed, platform-independent communication bus. FireWire interconnects digital devices such as digital video cameras, printers, scanners, digital cameras, and hard drives. FireWire is also known as IEEE 1394, i.Link (Sony proprietary), and linear heat detecting cable (LHDC) in the U.K.

firmware
Program that is embedded in a silicon chip rather than stored on a floppy disk.

Flash memory
Rewritable memory chip that retains data after the power is turned off.

flat-head screwdriver
Tool used to loosen or tighten slotted screws.

floppy disk drive (FDD)
Device that spins a magnetically coated floppy disk to read data from and write data to it.

floppy drive data cable
External cable that transfers data between the computer and the floppy drive.

form factor
Physical size and shape of computer components. Components that share the same form factor are physically interchangeable.

format
To prepare a file system in a partition to store files.

Front Side Bus (FSB)
This bus connects the CPU to main memory on the motherboard.

full backup
Backs up all files on a disk. Also called a normal backup.

full-duplex transmission
Data transmission that can go two ways at the same time. An Internet connection using DSL service is an example.

function key (Fn key)
Modifier key usually found on laptop computers. It is used in combination with other keys to perform specific functions.

gamepad
External controller used as an input device, primarily for gaming.

gigahertz (GHz)
Common measurement of a processor equal to one billion cycles per second.

Global System for Mobile Communications (GSM)
World-wide cellular network.

Graphical User Interface (GUI)
Interface that allows the user to navigate through the operating system using icons and menus.

graphics application
Creates or modifies graphical images. The two types of graphical images include object- or vector-based images, and bitmaps or raster images.

Graphics Device Interface (GDI)
Windows component to manage how graphical images are transmitted to output devices. GDI works by converting images to a bitmap that uses the computer instead of the printer to transfer the images.

grayware
Spyware that installs on a computer without being prompted and downloads additional applications without permission from the user.

half-duplex transmission
Data transmission that can go two ways, but not at the same time. A telephone and two-way radio are examples.

handshaking sequence
Series of short communications that occur between the two modems. This establishes the readiness of the two modems and computers to engage in data exchange.

handwriting recognition
Ability of computer, especially mobile devices, to recognize letters and numbers written by hand and convert them to ASCII text.

Hard Disk Drive (HDD)
Device that stores and retrieves data from magnetic-coated platters that rotate at high speeds. The hard drive, or HDD, is the primary storage medium on a computer.

Hardware Abstraction Layer (HAL)
Library of hardware drivers that communicate between the operating system and the hardware that is installed.

Hardware Compatibility List (HCL)
Utility that verifies existing hardware is compatible with an operating system.

hardware firewall
Hardware device that filters data packets from the network before reaching computers and other devices on a network.

hardware
Physical electronic components that make up a computer system.

Hayes-compatible command set
Set of AT commands that most modem software uses. This command set is named after the Hayes Microcomputer Products Company, which first defined them.

headphone jack
Socket that is used to attach an audio output device.

heat sink and fan assembly
Device that dissipates heat from electronic components into the surrounding air.

Hertz (Hz)
Unit of frequency measurement. Hz is the rate of change in the state, or cycle, in a sound wave, alternating current, or other cyclical waveform. Hertz is synonymous with cycles per second, and it describes the speed of a computer microprocessor.

hex driver
Driver used to tighten nuts. Sometimes called a nut driver,

Hibernate/Standby indicator LED
Light that shows if the computer is in standby or hibernate mode.

hierarchical star topology
Extended star topology where a central hub is connected by vertical cabling to other hubs that are dependent on it.

High Data Rate DSL (HDSL)
Provides a bandwidth of 768 kbps in both directions.

HKEY_
Designation at the beginning of Windows Registry boot file names.

host
Computer system on a network. Similar to the term node except that host usually implies a computer system, whereas node generally applies to any networked system, including access servers and routers.

hot-swappable interface
Allows peripherals to be changed while the system is running. USB is an example.

hub
1. Generally, a term used to describe a Layer 1 device that serves as the center of a star-topology network.
2. Hardware or software device that contains multiple independent but connected modules of network and internetwork equipment. Hubs can be active (where they repeat signals sent through them) or passive (where they do not repeat, but merely split, signals sent through them).
3. In Ethernet and IEEE 802.3, an Ethernet multiport repeater, sometimes referred to as a concentrator.

Hypertext Markup Language (HTML)
Page-description language used by browser applications such as Windows Internet Explorer or Mozilla Firefox.

Hypertext Transfer Protocol (HTTP)
Standard used to transfer or convey information on the World Wide Web. HTTP is a communication protocol that establishes a request/response connection on the Internet.

Hypertext Transfer Protocol Secure (HTTPS)
A protocol that uses authentication and encryption to secure data as it travels between the client and Web server.

I/O shield

Grounded metal plate installed in the rear of the case that enables the motherboard connectors to be accessed from the outside of the case.

icon

Image that represents an application or a capability.

IEEE 802.1

IEEE specification that describes an algorithm that prevents bridging loops by creating a spanning tree. The algorithm was invented by Digital Equipment Corporation. The Digital algorithm and the IEEE 802.1 algorithm are not exactly the same, nor are they compatible.

IEEE 802.11a

An IEEE 802.11 extension that applies to wireless LANs operating in the 5GHz band with transmission rates up to 54 Mbps.

IEEE 802.11b

An IEEE 802.11 extension that applies to wireless LANs operating in the 2.4 GHz band and providing transmission rates up to 11 Mbps.

IEEE 802.11g

An IEEE 802.11 extension that applies to wireless LANs operating in the 2.4 GHz band with transmission rates up to 54 Mbps over short distances.

IEEE 802.11n

An 802.11 extension that uses additional transmitter and receiver antenna for increased data throughput over a wider range. This standard theoretically supports transmission rates up to 540 Mbps.

IEEE 802.12

IEEE LAN standard that specifies the physical layer and the MAC sub layer of the data-link layer. IEEE 802.12 uses the demand priority media-access scheme at 100 Mbps over a variety of physical media.

IEEE 802.15.1

An 802.15 extension that defines Bluetooth wireless technology, a short-range wireless technology designed to provide connectivity between portable or fixed-configuration devices without the need for using cabling.

IEEE 802.2

IEEE LAN protocol that specifies an implementation of the LLC sub layer of the data-link layer. IEEE 802.2 handles errors, framing, flow control, and the network layer, Layer 3, service interface. Used in IEEE 802.3 and IEEE 802.5 LANs.

IEEE 802.3

IEEE LAN protocol that specifies an implementation of the physical layer and the MAC sub layer of the data-link layer. IEEE 802.3 uses CSMA/CD access at a variety of speeds over a variety of physical media. Extensions to the IEEE 802.3 standard specify implementations for Fast Ethernet. Physical variations of the original IEEE 802.3 specification include 10BASE2, 10BASE5, 10BASE-F, 10BASE-T, and 10Broad36. Physical variations for Fast Ethernet include 100BASE-T, 100BASE-T4, and 100BASE-X.

IEEE 802.3i

Physical variation of the original IEEE 802.3 specification that calls for using Ethernet type signaling over twisted pair networking media. The standard sets the signaling speed at 10 megabits per second using a baseband signaling scheme transmitted over twisted pair cable employing a star or extended star topology.

IEEE 802.4

IEEE LAN protocol that specifies an implementation of the physical layer and the MAC sub layer of the data-link layer. IEEE 802.4 uses token-passing access over a bus topology and is based on the token bus LAN architecture.

IEEE 802.5

IEEE LAN protocol that specifies an implementation of the physical layer and MAC sub layer of the data link-layer. IEEE 802.5 uses token passing access at 4 or 16 Mbps over shielded twisted-pair (STP) cabling and is similar to IBM Token Ring.

IEEE 802.6

IEEE MAN specification based on DQDB technology. IEEE 802.6 supports data rates of 1.5 to 155 Mbps.

impact printer

Class of printer that includes dot matrix and daisy wheel.

incremental backup

Procedure to back up all the files and folders that have been created or modified since the last full or normal backup.

infrared (IR)

Electromagnetic waves whose frequency range is above that of microwaves, but below that of the visible spectrum. LAN systems based on this technology represent an emerging technology.

infrared port

Line-of-sight wireless transceiver that is used for data transmission.

infrared scatter

Infrared signal that is bounced off ceilings and walls. Devices are able to connect without the line of sight, but data transfer rates are lower and distances are shorter.

inkjet printer

Type of printer that uses liquid-ink–filled cartridges that spray ink to form an image on the paper.

input/output (I/O)

Any operation, program, or device that transfers data to or from a computer.

input/output (I/O) address

Unique hexadecimal memory address that is associated with a specific device on a computer.

installation CD

Compact disc that includes new software with drivers and manuals. Additionally, may include diagnostic tools and trial software.

instant messaging (IM)

Real-time text-based method of communication conducted over a network between two or more users.

Institute of Electrical and Electronics Engineers (IEEE)

Organization that oversees the development of communication and network standards.

insulation

High resistance material that inhibits the flow of current between conductors in a cable.

Integrated Drive Electronics (IDE)

An early drive controller interface that uses a 40-pin connector to connect drives.

Integrated Services Digital Network (ISDN)

Communication protocol, offered by telephone companies, that permits telephone networks to carry data, voice, and other source traffic.

interface

1. Connection between two systems or devices.
2. In routing terminology, a network connection.
3. In telephony, a shared boundary defined by common physical interconnection characteristics, signal characteristics, and meanings of interchanged signals.
4. The boundary between adjacent layers of the OSI model.

Interior Gateway Protocol (IGP)

Internet protocol that is used to exchange routing information within an autonomous system. Examples of common Internet IGPs include EIGRP, OSPF, and RIP.

International Electrotechnical Commission (IEC)

Industry group that writes and distributes standards for electrical products and components.

International Organization for Standardization (ISO)

International organization that sets standards for networking. ISO developed the OSI reference model, a popular networking reference model.

Internet

Largest global internetwork that connects tens of thousands of networks worldwide.

Internet Architecture Board (IAB)

Board of internetwork researchers who discuss issues pertinent to Internet architecture. Responsible for appointing a variety of Internet-related groups such as the IANA, IESG, and IRSG. The IAB is appointed by the trustees of the ISOC.

Internet Control Message Protocol (ICMP)
Used for network testing and troubleshooting, it enables diagnostic and error messages. ICMP echo messages are used by the ping utility to determine whether a remote device is reachable.

Internet Message Access Protocol (IMAP)
Used by local e-mail clients to synchronize and retrieve e-mail from a server.

Internet Protocol (IP)
Network layer protocol in the TCP/IP stack that offers a connectionless internetwork service. IP provides features for addressing, type-of-service specification, fragmentation and re-assembly, and security. Documented in RFC 791.

Internet service provider (ISP)
Company that provides Internet service to home users, such as the local phone or cable company.

Internetwork Packet Exchange/Sequenced Packet Exchange (IPX/SPX)
Used by Novell Netware; IPX is a connection-less communication and SPX is the transport layer (Layer 7 of the OSI model).

interrupt request (IRQ)
A request from a device for communication with the CPU.

IP address
Unique number that devices use in order to identify and communicate with each other on a computer network utilizing the Internet Protocol (IP) standard.

ISDN DSL (IDSL)
A method of using DSL over ISDN lines. The transfer rates are only 144 kbps, but the connection is always on and does not require the call setup found with an ISDN connection.

Java
Programming language for applets to run within a web browser. Examples of applets include a calculator or a counter.

JavaScript
Programming language developed to interact with HTML source code for interactive websites. Examples include a rotating banner or a popup window.

jumper
Electrical contact points used to set a hard drive as master or slave.

kernel
The kernel is responsible for managing memory, processes, tasks and disks. It is the central module of the Windows operating system.

keyboard
Input device with multi-functional keys.

keyboard port
PS/2 socket used to attach an external keyboard.

Keyboard, Video, Mouse (KVM) switch
A hardware device that makes it possible to use a single keyboard, monitor and mouse to control more than one computer.

kilobytes per second (KBps)
Measurement of the amount of data that is transferred over a connection such as a network connection. A data transfer rate of 1 KBps is a rate of approximately 1,000 bytes per second.

laptop battery
Rechargeable battery that powers the laptop.

laptop connector
Socket that is used to attach the laptop to a docking station.

laptop keyboard
Input device that includes alphanumeric, punctuation, and special function keys.

laptop latch
Lever used to open the laptop lid.

laptop
Small form factor computer designed to be mobile, but operates much the same as a desktop computer. Laptop hardware is proprietary and usually more expensive than desktop hardware.

laser printer
Type of printer that uses static electricity and a laser to form the image on the paper.

latent image
In laser printers, the undeveloped image.

LCD monitor
Output device that passes polarized light through liquid crystals to produce images on the screen.

Light-Emitting Diode (LED)
Type of semiconductor that emits light when current is passed through it. The LED indicates whether components inside the computer are on.

Lightweight Extensible Authentication Protocol (LEAP)
A wireless security protocol created by Cisco to address the weaknesses in WEP and WPA.

line of sight
Characteristic of certain transmission systems such as laser, microwave, and infrared systems in which no obstructions in a direct path between transmitter and receiver can exist.

line-in connector
Socket that is used to attach an audio source.

Linux
An open-source operating system that was derived from Unix and can be run on several types of computer platforms.

Liquid Crystal Display (LCD)
Type of light-weight, high-resolution display that works by blocking light rather than creating it.

Local Area Network (LAN)
Communication network that covers a small geographical area and is under the control of a single administrator.

local security policy
Combination of security settings that define the security of the computer on which the settings reside.

logical drive
Section that a partition is divided into.

logical topology
Actual method (ring or bus) by which different computers and other equipment in a network communicate with one another. Contrast with physical topology.

loopback plug
Diagnostic tool that redirects signals back to the transmitting port to troubleshoot connectivity.

MAC address
Standardized data link layer address that is required for every port or device that connects to a LAN. Other devices in the network use these addresses to locate specific ports in the network and to create and update routing tables and data structures. MAC addresses are 6 bytes long and are controlled by the Institute of Electrical and Electronics Engineers (IEEE). Also known as a hardware address, a MAC-layer address, burnt-in address, or a physical address.

Main Distribution Facility (MDF)
Primary communications room for a building. Also, the central point of a star networking topology where patch panels, hubs, and routers are located.

malware
Term taken from the words malicious and software. Malware is software designed to infiltrate or damage a computer system without the consent of the user.

man-in-the-middle
An attack that tries to read or alter information being sent between two computers.

Master Boot Record (MBR)
Program on the first sector of a hard disk that starts the boot process. The MBR determines which partition is used for booting the system and then transfers control to the boot sector of that partition, which continues the boot process. MBR allows programs such as DOS to load into RAM.

Material Safety and Data Sheet (MSDS)
A fact sheet that identifies hazardous materials.

Mean Time Between Failures (MTBF)
Average length of time that the device will work without failing. Information is found in the manual or on the manufacturer website.

media
The plural form of medium. The various physical environments through which transmission signals pass. Common network media include twisted-pair, coaxial and fiber-optic cable, and the atmosphere (through which microwave, laser, and infrared transmission occurs).

Media Access Control (MAC)
Lower of the two sub layers of the data link layer defined by the Institute of Electrical and Electronics Engineers (IEEE). The MAC sub layer handles access to shared media, such as whether token passing or contention will be used. Also the rules for coordinating the use of the medium on a LAN.

media-handling options
Options by which a printer handles media, including the orientation, size, and weight of the paper.

megabits per second (Mbps)
Common measurement of the amount of data that is transferred over a connection in one second. A data transfer rate of 1 Mbps is a rate of approximately 1 million bits or 1,000 kilobits per second.

megabyte (MB)
1,048,576 bytes (or approximately 1 million bytes).

megabit
1,048,576 bits (approximately 1 million bits).

megahertz (MHz)
One million Hz or cycles per second.

mesh grip
Tool attached to the end of a cable to help pull cable.

mesh topology
Method of connecting users that provides alternate paths for data. If one path is severed or unusable, the data can take an alternate path to its destination.

microphone
Audio input device.

microphone jack
Socket used to connect a microphone used for audio input.

microwave
Electromagnetic waves that range from 1 to 30 GHz. Microwave-based networks are an evolving technology gaining popularity due to high bandwidth and relatively low cost.

mobile processor
CPU that is optimized to use less power allowing laptop batteries to last longer.

modem port
RJ-11 jack that connects a computer to a standard telephone line. The modem port can be used to connect the computer to the Internet, to send and receive fax documents, and to answer incoming calls.

modulator/demodulator (modem)
Device that converts digital computer signals into a format that is sent and received over an analog telephone line.

Molex power connector
Four-wire computer power connector used to connect many devices such as optical drives and hard drives.

monitor
Display device that works with the installed video card to present output from a computer. The clarity of a CRT monitor is based on video bandwidth, dot pitch, refresh rate, and convergence.

motherboard
Main printed circuit board that connects all the components of the computer such as the CPU, BIOS, memory, mass storage interfaces, serial and parallel ports, expansion slots, and controllers required for standard peripheral devices.

mouse port
PS/2 socket that is used to attach an external mouse.

MSCONFIG
Windows utility designed to aid in the troubleshooting of the operating system. Allows the user to edit start-up applications and access the BOOT.INI, SYSTEM.INI, and WIN.INI files.

multimedia extensions (MMX)
A multimedia instruction set used by Intel CPUs to manage multimedia operations that are normally handled by separate sound cards or video cards.

multimeter
Troubleshooting tool that measures electrical voltage, resistance, and current.

multimode
Optical fiber that has a thicker core than single-mode. It is easier to make, can use simpler light sources, such as LEDs, and works well over short distances. This type of fiber allows light waves to be dispersed into many paths as they travel through the fiber.

multiprocessing
To enable programs to share two or more CPUs.

Multipurpose Internet Mail Extensions (MIME)
Standard that extends the e-mail format to include text in ASCII standard, as well as other formats such as pictures and word processor documents. Normally used in conjunction with SMTP.

multitask
To run two or more applications at the same time.

multithread
To divide a program into smaller parts that can be loaded as needed by the operating system. Multithreading allows individual programs to be multitasked.

multi-user
Two or more users running programs and sharing peripheral devices, such as a printer, at the same time.

My Computer icon
Desktop icon that provides access to the installed drives and other computer properties.

Near Letter Quality (NLQ)
Quality of print that is better than draft quality, but not as good as letter quality.

needle-nose pliers
Tool with long and slender jaws that can be used to grasp small objects.

NetBios Extended User Interface (netBEUI)
A protocol used primarily on small Windows networks. NetBEUI cannot be routed, but it can be used with a routable protocol, such as TCP/IP.

netiquette
Etiquette guidelines for proper posting to forums and communicating over the Internet.

NetView
IBM network management architecture and related applications. NetView is a virtual telecommunications access method (VTAM) application used for managing mainframes in Systems Network Architecture (SNA) networks.

network
Group of two or more electronic devices, such as computers, PDAs, and smartphones which communicate with each other to share data and resources.

Network Access Point (NAP)
Point at which access providers are interconnected.

network administration
Task of maintaining and upgrading a private network that is done by network administrators.

Network Basic Input/Output System (NetBIOS)
An API used by applications on an IBM LAN to request services from lower-level network processes, such as session establishment and termination.

network cable
Physical media used to connect devices together for communication.

network file services
Allow documents to be shared over a network to facilitate the development of a project.

network indicator LED
Light that shows the status of the network connection. The green link light indicates network connectivity. The other LED light indicates traffic.

Network Interface Card (NIC)
Computer interface with the LAN. This card typically is inserted into an expansion slot in a computer and connects to the network medium.

Network Layer
Layer 3 of the Open System Interconnection (OSI) reference model. This layer provides connectivity and path selection between two end systems. The Network Layer is the layer at which routing occurs. The OSI reference model includes Application Layer, Presentation Layer, Session Layer, Transport Layer, Network Layer, Data Link Layer, and Physical Layer.

Network Operating System (NOS)
Operating system designed specifically to provide additional network features.

network printer
Printer connected to the computer network that is set up to be shared by multiple users.

network server
Computer that provides some network service, such as file sharing, and is capable of handling multiple users and multiple jobs.

network topology
Way that computers, printers, and other devices are connected.

networking media
Material (either cable or air) by which signals are sent from one network device to another.

New Technology File System (NTFS)
Type of file system that provides improved fault tolerance over traditional file systems, and also provides file-level security.

nibble
Half a byte, or four bits.

node
1. The endpoint of a network connection or a junction common to two or more lines in a network. Nodes can be processors, controllers, or workstations. Nodes, which vary in routing and other functional capabilities, can be interconnected by links, and serve as control points in the network. Node is sometimes used generically to refer to any entity that can access a network, and is frequently used interchangeably with device.
2. In Systems Network Architecture (SNA), the basic component of a network, and the point at which one or more functional units connect channels or data circuits.

noise
Interference, such as EMI or RFI, that causes unclean power and may cause errors in a computer system.

non-bootable disk
Damaged or missing disk, or a disk that does not contain one or more system boot files.

northbridge
One of the two chips in the core logic chipset of a PC motherboard. It typically handles communications between the CPU, RAM, AGP, PCIe, and the southbridge core chip. Also called a Memory Controller Hub (MCH).

NSLOOKUP
Command that returns the IP address for a given host name. This command can also do the reverse and find the host name for a specified IP address.

NTDETECT
Program used by Intel-based systems to detect installed hardware.

NT Loader (NTLDR)
A program loaded from the boot sector of a hard drive that helps Windows load and displays the Microsoft Windows startup menu.

Num lock indicator LED
Light that shows the on/off status of the 10-key number pad.

Ohm's Law
The mathematical relationship between current, resistance, and voltage where voltage is equal to the current multiplied by the resistance.

Open Graphics Library (OpenGL)
An API that is built into Windows to improve performance.

Open System Interconnection (OSI) model
A networking guideline for implementing protocols across seven layers to ensure interoperability between different vendors and technologies.

Operating System (OS)
Software program that performs general system tasks, such as controlling RAM, prioritizing the processing, controlling input and output devices, and managing files.

optical drive activity indicator LED
Light that shows drive activity.

optical drive
Disk drive that uses a laser to read and/or write CDs and DVDs.

packet
Logical grouping of information which includes a header that contains control information and usually user data. Packets are most often used to refer to network layer units of data. The terms datagram, frame, message, and segment are also used to describe logical information groupings at various layers of the Open System Interconnection (OSI) reference model and in various technology circles.

Packet Internet Gopher (ping)
Simple but highly useful command-line utility that is included in most implementations of TCP/IP. Ping can be used with either the host name or the IP address to test IP connectivity.

Determines whether a specific IP address is accessible by sending an ICMP echo request to a destination computer or other network device. The receiving device then sends back an ICMP echo reply message.

Page Description Language (PDL)
Code that describes the contents of a document in a language that the printer can understand.

pages per minute (ppm)
Designation for measuring the speed of a printer.

Parallel Advanced Technology Attachment (PATA)
Standard for connecting hard drives and optical drives into computer systems and uses a parallel signaling technology.

Parallel ATA (PATA) data cable
Internal cable that transfers data between the motherboard and an ATA drive.

parallel cable
External cable that connects the parallel port of the computer to a printer or another parallel communications device. Also known as a printer cable.

parallel port
Socket used to connect a device such as a printer or scanner.

partition
To divide memory or mass storage into isolated or logical sections. Once a disk is partitioned, each partition will behave like a separate disk drive.

PC Card
Expansion card used in laptops to conform to PCMCIA standards.

peer-to-peer computing
Each network device runs both client and server portions of an application. Also describes communication between implementations of the same Open System Interconnection (OSI) reference model layer in two different network devices.

Personal Computer Memory Card International Association (PCMCIA)
Industry trade association that defines laptop expansion card standards.

personal digital assistant (PDA)
Stand-alone, hand-held device with computing and communicating abilities.

Phillips-head screwdriver
Tool used to tighten or loosen cross-head screws.

phishing
Type of spam intended to persuade the recipient to provide the sender with information that will enable the sender to access personal information of the recipeint.

Physical Layer
Layer 1 of the Open System Interconnection (OSI) model. The Physical Layer defines the electrical, mechanical, procedural and functional specifications to activate, maintain, and deactivate the physical link between end systems. The OSI reference model includes Application Layer, Presentation Layer, Session Layer, Transport Layer, Network Layer, Data Link Layer, and Physical Layer.

physical topology
Physical layout of the components on the network.

piezoelectric
For printers, an electrically charged plate changes the size and shape of the nozzle. This change in size causes the nozzle to act like a pump. The pumping action forces ink out through the nozzle and onto the paper.

plain old telephone service (POTS)
The regular phone system which typically uses analog signals to transmit voice and data. Sometimes called Public Switched Telephone Network (PSTN).

platen
Large roller in a dot matrix printer that applies pressure to keep the paper from slipping. If a multiple-copy paper is used, the platen gap can be adjusted to the thickness of the paper.

Plug-and-Play (PnP)
Technology that allows a computer to automatically configure the devices that connect to it.

Point Of Presence (POP)
Point of interconnection between the communication facilities provided by the telephone company and the main distribution facility of the building.

port replicator
Fixed base unit where a laptop is inserted and able to connect to peripheral devices.

Post Office Protocol (POP)
A protocol used to retreive e-mail from a mail server. The current version is version 3.

power adaptor
Device that transforms AC to DC to provide electricity to the computer and charge the battery.

power button
Control that turns a device on and off.

power cable
External cable consisting of color-coded conductors that transfer electricity to a computer and attached electrical devices.

Power Line Communication (PLC)
Communication method that uses power distribution wires (local electric grid) to send and receive data.

power on indicator LED
Light that shows the on/off status of the laptop.

power supply
Converts AC (alternating current) into the lower voltages of DC (direct current) which powers all components of the computer. Power supplies are rated in watts.

Power-On Self-Test (POST)
Diagnostic test of memory and hardware when the system is powered up.

Presentation Layer
Layer 6 of the Open System Interconnection (OSI) reference model. This layer ensures that information sent by the Application Layer of one system will be readable by the Application Layer of another. The Presentation Layer is also concerned with the data structures used by programs and therefore negotiates data transfer syntax for the Application Layer. The OSI reference model includes Application Layer, Presentation Layer, Session Layer, Transport Layer, Network Layer, Data Link Layer, and Physical Layer.

preventive maintenance policy
Detailed program that determines maintenance timing, the type of maintenance performed, and the specifics of how the maintenance plan is carried out.

preventive maintenance
Regular and systematic inspection, cleaning, and replacement of worn parts, materials, and systems.

primary corona wire
Voltage device that erases the charge on the printing drum. Also called the grid or conditioning roller.

primary partition
First partition on a hard drive. A primary partition cannot be subdivided into smaller sections.

Primary Rate Interface (PRI)
Integrated Services Digital Network (ISDN) interface to primary rate access. Primary rate access consists of a single 64-Kbps D channel plus 23 (T1) or 30 (E1) B channels for voice or data. Compare to BRI.

print resolution
Number of tiny dots that the print head is capable of placing per inch on the paper when forming an image.

Printer Control Language (PCL)
Developed by Hewlett-Packard to allow software applications to communicate with HP and HP-compatible laser printers. PCL is now an industry standard for most printer types.

printer driver
Software that must be installed on a PC so that the printer can communicate and coordinate the printing process.

printer network interface card
Adapter that the printer uses to access the network media.

printer queue
Temporary holding area for print jobs. The jobs in the queue are fed to the printer when it is ready for the next job.

printer-output options
Determine how the ink or toner is transferred to the paper and include color management, print quality, and speed.

Programmable Read-Only Memory (PROM)
A memory chip on which data can be written only once after it is manufactured.

protected mode
Allows programs to access more than 1 MB of physical memory, and protects against misuse of memory, such as programs that can not execute a data segment, or write into a code segment.

protocol
1. Formal description of a set of rules and conventions that govern how devices on a network exchange information.
2. Field within an IP datagram that indicates the upper layer (Layer 4) protocol that sent the datagram.

Protocol Data Unit (PDU)
A unit of data that is specified in a protocol of a layer of the Open System Interconnection (OSI) Model. For example, the PDU for Layer 1 is bits or the data stream, Layer 2 is framing, Layer 3 is the packet, and Layer 4 is the segment.

proxy
Entity that, in the interest of efficiency, acts on behalf of another entity.

Public Switched Telephone Network (PSTN)
General term that refers to the variety of telephone networks and services in place worldwide. Sometimes called plain old telephone service (POTS).

Radio Frequency (RF)
Generic term that refers to frequencies that correspond to radio transmissions. Cable TV and broadband networks use RF technology.

Radio Frequency Interference (RFI)
Radio frequencies that create noise that interferes with information being transmitted across unshielded copper cabling.

Random Access Memory (RAM)
Memory that temporarily stores data for processing by the CPU. Also called physical memory.

Read Only Memory (ROM)
Memory that permanently stores prerecorded configuration settings and data on a chip, that can only be read. This type of memory retains its contents when power is not being supplied to the chip.

Reduced Instruction Set Computer (RISC)
Architecture that uses a relatively small set of instructions. RISC chips are designed to execute these instructions very rapidly.

Redundant Array of Independent Disks (RAID)
Provides fault tolerance to prevent loss of data in the event of a disk drive failure on a network server. Also known as Redundant Array of Inexpensive Disks.

Regedit
Windows application that allows users to edit the registry.

registry
System-wide database used by the Windows operating system to store information and settings for hardware, software, users, and preferences on a system.

Remote Access Server (RAS)
Server that is dedicated to users that need to gain access to files and print services on the LAN from a remote location.

Remote Installation Services (RIS)
Ability to download a Windows operating system installation across the network. This install can be requested by the user or forced onto the computer by the administrator.

removable drive
Drive that can be removed from a computer to transport data.

replay attack
An attack that intercepts data, such as passwords, sent across a network so that the intercepted passwords can be resent later to gain access.

resistance (r)
Measurement, expressed in ohms, of the opposition of a material to the flow of current.

resolution
Number of distinct pixels in each dimension that can be displayed on a computer screen. The higher the resolution, the better quality the screen display is. Also referred to as display resolution.

restore point
Utility in Microsoft's Windows Me, XP, and Vista operating systems. It allows the rolling back of system files, registry keys, and installed programs to a previous state in the event of a system failure. User data is not affected by performing a restore point.

ring topology
Network topology that consists of a series of repeaters connected to one another by unidirectional transmission links to form a single closed loop. Each station on the network connects to the network at a repeater. While logically a ring, ring topologies are most often organized in a closed-loop star.

router
A network layer device that uses one or more metrics to determine the optimal path along which network traffic should be forwarded. Routers forward packets from one network to another based on network layer information. Occasionally called a gateway, although this definition of gateway is becoming increasingly outdated.

Routing Information Protocol (RIP)
Interior Gateway Protocol (IGP) supplied with UNIX Berkeley Standard Distribution (BSD) systems. The most common IGP on the Internet. RIP uses hop count as a routing metric.

safe mode
Option when booting the system that loads only the basic devices that Windows needs to run. It is used for troubleshooting.

satellite communication
The use of orbiting satellites to relay data between multiple earth-based stations. Satellite communications offer high bandwidth and broadcast capability at a cost that is not related to distance between earth stations. Because of the altitude of the satellite, satellite communications can be subject to long propagation delays.

SCANDISK
Windows utility used to examine all files on a drive.

sector
The smallest unit that can be accessed on a disk. A sector is a segment within a track on a disk.

Secure Socket Host (SSH)
Provides secure access to a remote computer using strong authentication and encryption.

security key fob
Small radio system that communicates with the computer over a short range. The computer must sense the signal from the key fob before it will accept the user login name and password.

security keyhole
Hard point in the case that is used to attach a security cable.

segment
Portion of a computer network in which every device communicates using the physical layer of the OSI Model. Hubs and repeaters extend and become part of a network segment, while switches and routers define and separate network segments.

semiconductor
Material used to make computer chips that can be either a conductor or an insulator, depending on the control signals applied to it. The most common semiconductor materials are silicon and germanium. These materials then have other materials added to them to increase conductivity.

Serial ATA (SATA)
Standard that uses a serial link for connecting drives in a computer.

serial cable
External cable that connects the serial port on the computer to a peripheral device.

serial data transfer
Movement of single bits of information in a single cycle.

serial port
Socket that is used to connect a device such as a mouse or trackball.

serial transmission
Method of data transmission in which the bits of a data character are transmitted sequentially over a single channel.

server
Repository for files, or other resources, that can be accessed and shared across a network by many users.

service level agreement (SLA)
Contract that defines expectations between an organization and the service vendor to provide an agreed upon level of support.

Service Set Identifier (SSID)
A unique identifier, often the network name, used by wireless devices to connect to a wireless access point.

Session Layer
Layer 5 of the Open System Interconnection (OSI) reference model. This layer establishes, manages, and terminates sessions between applications and manages data exchange between presentation layer entities. The OSI reference model includes Application Layer, Presentation Layer, Session Layer, Transport Layer, Network Layer, Data Link Layer, and Physical Layer.

Shielded Twisted Pair (STP)
Two-pair wiring medium used primarily for token ring networks. STP cabling has a layer of shielded insulation to reduce electromagnetic interference (EMI). Compare with UTP.

shortcut
Keyboard combination that activates a command.

Simple Mail Transfer Protocol (SMTP)
E-mail protocol used by servers to send ASCII text messages. When augmented by the MIME protocol, SMTP can carry e-mail with pictures and documents. SMTP is sometimes used by e-mail clients to retrieve messages from an e-mail server. However, due to the limited ability to queue messages at the receiving end, other protocols such as POP or IMAP are typically used to receive e-mail.

simplex
Capability for data transmission in only one direction between a sending station and a receiving station.

Single Inline Memory Module (SIMM)
A small circuit board that can hold nine RAM chips with a bus that is 32 bits wide.

single-mode
Fiber cable that has a very thin core. Uses a high-energy laser as a light source and can transmit signals over longer distances than multi-mode fiber optic cable.

site survey
Physical inspection of the building that will help determine a basic network topology.

Small Computer System Interface (SCSI)
Parallel interface standard that supports multiple devices on the same cable and achieves faster data transmission rates than standard buses.

Small Computer System Interface (SCSI) cable
External or internal cable that connects the SCSI controller to SCSI ports of multiple internal and external devices.

Small Outline DIMM (SODIMM)
A smaller, condensed version of DIMM that provides random access data storage that is ideal for use in laptops, printers, and other devices where conserving space is desirable.

smart card
Credit card sized device that includes a processor and memory, used to store information and authenticate network users. Smart cards provide two-factor identification because the user must have both the card and a password to access the network.

smartphones
Cell phones with the computing capabilities of a PDA.

social engineering
The act of gathering secure information by conning an individual into revealing information they do not realize can be used to attack a computer network.

software firewall
Application on a computer that inspects and filters data packets.

solenoid
Coil of wires that form electromagnets that fire the pins in the dot matrix printer.

solid-ink printers
Printer that uses solid sticks of ink rather than toner or ink cartridges. Solid-ink printers produce high-quality images. The ink sticks are nontoxic and can be handled safely.

sound card
Integrated circuit board that enhances the audio capabilities of the computer.

southbridge
Chip that implements the slower capabilities of the motherboard. It is connected to the CPU through the northbridge chip. Also known as the Input/Output (I/O) Controlling Station (ICH).

spam
Unsolicited e-mail.

speaker
Audio output device.

spike
Sudden increase in voltage that is usually caused by lightning strikes.

spoof
To gain access to resources on devices by pretending to be a trusted computer.

spooling
Process of loading documents into a buffer (usually an area on a hard drive) until the printer is ready to print the documents.

spyware
Malware that monitors activity on the computer. The spyware then sends this information to the organization responsible for launching the spyware.

Standby Power Supply (SPS)
Battery backup that is enabled when voltage levels fall below normal.

standoff
Barrier used to physically separate parts.

star topology
LAN topology in which end points on a network are connected to a common central switch by point-to-point links. A ring topology that is organized as a star, and implements a unidirectional closed-loop star, instead of point-to-point links.

static RAM (SRAM)
Type of RAM that retains its contents for as long as power is supplied. SRAM does not require constant refreshing, like dynamic RAM (DRAM).

Static Random Access Memory (SRAM)
Memory that holds data as long as there is voltage applied. Used mainly as cache memory for the CPU.

Streaming Single-instruction-multi-data Extensions (SSE)
A multimedia instruction set that is an enhancement to the MMX instruction set.

stylus
Writing utensil. Typically used as an input method for the touch-sensitive screens of PDAs and graphics tablets.

subnet mask
Second group of numbers used when configuring an IP address on a device. The subnet mask is used by end devices to determine the network portion of an IP address.

subnetting
Logical division of a network. It provides the means to divide a network, and the subnet mask specifies how it is subdivided.

surge
Any voltage increase above 110 percent of the normal voltage carried by a power line.

surge protector
Suppressor that regulates the voltage going to a device.

surge suppressor
Device that makes sure that the voltage going to another device stays below a certain level.

S-video port
Four-pin mini-DIN connector that is used to output video signals to a compatible device. S-video separates the brightness and color portions of a video signal.

switch
1) Operation that is added to a DOS command to modify the output of that command. 2) A Layer 2 network device also known as a multiport bridge.

Symmetric DSL (SDSL)
Version of a Digital Subscriber Line (DSL) service that provides the same speed for uploads and downloads.

Symmetric encryption
Encryption that requires both sides of an encrypted conversation to use an encryption key to be able to encode and decode the data. The sender and receiver must use the same key at the same time.

SYN flood
Randomly opens TCP ports, tying up the network equipment or computer resources with a large amount of false requests, causing sessions to be denied to others. Also

Synchronous Dynamic RAM (SDRAM)
A type of DRAM that can run at higher clock speeds than conventional RAM.

System Restore
Windows XP service that runs in the background and allows the user to restore the OS to a predefined point in time.

tape drive
Device used for data backup on a network server drive.

Task Manager
Displays active applications and identifies those applications that are not responding so that they can be shut down.

Taskbar
Utility within Microsoft Windows that graphically represents open applications, computer contents, and other information. Also provides a way to quickly access these resources.

TCP/IP Model
Developed by the U. S. Department of Defense, this Internet Architecture Model describes the components and functions of networks using four layers.

Telecommunications Industry Association (TIA)
Organization that develops standards that relate to telecommunications technologies. Together, the TIA and the Electronic Industries Alliance (EIA) have formalized standards, such as EIA/TIA-232, for the electrical characteristics of data transmission.

telnet
Remote access application used to provide remote terminal access between hosts on a network. As a troubleshooting tool, telnet can verify the application layer software between source and destination stations. This is the most complete test mechanism available for the OSI Model.

thermal paper
Chemically treated paper with a waxy quality. It becomes black when heated. Most thermal printer print heads are the width of the paper. The paper is supplied in the form of a roll.

thermal printer
A printer that marks special thermal paper by applying heat to areas of the paper that are to be darkened to represent characters.

Thicknet
Coaxial cable that was used in older networks and operated at 10 megabits per second with a maximum length of 500 meters. Also called 10BASE5.

Thinnet
Coaxial cable that was used in older networks and operated at 10 megabits per second with a maximum length of 185 meters. Also called 10BASE2.

three claw part retriever
Tool used to retrieve and manipulate small parts.

Token Ring network
Uses a ring topology and a token-passing methodology to create collision-free data transmission.

toner
Powder-type ink used in laser printers and photocopiers to form text and images on printer paper.

topology
Actual physical layout of a network or in the case of a logical topology, the signal or data flows in a network.

torx screwdriver
Tool used to tighten or loosen screws that have a star-shaped depression on the top, a feature that is mainly found on laptop screws.

touch screen
Interactive LCD or CRT monitor that detects when something is pressed on it.

touchpad
Pressure-sensitive input pad that controls the cursor.

tracert
Windows utility that traces the route that a packet takes from source computer to destination host.

track
Complete circle around a hard drive platter made up of groups of 512-byte sectors.

trackball
Ball that is rotated to control the cursor.

trackpoint
Input stick that controls the cursor.

Transmission Control Protocol (TCP)
Primary Internet protocol for the delivery of data. TCP includes facilities for end-to-end connection establishment, error detection and recovery, and metering the rate of data flow into the network. Many standard applications, such as e-mail, web browser, file transfer, and Telnet, depend on the services of TCP.

Transmission Control Protocol/Internet Protocol (TCP/IP)
Common name for the suite of protocols developed by the U.S. Department of Defense (DoD) in the 1970s to support the construction of worldwide internetworks. TCP and IP are the two best-known protocols in the suite.

Transport Layer
Layer 4 of the Open System Interconnection (OSI) reference model. This layer is responsible for reliable network communication between end nodes. The Transport Layer provides mechanisms for the establishment, maintenance, and termination of virtual circuits, transport fault detection and recovery, and information flow control. The OSI reference model includes Application Layer, Presentation Layer, Session Layer, Transport Layer, Network Layer, Data Link Layer, and Physical Layer.

Trojan threat
Programming code that appears to be legitimate software, but is actually malicious programs that can cause serious damage by deleting or damaging files on a computer.

troubleshooting
Systematic approach to locating the cause of a fault in a computer system.

tweezers
Tool used to retrieve and manipulate small parts.

twisted pair
A pair of insulated wires wrapped together in a regular spiral pattern to control the effects of electrical noise. The pairs can be shielded or unshielded. Twisted pair is common in telephony applications and in data networks. Category 3, Category 5, Category 5e, and Category 6 twisted pair cables all contain 4 twisted pairs in a common jacket.

unattended installation
Custom installation of an operating system with minimal user intervention. Windows performs unattended installations by using an answer file called unattend.txt.

Uninterruptible Power Supply (UPS)
Battery backup that provides a continuous and reliable power source in the event of power failure.

universal bay status indicator LED
Light that shows that a device is installed in the laptop bay.

Universal Serial Bus (USB) cable
External cable that connects the USB port on the computer to a peripheral device.

Universal Serial Bus (USB) port
External, hot-swappable, bi-directional connection for USB cables connecting to peripheral devices.

Universal Serial Bus (USB)
External serial bus interface standard for the connection of multiple peripheral devices. USB can connect up to 127 USB devices at transfer rates of up to 480 Mbps, and can provide DC power to connected devices.

UNIX
Operating system that is used primarily to run and maintain computer networks.

Unshielded Twisted Pair (UTP)
Four-pair wire medium used in a variety of networks. UTP is rated in categories, with higher categories providing the best performance and highest bandwidth. The most popular categories are Category 3, Category 5, Category 5e, Category 6, and Category 6A.

User Datagram Protocol (UDP)
Connectionless service for delivery of data with less overhead than TCP and designed for speed. Network management applications, network file system, and simple file transport use UDP.

user interface
Part of the operating system that allows the user to communicate with the computer. User interfaces can provide a Command Line Interface (text) or Graphical User Interface (GUI).

user profile
Specific setting for the user who is logged on to the computer.

ventilation
Series of vents that allow hot air to be expelled from the interior of the device.

very high data rate DSL (VDSL)
Broadband data transfer capable of bandwidths of 13 Mbps to 52 Mbps.

video accelerator card
Integrated circuit board that contains a processor and memory to increase the speed of video graphics. Video accelerator cards are primarily used for 3D and gaming applications.

video adapter
Integrated circuit board that stores digital data in VRAM and converts it to analog data.

Video Graphics Array (VGA)
Supplies analog video to an analog monitor. The connector is a 15-pin D-sub type connector.

video memory
Dedicated random access memory on a video graphics adapter (video RAM or VRAM).

video surveillance equipment
Used to record images and sound for monitoring activity.

virtual memory
Memory created and controlled by the operating system by manipulating free hard disk space to mimic more RAM than is actually installed in the system.

Virtual Private Network (VPN)
Encryption system that protects data as it travels, or tunnels, over the Internet or other unsecured public network.

virtual
Something that is conceptual rather than something that is physical.

Virus Scan
Utility that checks all hard drives and memory for viruses.

virus
In computer terms, a malicious piece of software or code that can copy itself and infect a computer without the knowledge or permission of the user. Some viruses are benign and do not adversely affect a computer, while other viruses can damage or delete operating system and data files.

Voice over IP (VoIP)
Method to transmit telephone calls over the Internet using packet-switched technology.

voltage (V)
Force that creates a current by moving electrons. Electromotive force or potential difference expressed in volts.

volume control
Button that adjusts audio output.

warm boot
Restarting a computer that is already turned on without first turning it off.

What You See Is What You Get (WYSIWYG)
Printer output that matches what the user sees on-screen.

Wide-Area Network (WAN)
Data communications network that serves users across a broad geographic area and often uses transmission devices provided by common carriers. Frame Relay, SMDS, and X.25 are examples of WANs.

Wi-Fi Protected Access (WPA)
Security standard for Wi-Fi wireless technology. Provides better encryption and authentication than earlier WEP system.

Wi-Fi Protected Acess 2 (WPA2)
An improved version of WPA which supports robust encryption and higher levels of security.

Wi-Fi
Brand originally licensed by the Wi-Fi Alliance to define the embedded technology of a wireless network, and is based on the IEEE 802.11 specifications.

Windows Explorer
Windows utility that graphically represents the file-management structure.

wire cutters
Tool used to strip and cut wires.

Wired Equivalent Privacy (WEP)
First-generation security standard for wireless technology.

Wireless Access Point (WAP)
Device that connects wireless devices to form a wireless network. An access point usually connects to a wired network, and can relay data between wired and wireless devices. Connectivity distances can range from several feet or meters, to several miles or kilometers.

wireless connection
Connection to a network using radio signals, infrared technology (laser), or satellite transmissions.

wireless indicator LED
Light that shows activity of the wireless network connection.

wireless network
Extension of a wired network using radio frequency (RF) signals to connect to access points. Wireless signals can be repeated to additional access points, extending the distance of the network.

wireless NIC
Expansion card that enables a computer to connect to a wireless modem using RF signals.

Wireless Transport Layer Security (WTLS)
Layer that provides security for mobile devices that use Wireless Applications Protocol (WAP).

workgroup
Collection of workstations and servers on a LAN that are designed to communicate and exchange data with one another.

worm
A program that replicates itself across a computer network and usually performs malicious activity.

Zero Insertion Force (ZIF) socket
Chip socket that permits the insertion and removal of a chip without using tools or force.

zombie
A computer that has been infected with programming code so that the computer can be used to launch DoS attacks.